To those who serve now…
With gratitude to those who served then…
That we all might live in freedom tomorrow.

CONTENTS

PRELUDE TO THE WAR IN THE PACIFIC

(1930–1941)

✪ **PEARL HARBOR, HAWAII**
SUNDAY, 21 MARCH 2004
0800 HOURS LOCAL

For Americans, World War II began here on a Sunday morning not much different from this one. The air is clear and crisp. Puffy white clouds punctuate the blue sky, and the sun, still low on the horizon, is already bright. A bugle sounds the notes for colors, and ashore, off in the distance, a church bell summons people to worship. This morning, here on the waters of Pearl Harbor, naval ensigns flutter from their halyards in a light breeze as sailors go about their duties on the decks of haze-gray Navy hulls. These are sights and sounds that would have been impossible to see or hear at this hour on 7 December 1941.

Every time I have visited Pearl Harbor I have tried to imagine what it must have been like at 0755 that Sabbath morn as 183 Japanese planes, led by Commander Mitsuo Fuchida, came roaring in on the first wave of the surprise attack. Even though the USS *Ward*, an aging World War I–era destroyer, had fired upon and sunk a two-man midget submarine just outside the harbor an hour before the air assault began, the Japanese pilots approached unchallenged. The dive-bombers struck first, taking out most of the land-based aircraft on Ford Island, as well as Ewa, Wheeler, Bellows, Kaneohe, and Hickam Fields. Two minutes later, torpedo bombers swept in low and fast—the first wave hit every outboard capital vessel tethered on Battleship Row. The venerable USS *Arizona*, tied up beside the USS *Vestal*, a repair ship, had already been struck by aerial torpedoes when a Japanese bomb plunged into the forward fourteen-inch powder magazine. The resulting explosion sent the ship and 1,102 men to the bottom before the attack was five minutes old.

By 0945, when the second wave of Japanese attackers finished spewing death and destruction from bombs, torpedoes, machine guns, and 20 mm cannon fire, 2,403 Americans—military and civilian—were dead or dying, and 1,178 others had been wounded. Of the ninety-six warships at Pearl Harbor, eighteen had been sunk or severely damaged. Five of the eight Pacific Fleet battleships, the U.S. Navy's primary strike force, were on the bottom or out of commission. Of the 388 Army, Navy, and Marine aircraft based in Hawaii, 199 had been damaged or destroyed and fewer than a hundred were left usable. As the Americans tended the wounded, fought fires, rescued shipmates, and tried to salvage sinking vessels, six Japanese carriers 200 miles north of Oahu recovered their aircraft and turned back west—escaping unscathed. Only twenty-nine of Fuchida's pilots failed to return.

The U.S. soldiers, sailors, airmen, and Marines in Hawaii were not the only Americans to fight the Empire of Japan on this "day of infamy." That evening, the Japanese struck our bases and facilities on Guam, on Wake Island, and in the Philippines. British and Dutch forces were assaulted in Hong Kong and Malaya. And on 8 December, while Congress debated a resolution to declare war, the Imperial Navy attacked Midway. These coordinated attacks, part of a master plan reluctantly devised by Fleet Admiral Isoroku Yamamoto, commander in chief of the Japanese Combined Fleet, were deemed in Tokyo to be a stunning military success.

But Pearl Harbor became something else that the emperor and most of his ambitious generals and admirals could not foresee as they celebrated their short-lived victory. Until the Japanese surrender in Tokyo Bay on 14 August 1945, Americans from every walk of life and every ethnic background would be motivated to serve in uniform, work harder, eat less, volunteer more, and buy war bonds—all with the rallying cry "Remember Pearl Harbor!"

✪ ✪ ✪

As a boy I had read about that "day of infamy," seen the pictures and newsreels, and later studied it at the Naval Academy. Then I visited this hallowed place while commuting to and from other wars. But it wasn't until I began interviewing those who were young men and women on 7 December 1941 that I began to grasp what that day was really like and what it meant to a generation of Americans. More than six decades after the event, every one of these warriors and their contemporaries, no matter where they were at the time, can recall exactly what they were doing and who they were with when they learned about the surprise attack on Pearl Harbor.

Many of them didn't even know where this Hawaiian naval base was when they first heard about the raid. But everyone knew what it meant: America was now in the war that most had hoped to avoid.

In the days after the attack, newspapers, magazines, and newsreels at local movie theaters quickly educated the American people about the geography of Hawaii—and the damage that had been done to America's Pacific Fleet. That same "Remember Pearl Harbor!" rallying cry became a call to battle for the legions of young men showing up at recruiting and induction centers.

It was a slogan that stuck, all the way across the broad expanse of ocean and the bloody battles of what came to be called the Pacific theater of war. Newspapers printed full-page maps of the region, and families tacked them up on kitchen and living room walls so that sweethearts, wives, parents, and siblings could keep track of where their loved ones were serving in the far reaches of that vast ocean. Tiny dots on those maps and locations with unpronounceable names became places to pray about in churches and weep over in the privacy of bedrooms.

The ocean that spanned those maps was anything but pacific during World War II. From the opening shots fired here at Pearl Harbor to the armistice signed in Tokyo Bay three years, eight months, and twenty-four days later, this body of water and its islands were the venue for the biggest air and naval engagements in history and some of bloodiest land battles ever fought.

The enemy that America was pitted against in the Pacific proved to be an implacable foe. Unlike our European adversaries—the Vichy French, Mussolini's Italian Legions, or the German Wehrmacht—no Japanese Imperial Army unit ever surrendered until the armistice was signed on the deck of the USS *Missouri* on 2 September 1945. The Japanese literally fought to the death.

Whether they served on air, land, or sea, the young Americans sent off to contend with the Japanese army, navy, and air force proved to be a remarkable lot. They are men and women often described in superlatives. Most were born in the aftermath of The War to End All Wars, were toddlers in the Roaring Twenties, and came of age during the Great Depression. Though few were unaffected by these events and the global economic catastrophe that began in America with the stock market crash of 1929, nearly all I've known have possessed a remarkable sense of optimism.

This generation grew up in an America that was still overwhelmingly rural. Their sources of information on current events were newsreels at neighborhood movie theaters, hometown newspapers, radio, and discussions over the family kitchen table. They matured in the harsh reality of "hard times:" devastating droughts in our agricultural heartland, massive Depression-induced unemployment, and increasing uncertainty as Bolshevism swept across Russia and Fascism took hold in Italy, Japan, Spain, and Germany.

Though most of those I interviewed for our *War Stories* documentaries and this book were just teenagers as war clouds gathered and broke over Asia and Europe in the 1930s, nearly all were familiar with the intrigues and events leading up to the conflagration. Yet few of them expected that America would be plunged into that awful cauldron. Most believed, as did their parents, that the broad, blue waters of the Atlantic and the Pacific insulated them from the troubles in faraway lands. Many cited the promises made by politicians of every persuasion who assured the American people that what was happening "over there" wasn't our fight.

Late in summer 1941—with Hitler dominating Europe and on the march toward Moscow, with Japanese forces controlling most of the Chinese coast and occupying Indochina, and with Britain being bombed daily—Congress began deliberations on the Selective Service Extension Act. The bill, authorizing the movement of American military personnel overseas and extending their term of service, was considered by opponents to be "jingoistic," "warlike," and too "provocative" for a "neutral nation." The hotly contested debate reflected the ambivalence of the American people on the issue of our involvement in "someone else's war." On 12 August 1941, the law passed the House of Representatives by a single vote.

Fewer than four months later, the attack on Pearl Harbor erased those uncertainties. For the young Americans already in service—and those now called up by the millions—it soon became obvious that while the war in Europe would be an Allied effort, the fight in the Pacific theater would be a predominantly American affair. They also quickly learned that they would face years of separation from those they loved, and they confronted the terrible prospect of death in a strange-sounding spot in the middle of an ocean most had never seen.

This book is about them. This isn't a book about war—it's about warriors. It isn't really a history book. It's about those who *made* history—the young Americans from every walk of life, from every part of this great nation, who came to serve with the words "Remember Pearl Harbor!" ringing in their ears.

Their self-effacing modest words are offered here as a memorial to heroic sacrifice in the crucible of dramatic and often deadly events that began with the attack on Pearl Harbor and ended with Japan's surrender in Tokyo Bay. Theirs is a war story that deserves to be told.

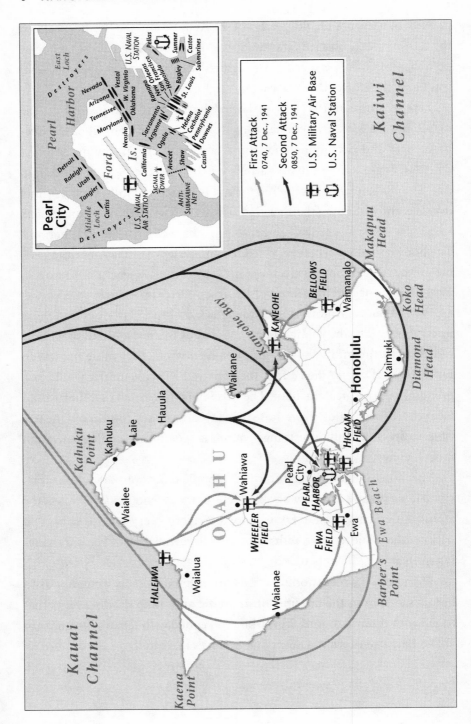

CHAPTER 1
WHO FIRED FIRST?
(7–8 DECEMBER 1941)

✪ **PEARL HARBOR, HAWAII**
SUNDAY, 7 DECEMBER 1941
0755 HOURS LOCAL

The first planes came in high, well above the ships and their sleeping crews in the anchorage. Some of the few sailors who were on deck actually waved, marveling at the sight of so many warplanes in the air that early on a Sunday. Then, across the water, came the sounds of explosions and firing from Ford Island and Hickam Field.

Just two minutes later, more aircraft, coming in low and fast, headed straight for the rows of battleships alongside Ford Island. The planes pulled up just in time to clear the masts of the assembled armada, but not before dropping aerial torpedoes from their bellies. The wakes of the torpedoes pointed like fingers toward the largest vessels of America's Pacific Fleet. As the 550-pound warheads detonated against the hulls beneath the water, those on deck could see the bright insignia on the wings of the green and silver aircraft as they swept overhead: a red circle representing the rising sun of Japan. Many of those sleeping or working below decks never even knew who killed them.

Within minutes of the first bombs and torpedoes, radio operators at shore stations and aboard several of the ships under attack sent out the message "AIR RAID PEARL HARBOR THIS IS NO DRILL." Weeks later, intelligence officers found a recording of another radio transmission. At 0753 hours that morning, Commander Mitsuo Fuchida, leader of the airborne assault, had sent a coded signal to Vice Admiral Chuichi Nagumo, commander in chief of the Japanese navy's First Carrier Strike Force and the forty-nine Kate bombers, forty Kate torpedo bombers, fifty-one Val dive-bombers, and forty-three "Zeke" fighter attack planes accompanying him on the first wave of the raid. The message confirming that they had achieved complete surprise was one word, repeated three times: "TORA, TORA, TORA!"

✪ ✪ ✪

Burlingame Airchive

Mitsuo Fuchida led the air attack on Pearl Harbor. After the war he was converted to Christianity by Jake DeShazer, one of the Doolittle Raiders and a former POW.

Fuchida's message was accurate. The Japanese air attack caught the U.S. Army, Navy, and Marines in Hawaii incredibly unprepared. By 0945, a second wave of 167 attack aircraft had added to the devastation, then wheeled north to return to their six carriers: the *Akagi*, the *Kaga*, the *Soryu*, the *Zuikaku*, the *Hiryu*, and the *Shokaku*. Pearl Harbor, the largest naval anchorage in the Pacific, was littered with sunken and burning American warships; the best dry-dock and ship repair facilities west of California were in shambles; only 25 percent of the aircraft based in Hawaii were still in operation; and there were 3,581 American casualties.

It was a disaster of historic proportions. Yet it failed in its principal goal: keeping the U.S. Navy from launching a westward offensive against Japan until the emperor's armed forces had seized sufficient territory to secure the Home Islands and their "Greater East Asia Co-Prosperity Sphere."

Conceived by Fleet Admiral Isoroku Yamamoto, the brilliant, fifty-seven-year-old commander of Japan's Imperial Combined Fleet, the surprise attack was code-named Operation Z—after Admiral Togo's famous "Z" signal before the Japanese victory against the Russian navy at the Battle of Tsushima in 1905.

Yamamoto, Harvard-educated and highly regarded in the United States, where he had served as a naval attaché, had initially urged his colleagues to avoid war with the Americans. Overruled by the Imperial General Staff, he set to work on a plan to do even greater damage to the Americans.

National Archives

Yamamoto was a lifelong gambler, and he drafted a war plan that was bold and brilliant, but risky. He told the Japanese military planners, "If we are to have a war with America, we will have no hope of winning unless the U.S. fleet in Hawaiian waters can be destroyed." It meant annihilating America's Pacific Fleet before it could sortie toward Japan, and it required that the Imperial Army seize key bases in the Philippines and Guam, with near simultaneous strikes against the British in

Admiral Yamamoto was the strategist of the Pearl Harbor attack and CINC of the Imperial Combined Fleet until American pilots shot down his plane in 1943.

Hong Kong and against Dutch possessions in Indonesia.

He told the Imperial General Staff that "if successful," the raid would enable them to hope for a short, limited war, after which Japan would quickly sue for peace on its own terms. The overall concept was approved by the General Staff by June 1941. Yamamoto then set his best naval planners to the most difficult part of the task: a surprise air assault of unprecedented size against Pearl Harbor, 4,000 miles from Japan. By August, working around the clock in absolute secrecy, Rear Admiral Takajiro Onishi and his fellow naval aviators Minoru Genda and Mitsuo Fuchida were able to deliver a final attack plan requiring six aircraft carriers and more than 350 aircraft.

In early September 1941, the Japanese Imperial General Staff approved Yamamoto's daring war plan, and fleet units commenced a rigorous period of pre-attack training, though they were not told their target. By early November, the six carriers, two battleships, three cruisers, nine destroyers, thirty submarines, and eight tankers—constituting Nagumo's First Carrier Strike Force—began to assemble at Tankan Bay in the Kurile Islands, Japan's northernmost and remotest naval base. On the night of 26 November, this armada, the mightiest battle fleet ever assembled in the Pacific, was ordered to sortie into the frigid waters of the north Pacific and head east. Once out of port and sailing without lights under strict radio silence, the captains of the fifty-eight ships opened envelopes containing their secret orders and learned their target: Pearl Harbor.

✪ ✪ ✪

Meanwhile, as Nagumo's force steamed undetected toward its objective, the Americans at Pearl Harbor were woefully unprepared for the coming onslaught. Some, including Admiral Husband E. Kimmel, commander in chief of the Pacific Fleet, and Lieutenant General Walter C. Short, commanding general of the U.S. Army's Hawaiian Department, believed that they would have sufficient advance knowledge of any Japanese attack.

Both Kimmel and Short knew that American cryptographers had broken the Japanese Purple code, giving senior U.S. officials access to Tokyo's diplomatic messages. Using intercepts of cables sent from Tokyo to the Japanese ambassadors in Washington, the Department of the Navy issued a "war warning" to the Pacific Fleet headquarters on 27 November—the day after Nagumo's battle group departed Japanese waters.

On 2 December, the U.S. code-breakers intercepted a message to all Japanese diplomatic and consular posts to destroy their code and cipher material and burn all classified documents. Based on this intercept and one directing the Japanese consulate in Honolulu to continue reporting on U.S. fleet activities at Pearl Harbor, another "war warning" message to all units in Hawaii was issued by the War and Navy Departments. Still, both commanders and their staffs believed that they had several weeks—if not a month or more—to prepare.

They had not ignored the situation. Ever since President Roosevelt had "indefinitely" stationed the entire Pacific Fleet in Hawaii in May 1940, naval officials had been complaining about the risk from Japan. In October 1940, the fleet commander, Admiral James O. Richardson, visited Washington to personally point out their deficiencies to Navy Secretary Frank Knox. Shortly after Richardson turned command over to Admiral Kimmel on 1 February 1941, almost one-quarter of the Pacific Fleet was transferred to the Atlantic to help contend with the German submarines wreaking havoc on Lend-Lease shipments to England. Though his organizational tables called for six twelve-plane squadrons of patrol aircraft, Kimmel had only forty-nine operational patrol planes available.

Because the Army was responsible for defending Hawaii, General Short's requests for men and matériel were equally severe. He had requested 180 B-17 bombers, but had only six that were flyable, and all his fighters were obsolete. Though the Army had only 102 out of the 233 anti-aircraft guns that were deemed necessary, thousands of them were being shipped to our struggling British and Soviet allies. And while five of the new, highly secret mobile radar

Admiral Husband E. Kimmel planned for traditional naval war and didn't foresee the importance of aircraft. He became a scapegoat for the attack on Pearl Harbor.

units had been delivered to Hawaii in November, few operators had been trained. Worse still, because the Army and Navy in Hawaii operated independently, with no unified command structure, even if a radar operator detected an incoming attack, the Army had no other means of alerting the Navy besides a phone call to the Fleet headquarters.

Uppermost in the mind of Admiral Husband Kimmel was the security of his ships, oil storage tanks, and naval aircraft. His long-range reconnaissance aircraft could fly 750 miles on patrol and sink any submarines in sensitive areas, especially at the entrance to Pearl Harbor. Kimmel regarded enemy submarines as the most serious threat to his fleet. Across the mouth of the harbor, the Americans had installed an anti-sub, anti-mine, and anti-torpedo net that extended almost to the bottom of the harbor floor, only forty-five feet deep. Though the anti-submarine net was highly classified, and the area around it designated as a restricted zone that was off-limits to civilian or foreign vessels, the Japanese were fully aware of it. German agents and Japanese spies routinely gathered remarkably detailed intelligence on our installations, ships, and aircraft. More than half a dozen reports provided data on the net at the harbor entrance.

Unaware of the magnitude and accuracy of the Japanese espionage but concerned about the inadequacies they had reported back to Washington, both Admiral Kimmel and General Short believed that they had done all they could to prepare for war. Warned of possible sabotage to his aircraft, General Short ordered them to be grouped close together so that they could be more easily guarded at Hickam and Wheeler Fields.

All combatant ships in port were ordered to maintain Readiness Condition Three, allowing for a 25 percent watch set on the guns and an ability to get under way in twelve hours. In the early morning of 7 December, Admiral Kimmel, trying to save on spare parts and aircrews, dispatched only three of his scarce long-range PBYs out on patrol—but none of them were sent north of Oahu, where Nagumo launched his air strikes. Both Kimmel and Short went to bed on Saturday 6 December believing that they had plenty of time before Japan launched an attack. They were, of course, dead wrong.

✪ ✪ ✪

It might appear from the results that all went exactly according to Yamamoto's plan, but that wasn't so. In Tokyo, at the last minute, Prince Hiroyasu Fushimi insisted that the attack include some special weapons that were hidden away at the top-secret Kure Naval Base. These weapons—so secret that only a handful of Japanese military officers knew about them—were midget submarines. The Japanese had been quietly working on these specialized subs for years. Fushimi was convinced that they could penetrate the highly secure Pearl Harbor. He wanted five of them to be included on the mission so that by attacking U.S. ships right at their docks, the submarine service would be part of the great victory over the American fleet.

The undersized subs, seventy-eight feet long and six feet high, were significantly smaller than conventional submarines. Displacing only forty-six tons, they had room for just two crewmen, specially trained for this mission.

Yamamoto was at first reluctant to include the unproven submarines in the attack, fearing that they could cost him the advantage of surprise if they were detected before his aircraft were over the target. Fushimi's tiny subs would have to be moved into position hours ahead of the planned attack, risking the possibility of detection and thereby alerting the American military to the impending air strike.

The midget subs, officially called Special Purpose Submarines (SPS), had been under development since the late 1930s and had been subjected to intensive testing by the Imperial Navy at the secret base in Kure. But they were a new weapon, dependent on unproven tactics. Yamamoto, not only skilled in the art of war but also wise to political realities, understood that Prince Fushimi had powerful allies in the emperor's household, so he reluctantly modified his plan of attack to include the midget subs.

Five I-Class submarines, Japan's largest, were fitted with special cradles enabling each "mother sub" to carry an SPS behind the conning tower. Yamamoto designated the group as the Special Attack Unit.

The 600-horsepower, battery-powered mini-subs were capable of twenty-three knots surfaced and nineteen knots submerged, but only for two hours. At two knots they could run for nearly ten hours submerged, if the two-man crew didn't run out of air first. Because of these limitations, Yamamoto ordered the Special Attack Unit I-boats to approach within ten miles of Pearl Harbor early on the morning of 7 December, fan out around the entrance, and launch their midget submarines. The mother subs would then retreat to a rendezvous point off Oahu and await the return of the SPSs after the attack.

Each SPS was outfitted with two Type 97, eighteen-inch-diameter torpedoes. There was nothing "midget" about these weapons—each had a

772-pound warhead. When fired from the vertical tubes at the bow of the subs, they could run up to three miles at fifty miles per hour. The midget subs were also packed with high-explosive charges that could be detonated by the crew, effectively making the subs suicide bombs.

Once released by their mother subs, each SPS was to make its way through the anti-submarine nets and into the harbor to launch its torpedoes at the U.S. ships moored around Ford Island.

Ten men had been chosen and trained for the two-man crew of each midget sub. They had to be able to tolerate confinement in a tiny space for long periods of time; be able to withstand extreme cold and heat; and be able to endure the foul air and the buildup of sulfuric acid gases given off by the sub's lead-acid batteries. Those serving on Japanese midget subs had to have not only no fear of death, they had to *expect* to die.

Early on the morning of 7 December, while Nagumo's six carriers were preparing to launch aircraft 230 miles north of Oahu, the five mother subs of the Special Attack Unit arrived on station off the mouth of Pearl Harbor. Navy Lieutenant Kichiji Dewa was aboard the mother ship for SPS I-16*TOU*, one of the midget subs. (The midget subs didn't have individual names like all of the large ships. Instead, they were referred to by the designation of their mother ships, followed by the suffix *TOU*.) He spoke by telephone to the officer inside the SPS as the tiny vessel prepared to disconnect from its mother ship, wishing that he were one of the ten brave men in the five midget subs headed for Pearl Harbor.

▯ ▯ ▯

SIGNALMAN KICHIJI DEWA
Aboard Submarine *Chiyoda*
6 December 1941
2210 Hours Local

We were the chosen ones among the chosen. We had realized the importance of our mission, so despite the kind of work we were doing, there was not much dreading. We were gradually making progress in training for the port and harbor assault.

When I went on the *Chiyoda*, I did a lot of training and learned many spiritual lessons [as] the "chosen ones among the chosen." It was maybe two months after I went on the *Chiyoda* that I really started to become aware of my status as a crew member of the SPS. I felt that we were working on something really important.

During training they created what is called "port and harbor assault." The strategy was that when SPSs encountered enemy warships, the first thing they tried to do was lessen the numbers of warships, battleships, and troops—to decrease the enemy military units. The SPS was to be used for this "reduction of enemy forces" plan.

While we were submerged, we devoted ourselves to sleep. When we surfaced at night, we maintained the ship. Our major duties were charging the batteries and ventilation. Since we carry large batteries, if we leave the hatch closed all day long, a lot of gas gets generated. And if the motor is turned on with that generated gas, it can spark and blow up. Someone actually died from an explosion, so we were constantly careful about that. Otherwise, it was cleaning the ship. Bilge, filthy water, would accumulate. We can't just leave it, especially in places like the motor room.

After we loaded the SPS on the mother submarine and sailed, it was officially announced by the captain that our target was Pearl Harbor.

I heard that the upper staff officers weren't going to grant permission [for the mission] unless there were arrangements for the crew members to return alive, but I don't think the commanding officer, Lieutenant Commander Masaji Yokoyama, expected to return alive. He used to say, "There is a saying, 'Kill the small insect to get the big insect.'"

Basically, even if they were to succeed with the assault and return, the U.S. was no doubt going to track us down, and once they did, the existence of the mother ship would be discovered, and if it were attacked, we would lose everything. So it would be for the best if just the two in the SPS died. That was our way of thinking. I don't think anyone expected to come back.

When they were leaving, they were dressed in the uniforms that airplane pilots wore. They took their Japanese sword and food we prepared for them.

On the night of 6 December, I was in charge of the phone connecting the [mother] ship and the SPS. I was talking about maintenance and ordinary things. On the other end, Lieutenant Commander Masaji Yokoyama, the commanding officer of the SPS, spoke, thanked us for the job well done, and things like that. Both of us were matter-of-fact. It was just an ordinary conversation. We weren't really thinking about death. We were only thinking about carrying out our duties properly.

✪ PACIFIC OCEAN
ONE MILE SOUTH OF OAHU
SUNDAY, 7 DECEMBER 1941
0245 HOURS LOCAL

Once released from their "mother subs," the skippers of the midget subs tried to find a way into the harbor so they'd be in place around Ford Island when the aerial attack started.

The crews of the midget subs could see the lights of Honolulu through their periscopes and hear big-band jazz music coming from the local radio stations—the same ones whose signals had guided the mother subs to the release point ten miles from the harbor mouth. Getting this far had been relatively easy. Slipping undetected through the anti-submarine net into the anchorage behind or beneath one of the American ships as it entered the harbor presented a much more formidable challenge.

The commander of the five-sub Special Attack Unit, twenty-nine-year-old Lieutenant Commander Naoji Iwasa, had been a Japanese test pilot. He had trained the other nine men and emphasized the importance and seriousness of their task. He hadn't exactly said that theirs was a suicide mission, but none doubted that it was. "No one intends for us to come back," Iwasa had told his men. Iwasa, the skipper of the mother ship I-22, was also skipper of the SPS I-22*TOU*. Iwasa was the oldest of all the crew members, and his crewman was Naokichi Sasaki, an expert kendo swordsman.

Lieutenant Commander Masaji Yokoyama, the skipper of SPS I-16*TOU*, was assisted by Petty Officer Sadamu Uyeda, a quiet mountain boy.

Skipper Shigemi Furuno of SPS I-18*TOU* had told his parents that he couldn't get married because he had to be ready to die at any moment. His crewman was Petty Officer Shigenori Yokoyama.

Ensign Akira Hiro-o, the skipper of SPS I-20*TOU*, at twenty-two years old, was the youngest of the midget submariners. Petty Officer Yoshio Katayama, a farm boy, was his crewman and engineer.

Ensign Kazuo Sakamaki was the skipper of SPS I-24*TOU*, along with crewman Chief Warrant Officer Kiyoshi Inagaki.

✪ ✪ ✪

At 0342 hours, the minesweeper USS *Condor*, on patrol just outside the harbor entrance, sighted what appeared to be a submarine periscope following in the wake of the USS *Antares* as she steamed slowly toward the harbor, waiting for the submarine net to drop at dawn so she could enter. The crew of the *Condor* immediately broadcast a warning over the radio: "SIGHTED SUBMARINE ON WESTERLY COURSE SPEED FIVE KNOTS." Alerted by the *Condor*, the crew of the *Antares* also spotted the sub and repeated the message. The calls were heard by a PBY reconnaissance aircraft overhead and by the USS *Ward*, an ancient four-stack destroyer manned by Navy Reservists from the upper Midwest under a brand new captain, Commander William Outerbridge.

Aboard the *Ward*, Fireman First Class Ken Swedberg, a fresh-faced Navy Reservist from St. Paul, Minnesota, was at his "general quarters" battle station within seconds of the alert. As he peered into the darkness, his first thought was that it had to be one of Hitler's submarines.

▢ ▢ ▢

FIREMAN FIRST CLASS KEN SWEDBERG, USN
Aboard USS *Ward*, Pearl Harbor
7 December 1941
0630 Hours Local

I was a Fireman First Class, which meant I was normally in the boiler rooms. This is what I was trained for. But my job for "general quarters"

was topside, up on deck, assigned to a World War I balloon gun designed to shoot down dirigibles.

About one o'clock Saturday afternoon, 6 December, the captain called a "general quarters" drill to test his reserve crew. This was his first drill, and I think he was very wise to do that, as it later proved. We went to battle stations and I manned my three-inch gun up on the bow, right below our main battery, the number-one four-inch gun. We went through our drills and the captain was pleased, so we went back to our regular watches.

There was a wire mesh net that was drawn across the harbor entrance at dusk. It normally wouldn't open again until dawn. At night we'd make lazy figure eights outside the harbor entrance, sounding with our relatively new sonar. At 3:45 AM on the morning of 7 December, one of the minesweepers, the USS *Condor*, sighted what they thought was a periscope. We went to "general quarters," raced over there, and searched for about an hour, but found nothing. And so then we went back on our patrol.

At daybreak, about six-thirty, just as the harbor was coming alive, the USS *Antares* was standing off, waiting for the net to open so they could enter Pearl Harbor. And in the wake of the *Antares* we spotted this sub conning tower, about four feet out of the water, following the *Antares*, obviously intending to follow the supply ship into the harbor. We went to "general quarters" immediately, and as we raced over to it, a PBY overhead dropped a smoke bomb to mark the position for us. As I manned my gun on the bow, I could see we were coming up pretty fast.

I've got a front-row seat. As we approached it, it looked as though we were on a collision course. Everybody was starting to brace themselves. But at the last minute, the captain veered to port. When he did, the starboard, or right side, raised up a little. Our naval guns could not depress down that far, so when we fired, the first shell, from number-one four-inch gun, went over the conning tower.

By now we were almost parallel to the sub, and number-three gun on top of the galley deck, on the starboard side, trained on it and fired. We were so close that the fuse didn't travel far enough to arm, but the projectile put a hole right through the conning tower. It was a relatively small hole, but the sub took on water and started to sink. Obviously it filled up with water pretty quick.

We thought it was a German U-boat and released four depth charges set for a hundred feet. With the added weight of the water she had taken on, the sub lost her buoyancy and she settled like a rock—in twelve hundred feet of water.

We stayed at "general quarters," and the captain gave the order to break out the Springfield rifles. About an hour or so later, two planes came at us from inside the harbor and we could see the "meatballs," the red suns, painted on their wings. Our new anti-aircraft guns fired at the planes, and that's really what saved us, because they broke off their attack. We got a splash on one side, a splash on the other side. And that was as close as we came to getting any hits.

By 8:15, we could see the smoke and explosions ashore. About that time the captain told us that he had received a radio message that "this is no drill."

⊗ ABOARD USS WARD
PEARL HARBOR
7 DECEMBER 1941
0645 HOURS LOCAL

After relaying what he had seen up on the bridge, Ken Swedberg busied himself at his gun station. At 0653, Commander Outerbridge transmitted a message to the commandant, 14th Naval District: "WE HAVE ATTACKED, FIRED UPON AND DROPPED DEPTH CHARGES UPON SUBMARINE OPERATING IN DEFENSIVE SEA AREA. STAND BY FOR FURTHER MESSAGES."

The crew of the *Ward*, though all Reservists assigned to an aging destroyer, had been trained well and responded quickly.

As Ken Swedberg correctly surmised, the four-inch shell fired by the *Ward*'s number-three turret had not traveled far enough to arm. But even without exploding, the shell had done its damage. The round that hit the conning tower killed the Japanese skipper and the sub took on water. After sinking the Japanese midget sub, the *Ward*'s crew continued to salvo depth charges into the harbor, assuming correctly that there were probably other submarines in the waters.

The PBY patrol plane that Ken Swedberg had seen from the deck of the USS *Ward* was being flown by Lieutenant (jg) Bill Tanner, a twenty-four-year-old pilot from San Pedro, California. He was a graduate of USC and had joined the Navy in 1938, had trained in Pensacola, Florida, and had been stationed in San Diego until his squadron had ferried their twelve PBYs to Kaneohe Bay, on the northeast coast of Oahu, earlier that year. Tanner had responded to the radio calls from the *Antares* and the *Condor* and was flying over the area where the sub was last sighted. In the gray dawn of the morning, Captain Tanner thought he saw something and banked his plane for another look. His stomach fluttered a little when he spotted the subs—at least two, maybe three of them, in waters below—scarily close to the ships anchored just beyond the anti-submarine net, *inside* Pearl Harbor. He dropped smoke signal flares into the water where he had spotted the midget subs and then radioed a message to the air base telling of his discovery.

Tanner turned his PBY around and headed back to the spot where he had dropped the smoke containers. He readied his plane for dropping depth charges on the target to try to sink the enemy subs that he'd discovered in the Hawaiian waters.

A PBY plane like the one that detected the midget subs.

⬚ ⬚ ⬚

CAPTAIN WILLIAM (BILL) TANNER, JR., USN
Navy Air Recon PBY
Pearl Harbor Patrol Area
7 December 1941
0630 Hours Local

The PBY was a very slow, cumbersome airplane, but it had great range. It had a crew of eight and two engines, and was a seaplane used for long-range reconnaissance. They flew on patrol about 700 or 800 miles and returned. They were not fighter airplanes; it was strictly reconnaissance, but we had guns if we were attacked.

On the morning of 7 December, it was our turn to fly patrol, and as a matter of fact, it was the first real patrol that I had flown as a command pilot. I had just been made a patrol commander the week previous. I took off before dawn, along with two other airplanes, one flown by Fred Meyers and another by Tommy Hillis. We flew out of Kaneohe Bay on the north side of the island of Oahu, around Barber's Point, turned east, and flew south of Pearl Harbor, with the island about two miles offshore. Then we veered slightly to the southeast and followed the line of the islands of Maui and Lanai toward the big island—about a hundred miles—and then we'd turn, and return on a parallel course twenty miles further to sea. That's what I was supposed to do. The other two airplanes had slightly different patrols, to the north and east of where I was.

I saw it, and the copilot saw it too—what looked to be a buoy in the water, but a moving buoy. We had never seen anything quite like it. There was no question in our minds that it was an enemy submarine. It looked like it was on a course directly heading toward Pearl Harbor. We looked off to the left and saw the *Ward* steaming toward the object. We were too close to do anything about arming bombs, so we dropped two smoke signal flares on the object to help the *Ward* close in on it.

We turned left to circle and come back and see what was happening, and as I turned the airplane, the *Ward* was firing at the submarine. From what we could tell, it looked like the first shot went high, and the second shot I thought was high because I saw it splash in the water behind the submarine.

There was no question that it was an enemy submarine because our subs were not allowed to be submerged in that area, and we were ordered to attack any submerged submarine we sighted in the restricted zone. We completed our circle, came around, and dropped our two depth charges. The *Ward* followed its gun attack by dropping depth charges as it went over the spot where the submarine was.

We reported, "SANK ENEMY SUBMARINE ONE MILE SOUTH OF PEARL HARBOR." We sent it in code, not by voice, back to our headquarters. We had no indication we were at war but we sent it in Morse code, just as we were supposed to. We got an answer from our base that said, "VERIFY YOUR MESSAGE." And so we did, and our base told us to remain in the area until further notice.

We circled there for some time. When we didn't see anything other than what we had already reported, Fleet Air Wing One sent us a message to resume patrol.

✪ ABOARD JAPANESE SPS I-24TOU
PEARL HARBOR OUTER PERIMETER
7 DECEMBER 1941
0650 HOURS LOCAL

Twenty-three-year-old ensign Kazuo Sakamaki, stripped to just a loincloth, sat at the periscope of his midget submarine. Because he had no radio contact with the other SPS boats, he was unaware that one of them had just been sunk. He panned the periscope around to see if the USS *Antares*, the supply ship waiting outside the harbor, had been given clearance yet to move inside the bay and on to the docks. If the *Antares* was moving in that direction, then that would mean the underwater anti-sub net was open and Ensign Sakamaki could maneuver his midget sub, submerged below and behind the *Antares*, to get inside the harbor next to all the U.S. Navy ships at anchor around Ford Island. Sakamaki's orders called for him to get inside the harbor and launch his two torpedoes and "sink as many ships as he could," any way that he could. His orders made aircraft carriers the first priority, then battleships, followed by heavy cruisers. If the American carriers were not there, the Japanese submariners decided that their primary target should be the battleship USS *Pennsylvania,* the flagship of Admiral Husband Kimmel, commander of the U.S. Pacific Fleet.

It had been more than seven hours since the midget sub had been released from the mother sub some ten miles away, and by now the sulfuric acid gases were building up inside the cramped sub.

But Ensign Sakamaki had more problems inside his tiny sub than the buildup of toxic gases. Ever since they had detached from I-24, the minisub's gyroscopic compass—his primary means of navigation—had been malfunctioning. He and his crewmate, Petty Officer Kiyoshi Inagaki, had been working for the past several hours to try to repair the gyrocompass but had been unsuccessful. Eager to participate in the attack, they were both growing increasingly anxious that they would not make it inside the harbor before the air attack began, in little more than an hour.

Sakamaki's duty was to steer the midget sub, and Inagaki's job was to operate the ballast and trim valves. Working together, they tried to navigate toward the mouth of the anchorage by recalling the detailed charts of Pearl Harbor that they had memorized while en route across the Pacific from Japan. They, along with the other four midget sub crews, had been required to memorize all the pertinent details and layouts of not just Pearl but four other harbors as well: Singapore, Hong Kong, Sydney, and perhaps most frightening to the Americans, had they known about it, San Francisco.

✪ USS MONAGHAN, DD-354
PEARL HARBOR
7 DECEMBER 1941
0755 HOURS LOCAL

A little more than an hour after the USS *Ward* sank a sub outside the anchorage, the USS *Curtiss,* a seaplane tender, and an auxiliary ship, the USS

Medusa, also sighted one of the midget subs—this time *inside* Pearl Harbor. They immediately sent messages to the USS *Monaghan*, a destroyer that had just gotten under way. But as the *Monaghan* got up steam to race toward the new contact, the sky was suddenly filled with planes and all hell broke loose around them.

As Japanese aircraft dropped bombs and torpedoes, strafing the American airfields, barracks, and fleet, only one SPS midget sub penetrated the harbor. It launched a torpedo at the *Curtiss*, which by now had also been severely damaged after a Japanese plane had crashed into it. Despite fighting fires inside her hull and defending against other aircraft, the crew of the tender replied to the torpedo attack with a salvo of gunfire that scored a direct hit on the sub's conning tower.

The underwater missile intended for the tender missed and struck a dock at Pearl City. But the torpedo's wake alerted lookouts on the USS *Monaghan*. With anti-aircraft guns blazing at swarming Zeros, the destroyer, belching black smoke to hide it from the aerial attack, charged at the minisub, which then fired its second torpedo at the bow of the oncoming American vessel. The shot went wide, and seconds later, the *Monaghan* rammed the sub at high speed, crumpling its stern like a discarded cigarette. For good measure, before clearing the blazing harbor, the *Monaghan* dropped depth charges on the damaged sub. She sank quickly into the mud at the bottom of the anchorage.

By the time Commander Fuchida's second wave of aircraft reached Pearl Harbor, the *Monaghan* had joined the *Ward* and several other U.S. combatants—including the cruisers *Phoenix*, *St. Louis*, and *Detroit*, and destroyers *Tucker*, *Bagley*, *Dale*, *Henley*, and *Phelps*—outside the anchorage. There they joined in the attack on two other SPS midget submersibles—one of which was detected and believed sunk by depth charges after it fired its torpedoes at the USS *St. Louis*. Though never confirmed, a fourth midget sub was initially presumed to have been sunk about a mile outside the harbor during one of several depth charge attacks by American destroyers that ensued during the afternoon of 7 December and the morning of the following day.

Yamamoto's misgivings about the SPS attack were proving to be well founded. But for one of the midget sub skippers, Ensign Kazuo Sakamaki, the attack would prove to be the most ignominious event of his life.

□   □   □

ENSIGN KAZUO SAKAMAKI
Aboard SPS I-24 *TOU*
Oahu, Hawaii
8 December 1941

The National Museum of the Pacific War

We were under severe orders to keep our mission secret, so we couldn't surface or make any noise. Two destroyers were working the area, patrolling. When I approached, they dropped many depth charges. I tried again to pass the patrol and get into the harbor. We were instructed to try to get past the anti-submarine net, and even cut the net if necessary to get into the harbor.

We rushed the net and cut the wire mesh, trying to enter so we could get to our rendezvous point inside, but it was so hard, impossible to make a good course because my gyrocompass did not work. Then we got caught on the reef. We tried for four hours to try and get moving, but could not.

The next day, 8 December , just before dawn, we emptied the ballast tanks. I ordered my crewman to abandon ship. At that time, both of us were overwhelmed by the bad air inside the submarine.

Before I knew it I was floating in the sea, hurt. I cannot be sure, but maybe when we jumped into the water we got injured on the coral. I don't know. Waves—big waves—pushed me to the island, in front of the American airfield.

I was unconscious . . . and remembered nothing. I was captured.

□   □   □

By the night of 7 December, the sole surviving midget sub, piloted by Ensign Sakamaki, was in dire straits. Its gyrocompass inoperable and batteries nearly depleted, the sub drifted east until it ran aground on a coral reef off Bellows Field late that night. Sakamaki and his junior officer, Inagaki, were forced to abandon ship. Before doing so, they set a detonator on an explosive device to keep their sub from falling into American hands. Then they swam for the shore, fewer than a hundred yards from where the sub ran aground. Unfortunately for the hapless Sakamaki, the explosive charge failed to work as advertised and the sub did not self-destruct and sink. Worse still, Inagaki either drowned or committed suicide, and the exhausted Sakamaki, injured from the coral and sick from the poisonous fumes that had filled the submarine, barely made it ashore, where he finally collapsed, unconscious.

The next thing he recalls is a Colt .45 automatic pistol being held against his head by an American soldier, yelling at him in English to get up. The soldier holding the pistol was Corporal Akui of the Hawaii National Guard. He had just made Ensign Kazuo Sakamaki, Imperial Navy, the first Japanese prisoner of war.

□ □ □

SECOND LIEUTENANT STEVE WEINER, US ARMY
Bellows Field Communications Shack
Pearl Harbor
7–8 December 1941

Early Sunday morning, just as the attack began, there was a four-engine plane that buzzed our field. Now, Bellows Field is just a short strip, used for gunnery practice for P-40 fighter planes. And when this plane passed over, we thought it was the Navy, but they didn't have four-engine planes. Moments later, there was a crash. A B-17 trying to land on our strip had overrun our runway and crashed into the ditch at the far end. Those of us that were in the BOQ [Bachelor Officers' Quarters] got dressed quickly, ran down to the plane, and found that the crew was semi-hysterical. They had been shot up—some of them were bleeding, and you could see where the plane had been shot at.

We asked them, "What do you mean, you were attacked? Who attacked you?"

And while we were trying to make sense of the situation, a flight of Japanese fighter planes came in and started strafing us, and we all ran for cover. I ran to the operations shack, where there was a space between the floor and the ground. I stayed there until the attackers left.

After the attack, the armory was opened. None of us had carried arms before, but now we could take whatever we wanted. We each took .45s and M1 rifles, but there was no loose ammunition for the rifles. All they had were bandoliers for the .30-caliber machine guns, but the shells fit the rifles. So we wrapped bandoliers around us.

We were advised to pair off, dig a foxhole, and be prepared for hand-to-hand combat. By late afternoon I paired off with a young pilot from Texas. He was greener than me, and neither of us had ever fired a gun. So it starts to rain, and it was a miserable time, and we're sitting commiserating with each other—how it might be our last day on earth. He was sitting on my right, and because it was raining he took out his handkerchief to wipe his rifle, and he fired it across my lap. And I almost became a Pearl Harbor Purple Heart recipient on the first day of the war!

Later, after dark, we were sitting in the foxhole, and we saw two figures walking toward us from the ocean, about a hundred yards from where we were. When they got close enough, we saw that one was Corporal Akui, who had been stationed at the end of the runway. He was a member of the Hawaiian National Guard, leading a prisoner who was nude, with the exception of a loincloth. The corporal turned him over to us.

I asked, "Where did you get him?"

Corporal Akui said, "He walked right out of the water."

I think he was happy to turn him over to us. We, in turn, were looking to turn him over to a higher authority, so we took him to the operations shack. We sat him down and could see that he had been in the water for a number of hours. His skin was all wrinkled and he looked distressed, so we put a blanket around his shoulders and gave him some water and crackers. We tried to get some intelligence but he was defiant. He just looked from one face to the other, and we realized that we weren't getting anywhere with him. We decided that two young second lieutenants with no experience in interrogation weren't likely to get this guy to talk.

After an hour of attempted interrogation we realized we weren't getting anywhere. We didn't know who he was or where he came from and kept hoping that a senior officer would show up and take him off our hands.

Then, all of a sudden, after about two hours of just sitting there, the prisoner finally spoke. In crude English he asked for a paper and pencil. He wrote, "I Japanese Naval Officer. My ship catch on coral. I jump in water, swim to this airplane landing. I no tell about ships. Kill me in an honorable way." And he signed his name, Kazuo Sakamaki.

Well, early Monday morning, we see a conning tower sticking up, about a hundred, or a hundred and fifty yards offshore. We couldn't get very close—we were on shore—this was still in the water, and it wasn't accessible. I don't know who arranged it, but somebody from the base swam out to the sub with a towline, and with a jeep we pulled it in. We also found the body of an enlisted Japanese sailor. It washed ashore later that morning. Never in our wildest dreams did we think that we'd be attacked by midget submarines.

□   □   □

Ironically, these little-known facts of history are often overshadowed by the other events that originated in the skies over Pearl Harbor. This footnote to that "Day of Infamy" has been brought to light by a handful of warriors and historians from both sides of the hostilities.

For more than sixty years, members of the destroyer *Ward*, the *Monaghan*, and others had maintained that they had sunk three of the Japanese midget subs shortly before and during the infamous air attack. Yet, except for the captured sub commanded by Ensign Sakamaki—his sub is on display at the National Museum of the Pacific War in Fredericksburg, Texas—no evidence could ever be found to prove the claim that at least three other subs were sunk. Photographs taken during the aerial attack bear out evidence of a sub's presence in the harbor, but couldn't prove that any of them were sunk.

Then in 1960, off Keehi Lagoon, Navy divers found a midget sub during practice exercises. On 28 August 2002, just a few miles outside the mouth of Pearl Harbor, another was discovered. A research submarine from Hawaii Undersea Research Laboratory made a discovery that confirms that the *Ward* fired the first shot and scored the first victory over the Japanese attackers.

John Wiltshire, director of the Hawaii Undersea Research Laboratory, told me the *Ward* did indeed sink the midget sub. He showed me a four-inch hole in the starboard side of the conning tower—a shot that even John Wayne would have had trouble making. Wiltshire said, "This is the midget sub sunk by the USS *Ward* on the morning of December 7, 1941. It was found over 1,200 feet down on the ocean floor, just a few miles outside Pearl Harbor. It vindicates the crew of the USS *Ward*. It shows that, in fact, the crew of the *Ward* accomplished that dramatic first kill with an incredible shot from an ancient deck gun."

During that first battle of World War II, the U.S. defenders nailed four of the five midget subs, having sunk three and captured the fourth, Ensign Sakamaki's, after it ran aground. The fifth sub was variously believed to have been sunk outside the harbor on 7 or 8 December, or to have escaped altogether. Twelve hours after the attack on Pearl Harbor, U.S. code-breakers intercepted a Japanese fleet message thought to have originated on the fifth midget sub: "SUCCESSFUL SURPRISE ATTACK."

But after the war, it was concluded that the fifth sub had been lost trying to rendezvous with the mother sub—and it's still out there somewhere in the Hawaiian waters. All five mother ships waited two days for the midget subs to return. None did.

In the aftermath of the attack, Admirals Nagumo and Yamamoto would be decorated by Emperor Hirohito for their victory. Admiral Husband Kimmel and General Walter Short were relieved of command just ten days after the attack. Though both men asked for courts-martial to clear their names, neither request was granted.

And as for American forces at Pearl Harbor? Other than the irreplaceable lives lost, the attack was not as devastating as it might have been. Half the Pacific Fleet, including its three carriers—the *Enterprise*, the *Lexington*, and the *Saratoga*—were out of port on various assignments. Because the Japanese neglected to attack the shipyards, salvage and repair work on damaged vessels began almost immediately. Of the battleships that the Japanese thought they had sunk forever, only the *Arizona* and the *Oklahoma* (and the target ship *Utah*) were total losses. The *West Virginia*, the *California*, the *Nevada*, the *Pennsylvania*, the *Maryland*, and the *Tennessee* were all repaired and saw action later in the war. And the same was true for the cruisers *Helena*, *Honolulu*, and *Raleigh*. Other than the destroyers *Cassin* and

National Archives

Japanese Midget Sub

Downes and the repair ship *Sotoyomo*, which were damaged beyond repair, every other vessel hit during the attack was fixed and returned to duty.

Fuchida's pilots also ignored two other targets that would prove critical to the United States in the days ahead: Untouched by a single Japanese bomb or bullet was the enormous fleet fuel farm, where millions of gallons of fuel oil and aviation gas were stored. And in perhaps the greatest error of all, not one of the U.S. submarines in port at the time of the attack was touched. Yamamoto's Combined Fleet would soon feel the consequences of these mistakes.

A total of 350 Japanese aircraft carried out assaults on the *Utah*, the *Raleigh*, the *Helena*, the *Arizona*, the *Nevada*, the *California*, the *West Virginia*, the *Oklahoma*, and the *Maryland*. The U.S. Pacific Fleet was nearly decimated. At the same time, attacks on nearby air bases severely crippled America's air assets. Kaneohe Naval Air Station lost thirty-three out of thirty-six of its Catalina PBY flying boats. Hickam Field and the base at Ford Island suffered extensive damage to the runways, to aircraft parked on the fields, and to barracks and BOQ buildings housing the military personnel.

Some ninety-eight ships, about half of the U.S. Pacific Fleet, were in port the day of the attack. Miraculously, the other half of the American fleet was elsewhere in the Pacific on that fateful day. All of her carriers, most of her heavy cruisers, and about half of her destroyers were at sea when the attack occurred. That lucky break would help the United States greatly when America fought back, determined to rebound.

Luck, or Providence, played a key role that day for America.

CHAPTER 2
THE FALL OF THE PHILIPPINES
(JANUARY 1942)

Without pausing to celebrate the successful attack on Pearl Harbor, Admiral Yamamoto launched phase two of his ambitious Operation Z war plan. Though the calendar shows the date of these events as 8 December, they all took place within hours of the attack on Pearl Harbor because of the International Date Line.

As Admiral Chuichi Nagumo's First Carrier Strike Force steamed west toward Kure, Japan, he detached the carriers *Soryu* and *Hiryu*, accompanied by the cruisers *Tone* and *Hiru*, along with two destroyers, all with orders to attack the tiny American garrison on Wake Island. At 1150, less than four hours after they had seen action in Hawaii, some of the same pilots and aircraft bombed the U.S. base on Wake, destroying eight of the twelve brand-new Marine aircraft that had just been delivered on 6 December by the USS *Enterprise*.

Two hours later, aircraft from the Japanese 2nd Fleet, commanded by Vice Admiral Nobutake Kondo, attacked the British bastions at Hong Kong and Singapore, in preparation for full-scale invasions.

Five hours afterward, while flames still burned in the battered hulls of America's Pacific Fleet in Hawaii, and despite radio and telegraph messages reporting on the Pearl Harbor attack, Japanese aircraft launched from Formosa scored a successful surprise air assault on U.S. facilities in the Philippines. The 160-plane contingent of the Army Air Force that General Douglas MacArthur had been so painstakingly building to defend the islands the United States had sworn to protect was shattered—at a cost of just seven downed "Zero" fighters. The air raid eased the way for an invasion of the archipelago by more than 43,000 troops under the command of General Masaharu Homma.

Within six hours, bombs fell on Agana, the capital of Guam, and on all of the island's U.S. air and naval bases. This too preceded an invasion, making Guam the first U.S. territory to be seized by Japan.

Twelve hours after the attack on Pearl Harbor ended, it was just beginning at the tiny atoll of Midway. Japanese destroyers, attempting to put the island's runway out of commission with naval gunfire, came in so close that Marine artillerymen were able to fire back. The tiny garrison rejected the Japanese order to surrender.

National Archives

Vice Admiral Chuichi Nagumo was CINC of the Imperial Navy's First Carrier Strike Force.

The day after the Pearl Harbor raid, the U.S. Congress declared war against Japan. Invoking terms of their Tripartite Pact, Germany and Italy responded on 11 December by simultaneously declaring war against the United States.

Within forty-eight hours of the surprise attack on Hawaii, every major American and Allied base west of California had been attacked. The Japanese had seized Bangkok, Thailand, and Tarawa and Makin in the Gilbert Islands, and the American garrisons in Shanghai and Tientsin, China, had surrendered. Off Singapore, the British had lost their two largest capital ships in the Pacific, the battleship *Prince of Wales* and the battle cruiser *Repulse*, along with 840 British sailors.

These near-simultaneous strikes throughout the western Pacific, thought by most military officers of the day to be impossible, were the consequence of Yamamoto's meticulous operational and logistics planning. Their success also demonstrated the appalling condition of American intelligence and the abysmal state of American preparedness for war.

✪ HQ ASIATIC FLEET
MARSMAN BUILDING
MANILA, PHILIPPINES
8 DECEMBER 1941
0330 HOURS LOCAL

A little over half an hour after the attack on Pearl Harbor had begun, a Navy radio operator in the Asiatic Fleet headquarters in Manila received a message from Hawaii that the Pacific Fleet was under attack. The message concluded with the phrase "THIS IS NO DRILL." The radioman immediately awakened his duty officer, who in turn had the message delivered to Rear Admiral W. A. Glassford, commander of the American Asiatic Fleet.

The admiral, awakened at 0415, read the message and instructed that a copy be sent via his aide to General Douglas MacArthur, the senior American officer in the Philippines.

MacArthur, shown the message at 0445, ordered a coded dispatch sent to his senior staff and subordinates alerting them of the attack on Pearl Harbor. At 0530 in the Philippines, MacArthur's headquarters received a second coded cable, this one from the War Department in Washington, advising him that

General Douglas MacArthur

Japan had launched an "unprovoked surprise attack" on Hawaii and that war was "likely." More details were promised.

At 0800, news bulletins broadcast over shortwave and by standard commercial stations in Manila—and heard at nearby Clark Field—informed the population and MacArthur's troops, giving them a rough outline of what had happened at Pearl Harbor. By breakfast time, it seemed as though nearly everyone in the Philippines knew that the Japanese had attacked the Americans in Hawaii.

What they did *not* know was that in the predawn hours, about the time the first message came in from Pearl Harbor, hundreds of Japanese planes had taken off from bases in Formosa, en route to the Philippine Islands. The Japanese pilots flying the mission were worried—believing that by the time they arrived over the Philippines, the Americans would be ready for them. But as it turned out, they needn't have been concerned. MacArthur never ordered a defensive alert.

At about 0900, aircraft spotters on northernmost Luzon reported Japanese army bombers flying south toward Manila. U.S. planes were launched from Clark Field to intercept them, but the Japanese aircraft avoided a confrontation and detoured to another target, bombing barracks and other facilities at Baguio and Tuguegarao. At about 0930, the enemy bombers turned north and headed back to Formosa.

Lulled into believing that was the full extent of the Japanese attack, U.S. Army Air Corps officers at Clark Field ordered the fighters to return to base. Then, at 1130, as the U.S. aircraft were on the ground refueling, a second, much larger formation of Japanese bombers was picked up by radar. Fifteen minutes later, Colonel Alexander Campbell, the base warning officer, sent a Teletyped, coded message to Clark Field reporting that a huge formation of enemy planes was headed that way. For whatever reason, the message was never received.

U.S. fighter planes of the 34th Air Squadron from nearby Nielson Field were scrambled and sent to intercept the Japanese planes and to defend Clark Field. Planes from the 17th Air Squadron were launched to protect the Bataan Peninsula, while the 21st Air Squadron flew toward Manila. From its base at Iba, the 3rd Pursuit Squadron took off about noon to meet the Japanese formation over the South China Sea.

But none of the planes at Clark Field had been sent aloft. All except one of the B-17 bombers were still parked, wingtip to wingtip, on the airfield apron, when the first twenty-seven Mitsubishi bombers struck. Fifteen minutes later, another twenty enemy aircraft bombed and strafed Clark and Nichols Fields. And then a third wave of thirty-four Zeros dropped their munitions on—and then strafed—the American B-17s and P-40s lined up below. The American planes, fully fueled and loaded with bombs and ammunition, ignited like a fireworks display as the Japanese bombs and incendiary cannon rounds found their mark.

American losses during the hour-long Japanese air assault were staggering, just as they had been in Hawaii. Though there were only fifty-three American fatalities and a hundred wounded, the damage and destruction to U.S. aircraft was catastrophic.

Although some in the press described the Japanese air strikes on the Philippines as a second Pearl Harbor, the similarities ended with the surprise air attack. Unlike those in Hawaii, the air attacks of 8 December were just the prelude to the onslaught on the Americans and our Filipino allies. The Japanese had come to stay.

As Admiral Glassford's diminished Asiatic Fleet prepared to flee south to link up with Dutch and British ships in the East Indies, Japanese ships were already landing the first of 43,000 soldiers from General Homma's 14th Imperial Army. Arrayed against them, without air support and cut off from resupply or reinforcement, were the 15,000 American and 80,000 poorly equipped Filipino troops led by General Douglas MacArthur. Among them were some remarkable heroes.

✪ ✪ ✪

Dick Gordon volunteered on 5 August 1940 by walking into the U.S. Army recruiting center on Whitehall Street in downtown Manhattan. There, Gordon was offered his choice of where he wanted to go, so he chose the Philippines—suggested by the Army recruiter, who told him life there was pretty good. The recruiter had waxed eloquent about the beautiful tropical climate, warm breezes, and pristine beaches.

And that's just the way it was when Private Gordon arrived in the winter of 1940–1941. They drilled only until eleven-thirty in the morning, and stayed out of the hot afternoon sun, and, except for the midday heat, the weather was great, especially compared with the snow, wind, and sleet of New York. Private Gordon really thought he had it made—that is, until things began to take a decided turn in a different direction.

Lanky, six-foot-two, twenty-year-old Army Air Corps Private John Cook was a medic. He had enlisted in the Army Air Corps in Salt Lake City, Utah, and was assigned to the 90th Reconnaissance Squadron when the unit shipped out for the Philippines.

Corporal Ralph Rodriguez, Jr. was a twenty-three-year-old from New Mexico's 515th National Guard, in an Army anti-aircraft unit that had been dispatched to the Philippines after Congress extended the Selective Service Act just months earlier. All of his training was as a medic. When the Japanese invaded, he knew almost nothing about being a gunner or a rifleman.

Twenty-one-year-old Andy Miller from Nebraska was a private in the 19th Airborne Squadron of the Army Air Corps, stationed at Nichols Field. He regarded this as pretty good duty. The food was decent and the work wasn't too hard. It was a long way from home, but jobs were scarce in the Great Plains. But after the Japanese arrived, the bleak drought and Depression in Nebraska would start to look pretty good.

□   □   □

SERGEANT RICHARD GORDON, US ARMY
Assigned to U.S. Army Hospital
Manila, Philippines
8 December 1941

Things were great until around the summer of 1941, when it became a reality that the United States intended to defend the Philippine Islands in the event of war with Japan.

Troops began to arrive, ammunition began to arrive, and matériel began to arrive. And the men came. Many arrived in October and November wearing winter clothing from the States. Once the U.S. forces began the buildup, training began to accelerate.

I guess that's when we first became aware of the fact that we would probably be at war with the Japanese real soon. But no one said, "I wanna go home," because—quite frankly—nobody ever believed that we weren't ready for them. From our point of view—the lowly private's point of view—we never thought anybody would have the nerve to attack the Philippines.

When they bombed Pearl Harbor in December, it was a shock...we thought it'd be the Philippines first. The talk in the barracks was that everybody in Washington expected the Philippines would be the first target of the Japanese.

When we heard the news of the attack on the radio that morning, a lot of the men asked, "Where's Pearl Harbor?" I happened to have come through Pearl Harbor, so I had a good idea of where it was. But, yeah, it came as a shock. Suddenly war was thrust upon us. And what was a nice, peaceful existence suddenly became a tough situation.

Immediately after Pearl Harbor, in fact within eight hours, the Japanese struck the Philippines and caught all of our planes sitting on the landing fields, just like they did in Pearl Harbor. They wiped out the Army Air Corps. That's when we knew we were in deep trouble, because now we had no airpower of any kind.

The Japanese people in Manila had trinket shops, which we would shop in on Sunday. But by Monday, 8 December, they were wearing uniforms and sniping at us.

About three days after they bombed Pearl Harbor and that first attack on the Philippines, they bombed us again—but this time it was all over the place, so they moved us into Bataan, and much of the Filipino army was sent north by General MacArthur to defend against Japanese invasions. Within two days, the Japanese army just poured through. The Filipino army just wasn't ready. They weren't fit and hadn't been properly trained for combat.

□ □ □

PRIVATE ANDREW MILLER, US ARMY
19th Air Base Squadron, 20th Group
Nichols Field, Philippines
8 December 1941

I was at Nichols Field and I didn't have to go on guard duty till midnight, so I went to the theater and I saw the first half of *Gone with the Wind*. I planned to go back the next night—when I didn't have duty—to see the second half. But as it turned out, I had to wait four years to get to see the second half of that doggone movie.

At midnight I went on guard duty, and about four o'clock in the morning the sergeant said, "Wake me up at six." And then he told me that Pearl Harbor had been hit and all of us were dumbstruck. We couldn't figure out why those guys in Hawaii hadn't been on alert. We'd been on alert for a couple of weeks and it just threw us.

But then, later that same day, we got caught with our own pants down. I guess in war nothing ever goes quite the way it's supposed to.

☐ ☐ ☐

PRIVATE JOHN COOK, US ARMY
Fort McKinley, Philippines
8 December 1941

I was asleep in the barracks when the NCO in charge came in about three-thirty on Monday morning, turned on the lights, and shouted, "The Japs have bombed Pearl Harbor!" We had a formation outside and had to put on our field gear in the dark. . .from gas mask to helmets, fatigues, and everything. I was stationed at the hospital when we got our first patient early that morning from Nichols Field. I can still see that poor devil lying on the operating table. His heart was pumping the blood through his body, and he was all ripped up—his arm was torn off, and there was a great big gaping hole in his side.

After we'd finished surgery, there was a bunch of fighter planes scurrying, and we thought they were Americans. Then we heard the *rat-a-tat-tat* and we took it serious. Some of the trees out there are pretty huge. They must have been thirty-six inches in diameter, and we got behind them. When the planes left we looked around the tree, and there were ridges cut three inches deep into the other sides. How none of us were killed I'll never know.

▢ ▢ ▢

CORPORAL RALPH RODRIGUEZ, JR., US ARMY
Fort McKinley, Philippines
8 December 1941

It was Monday and I went to Catholic mass that morning. As we were coming out of the chapel, some airmen approached us and told us that the Japanese had bombed Pearl Harbor and the damage was great. I couldn't imagine what really happened but I figured maybe we're next. But all the anti-aircraft units of our regiment were already deployed around the airfield and they were ready. At least that's what we thought.

I was a medic and I wasn't supposed to carry a gun. I couldn't find any of the other medics from my unit, so I headed for the hospital. But on the way, a group of Japanese airplanes flew over. They were strafing the airfield. I saw a soldier with two boxes of ammunition running toward a machine gun mounted on a tripod and he hollered at me, "Give me a hand!"

Even though I'm not supposed to help carry a gun or anything, I fed the belts of ammo into the machine gun while he fired at four planes that tried to hit us. The bullets were going by us and this guy said, "We'll take those two—don't get too far away." Every time a plane would shoot at us, we'd shoot right back at it.

Well, after the first set of planes dropped their bombs, there was a kind of a lull and we got some more ammunition. Then more Japanese planes showed up. These were dive-bombers and even though we fired the gun a lot, I don't know if we hit any of them.

Nichols Field took a terrible pounding that day. It made us feel good to be able to shoot back. A lot of people didn't get to do that. Later that day, about four o'clock, I was sent to Manila to tend the wounded. We stayed there until Christmas Day, ready to fight.

✪ AMERICAN FAR EAST COMMAND
MANILA, PHILIPPINES
13 DECEMBER 1941
1230 HOURS LOCAL

Japanese attacks continued for the next several days. On 9 December, Nichols Field was attacked again with the same intensity that had rained down on Clark Field the day before. And more attacks followed for the next three days.

American airpower was soon reduced to nil. Four days after hostilities commenced, only six P-35 fighter planes were still operational, and though the mechanics managed to get a few of the obsolete P-26s running, they were no match for the Zekes and Zeros—even though the Japanese had to conserve fuel to make the long flight from Formosa to southern Luzon.

From more than a hundred P-40s that had been functioning a week earlier, the Americans now had fewer than two dozen. Only a handful of bombers were still able to fly, and half of those were limited to low altitudes.

On 12 December, more than one hundred Japanese aircraft raided Manila and the surrounding military bases. On 13 December, they attacked with almost 200 planes. The next day, General MacArthur ordered the remnants of the Asiatic Fleet to depart for safer waters and the remaining long-range B-17s to fly south to Australia. Two days after they were gone, the Japanese aircraft carrier *Ryujo* moved into close range to finish the work that the long-range aircraft had started from Formosa. By then, MacArthur's Far East Air Force was useless. And with no fleet or air cover for protection, the 15,000 green American draftees and Reservists and

80,000 poorly trained and equipped Filipino soldiers digging in on southern Luzon could do little but wait for General Homma's 43,000 battle-hardened 14th Army to arrive. They didn't have long to wait.

☻ BATAAN PENINSULA
THE PHILIPPINES
22 FEBRUARY 1942
1140 HOURS LOCAL

General Homma's troops began their three-pronged attack on Luzon by first seizing the tiny island of Bataan—north of the main island—on 8 December. While MacArthur's air force was being pounded by air raids, the Japanese marched ashore and overwhelmed the garrison guarding the airfield. Homma now had a refueling stop for his bombers returning to Formosa from their raids to the south.

Japanese landings on the north and west coasts of Luzon followed on 10 December, and a regimental-sized force was deployed from the Palau Islands to secure the port of Legaspi on 12 December, effectively isolating the U.S.-Filipino army in central Luzon. For the next ten days, the Japanese consolidated their supply lines and mercilessly suppressed any opposition they received from the civilian population.

General Homma commanded the Japanese army occupying the Philippines.

On 22 December, General Homma landed forty-eight divisions virtually unopposed across beaches and ports in Lingayen Gulf and followed up by landing 10,000 fresh troops—shipped all the way from Japan—at Lamon Bay on Christmas Eve. Surrounded, and faced with a catastrophic collapse of his food-, fuel-, and ammunition-starved army, General MacArthur reluctantly ordered a phased withdrawal of all U.S. and Filipino troops to the thick jungles and volcanic mountains of the Bataan Peninsula and declared Manila an open city—a city that is not defended by a military force and is not allowed to be bombed under international law. The Japanese, ignoring international conventions, continued to bomb it anyway.

Christmas Day brought no relief to the beleaguered Americans and their Filipino allies. On the northern Bataan Peninsula, the Japanese succeeded in breaking through the Allied lines along the Agno River, killing or capturing nearly 5,000 men—troops MacArthur could ill afford to lose as he waited for reinforcements from the United States.

At 1745 on New Year's Eve, as the first Japanese troops swarmed into Manila, Imperial Air Force aircraft operated from captured Philippine airports and bases—and pounded the defenders on Bataan. Lack of medical supplies and hospital facilities created a medical nightmare for the hundreds of casualties inflicted daily on the peninsula's front lines. The Allied troops suffering from malaria and other tropical diseases continued to fight untreated. By 10 January, rations were cut to one meal per man per day.

For the next forty-five days, Bataan was a bloody war of attrition. General Homma, increasingly pressured by Tokyo to finish the campaign, was forced back with heavy casualties in three failed attempts to land forces behind the American–Filipino lines at night. The tenacious defenders gave ground slowly, falling back only when overwhelmed by superior numbers or when ammunition supplies were depleted. On 22 January, General MacArthur gave the order to withdraw to prepared positions on the road connecting the towns of Pilar and Bagac. It would be Bataan's final defense line.

Through the first two weeks of February, the defenders beat back a dozen concerted Japanese assaults. From his headquarters on the island fortress of Corregidor, at the mouth of Manila Bay, MacArthur continued to beseech Washington for aid. Though the Allied troops were pounded daily by Japanese air raids and raked by naval gunfire, the island's deep defenses anchored the rear of those trapped on the peninsula. The Allies became increasingly confident that they could hang on until relief arrived from the United States despite the appalling conditions on Bataan. Among the troops on the line, there were rumors that a force was being assembled in Hawaii to arrive "any day now."

On 15 February, the defenders' hopes were dashed by news that the Japanese had captured Singapore. This prompted a widespread realization that the victory would free up tens of thousands of fresh troops and planes for Homma to throw against them.

Five days later, fearing that Philippine president Manuel Quezon would be captured in a Japanese breakthrough, General MacArthur convinced him to depart his homeland and prepare a government in exile. Under cover of darkness, President Quezon embarked on a U.S. submarine for Australia. Two days later, President Roosevelt issued secret orders to General MacArthur, directing him to leave the Philippines as well and establish a new headquarters as commander in chief, South Pacific, in Australia. It was the first confirmation that there would be no forces dispatched to rescue "the battling bastards of Bataan."

MacArthur, conscious of what his departure would mean to his long-suffering soldiers, was loath to carry out the order. He knew that rations had been cut from the prescribed 4,000 calories a day for a combat soldier to half of that, and soon they would have to be cut again.

He was likewise aware that his troops were already scrounging to supplement their scant rations. They were eating horses, pythons, caribou, monkeys, mules, iguanas, snails, and whatever else they could get their hands on. Milk, coffee, and tea had long since disappeared. MacArthur's men were beginning to starve.

When a quartermaster found some harvested, unhusked rice on the Bataan Peninsula, he brought all 250 tons of it to an undamaged rice mill to be milled. But the rate of consumption was fifteen tons of rice a day for the 80,000 troops—so the 250 tons of rice lasted fewer than three weeks.

Food was only one of the necessities in serious shortage. Medical supplies were almost exhausted, and medicines—especially morphine and plasma—were running out. The medics and surgeons had to improvise to save lives and keep even the most minor wounds from becoming dangerously infected. Many died of malaria who would have survived and recovered if they'd had quinine, but it was now nearly all gone. So, too, were other lifesaving drugs, like sulfa for treating infections. Vitamin deficiencies were likewise becoming apparent, with bleeding gums, and nearly every soldier had some kind of upper respiratory infection and a constant cough.

The climate and constant combat were also taking a toll on uniforms. Most of the men were missing parts of their clothing. Many had lost their boots or shoes. What remaining garb was left became torn and ragged and ordinarily would have been considered unserviceable. But nothing was thrown away.

Fortunately, most of the Americans didn't know their situation was as hopeless as it was. Many thought only their own unit was low on food and other necessities, and that help was on its way. If they had known the truth, they might have given up completely.

These were the realities that Douglas MacArthur confronted as he anguished over how to follow the orders of his commander in chief and still meet his responsibilities to his men. After conferring with his closest aides and General Jonathan Stilwell, he reorganized the defenses on Corregidor and Bataan and made plans to depart. On the night of 11 March, he and a few members of his general staff boarded four PT boats and headed for Mindanao. Addressing his men, he promised, "I shall return."

✪ ✪ ✪

After three harrowing days and nights avoiding Japanese ships and aircraft, MacArthur and his party arrived on Mindanao in the middle of the night. There, he and his staff boarded a U.S. aircraft for Australia. It marked the beginning of the end for the Philippine defenders.

On the night of 15 March, the Japanese launched an all-out artillery barrage against the last American–Filipino line of defense. On 20 March, President Roosevelt named General Jonathan Wainwright commander of all U.S. forces in the Philippine theater of operations. The following day Wainwright moved his headquarters to Corregidor and placed General Ed King in command of all Filipino and American forces on Luzon.

The Japanese, now aware of MacArthur's narrow escape, blanketed Bataan and Corregidor with leaflets promising good treatment to those who surrendered and lampooning MacArthur for "running away" from the Philippines and "abandoning them to starve and be killed." Ironically, the

Americans began to look forward to the Japanese leaflet drops—they used them for toilet paper.

By the end of March, the Japanese begin using radio broadcasts to add emotion to their propaganda. U.S. troops also received American broadcasts. In one, MacArthur himself pledged, "Help is on the way from the United States. Thousands of troops and hundreds of planes are being dispatched."

If only it's true... became the fervent hope of the defenders. But by 1 April, it was apparent to all that there would be no new supplies and no reinforcements.

No one from Washington ever told the troops in the jungles of Bataan that help was *not* on the way. They were, in fact, led to believe just the opposite. Three months of jungle combat, starvation, and diseases such as malaria and dysentery had taken a huge toll on troop strength. By the first week of April, just 30 percent of the defending soldiers were combat effective. The American and Filipino patients in base and field hospitals surged to 12,000. Sickness killed more allied soldiers than the Japanese Imperial Army.

Major General Wainwright was given command of the Philippines when MacArthur fled. He was later forced to surrender Corregidor to the Japanese.

On 2 April 1942, the Japanese began their final offensive, with massive air and artillery bombardments. General Homma, desperate for a final victory, brought up tanks to support his infantry. After four grim days of intense fighting, it became clear that the Allied troops on Bataan could hold out no longer. It was obvious that further resistance meant a hopeless slaughter. Homma had made it clear he was ready to annihilate any remaining American and Filipino forces who resisted.

Before departing, MacArthur had instructed General Wainwright that even if food and ammunition failed to arrive, and though the Japanese might be poised to destroy the American and Filipino armies, that the troops should valiantly fight on and kill as many Japanese soldiers as possible.

Likewise, FDR, who knew of their plight, had ordered "no surrender" as far back as February. So the only order still in effect was "resist to the end."

But without food, medicine, or ammunition, and faced with increasing numbers of fresh, well-supplied enemy soldiers, following such an order would result in a slaughter of crushing, colossal proportions.

The remaining senior officers in the Philippines now had two choices: accept annihilation or consider surrender. General Ed King commanded the Philippine Army and the U.S. forces on Bataan. King felt that no sane man could consider anything but surrender. He sent word to General Wainwright asking for direction. Wainwright responded with a direct order: "Counter-attack!"

✪ GENERAL ED KING'S COMMAND POST
BATAAN PENINSULA, PHILIPPINES
8 APRIL 1942
0900 HOURS LOCAL

Sick with malaria, exhausted from days without sleep, and demoralized by the plight of his weary warriors, General King decided to ignore his superior's impossible order to "counter-attack" and instead to open negotiations with the Japanese commanders to end the fighting. At midnight on 7 April, and aware that he was acting on his own, King informed his staff of his decision. Several of his officers wept.

At dawn on 8 April, after destroying classified equipment and material and after seeing to the escape of dozens of nurses and some 2,000 men to Corregidor, General King sent two of his staff officers out in front of the U.S. lines carrying a dirty bedsheet as a makeshift white flag of truce. Having made contact with a Japanese officer, they were escorted to the command post of the nearest division commander, General Nagano. With "safe passage" assured, King came forward to meet with the Japanese general. Since Nagano didn't speak English, his aide, Colonel Nakayama, acted as interpreter.

The Japanese, believing that General King was an envoy of General Wainwright, refused to discuss terms of surrender with him. But King eventually convinced Nagano that he was there to surrender his own men, and didn't speak for Wainwright, the overall commander of the remaining forces in the Philippines.

Reluctantly, the Japanese accepted the unconditional surrender of only King's troops on Bataan—but not those still holding out on Corregidor. When asked to surrender his sword, an act of great significance for the Japanese, King had to admit that he'd left his ceremonial saber in Manila. Instead, he took his Colt .45 automatic sidearm and laid it on the table.

General King had now officially surrendered his troops, 66,000 Filipinos and 12,000 Americans. He believed that by surrendering, he had prevented a bloodbath. It was the largest contingent of U.S. Army troops ever to surrender to a foreign adversary. The only comparable event was the surrender of General Lee's army in the Civil War—that, coincidentally, had taken place at Appomattox on the very same day in 1865.

✪ JAPANESE POW COLUMN
BATAAN PENINSULA, PHILIPPINES
8 APRIL 1942
1700 HOURS LOCAL

By 1600 on the day General King surrendered his army, it had begun. All along the Bataan front, Americans and their Filipino allies were laying down their weapons and moving out onto roads and tracks in the muddy jungle to be placed in clusters of several hundred in long columns by Japanese soldiers. It quickly became apparent that their conquerors had no intention of abiding by any of the civilized norms for the treatment of prisoners of war (POWs).

For his part, General Masaharu Homma had a hopeless problem. He had no idea how to handle this many prisoners. Tokyo had given him instructions for how to deal with 25,000 prisoners, not the 78,000-plus that he now had—and that worried him. He had insufficient food, water, medicine, and transport for his own men—how could he possibly care for this many prisoners? And most troubling of all, he was already five months behind Tokyo's war plan schedule.

Homma devised the perfect solution. By the time they arrived at the POW camps, sixty-five to eighty-five miles north on the Bataan Peninsula, there had to be fewer POWs—a lot fewer.

The situation was ripe for atrocity. The American and Filipino POWs began the agonizing march to the prison camps in what would become a brutal, unorganized extermination of horrific proportions.

The anguish would continue for years in the prison camps, where the Americans and their Filipino allies would be tortured, starved, shot, and worked until they expired.

The initiation into this hell on earth began with the sixty-five-mile odyssey of hideous pain and suffering that came to be called the Bataan Death March. It turned out to be one of the darkest chapters not just of World War II but of any war, anywhere. As they struggled up the muddy jungle path toward their place of confinement, it was a good thing that these emaciated survivors were unaware of the words of Secretary of War Henry Stimson, just three weeks after the Japanese attacked. Commenting on the U.S. government's inability to relieve MacArthur's beleaguered garrison in the Philippines, Stimson was heard to remark, "There are times when men have to die."

CHAPTER 3
A HELL WORSE THAN WAR: THE BATAAN DEATH MARCH
(APRIL 1942)

At 1300 on 9 April 1942, after holding out for more than four agonizing months, the Allies finally ended the siege on Bataan. As ordered by General King, the 12,000 American and 66,000 Filipino soldiers on the peninsula reluctantly laid down their arms. Many had been wounded; even more were sick. Nearly all were exhausted, starving, and deeply demoralized.

Many felt betrayed by their leaders, who had long promised that help was on the way. MacArthur, for weeks derided as "Dugout Doug" for commanding from the deep concrete tunnels on Corregidor, was, by the time of the surrender, being disparaged for having departed to Australia for his new command. Though some men escaped to continue to fight as guerrillas, fewer than 2,100 of those who had endured the battle of Bataan made it across the channel to join the defenders on Corregidor, where General Jonathan Wainwright vowed to fight on.

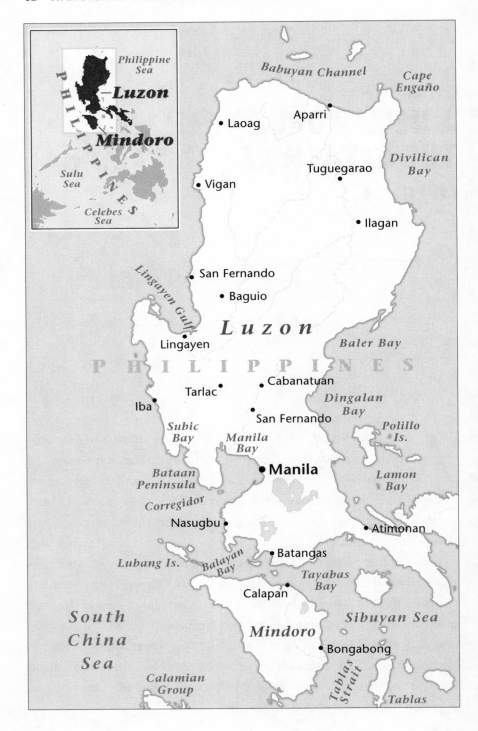

For the next twenty-six days, the Japanese pounded "the rock" nonstop with air strikes, naval gunfire, and artillery. Many of the rounds fired at the fortified island were made in America and had been captured on Bataan. By 6 May, Corregidor's "holdouts" could endure no more. General Wainwright surrendered unconditionally that afternoon. By noon the following day, the Japanese had assembled enough small boats and barges to begin transferring 15,000 dazed American and Filipino prisoners from the battered island to Mariveles, on the southern tip of the Bataan Peninsula. On 8 May, they began the long trek north, following the bloody footsteps of their countrymen on the "march of death."

Bataan Death March

Among those who were surrendered on Bataan on 9 April, others who escaped to fight as guerrillas, and the handful of "holdouts" who joined Wainwright on Corregidor were Sergeant Richard Gordon, Private Andrew Miller, Private John Cook, and Medic Ralph Rodriguez, Jr. Their eyewitness accounts of what they and their comrades endured are testament to the worst and best of humanity: horrific cruelty and incredible courage.

◻ ◻ ◻

SERGEANT RICHARD GORDON, US ARMY
Bataan Peninsula, Philippines
9 April 1942

When MacArthur realized that he could not stop the Japanese with his Filipino army, he reverted to War Plan Orange, which dictated that we withdraw into Bataan itself. What he failed to do, though, was to bring the supplies for the Filipino troops that had already gone north to fight the Japanese that had landed on northern Luzon. The army left behind tons of food and stuff that we desperately needed later on Bataan. So when we moved over to Bataan, we were already short of rations.

On 12 January [1942], MacArthur issued orders to cut the rations in half. And on 6 February or thereabouts, they cut the rations in half again. And in March we cut them again. So by the time the Japanese were closing in on us, in April, we were already living on fewer than 1,000 calories a day. And it's totally impossible, given the environment of that area and the rugged terrain, to fight on under 1,000 calories a day.

Most of the supply ships had been sunk by the Japanese, who had a tight blockade around the island of Luzon. We ate canned salmon and rice twice a day during the last two months of fighting on Bataan. We kept holding out, figuring things had to get better. In the meantime, the weight of the men dropped off something fierce. And before we knew it, there was no combat effectiveness whatsoever.

And then disease came in. Men came down with malaria and dysentery, and it spread like wildfire. By the end of March they were committing 1,000 malaria patients a day to the field hospitals. That left us with only about 30 percent of the troop strength to fight off the Japanese by the time we began the final retreat to the bottom of the peninsula, in the hopes of escaping from Bataan.

Later on I heard that Henry Stimson, the secretary of war, made the statement "There are times when men must die." But it's a good thing I never heard about that remark until after the war.

We sort of figured out that help would *not* be forthcoming. It never happened. But you know, from my point of view as a professional soldier, I could accept it. But most of the men were youngsters just drafted into the military, or National Guardsmen who had no training to speak of. For them it was a much more precarious situation.

By the first week of April it was pretty clear that our military wasn't going to be able to rescue the Philippines. We knew it all depended on the American Navy coming to our rescue. But since Pearl Harbor was destroyed, that pretty well sealed our fate.

The first realization that we were in really deep trouble was when the order came to lay down our arms and surrender to the Japanese. Until then we didn't think that surrender was possible. Many of the men cried when that order was issued. As bad as things had gotten, we were still holding out hope that somehow Uncle Sam would be able to bail us out. We'd been promised it so often right along for the four months that we were in Bataan that we had come to believe it. We believed it because President Roosevelt made a speech to that effect—that arms, equipment, and everything else was coming our way. General MacArthur had said, "Hold on . . . don't give any ground. Food and help are on the way, hundreds of planes, and thousands of men." And of course, you live on those rumors. But the rumors never came true. On 9 April we found out that nothing was coming.

General Ed King had absolutely no choice other than to surrender, and it took a great deal of courage, knowing full well that he might be court-martialed after the war. General King knew he had the lives of [66,000 Filipinos and 12,000 Americans] in his hands. But the Japanese did not want to accept General King's surrender. And there never was an official document called the surrender of Bataan. General King placed his .45-caliber pistol on the table they were sitting at and turned himself over to the Japanese. He wasn't allowed to come back to the troops, but word came back by one of the staff officers that the surrender was in effect.

But I didn't surrender. I went with a group of other soldiers and my friend Elmer Parks further up the mountain to a place called Mount Bataan, in the hopes that we could avoid surrender. Two or three days later, we were scrounging for food or anything that was left behind, because we couldn't find anything on the mountain. And when we came down, we ran into a Japanese patrol. They captured us, and about fifteen Japanese soldiers came out from the underbrush and began to beat the living daylights out of us. They took everything we had and walked us down the hill to where the main group was. As I passed I saw a U.S. soldier tied to a tree—he'd been bayoneted. It was Major James Ivey from San Antonio, Texas, and they'd used him for bayonet practice. He was bare from the waist up, and blood was still spurting out of the wounds.

Bataan Death March

The Japanese took us to a staging area, an assembly point for thousands of our soldiers, and threw us into this enclosure. At this time I lost contact with Elmer Parks, and didn't find him again for forty years.

When they threw us into this stockade it was the middle of the night and pitch dark and you couldn't see anything. And there were thousands of men all over the place, lying down out of sheer exhaustion. There was no order or discipline, just thousands of men lying in an open field. There were no latrines, and the men who were wounded or who had malaria or dysentery just relieved themselves where they lay. The place was covered with feces and was a terrible mess. I found a place and lay down, waiting for the night to pass.

□   □   □

PRIVATE ANDREW MILLER, US ARMY
Nichols Field, Philippines
6 May 1942

After the first air attacks in December, we were moved from Nichols Field to Bataan—a peninsula with Manila Bay on one side and on the other side was the South China Sea. The Harbor Defense Group and their big guns on four different islands in the mouth of the bay protected the entrance to the bay. Corregidor was the biggest and best fortified of these islands. The idea was to hold out until the Navy could escort ships over to support us. Well, it never happened.

When my unit got sent to Bataan we were positioned at about kilometer mark 133. I guess you'd call it the front line, but the Japs called it the main line of resistance. The Jap offensive started on 3 April on our left flank. They never shot where we were at all. They'd send an occasional artillery round just to let you know that they knew you were there. On the night of 6 April the medics came in and took the men who had malaria the worst back to one of the hospitals.

On the afternoon of the eighth, we were on a hill, and they weren't too far away from us, and quite a few men got hit. For some of the men the only thing we could do was ease their pain with a shot of morphine, because there was no way you could save them.

But the sun finally came up and somebody told us that they were trying to arrange a surrender. Well, we didn't think that was such a good idea. So we made it down to the beach and found an outrigger canoe. Then we started out for Corregidor, which was not such a smart move. The tide was going out, and there's a current in the bay. We got out about a quarter mile or so, looked over to Corregidor, and saw nothing but smoke and dust. We looked back at Bataan and it was the same thing—a lot of fire, everything was a mess. Airplanes were all over the place. Looking out in the bay [we could see] silhouettes of the Jap navy out there. You couldn't go to Manila, and the water was full of sharks.

I escaped, and got over to Corregidor. My hunch was right. They had more food over there and it was much better. I stayed for almost four weeks, until Corregidor surrendered.

◻ ◻ ◻

PRIVATE JOHN COOK, US ARMY
Fort McKinley Base Hospital
9 April 1942

Three days before the surrender, the Japanese launched a big offensive with a lot of air and artillery strikes. I was on the front line, up on a lookout tower, about fifty feet up on this platform built between two trees. It was in the morning and I was supposed to give a warning with a siren if the Jap planes came over. But they came in over Mount Mariveles, in the sun, about 9:30 and they dropped a 550-pound bomb and blew up eighty-eight people in the hospital ward even though it was marked with a big red cross.

We worked for three days and nights without sleep, and the night before the surrender the nurses were ordered on a bus and aboard a barge for Corregidor.

When we got the order to surrender, the medics at Hospital Number One used a piece of white sheet and Colonel Duckworth had the folded-up flag, and on top of that he had his web belt and his .45. The officers and senior NCOs took our guns and presented them to the Japanese Tank Corps.

✪ JAPANESE-HELD TERRITORY
AMERICAN POW COMPOUND
BATAAN PENINSULA, PHILIPPINES
MID-APRIL 1942

It quickly became apparent to the prisoners on Bataan that their ordeal had not ended when the guns fell silent. The Japanese had no food, water, clothing, or medicine to spare. In fact, many of General Homma's soldiers guarding the prisoners were in as bad or worse shape than their American and Filipino captives. Japanese troops immediately "searched for weapons"—an excuse for stripping the prisoners of anything of value, not just watches, rings, rank insignia, and cigarettes, but boots, mess gear, canteens, packs, even clothing—the very things the prisoners would need most to survive captivity.

Once the "search" was complete, the prisoners were randomly counted off into groups of one to three hundred men and led off into the jungle. As soon as one cluster departed, another was formed up and marched off—ignoring any U.S. or Filipino unit integrity that might have kept comrades together to help one another.

By 12 April, all organization for moving tens of thousands of thirsty, wounded, sick, and starving men into the interior of Luzon had completely collapsed. There were far too few Japanese guards to keep order with such a huge number of prisoners and there was no order in the ranks whatsoever. When problems arose on the muddy, blood-soaked path, the guards used their bayonets and swords—their officers had ordered them not to "waste" ammunition—in

A Japanese soldier beheads a U.S. prisoner.

National Archives

order to keep the prisoners from getting out of hand. Deadly incidents happened infrequently at first, but quickly escalated in number as the march north degenerated into a chaotic, genocidal extermination. Weak and terrified American and Filipino troops who did not instantly follow orders or who fell out of ranks from wounds, sickness, hunger, or thirst were disemboweled or beheaded.

For most of those at the front of the column, the "march of death" took only a few days. But for the vast majority—perhaps as many as 50,000 others—farther back in the pathetic procession, it was a matter of weeks. And although there are no official reports, because the Japanese kept no records and the Allied officers weren't allowed to, survivors estimate that more than 2,000 Americans and as many as 10,000 Filipinos perished on the trek.

The Japanese also killed hundreds of Filipino civilians, often for merely showing basic human kindness to the prisoners. In one horrific, well-documented incident, a Japanese soldier used his bayonet to disembowel a pregnant Filipino woman and ripped the woman's unborn baby from her abdomen for her "crime" of offering some food to an American POW. The Japanese soldier then "mercifully" killed both mother and child.

Battling Bastards of Bataan

Camp O'Donnell POW compound

Several thousand prisoners were routed to the little railhead town of San Fernando, where they were loaded aboard narrow-gauge railroad cars. In stifling heat, they were packed in so tightly that when the weakest expired from suffocation, wounds, heat exhaustion, or disease, they had nowhere to fall. Many of the men had dysentery and couldn't control their bowels, and as a result the floors were covered with diarrhea, urine, and vomit. The stench was unbearable. When the train finally arrived at Kapas, the Japanese opened the boxcar doors and the prisoners tumbled out. The bodies of those who had died during the journey were tossed outside into a pile, drenched with gasoline, and burned.

The terrible trek was a prelude to the horrors that would follow. Afterward, survivors estimated that there was a dead body every ten to fifteen feet along the entire route of the Death March. Yet there would be many times over the course of their confinement when the living would envy the dead.

By 24 April, more than 54,000 American and Filipino prisoners were crammed into an area of less than one square mile in western Luzon. The captives called this hellish place Camp O'Donnell. The Japanese called it a "prisoner processing center."

Malnourished and weak, many prisoners were too feeble to even go inside huts and were laid out on palm-frond mats. There was scant shade; the sun beat down upon them unmercifully. As they lay in their own feces, ravaged by swarms of flies and mosquitoes, they were plagued by malaria, gangrene, dysentery, typhoid fever, and other tropical diseases the doctors had never seen before. Men began dying at the rate of fifty a day. And then things got worse. Within six weeks, one of every six Americans who had survived the Death March was dead.

When they could, the POWs would bury the deceased. But it was the beginning of the rainy season and the torrential downpours constantly washed the bodies out of the shallow graves. The Japanese guarding the prison didn't seem to care. They had built Camp O'Donnell as a place from which they could ship "healthy" POWs to Japan and Manchuria as slave laborers. Those too weak or wounded to be shipped out were simply moved a few miles farther into the jungle to other camps, like the infamous Camp Cabanatuan, to await death or release. Few dared hope of escape or rescue.

▯   ▯   ▯

SERGEANT RICHARD GORDON, US ARMY
Camp O'Donnell POW Camp
Luzon, Philippines
May 1942

The day after the surrender, the Japanese got us up at the crack of dawn and started marching us north, in groups of about 300 at a time. It was every man for himself. A lieutenant colonel had been wounded and he was unable to stand. They put him on a stretcher and asked for volunteers to carry him. I was one of four who carried that man all day long. We kept asking for relief, because it was hot and getting hotter. No one came near us to relieve us. When we put that man down that night we went in four different directions, because we knew that the next day, if we were still on the detail, we would not physically be able to make that march.

I think that the Japanese made sure they didn't let units march together. Units are much more difficult to control than a loose group of prisoners. Generally speaking, they didn't allow that to happen, and just broke up our military units.

One loose group of 300 would lead the first day, and another group would lead the next. We wondered how the Japanese would treat us. What they had done in China had been played on newsreels almost nightly in Manila theaters. We saw what they did to Chinese women and soldiers— raping, beheading, shooting—so we knew what they were capable of. But naively, we didn't think that we would have to suffer that inhumane treatment as Americans. But we did.

When General King had tried to arrange to use our own vehicles to transport us out of the Bataan area, the Japanese refused.

They gave us no food at all. Some may have gotten a rice bowl somewhere, but not in my case. They would not let you break ranks to go for water. They would allow stops for water, but they were few and far between. So as a result, men would break ranks and go to some stagnant pool on the side of the road and begin to drink. And the Japanese would yell, get them back in ranks—or if they wouldn't get in ranks fast enough, they shot them.

In my case, training was the difference between my survival and perhaps not surviving, because I had been trained in how to preserve water. I had one canteen, and I would put a little of that water in my mouth, swish it around, get a little trickle down my throat, and spit the rest back into my canteen. Hardly Emily Post etiquette, but an effective way to keep what water you had.

But most of these men came overseas untrained and not acclimated to the Philippine climate. They couldn't tolerate it. The sun in the Philippines is incredibly hot, especially at noontime. And every day at noon on that march, the Japanese would stop us. Every time they stopped they conducted a shakedown. We were all warned before the surrender, just before we were all captured, to have nothing on us that was Japanese. We were told not even to keep some of the propaganda leaflets that they dropped on Bataan, which [they felt] showed that you had ignored their offer of surrender. But many of us had money we had taken off dead Japanese soldiers during the fighting. In my case I had a diary that some Japanese writer had kept. I got rid of it real quick—even before the surrender. If they caught you with something like that, there was an immediate execution.

Each time we stopped on the march, the Japanese put us into an open field with no shade, no trees around, and made you take your hats off and sit there all through their lunch hour. That was deliberate. It made you lethargic, to the point that you were in a stupor. That way you couldn't run away.

I saw a young American soldier who passed out from trying to walk in that heat. He just collapsed where he was, close to the road. A Japanese tank, moving south as we moved north, deliberately ran over him. And behind that tank, the other tanks swerved to run over him.

A Filipino soldier in the column ahead of us was alongside the road as our column passed. He was on his knees and I watched as a Japanese soldier beheaded him. I don't know why.

I saw a Japanese soldier beat a woman with the butt of a rifle because she was trying to hand food to one of the prisoners.

We marched like this for—in my case—eight days. They knew we were dying for food and water, and they weren't going to let us have it.

At the end of the eight days, we arrived at a huge metal warehouse that had held thousands of sacks of rice. But it was empty when we got there. The Japanese pushed us inside that warehouse, as many prisoners as they possibly could squeeze in. We were standing like the subway at rush hour.

When we were all inside they shut the windows and door. The sun beat down on that place and men died in the night because of the heat and closeness, and from being ill to begin with.

The next morning when they opened the door for us to come out, there were a lot of dead men left behind. The Japanese took those people and threw them into a big open hole, poured gasoline on them, and set fire to them.

We were marched further up the road to a town called San Fernando, where they had trains with boxcars waiting for us. They shoved as many people into those boxcars as they could get inside, standing up, with no room to move. Every now and then, some would die, but we were packed in so tight, they couldn't fall down. We finally ended that train ride, and when we got out of those cars, there were dead men in every car. Once again, the Japanese piled them off to the side and set fire to them.

When we got to our destination we started marching again. Men were dehydrated from being in that warehouse, in the boxcars, and being forced to sit in the noonday heat, and many more of them died.

If we had known it was going to be eight days of inhumane treatment and abuse, with so many dying or executed, I think there might have been an attempt at mass escape, despite the risk. But no one had any idea how long it was going to take, because the Japanese kept telling us, "Just a little way up the road we will stop for food and water." It was a lie, of course, but they kept telling us that, like bait dangling in front of you. Those things never materialized.

The Japanese marched us to a place called Camp O'Donnell, which was to be our first prison camp. We had to stand in the hot sun and wait about an hour or so, until the camp commander came out. He gave us the full, ten-course description of what would happen if we tried to escape. We were searched, and if they found anything they didn't like, those people were executed on the spot.

The conditions at Camp O'Donnell were indescribable. We were assigned to certain barracks, and we found ourselves with a single water pipe for 3,000 men. Men went without water even in that prison camp, many of them too weak or sick to wait in line for hours for a drink.

We thought that when we got to O'Donnell that our lot in life had improved, only to find ourselves in the Black Hole of Calcutta. I was ordered to burial duty, and after a while you couldn't even recognize the corpse you were taking out. So I could very easily have buried my friends and never known it.

□   □   □

CORPORAL RALPH RODRIGUEZ, JR., US ARMY
Camp O'Donnell POW Camp
Luzon, Philippines
May 1942

Before the surrender I packed my medic's bag with a couple of bottles of paregoric and a good-sized bottle of iodine. And those are the two things that I used throughout the Death March. I put iodine in the water and the paregoric to give out because it numbs pain a little and helps if you have diarrhea. It also has alcohol in it, and it builds you up a little bit.

I barely got through the areas where they stood you one against the other. I guess from lack of air or something, I passed out. A lot of the men hadn't eaten for at least two, three days or more. You can't march very far in a hundred degrees, much less half-starved. On the first night, there were some people ahead of us—the airfield was full of people. During the evening, late, we started coming across men who were sitting down or couldn't move, or were lying down sick, asking for help. Right away the medics started to try to help them out, but as soon as you start helping them, here come the Japs with their bayonets.

The Japanese struck the butt of the rifle in one man's face, broke all his teeth and nose and everything. I saw the Japanese pursue one who got behind a fruit stand and he shot him, and then he came up cleaning his bayonet.

One time they made us run—maybe because they were just mean. God was with us, for after making us run, they stopped us about two, three o'clock in the morning. We lay down alongside the road. I couldn't find any comfortable spot to lie down, because it looked like a bunch of rocks. But the "rocks" happened to be turnips. And we all ate turnips. I ate my share of them after cleaning the dust off a little bit.

☐ ☐ ☐

PRIVATE ANDREW MILLER, US ARMY
Camp O'Donnell POW Camp
Luzon, Philippines
June 1942

After the surrender of Corregidor they put us on ships and took us across Manila Bay to a town called Maclarin, right outside the base where I started the war, at Nichols Field.

Then they marched us the full length of Dewey Boulevard to Bilibid Prison, the equivalent of Atlanta or Leavenworth. They herded us all in there. After a couple of days they started to take us out, 1,500 at a time, put us on trains, and took us to a town where we would stay overnight. The first four groups of 1,500 ended up at Cabanatuan Three, and there were 6,000 men there.

The first four days of June 1942, the majority of the men from Camp O'Donnell were moved. That place was a mess. A lot of men died there.

☐ ☐ ☐

PRIVATE JOHN COOK, US ARMY
Camp O'Donnell POW Camp
Luzon, Philippines
May 1942

When we got to Camp O'Donnell there were around 200, 250 deaths a day. Filipinos and Americans were dying. They would put two bodies that were so scrawny on one of the straight pole field stretchers, and they would carry it to the burial ground. They would dump them in the open pit.

When I got to Camp O'Donnell most of us had malaria and beriberi. I didn't know that we had diphtheria, dysentery, typhoid fever, and stuff like that. The sickest people had yellow jaundice, typhoid fever, or dysentery. They were so skinny it was pathetic and you thought they were about ready for their graves.

One morning I had mess duty and was stirring the *lugow* pot—like a rice pot—with this fellow Clark. We were working on the Zero Ward. Zero Ward meant that you were there because you were expected to die soon. At that time there were about twelve of these scrawny guys on Zero Ward. It was just getting daylight and the poor fellows were standing there with their beat-up mess kits waiting for rations. Then I said, "Clark, come here." And I pointed to a rat in the cooking pot, in the *lugow* for breakfast. "Clark, we can't eat this stuff. What are we gonna do?"

Clark said, "I'm gonna go back behind the stove and push down the window. And you just flip it out there and they'll never see it."

I flipped that darn rat out there and there were ten or twelve guys who saw it and soon there wasn't one scrap of that rat. They ate it, bones and all.

✪ PHILIPPINE ISLANDS
AUGUST 1942

Within weeks of the fall of Corregidor, Filipino civilians—many with relatives inside the complex of Japanese POW camps—began to get word to the outside world about what had happened on the Death March and about conditions inside the camps. U.S. and Filipino guerrillas, operating in the jungle-covered volcanic mountains, passed information about the camps and the POWs to allied intelligence officers. And while conditions inside the camps remained deplorable, the Philippine underground was eventually able to smuggle small amounts of medicine and some supplies into the camps.

Claire Phillips was the American bride of Sergeant John Phillips, fighting with the 31st Infantry when Bataan surrendered. He was sent to Cabanatuan, where he died of malaria, dysentery, and malnutrition. Claire, alone and living in Japanese-occupied Manila, was determined to avenge her husband's death. She made contact with a Philippine resistance organization, which provided her with false Italian identity documents. Since Rome and Tokyo were allies, this would keep the Japanese from becoming suspicious of the attractive young American.

Claire, now known as "Dorothy Fuentes," started a nightclub for Japanese officers.

She called it Club Tsubaki and opened its doors in October 1942. "Tsubaki" meant "camellia" in Japanese and also meant "hard to get." The beautiful Filipino women who worked with "Dorothy" in Club Tsubaki were

FNC *War Stories*

Claire Phillips

amazingly effective in eliciting information and military intelligence from the officers who frequented the club. The Japanese nicknamed Claire "High Pockets," because she had a habit of hiding her tips in her bra. Unbeknownst to her generous customers, Claire used the money to buy quinine and other medicines that the Philippine resistance organizations smuggled into the POW camps.

Courtesy Taylor family

Robert Taylor

A key member of Claire's spy and smuggling web was a highly respected and devout Army chaplain, Major Robert Taylor. Ironically, it was the gift of a signed Bible from "High Pockets" to Chaplain Taylor that almost got them both killed.

Shortly before the United States liberated the Philippines, a prison guard conducting a routine search of the chaplain's belongings found the Bible. Within days, Japanese military intelligence arrested Claire. Though they tortured her and the chaplain, neither of them divulged what they knew of the other. Both survived the experience, and after the war, both the U.S. and Philippine governments recognized Claire for her heroism.

The courage of Claire Phillips, Chaplain Robert Taylor, and hundreds of others—mostly Filipinos—helped to ease the desperate plight faced by tens of thousands of prisoners seized in the most ignominious defeat ever suffered by the U.S. Armed Forces. Unfortunately, the good news of their bravery would remain unknown to all but a few Americans for several more years. And in the months after Pearl Harbor, good news was something the American people desperately needed.

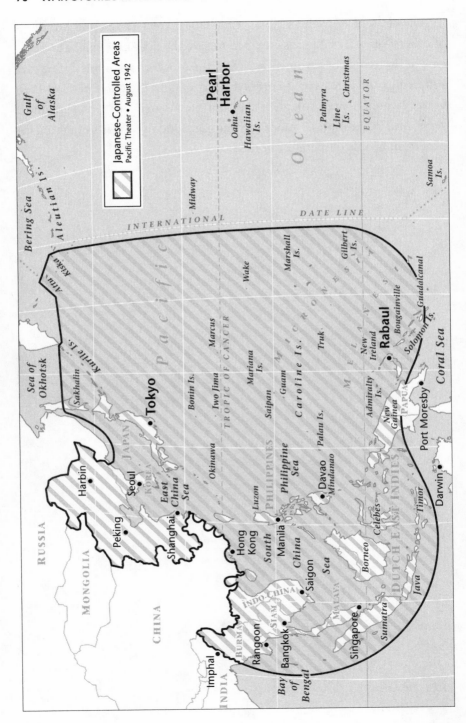

CHAPTER 4
REVENGE FOR PEARL HARBOR: THE DOOLITTLE RAID
(APRIL 1942)

Stunned by the surrender on Bataan and the broad scale of Japanese attacks in the Pacific, many Americans saw the war they had sought to avoid as a succession of military disasters. Pearl Harbor had awakened the "sleeping giant," but since December 1941 it had seemed as though there was little that the giant could do to stop the onslaught.

On 1 January 1942, representatives of twenty-six countries, calling themselves the United Nations, signed the Atlantic Charter, drafted by Roosevelt and Churchill. In it, the signatories pledged to "wage total war" against the German-Japanese-Italian Axis. But the document had little immediate effect on the global battlefield. The headlines in U.S. newspapers continued to carry a steady stream of bad news from around the world.

In the Pacific, it certainly appeared as though the Japanese were invincible. Guam—the first American territory to be seized by a foreign power—fell only hours after the attack on Pearl Harbor. The tiny garrison of Marines and sailors on Wake Island had fought back valiantly against overwhelming odds but had finally succumbed on 23 December. Forty-eight hours later, on Christmas Day, the British surrendered Hong Kong, the crown jewel of their Far Eastern colonies.

The Japanese didn't take time off to celebrate the new year or their victories. As they reinforced General Homma's effort to crush opposition in the Philippines, they moved simultaneously to seize French Indochina, Thailand, Malaya, and the oil-rich Dutch East Indies, and moved against the British in Burma. By 15 February, when Singapore fell—just over two months after Pearl Harbor—the Japanese had killed or captured more than 150,000 British, Australian, Dutch, and Indian troops. Four days after the fall of Singapore, Japanese carrier-based aircraft bombed Darwin, Australia, sinking thirteen Allied ships and razing the port.

On 23 February, a long-range I-class submarine shelled the coast of northern California and incendiary flares attached to small balloons started forest fires in Oregon. Though militarily insignificant, the attacks on the U.S. mainland caused panic in Washington. The American press, distracted by these events, barely covered a real disaster on 27 February in the Java Sea. There the Japanese destroyed a hastily cobbled together U.S.-British-Dutch task force and eliminated the last remnant of Allied naval power anywhere near their Home Islands or newly seized possessions. From that point on, the Americans were virtually fighting alone against the Japanese in the Pacific.

In an effort to slow the Japanese advance, every available submarine and all three carrier battle groups of the Pacific Fleet were thrown into the fight. Though poor torpedoes and inexperienced crews limited the initial effectiveness of the U.S. subs, the carriers scored some successes.

Between 1 February and the end of March, Vice Admiral William "Bull" Halsey with the USS *Enterprise*, Rear Admiral Jack Fletcher on the USS *Yorktown*, and Vice Admiral Wilson Brown aboard the USS *Lexington* conducted a series of fast carrier raids over vast areas of the southwest Pacific. Japanese installations, ships, and forces were hit in the Marshall Islands, the

Solomons, and the Bismarck Archipelago, and successful attacks were conducted against Kwajalein, Marcus, and Wake Islands.

Though these fast carrier raids did little serious long-term damage to the Japanese, U.S. commanders and pilots were quickly gaining skill and proficiency against their far more experienced adversaries. Using newly built fleet oilers and fast resupply ships, the U.S. carriers perfected the ability to replenish under way, allowing them to stay at sea for months at a time. The pilots were improving as well, and the names of U.S. naval aviators were becoming known to the American people, desperate for good news on any front. While battling Japanese bombers sent out to find the *Lexington*, Lieutenant Edward "Butch" O'Hare became the Navy's first ace—achieved by downing five enemies—and was lionized in the press.

Yet as dramatic and courageous as these fast carrier raids were to the American people and the participants, they were still defensive operations, hitting at but not stopping the Japanese advance. By mid-April 1942, the Japanese had seized virtually all the territory they needed to assure the availability of strategic resources and materials for their war effort. And once the Philippines fell, they would be able to secure their entire southern flank—and neutralize Australia as an Allied base.

By the spring of 1942, the long string of defeats and near-calamities had many Americans grumbling that it was "time to fight back." In Washington, congressional leaders complained to FDR that Radio Tokyo was broadcasting taunts that the Japanese Home Islands "were invincible and could never be attacked."

But in April 1942, striking at Japan itself seemed nothing short of impossible. Land-based bombers in China and Australia didn't have the range to make it to Tokyo and return. Naval air raids were out of the question. Carrier-based aircraft had to be within 200 miles of their target—300 at the very most—and it was going to be many months, if not years, before the U.S. Pacific Fleet, ruined at Pearl Harbor, could be rebuilt strong enough to seriously challenge the Japanese navy west of Hawaii.

Fast carrier raids like those conducted by Halsey, Brown, and Fletcher helped keep the Imperial Fleet off balance—it wasn't the same as going on the offensive. And in April of 1942, with the collapse of the Philippines—even with Wainwright holding out on Corregidor—almost everyone assumed that hitting the Japanese at home was impossible.

But those who were so despondent didn't know that the U.S. Navy and Army had been working together for months on a daring plan to do just that. And they hadn't reckoned on Jimmy Doolittle.

✪ ATLANTIC OCEAN
U.S. NAVY CARRIER USS HORNET
NORFOLK, VIRGINIA
MID-JANUARY 1942

Two weeks after the attack on Pearl Harbor, Navy Captain Francis Low, a submarine officer on the staff of the chief of naval operations, Admiral Ernest J. King, was dispatched from Washington to Norfolk, Virginia. His mission was to determine what could be done to expedite the delivery of a brand-new carrier, the USS *Hornet*. While there, Low happened to observe some U.S. Army Air Corps bombers practicing takeoffs and landings from nearby Langley Field. Because the airfield was also used to train Navy pilots, it had the outline of a carrier deck painted on the runway. As Captain Low watched the Army bombers practice "touch and go" landings and takeoffs, his imagination took over.

Admiral Ernest J. King, chief of naval operations during World War II.

Returning to Washington, Low broached an idea with Admiral King that lesser men might have rejected, for fear of having their service loyalty—or even their sanity—questioned: "Sir, I'm wondering . . . would it be possible for Army bombers to take off from a carrier?"

No one had ever tried it before, but King, rather than rejecting the query out of hand, instantly grasped its importance. If a long-range Army bomber could take off from a carrier, the U.S. vessel—and those that accompanied it—wouldn't have to get nearly as close to the target as smaller, shorter-range Navy aircraft did. With the Far East Air Force eliminated and the Philippines under siege, it might be the only way America could strike back at Japan for months or years to come.

Admiral King put the submarine officer to work on the concept and told him the goal was to find a way to attack the Japanese Home Islands. Although he wasn't a pilot, Low understood that even if a fully loaded bomber could take off from a carrier, it was solving only half the problem. No large bomber could land on a carrier, and unless he could come up with a place for the Army aircraft to land, it would end up being a one-way suicide mission. Was there somewhere they could safely land?

General Henry "Hap" Arnold, commander, U.S. Army Air Forces.

Captain Low believed that the U.S. bombers might make it to a friendly base in China, where General Claire Chennault and a group of American "volunteers" were helping Chiang Kai-shek's Nationalist Forces fight the Japanese. Unsure, he went back to King for advice.

Admiral King took the idea up to General Henry "Hap" Arnold, the Army Air Corps chief of staff. Intrigued, General Arnold immediately called his friend Lieutenant Colonel James H. "Jimmy" Doolittle for advice. Doolittle was a stunt flier, test pilot, and Army Air Corps officer. Yet Doolittle wasn't just a brash hotshot. He'd also earned a degree in aeronautical engineering at MIT so he would fully understand the science of flight as well as its daring mystique. He was the kind of pilot who needed to know firsthand just how high a plane could go, how fast it could fly, and just what it was made of.

Doolittle had become a charismatic and popular figure in the 1920s and '30s winning just about every aviation trophy available. His fame and notoriety were second only to Charles Lindbergh's. Doolittle had helped to develop the first high-octane aviation fuel and had pioneered instrument flying in 1929. After covering the windshield of his airplane with a hood, he became the first person to fly a course and land "blind," using only the plane's instruments to guide him.

But that was old news by now, and Hap Arnold had a new challenge for his daring friend. The general asked Doolittle, "Does America have a bomber that can take off in less than 500 feet and carry a 2,000-pound bomb load?" Arnold added that the planes had to have enough range to fly at least 2,000 miles and attack Japan.

Intrigued by the challenge, after several days of research, Doolittle told his boss that the only aircraft available for such a mission was the B-25, a relatively new twin-engine, land-based bomber, built by California's North American Aviation. Asked why he selected the B-25, Doolittle replied, "Because it's small...and has sufficient range to carry 2,000 pounds of bombs 2,000 miles." Arnold gave his assent and left it up to Doolittle to work out the details.

✪ HQ U.S. ARMY AIR CORPS
OFFICE OF LIEUTENANT COLONEL JAMES DOOLITTLE
WASHINGTON, D.C.
25 JANUARY 1942

The B-25 bomber Doolittle selected was trim—about fifty-three feet long (about the length of the typical semitrailer) and with a wingspan just a little over sixty-seven feet. Its right wingtip could just clear an aircraft carrier's island, the superstructure on the starboard side of the vessel. But the overriding question still had to be answered: Could it take off from an aircraft carrier?

Doolittle and the Navy tested the idea with a couple of stripped-down B-25s aboard the USS *Hornet*. The planes rolled down the deck, and at sixty knots—about sixty-five miles per hour—showing on the airspeed indicator, the big bombers lifted into the air before they got to the end of the carrier deck. So far, so good. But there still was no proof that a B-25 fully loaded with bombs, extra fuel, and crew could repeat the feat. Doolittle worked out the calculations and said it could be done—in theory.

That was good enough for Ernie King and Hap Arnold. Admiral King decided that the USS *Hornet* would be the ship, and Arnold told Doolittle that he could have as many B-25s as he needed for the operation.

The *Hornet* was the perfect choice for the mission. Brand-new, and outfitted at the then unheard-of cost of $31 million, it was the ship they had already used for testing the idea during her pre-commissioning trials.

Since only sixteen of the bombers would fit on the *Hornet* and still allow sufficient space on the 809-foot flight deck for a 500-foot takeoff roll, Doolittle now set out to find enough five-man crews to fly the mission. That should have meant he was looking for eighty men, but the forty-five-year-old lieutenant colonel needed only seventy-nine. Doolittle had convinced his superiors that he'd have to lead the attack, not just plan it.

USS *Hornet.* Doolittle's Raiders launched from her deck in April 1942.

Naval Historical Center

Doolittle began his search for aircrews by first asking the Army Air Corps to identify the best-trained B-25 unit. The 17th Bombardment Group, stationed at Pendleton Field, Oregon, was selected, and in early February 1942, the entire group was ordered to fly to Columbia, South Carolina, where they would be away from any possible enemy spies or collaborators. Once they arrived in South Carolina, Doolittle asked for volunteers to accompany him on a top-secret mission he described only as "dangerous." One hundred and forty-nine men volunteered, from which he selected ninety-nine.

Doolittle divided the men into twenty five-man flight crews, and dispatched them to Eglin Field, on the Gulf Coast of Florida, where they spent most of March practicing takeoffs from a 500-foot section of runway to approximate what it would be like to launch from a carrier deck. They also practiced low-level bombing runs by flying just above the whitecaps in the Gulf of Mexico.

During this Florida "shakedown" period, Doolittle had each B-25 retrofitted with extra 225-gallon fuel tanks in the bomb bay and in the crawlway behind the cockpit. Sixty-gallon fuel tanks replaced guns in the bottom turrets, so radios, batteries, and even the tail guns were removed. Broomsticks, painted black, were inserted in the turrets and blisters in hopes that any pursuing Japanese fighter planes would mistake them for real machine guns and think twice about getting too close. Doolittle also used this time to trim down his volunteers to the seventy-nine who would accompany him on the mission.

While the aircraft were being modified, Doolittle sent two lieutenants, Thomas Griffin and Davey Jones, to Washington, D.C., to learn all they could about the enemy from Army Air Corps intelligence. Without divulging their mission, Griffin and Jones collected maps and photographs of five different Japanese cities. Doolittle wanted American bombs to land on at least five different locations so that that the enemy propaganda machine couldn't hide the facts of the attacks from the Japanese people.

Twenty-six-year-old Dick Cole was among those who gave me their account of the mission. He was Doolittle's copilot, and the plane's navigator was Lieutenant Henry Potter, a twenty-two-year-old from South Dakota.

Lieutenant Bobby Hite, a farm boy from Texas, had planned to become an agricultural teacher but dropped out of college after three years and enlisted in the Army Air Corps. As a twenty-one-year-old copilot, he flew in the same B-25 as Corporal Jacob ("Jake") DeShazer, their bombardier.

      □   □   □

LIEUTENANT ROBERT HITE, US ARMY
Secret Training Site
Eglin Field, Florida
15 February 1942

We didn't know at the time that we were going to Japan. Jimmy said it would be very dangerous, but he couldn't tell us more. Everybody speculated that we were going to be sent to Europe. We just really didn't have a clue. Nobody mentioned an aircraft carrier, but the whole group volunteered anyway.

We were ready. We wanted to go with Jimmy Doolittle wherever he went. And I think, in our hearts and minds, we had the attitude "we can do it."

◻ ◻ ◻

LIEUTENANT HENRY ("HANK") POTTER, US ARMY
Secret Training Site
Eglin Field, Florida
15 February 1942

When we got to Columbia, South Carolina, Doolittle gathered the flight crews together in a hangar and briefed us, stating, "We're gonna need volunteers for a dangerous mission that will be of great importance to the American war effort." Nobody could figure out where he wanted us to go or what he wanted us to do when we got there, but if Jimmy Doolittle was going, we wanted to be there.

He sent us to Eglin Field in Florida, where the pilots learned how to take off at short distances and the rest of us got the additional training in navigation, bombing, and firing machine guns. I don't think that any one of us had any lack of confidence that we'd be able to make it. After all, we were flying with the premier pilot in the Air Corps at that time. If he couldn't do it, it wasn't going to be done.

✪ USS HORNET
NAVY TASK FORCE 16.2
SAN FRANCISCO BAY
1 APRIL 1942

Finally, after more than a month of arduous training exercises and flight maneuvers, the planes and men were ready. Doolittle sent the armada of B-25s from Eglin Field to McClelland Field, not far from Sacramento,

California. From there, on 22 March, the B-25s flew to Alameda Naval Air Station near Oakland, on San Francisco Bay.

During the nearly 3,000-mile trip to California, Doolittle had told his high-spirited aircrews to practice low-level flying. The young daredevils flew at practically cornstalk level, skimming over farmhouses, "hot-dogging" it across the country. They flew down through the Grand Canyon, and up and down the Sacramento Valley at an elevation of ten feet above ground level, sending farmers and fruit pickers scurrying for cover.

April Fool's Day, 1942, was the date picked for having everything ready. The following morning, the carrier and its seven escort ships, designated as Task Force 16.2, sailed from San Francisco Bay. Once well out to sea, the skipper of the *Hornet,* Captain Marc Mitscher, with Doolittle beside him, announced over the ship's PA system their objective—until now top secret information. The captains of the escorts did the same, telling all hands: "Now hear this—this task force is going to Japan." Those who were there remember the cheering that reverberated across the decks.

Northwest of Hawaii, the *Hornet* and her escorts rendezvoused with Task Force 16.1, consisting of the carrier USS *Enterprise*, with Admiral Halsey aboard, and eight escorts. Together, the seventeen ships raced northwest across the Pacific, heading for the spot in the ocean 412 miles from the Japanese coast that Doolittle and the Navy planners had chosen as a take-off point for the B-25s.

It was, for this high-risk mission, a sensible plan. U.S. naval intelligence officers knew that the Japanese had positioned picket ships along a perimeter 400 miles from their homeland. The warlords in Tokyo had done the math—they figured that the Americans would have to be no more than 300 miles from Japan in order to carry out any kind of attack with carrier-based aircraft. The U.S. Navy code-breakers also knew from intercepts of Japanese communications that the 26th Air Flotilla, with more than sixty bombers on alert, could take off on short notice and attack any U.S. vessel that the pickets sighted as far as 600 miles out—well before carrier-based task forces could launch an air attack on Japan.

Halsey's fleet steamed west maintaining total radio silence, hoping that the 10,000-man task force could make it to within 412 miles of the Japanese coastline without being detected. Doolittle's aircraft needed to be close enough to hit their targets and still have enough fuel to make it 800 more miles to recovery fields in China. After launching the bombers, the task force ships would turn and race south, hoping to be out of the area and beyond the range of any Japanese aircraft by the time they arrived at the launch site.

It was a superb plan—on paper. But the fliers were taking a huge risk. So were the aircraft carriers and their escorts. The *Hornet* and the *Enterprise* made up half of the entire carrier strength of the U.S. Pacific Fleet. If they were discovered and sunk by the Japanese, it could take years for America to rebound, rebuild its naval forces, and deal with the Imperial Navy.

Aboard the *Hornet*, the Army aircrews were kept busy rehearsing the mission and working on the planes—critical parts were even delivered to them by blimp. They had to memorize maps and targets, listen to intelligence briefings, learn about Japan's cities and culture, and review their options after the bombing runs.

Doolittle hoped that he had thought of everything. His plan called for Chinese guerrillas, under Chiang Kai-shek, to place radio beacons to lead the B-25s to safe landing fields in China. Still, his greatest anxiety was having enough fuel to reach them.

But if Doolittle had any doubts, he did not show it.

Corporal Jake DeShazer, from Salem, Oregon, was a cook for a sheep-herding camp before he joined the Army Air Corps in 1940 at the age of twenty-seven. He remembers being on KP duty when Pearl Harbor was bombed and thinking to himself, "Japan is really going to get it for this." DeShazer recalls standing alone on the *Hornet*'s flight deck, thinking, "I wonder how many more days I am going to spend in this world. Maybe I wasn't so fortunate after all to get to go on this trip."

On 16 April, in heavy seas, the sailors and Army airmen aboard the *Hornet* moved the B-25s to a parking area at the rear of the flight deck, where they would be ready to take off. The following day the weather deteriorated further. Halsey and Doolittle, concerned about the ability of the sailors and airmen to work on the open flight deck, ordered the planes fueled and bombs loaded, even though the task force didn't plan to be at the launch point until late on 19 April.

By darkness on 17 April, the airmen and deck crews were exhausted, but Halsey and Doolittle had done all they could to prepare. Now if they could just avoid the enemy picket ships and patrol craft, the *Hornet* might be able to get within 400 miles of Japan—and that edge might give the B-25s and their crews a chance of surviving the mission. But it wasn't to be.

✪ USS HORNET
TASK FORCE 16.2
650 MILES OFF JAPANESE COAST
18 APRIL 1942

In the predawn morning hours of 18 April, a radar operator on the *Enterprise* reported a "surface contact"—a ship—about ten miles from the carrier. Though the *Enterprise* was still more than 650 miles from Japan, Halsey ordered the entire task force to change direction to keep from being spotted by what had to be a Japanese ship. Then, at 0600, an American scout plane scouring the waters ahead of the American ships saw a Japanese patrol boat.

Hoping to sink the vessel before it could notify Japan of their presence, Halsey's cruiser, the USS *Nashville*, engaged with five-inch gunfire at 0738, and immediately afterward dive-bombers from the *Enterprise* attacked the picket ship. The *Nitto Maru*, designated as Japanese Naval Patrol Boat No. 23, sank in minutes. But not before the crew radioed Imperial Fleet HQ at Kure that three American aircraft carriers were headed for Japan.

Aboard the *Enterprise*, Navy code-breakers intercepted the *Nitto Maru*'s radio traffic, and though the *Nitto Maru* incorrectly warned that there were three American carriers, it still meant that, despite the weather, the task force was now in great jeopardy. So, too, was Doolittle's attack plan.

The *Hornet*, with the sixteen B-25s aboard, was still hundreds of miles away from its intended launch destination, and hundreds of miles more from the targets in Japan. Halsey had planned to steam west another thirty-two hours before launching the bombers, so that they would arrive over their targets on the night of 19 April—and be able to find their landing fields in China on the next morning.

Admiral Halsey and Doolittle now had to make a serious decision, and it had to be made quickly. The carriers couldn't proceed closer to the intended launch point, loath to engage an overwhelming Japanese naval force or provoke an attack by land-based bombers. But could the B-25s still make it to their targets—and then on to safety in China—if they launched now? If not, their only alternative was to abandon the mission. By signal light, from his flagship to the *Hornet*, Halsey presented the options to Doolittle.

The Army flight leader wasted no time in making a decision. Even though they were still nearly 700 miles from Tokyo, with almost no chance of reaching the recovery airfields in China after the bombing raid, Doolittle signaled back, "Let's go now."

Halsey ordered the task force to turn into the wind and gave the order to launch the aircraft. The admiral ended his message with, "Good luck, and God bless you."

Aboard the *Hornet*, Army airmen and sailors sprang into action as loudspeakers blared, "Army Air personnel, man your airplanes for immediate takeoff." The aircrews raced onto the flight deck and readied the sixteen bombers for takeoff as high winds and thirty-five-foot swells tossed the ships about like toy boats. With water breaking over her bow, the *Hornet* turned into the wind, now blowing at twenty-five to thirty knots.

To the uninitiated, the idea of trying to launch sixteen overloaded B-25s from the terrifyingly short, pitching deck of an aircraft carrier into the teeth of a raging gale might seem like madness. But to Jimmy Doolittle, the MIT engineer perched in the lead aircraft, the plane that had the shortest takeoff roll, the wind was now their ally. It offered hope that all his aircrews could succeed in doing what no one had ever done before—first, getting the planes, weighing nearly fifteen tons, into the air, and then bombing the Japanese homeland.

❑   ❑   ❑

CORPORAL JACOB "JAKE" DESHAZER, USAAF
Aboard the USS *Hornet*
18 April 1942

The announcement came: "Army personnel, get your airplanes ready; in ten hours will be takeoff." And just after they did that, the fog lifted up and we saw a Japanese ship. We could all see it. And one of our ships turned and shot into that Japanese ship and I could see it sinking. One end was up, the other end headed for the bottom of the sea. Right after that happened, they made the announcement: "Army personnel, man your airplanes, take off immediately!"

I saw Doolittle going out to his airplane; he was the first one off. We were all watching pretty close because his plane only had about 400 feet for takeoff on that aircraft carrier.

◻   ◻   ◻

LIEUTENANT ROBERT HITE, USAAF
Aboard the USS *Hornet*
18 April 1942
0920 Hours Local

Yeah, the space that we had for takeoff was from the island to the end of the flight deck, about 400 feet. So we had that much to get off of the carrier. But the secret of being able to do this was, we had about a thirty-knot wind that we were going into, a west wind. And the carrier was traveling at about close to thirty knots, so that gave us a wind across the deck of about sixty knots. This was very advantageous for what we were going to do. We used full flaps and full power on our B-25s, which was enough to lift us from the carrier.

The original plan was to take off in the evening and do our bombing raid at night. That changed after they sank the Japanese patrol boat that had radioed that we were coming. So Jimmy and the commander from the *Hornet*, and Halsey with the *Enterprise* decided we better get those B-25s off the deck and on the way.

The last thing that Jimmy said before we took off was, "We don't have any new information on the mission. And we'll have to do the best we can."

We knew he was a great pilot, so if Jimmy could do it, we were going to try it. Jimmy being the number-one aircraft was the first one off, and he did it perfectly. It gave us great confidence to know that it could be done, to see him make that takeoff.

Jimmy took off at 8:20 AM and we were the last aircraft, number sixteen, taking off at 9:20 AM, so it took one hour to get the American B-25s off of the Hornet.

Once we were at altitude, we made meticulous use of the mixture control and our rpm to minimize the flow of gasoline through the engine. The standard B-25 engine runs on about 150 to 160 gallons an hour, but we had our B-25 running at about 60 gallons per hour. We had planned to launch within about 400 miles of our target, but we actually took off about 700 miles out.

□   □   □

LIEUTENANT RICHARD ("DICK") COLE, USAAF
Aboard the USS *Hornet*
18 April 1942
0920 Hours Local

The first thing we heard that morning was the guns going off, from the cruiser that had spotted the picket ship. I was at breakfast when they started firing. And immediately we all put breakfast aside and ran up topside to see what was going on. Then, right away they announced over the PA system, "Army personnel, man your planes!" I had to run back down to where my quarters were and get my gear. For those of us who flew with Jimmy, the name of the game was to get to the airplane before the old man did.

I got there in time to help Fred Braemer and Paul Leonard pull the props through and make a walk-around check, and we were "air-available" when the boss came. There was a low overcast and the sea was running high enough where water was coming up over the bow. In fact, the area where we were got wet, and they had to put down some abrasive pads for some of the later airplanes because they were sliding back and forth on the deck.

As far as whether or not we were going to make it off the deck, I didn't even think about it. We had done the same thing off of a runway with not near as much headwind. I had no doubt about it. We were flying with the best pilot in the world and besides that, being a second lieutenant, I had to worry about flaps, landing gear—stuff like that.

✪ USS HORNET
TASK FORCE 16.2
650 MILES OFF JAPANESE COAST
18 APRIL 1942

A 16mm film made by a U.S. Navy combat cameraman that stormy morning shows the deck crew pulling the wheel chocks from the lead B-25. Then, at 0820, with both engines at max rpm and sea spray whipping down the deck, Jimmy Doolittle's plane lumbered just a few hundred feet and leapt into the air—a dozen feet before reaching the end the *Hornet*'s bow. The sailors on the flight deck let out a cheer. It could be done after all.

Doolittle's B-25 climbed immediately and circled, buzzed the *Hornet* to synchronize his magnetic compass heading with the ship's, and then headed west, while behind him the rest of the planes took off. One by one, the fifteen B-25s, each carrying 2,000 pounds of munitions, and nearly that much weight in fuel, along with five crewmen, followed Doolittle's example and took off.

The first six did it flawlessly. The seventh plane—its flaps mistakenly left up in the pre-flight tension—took off but slipped dangerously low as it left the deck of the carrier, almost dropping into the waves. But the pilot recovered in time and lifted his craft smoothly, up into the blustery skies with the rest of the bombers. The other nine B-25s followed without a hitch—almost.

Just before the last bomber cleared the deck, one of the sailors helping to launch the planes fell into the spinning prop of copilot Bob Hite and bombardier Jake DeShazer's B-25. Both men watched in horror as the blade tore off the sailor's arm, expecting that it had killed him. It wouldn't be until after the war that they would learn the sailor survived.

Admiral William "Bull" Halsey commanded U.S. Navy carrier forces, and was later CINC South Pacific forces.

Doolittle had instructed his pilots that once they were airborne, they had to maintain course just forty feet above the ocean at a speed of 150 mph in order to conserve fuel. As the Army bombers headed west, Admiral Halsey ordered the *Hornet*, the *Enterprise*, and their escorts to make a sharp U-turn and head for Pearl Harbor. The Doolittle Raiders were now completely on their own.

❑   ❑   ❑

CORPORAL JACOB "JAKE" DESHAZER, USAAF
Plane #16, Doolittle Raid
18 April 1942

When Doolittle got up, we all let out a big cheer and we knew it could be done. In my B-25, Bill Farrow was the pilot and the copilot was Bobby Hite. George Barr was the navigator, Harold Spatz was crew chief, engineer, and gunner, and I was the bombardier. There were five men on each airplane, all doing the same kinds of duties. They told me that when our wheels left the deck of the *Hornet*, I became a sergeant.

I really didn't know what was going to happen and I didn't speculate on it. I didn't think about it. If I got killed, I got killed.

✪ DOOLITTLE RAID
EN ROUTE TO TOKYO
550 MILES OFF JAPANESE COAST
18 APRIL 1942

The sixteen B-25s scattered in a loose formation spreading out more than 150 miles across the skies. To add to their fuel concerns, they were bucking a twenty-five miles per hour headwind. Soon they were out of sight of one another. That didn't matter, though. They had planned it this way. There was less likelihood of detection if they were spread out. They all had their own orders and flight plans; each aircraft had its own target list specifying where to drop its bombs.

A Japanese patrol plane at least 600 miles off the east coast of Japan spotted one of the bombers at 0945 and reported a single twin-engine, land-based plane flying toward the Home Islands. But back in Tokyo, the military intelligence people ignored the report—it had to be a mistake; no land-based enemy aircraft that large could fly that far out to sea.

That morning in Tokyo there was a routine air raid drill. The military and civilians took it in stride. Practice drills were commonplace and the people often took them for granted. After all, Tokyo was safe—the Japanese generals and Radio Tokyo had said so. And Emperor Hirohito had personally reassured them that they were safe from enemy attack. It was impossible for enemy aircraft to attack the city.

Just minutes after noon, the first of Doolittle's planes reached their target areas. Climbing to 1,500 feet to avoid being blown out of the sky by their own bombs, they lined up their targets in the bombsights.

At 1215, the Americans released their ordnance, and in fewer than fifteen minutes, Tokyo was ablaze from the B-25s' incendiary bombs.

The same thing happened in Osaka, Kobe, the Yokosuka Navy Yard, and three other Japanese cities. The raiders made it a point to seek out military targets, concentrating on factories believed to be serving the war effort, refineries, and docks, as well as any visible fuel and ammunition dumps.

After dropping their bombs, the B-25s descended to a hundred feet so as to present less of a target to Japanese anti-aircraft guns.

The anti-aircraft fire was ineffective, and though enemy fighter planes were aloft and others were sent up during the raids, not one of the B-25s was shot down. Several Japanese fighters tried to close in on some of the U.S. aircraft after they had dropped their bombs, but it was no easy task. After hitting their targets, the Americans were squeezing every bit of speed they could out of their planes, achieving speeds of up to 300 mph. Those B-25s that were threatened responded with the only weapons Doolittle had let them keep—two lightweight .30-caliber machine guns. At least two Japanese fighters that got too close were downed.

For Doolittle and his raiders, escaping Japanese anti-aircraft batteries and fighters over land wasn't the end of their jeopardy. By the time they had cleared the west coast of Japan and headed over the East China Sea, the B-25s had enough fuel to fly about 800 miles. Unfortunately, the safe area in China was 1,000 miles away. But as the American aircrews began reviewing procedures for ditching at sea, something happened that seemed contrary to the laws of nature. A storm came up and the winds shifted. It seemed impossible to the navigators, who knew that the prevailing winds always blew from the China Sea toward Japan. But that day, the headwinds that they had bucked all day turned into tailwinds, and began to blow them toward China.

It was, in the minds of some of the weary airmen, an answer to prayer— a miracle! The winds were now helping the bombers to make up some of the hundreds of additional miles they had had to fly when they took off early from the *Hornet*.

Still, the wind shift hadn't solved all their problems. None of the B-25s were able to pick up the homing signals in free China that were supposed to guide them to their recovery airfields. It was only later that they would learn that the plane dispatched to place the transmitting beacons had crashed in the same storm that helped extend the range of Doolittle's B-25s. Without those homing signals to guide them to friendly airfields, they were on their own.

Finally, nearly ten hours after they had bombed Japan, one by one, lost in a tropical storm, with fuel gauges at "empty," their engines began to sputter. Doolittle's crew and the men aboard ten other B-25s decided that their best option was to bail out before the planes went down. Four other bombers made forced landings on the Chinese coast, but one crashed into the sea while trying to ditch. The plane hit the water at more than a hundred miles per hour, and the five men inside were pulled beneath the waves, still strapped in their seats. Three of them managed to unbuckle themselves and get out before the plane sank. These survivors managed to climb into a rubber life raft and make it to land. Soon after, the three were captured by Japanese patrols.

Only one plane was able to locate an airfield for a landing—but that was because the pilot knew they wouldn't have enough fuel to get to China. He'd decided instead to head for Vladivostok, a Russian port in southeastern Siberia, some 500 miles west of Japan. When their B-25 landed, the Russians took the crewmen into custody and confiscated their bomber. Though the Soviets were ostensibly our "allies," the American flyers were kept in Siberia until they escaped about a year later, eventually making their way through Iran to the Middle East and back into Allied hands.

The B-52 in which Jake DeShazer served as bombardier made it almost 300 miles into China. It wasn't far enough. He and the other four men on his plane parachuted safely from their doomed aircraft, but were soon captured. The Japanese wasted no time in parading the Americans before the cameras for propaganda purposes. In all, eleven of the Doolittle Raiders were captured and became Japanese POWs. Three of them, DeShazer's crewmates, were executed to exact revenge for the bombings. Jake DeShazer survived to tell the story.

⬚   ⬚   ⬚

CORPORAL JACOB "JAKE" DESHAZER, USAAF
Plane #16, Doolittle Raid
3,000 Feet Above China
18 April 1942

Our airplane flew farther than any of the rest of them. At 10:30 at night we were at 3,000 [feet] and the pilot said, "We're going to have to jump. Jake, you're first."

I took a hold of the edge of the fuselage, pushed real hard, and jumped away from it. I counted to five real fast, pulled the ripcord, and the parachute opened up, and I thought, "I'm on the way now. I'm gonna get down." And sure enough, I hit the edge of some kind of a rice field.

I tried to find a road or something that night, but I just went around in circles, so I came back to the same place where I started, found a place where I could get in out of the rain, and the next morning I started out looking for a road or some telephone lines. I found some kids about fifteen years old who had uniforms on. So I went up to them and asked them if they were Chinese or Japanese. And one fellow said, "Me, China." I had my .45 all ready to go, because I was trying to find out if I was in free China or Japanese-occupied China. And they said, "Let's go down to the camp." It was only about a quarter of a mile away.

But when I got there, they surrounded me and every bayonet was pointed right at me. So I let them have my gun. They fed me and then I found out that I was in the hands of the Japanese military. They had captured all five of us. That started my three years and four months in a Japanese prison.

A few days later they flew us to Tokyo and started asking us questions. The hardest part was to be questioned for twenty-four hours and then taken down to our cells and maybe get a piece of bread to eat with a little rotten potato-peel soup.

When they did give us a little sleep, it would be only an hour or so. I was all tied up, and if I squirmed around, the guard would hit me on the side of the head with his club. It was more than I could stand.

We were kept in solitary cells and questioned for sixty days. Dean Hallmark got dysentery so bad that we'd have to carry him over to the toilet. Later on they took Hallmark, Farrow, and Spatz away and executed them.

▫   ▫   ▫

LIEUTENANT DICK COLE, USAAF
Plane #1, Doolittle Raid
3,000 Feet Above China
18 April 1942

Paul Leonard bailed out first, then Fred Braemer, then Hank, and then me. I tried to see when I was going to hit the ground, but it was foggy and I couldn't see how high I was, until all at once I felt some leaves brushing my face just before I hit the ground.

I was probably the luckiest guy in the bunch. My chute drifted over a pine tree and so I didn't hit the ground very hard. I don't really recall much except that I made it down safe.

I waited until dawn, took out my compass, and just started to walk west. Toward evening I came to the edge of a cliff. And down below, there was a military compound flying a Chinese nationalist flag, so I went down there.

An hour or so later, Bombardier Fred Braemer came walking down the same path that I had followed. Neither of us could speak Chinese, so after a while, Fred and I used hand signals to let them know we wanted to leave.

This group obviously had some means of communications and they knew where they wanted to take us. We ended up in a headquarters with the Chinese general in charge of that area. By the time we arrived, Doolittle was already there. And in the meantime we'd picked up the fifth member of our aircrew, Paul Leonard.

They kept us there for about a week. And then they put us on a kind of river junk to keep us moving. Japanese patrol boats were going up and down the river with searchlights but we were never challenged.

They eventually brought us ashore and moved us over land on foot until we ended up in Hen Yang. A few days later a C-47 came in and picked us up and took us to Chungking. From there I was fortunate enough to eventually be returned to the United States.

✪ ✪ ✪

Surprisingly, the first news of the raid came from Radio Tokyo, carrying broadcasts by Japan's furious military leaders, promising revenge. An announcement from Washington, a few hours later, was vague and terse: "American planes might have participated in an attack upon the Japanese capital." But by the following day, though details were still scant, newspaper headlines across the U.S. trumpeted the news: "Tokyo Bombed in Broad Daylight," "U.S. Warplanes Rain Bombs on Jap Empire," and "U.S. Bombs Hit Four Jap Cities." Pressed by reporters to explain how the B-25s had managed to get all the way to Japan, FDR said that they had launched from "Shangri-La."

But while Americans celebrated the feat, many of the participants were still suffering. Pilot Ted Lawson, whose plane had crashed into the sea, had a crushed leg, and by the time the flight surgeon, Thomas "Doc" White, found him, the leg was rotting from gangrene. Doc White figured that to save Lawson's life, the leg would have to go.

Operating in a nationalist Chinese jungle encampment, the surgeon gave Lawson a spinal injection with Novocain to numb the pain, then used a hacksaw to methodically cut through the fetid flesh and thick leg bone. Lawson remained conscious throughout the long procedure, and when it was over, he watched quietly as Doc sewed up the wound and then used a hypodermic syringe to take his own blood to transfuse the traumatized patient. As a nurse carried the sawed-off leg outside the tent to dispose of it, Lawson said, "Thanks, Doc."

Back home, little was initially known about the fate of most of the airmen. General Hap Arnold had received a coded message from Doolittle on 21 April, relayed through the nationalist Chinese. But all that Doolittle was able to report at the time was that the mission to bomb Japan was accomplished and that bad weather, not a shortage of fuel, might mean that all sixteen of the B-25s had been lost. He also informed Washington that five American fliers had survived.

By the time Doolittle arrived back in the United States, it was known that the Japanese had captured eleven of the airmen. What no one knew until much later was that they were all subjected to horrific torture and interrogation in an effort to discover how the attack could have taken place. Even after three of their number were executed by the Japanese, the Americans gave them only name, rank, and serial number.

All of the Doolittle Raiders were awarded the Distinguished Flying Cross for their heroism. FDR presented Lieutenant Colonel Jimmy Doolittle with the Medal of Honor and promoted him to brigadier general, allowing him to bypass the rank of colonel.

Of the eighty men who went on the mission, three were killed while jumping from their planes after the raid. Eleven were captured, and the Japanese executed three of them on 15 October 1942. Another prisoner died of maltreatment by his captors, and four others were released when the war ended, following three and a half years of imprisonment.

Most of the Doolittle Raiders were reassigned after they returned to the United States and volunteered to fly combat missions elsewhere. Ten of them were killed in action, in North Africa, Europe, and Indochina, and four others were shot down in the European theater and captured by the Germans, who held them for the duration of the war.

✪ ✪ ✪

At the U.S. Air Force Academy in Colorado Springs, a carefully protected display case holds eighty silver goblets, each engraved with the name of a Doolittle Raider. Every 18 April, the goblets are used at a reunion of the surviving Doolittle Raiders, in a private and emotional ceremony. They toast their comrades, living and dead, and reminisce. The goblets of those who have passed on since the last reunion are inverted inside the case. And one day soon, all the goblets will be upside down.

CHAPTER 5
AN AWAKENED GIANT: THE BATTLE OF THE CORAL SEA
(MAY 1942)

✪ **HQ U.S. PACIFIC FLEET**
PEARL HARBOR
OAHU, HAWAII
5 MAY 1942

Jimmy Doolittle's daring raid from the deck of the USS *Hornet* on 18 April 1942 did little damage to Japanese warmaking capability. But bombing the emperor's cities seriously alarmed military planners in Tokyo—and precipitated decisions they would soon regret.

Until the American B-25s struck their homeland, the generals and admirals of the Imperial military were uncertain as to where they would go next. Their advance through the western Pacific had taken less than half the time they had expected, and had cost them fewer than 5,000 casualties, fewer than 100 aircraft, and the loss of only one ship—a destroyer at Wake Island.

For most of March, the emperor's military staff wrangled over three competing strategies: attacking west against India and Ceylon (now Sri Lanka), pressing south against Australia, or moving east against Hawaii.

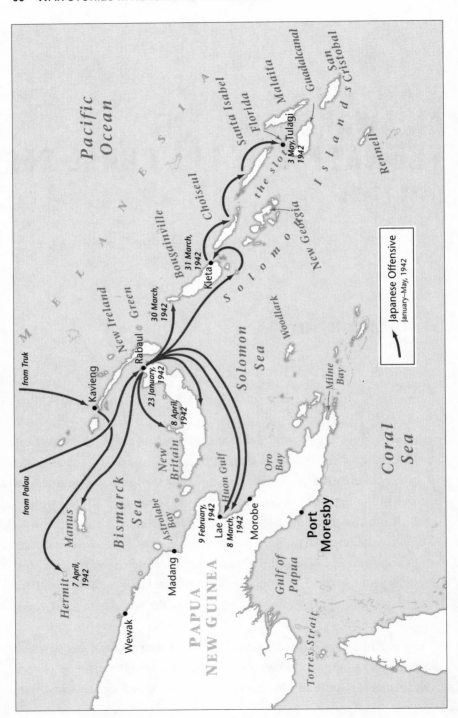

Yamamoto, believing that it was essential to destroy the U.S. Navy in a decisive battle, advocated an eastern offensive: seizing Midway and the Aleutians and, if the Americans didn't sue for peace, moving against Hawaii to precipitate an engagement that would eliminate the U.S. fleet once and for all. The Japanese naval general staff argued for attacking south to Australia, while the Imperial Army staff—already engaged in China, Burma, and the Philippines—opposed all three.

While the debate was being waged, Yamamoto dispatched Admiral Chuichi Nagumo's carriers west, into the Bay of Bengal, the Arabian Sea, and the Indian Ocean. Between 31 March and 9 April 1942, the "hero of Pearl Harbor" had raided the British bases on Ceylon, struck Royal Navy supply bases on India's east coast, sunk six British warships—including the carrier HMS *Hermes* and the heavy cruisers *Dorsetshire* and *Cornwall*—and virtually swept the Indian Ocean clean of British merchant vessels.

Naval Historical Center

Admiral Chester Nimitz

Instead of choosing one of the competing southern, western, or eastern strategic alternatives for their next step, flushed with the thrill of easy victories and filled with confidence, the warlords in Tokyo decided to pursue all three. That was the plan. Then Doolittle's raid changed everything.

In Hawaii, there was desperation but no indecision. Twenty-four days after the attack on Pearl Harbor, a tall, cool Texan, Chester W. Nimitz, had replaced Admiral Husband Kimmel as the commander of the Pacific Fleet. Nimitz had turned down the assignment a year earlier, telling friends, "I am so much junior to so many of the admirals, and if I take it, that will make me so many enemies."

But with the country at war, Nimitz set his personal concerns aside. On 31 December 1941, aboard the submarine USS *Grayling*, fifty-six-year-old Chester Nimitz had added his fourth star and taken command of a badly damaged U.S. Pacific Fleet with FDR's orders still in his head: *"Report to the Pacific and stay there until the war is won."*

The man who would become Yamamoto's nemesis was a long way from the hill country of Fredericksburg, Texas, where he had grown up in a tightly knit German-American community, raised by his mother, Anna, and grandfather, Charles. His father and namesake had died before he was born. As a young man he learned tolerance and forgiveness of mistakes. These qualities came out of personal experience. Nimitz had run his first ship, the destroyer USS *Decatur*, hard aground. At his court-martial he was reprimanded for "neglect of duty." He would later say, "Every dog deserves two bites." This colloquial and practical philosophy served him well as he sought to rebuild the shattered morale and demolished ships at Pearl Harbor.

The arrival of the *Yorktown* from the Atlantic shortly after the Pearl Harbor attack had brought U.S. carrier strength in the Pacific up to four—but on 11 January a Japanese sub torpedoed the *Saratoga* just 500 miles from Oahu. She would be out of the fight for five months. With only three carriers in operation, about the best Nimitz could manage during February and March were the fast carrier strikes by Halsey's *Enterprise*, by Admiral Wilson Brown's USS *Lexington*, and by Jack Fletcher's *Yorktown*.

These "hit and run" strikes, though incapable of stopping the Japanese advance into New Guinea and the Solomon Islands, reinforced Yamamoto's belief that the American carriers based in Hawaii had to be sent to the bottom. But before he could attack Hawaii, Midway would have to be taken. To that end, Yamamoto urged military planners in Tokyo to expedite operations in New Guinea, complete the construction of a major fleet anchorage at Rabaul, and complete the isolation of Australia. On 10 April, the general staff in Tokyo approved his plan, although they refused to fix a date for the seizure of Midway until the lifeline to Australia could be cut off from the U.S. mainland.

But Doolittle's raid threw them off their stride. Tokyo responded by accelerating its timetable. An invasion fleet and covering force were ordered to assemble immediately at Rabaul on the north coast of New Britain. The carriers *Shokaku* and *Zuikaku* were stripped from Admiral Nagumo and dispatched along with the light carrier *Shoho* to support the capture of Port Moresby, New Guinea, from which Japanese bombers could strike Darwin and Australia's Northern Territory. The war planners also decided to seize Tulagi, an island in the Solomon chain north of Guadalcanal, for use as an air and seaplane base. As soon as the invasion forces were safely ashore, the Japanese carriers would detach and assemble at a point in the central Pacific for the attack on Midway.

All these changes to the Japanese operations plans required that they fill the airwaves with hundreds of encrypted radio messages. But Imperial radio operators weren't the only ones listening.

Back in Pearl Harbor, inside a windowless vault called Station Hypo, U.S. Navy signals specialists carefully recorded each of the Imperial Fleet's encoded radio broadcasts—and then painstakingly decrypted them. The little-known facility—connected to arrays of antennas in northern Australia, on Midway, and around the Hawaiian Islands—was the creation of U.S. Navy Lt. Commander Joseph Rochefort, an eccentric forty-three-year-old mathematician who had spent several happy years with his family in Japan before the war,

Courtesy Donald "Mac" Showers

Station Hypo

becoming fluent in Japanese. He and his little team of code-breakers had been intercepting and unscrambling Japanese message traffic since before Pearl Harbor. And because he had missed the cable ordering the attack on 7 December, he had fully expected to be fired along with Admiral Kimmel. But Nimitz, recognizing the man's brilliance, and playing on his sense of duty, asked—not ordered—him to stay on.

The appeal to Rochefort's patriotism had the effect Nimitz intended, and the team the code-breaker had built remained essentially intact. Then, after providing additional personnel necessary to do the job, Nimitz changed the guidelines on the dissemination of Station Hypo's intercepts. Wary of leaks and keenly aware that politicians were looking over his shoulder, the admiral instructed Rochefort to stem the flow of information back to Washington. Instead, the decoded messages would first be given directly to him as the commander in chief of the Pacific Fleet, and Nimitz would determine which, if any, should be forwarded to Washington.

With additional personnel aboard, the rate at which intercepted Japanese messages could be decrypted improved dramatically. About the time that Doolittle was preparing for his raid on Tokyo, Rochefort, one of his Station Hypo colleagues, Navy Lt. Commander T. H. Dyer, and Commander Edwin Layton, Nimitz's intelligence chief, succeeded in breaking the Imperial Navy's JN-25 code. The Japanese fleet used this code to transmit thousands of messages daily. Station Hypo had been working with some 45,000 code groups, trying to translate them from Japanese into English. They considered themselves fortunate if they could recover 10 or 15 percent of a message. But sometimes that was enough.

By April 1942 Admiral Nimitz was getting solid intelligence from his Station Hypo code-breakers—he knew of Japanese ship movements even before many of Yamamoto's own ships' captains. In fact, some of the Japanese skippers never got the information themselves, a problem that plagued them throughout the war.

Among the team of bright young specialists that joined Station Hypo after Pearl Harbor was a farm boy from Iowa. Newly commissioned as an ensign, Mac Showers was ordered to Hawaii. He was told that his assignment was too sensitive to discuss with anyone.

☐   ☐   ☐

ENSIGN MAC SHOWERS, USN
PAC Fleet Signals Intelligence Center
Station Hypo
Pearl Harbor, Hawaii
20 April 1942

I arrived at Hypo in February 1942. I was an ensign and was told that I was being assigned to an intelligence unit that was working for the Pacific

Fleet. I went to the Navy yard and reported to Commander J. J. Rochefort. His office was in a basement that was relatively cold and damp, and people had to wear extra clothing in order to work comfortably down there. When I first saw Commander Rochefort, he was wearing a maroon smoking jacket and bedroom slippers. I was not particularly surprised. I figured a commander could do pretty much anything he wanted to. And it was uncomfortably cold. But I noticed that when he left, he didn't wear those outside. He was in his proper uniform.

Rochefort had a very strong feeling that at the beginning of the war he had failed his commander in chief by not giving him warning of the Japanese attack on Pearl Harbor. We now know there's no way he could have known about it, because it was executed in total radio silence, but Rochefort took it personally. This gave Rochefort a dedication to his task, which he passed on to his people.

The Japanese diplomatic service used a coding machine, which we replicated even before the war, allowing us to read their coded diplomatic traffic. But the Japanese navy didn't use that equipment. The Japanese military high command and their operating forces all used manual codes, which had to be encoded and decoded by hand using codebooks the size of an encyclopedia. For example, when they reported the sinking of their aircraft carriers, they had to go to the codebook and pick out a code group that represented the *Kaga*, and another one that represented the *Akagi*, and another one that represented the *Iru*, and then send their message by encoding that manually. And the recipient then had to decode it manually from an identical encyclopedic book, with all the code groups listed. That was the code system the Japanese navy used throughout the war. It was a laborious task.

Commander Edwin Layton was a good friend of Rochefort's. They had known each other a long time and had studied the Japanese language together in Japan for three years. Layton was somewhat more flamboyant, but more forceful. The two worked very closely together and trusted each other. Layton was a very persuasive individual and the perfect man to be Admiral Nimitz's intelligence officer.

Station Hypo set out to break the Japanese naval code, from thousands of messages transmitted every day in Morse signal. It was copied by intercept operators who tuned in on the frequencies that the Japanese were using. They had typewriters with Japanese characters. After those messages were copied, they would be sent down to our processing unit.

That was the name of the game: recover a "string" of code groups so that we could figure out the sense of the message from the code groups we had already broken. Little by little we were able to fill in the blanks and recover more words. This all came from a codebook that had thousands and thousands of code groups, each one meaning something, the name of a ship, the name of a person, the number or position, a place.

Rochefort would sit there in the basement producing this information, and give it to Layton, who would look it over, digest it, ask questions about it until he understood it. And then he would pass it to Admiral Nimitz.

By April 1942, we were able to read enough of the Japanese naval traffic to realize that they were preparing to mount a major operation in the South Pacific. It would put them within flying distance of Australia. We figured out enough about this operation to tell Admiral Nimitz what they were planning to do and when they planned to do it.

✪ BATTLE OF THE CORAL SEA
OFF THE SOUTHERN TIP OF NEW GUINEA
7–8 MAY 1942

By 29 April, the carriers *Shokaku* and *Zuikaku* sortied from Truk, and the light carrier *Shoho*, commanded by Vice Admiral Takeo Takagi, arrived on station to provide cover for the invasion of Port Moresby and the attack on Tulagi. But the code-breakers at Station Hypo knew exactly what was happening. In the Pacific Fleet war room, Nimitz could see on a large tabletop map of the Pacific the disposition of the Japanese carriers, transports, and battle cruisers—and even Japanese submarines deployed to provide a security perimeter around their two invasion forces.

Yamamoto, the master of the surprise attack, was certain no one would find them and that his battle plans could not be compromised. But they were. And best of all, thanks to Station Hypo, Nimitz even knew the date set for the invasions: 3 May for Tulagi and 9 May for Port Moresby.

Looking at the charts on his office walls and the little wooden ship symbols on the map board in the Pacific Fleet Command Center, Admiral Nimitz had a terrible choice to make. The *Hornet*'s arrival at Pearl Harbor after launching the Doolittle raid had brought the fleet back up to four carriers. But the *Enterprise* and the *Hornet* had taken a beating from the stormy north Pacific. Nimitz had no other capital ships available but the *Yorktown* and the *Lexington*. Furthermore, his two code-breakers, Layton and Rochefort, were telling him that they "suspected" that Yamamoto was also preparing a subsequent operation to seize Midway. Could Nimitz risk two of his four carriers trying to stop the Japanese invasion forces already steaming to take Port Moresby and Tulagi?

On 29 April, after talking it over with his staff, Nimitz gave the order for Rear Admiral Aubrey Fitch, fresh out of Pearl Harbor with the *Lexington,* to join Vice Admiral Jack Fletcher's *Yorktown*, which had been operating in the South Pacific east of Australia for several weeks. He also directed the cruiser *Chicago* to sortie

Admiral Jack Fletcher commanded naval assets in three of the five carrier battles of the Pacific—Midway, Guadalcanal, and Coral Sea.

from New Caledonia and link up with HMAS *Australia* and HMAS *Hobart*, two Australian cruisers under the command of Rear Admiral J. C. Crace of the Royal Navy. Nimitz ordered this somewhat more formidable task force, under the command of Vice Admiral Fletcher, to proceed northwest into the Coral Sea to stop the Japanese invasion forces.

On 1 May, the *Lexington* and the *Yorktown* made contact in the southern Coral Sea, west of Espiritu Santo Island. For a full day and a half, the two carriers steamed northwest toward New Guinea. On 3 May, using information from Station Hypo, Pacific Fleet HQ informed Fletcher that the Japanese were landing on Tulagi, so Fletcher left the *Lexington* to complete refueling from the fleet oiler *Neosho* and proceeded due north with *Yorktown* to do what he could to disrupt the invasion. At 0700 on 4 May, his aviators launched a series of three attacks against the transports anchored off Tulagi. Though the 12,000-ton carrier *Shoho* was supposed to be protecting the troop and supply ships, the *Yorktown's* pilots sent one transport to the bottom and damaged at least five landing barges. Then, before the Japanese could respond, Fletcher recovered his strike aircraft, turned the *Yorktown* south, and steamed at flank speed to rejoin *Lexington* on the morning of 5 May.

Though the Tulagi attack had done relatively little serious damage, the officers of the Japanese carrier striking force, commanded by Vice Admiral Takeo Takagi, were stunned. In Rabaul, where 4th Fleet commander Vice Admiral Shigeyoshi Inouye was coordinating the entire dual-invasion operation, there was an immediate effort to find the American carrier or carriers that had hit the Tulagi transports. But when long-range land-based bombers and patrol aircraft launched from Rabaul failed to find any American ships on 5 or 6 May, Inouye ordered the invasion covering force, including the *Shoho*, to break away from the invasion fleet headed for Port Moresby and head quickly south to find them. Meanwhile, Takagi was racing around the southern tip of the Solomons with the carriers *Shokaku* and *Zuikaku*, both veterans of the Pearl Harbor attack. By the night of 6 May, it was entirely possible that the *Lexington* and the *Yorktown*, heading straight toward the *Shoho* battle group and pursued from behind by the *Shokaku* and the *Zuikaku*, might be trapped between the two Japanese forces.

But once again Station Hypo provided the intelligence Fletcher needed. Alerted to the *Shoho* battle group, he dispatched scout planes at first light on 7 May. At 0815, one of the patrols reported "two carriers and four heavy cruisers" off the southern tip of New Guinea. Though this "sighting" conflicted with the Station Hypo information—and was soon proven to be incorrect—Fletcher decided to launch the attack groups from both *Yorktown* and *Lexington*.

At 1100, in the first attack ever made by U.S. pilots against an enemy carrier, ninety-three American torpedo and dive-bombers swarmed over the
Shoho, hitting her with thirteen bombs and seven torpedoes, sending the
carrier to the bottom in just minutes. In a radio call back to the *Yorktown*,
one of the strike leaders, Lieutenant Commander Robert E. Dixon, jubi-
lantly reported, "Scratch one flattop!"

While Fletcher was busy recovering his attack aircraft, the Japanese,
infuriated by the first sinking of a major Imperial Navy warship, launched
every land- and sea-based aircraft that would fly in an effort to find the
Americans. In less than an hour, aircraft launched from the *Shokaku* and
the *Zuikaku* found the American fleet oiler *Neosho* and the destroyer *Sims*
trailing more than 100 miles behind Fletcher's carriers. Mistakenly identifying the ships as a carrier and her escort, the Japanese pilots attacked
with bombs and torpedoes. At 1230, the valiant little destroyer went down
with most of her crew. Though the *Neosho* took seven hits, she miraculously managed to stay afloat until her crew could be rescued four days
later.

Two hours after the attack, land-based bombers launched from Rabaul
spotted Admiral Crace and his little flotilla of Australian and American
cruisers, steaming in the van of Fletcher's carriers. Once again the Japanese
aviators mistook the cruisers for carriers and dropped their bombs from
high altitude to avoid the furious anti-aircraft barrage from Crace's vessels.
When the Japanese pilots returned to Rabaul, they reported that they had
sunk a battleship and a cruiser—when in fact not one of the Allied ships
had been touched.

Late in the afternoon of 7 May, Admiral Tagaki, determined to avenge
the loss of the *Shoho*, decided to make one more effort to find the American carriers, which no Japanese aircraft had yet sighted. He ordered Rear
Admiral Tadaichi Hara, the commander of the carrier air wings, to choose
twenty-seven of his best pilots, all with night-operations experience, and
launch them into the darkening sky. Radar operators on the American carriers detected the inbound raid and vectored the combat air patrol to intercept. In the ensuing melee, nine of Hara's veteran pilots were blasted out of

the sky. A tenth Japanese aircraft was shot down by anti-aircraft fire when the pilot mistook the *Yorktown* for his own carrier and attempted to land. Eleven more Japanese pilots perished attempting to land on their own decks. When the ill-fated raid was over, only six of Hara's twenty-seven attackers were alive.

Before dawn on the next day, both Fletcher and Takagi had scouts in the air searching for the opposing carriers. Despite heavy overcast and squalls over the Japanese fleet, they spotted each other almost simultaneously at about 0800. Between 0900 and 0925 both the *Lexington* and the *Yorktown* launched their attack groups of torpedo planes and dive-bombers. But by 1030, when they arrived over the location where the Japanese carriers had been reported, only the *Shokaku* was visible in the squall line. The American aircraft unleashed everything they had on the carrier.

Unlike the success they had enjoyed the day before in attacking *Shoho*, the strike on *Shokaku* was almost a failure. Every American torpedo either missed or was a dud. Only three of the dive-bombers found their marks. But in the end, those three were enough to render the *Shokaku*'s flight deck unusable. No longer able to fight, Takagi ordered the ship to return to Truk before it became a target for another raid.

As the *Shokaku* sped away, the planes she and the *Zuikaku* had launched were swarming over the *Lexington* and the *Yorktown*. Anti-aircraft fire and the carriers' combat air patrols succeeded in disrupting the attack on the *Yorktown*, which managed to weather the assault, receiving only a single bomb hit that was insufficient to put her out of action. But the larger and less maneuverable *Lexington* was an easier target. Four bombs and two torpedoes found their mark, but for a while it appeared as though valiant efforts by her damage-control parties might keep her in action.

Then, at about 1245, after the attackers had disappeared over the horizon and she was recovering planes on her flight deck, the *Lexington* was rocked by a terrible explosion as gasoline vapors from a ruptured fuel line ignited deep inside her hull. About two hours later, a second, even larger explosion buckled her flight deck and set a raging inferno that forced Captain Frederick Sherman to order the crew to abandon ship.

The surviving crew members made it over the side to be rescued by destroyers while the *Yorktown* recovered *Lexington* planes still in the air. At 1930 she was still afloat but burning madly. Fletcher gave the order to sink her. A destroyer put five torpedoes into her side, and at 1936 the *Lady Lex* sank beneath the waters of the Coral Sea—becoming the first U.S. carrier lost to enemy action.

Aviation Mechanic Bill Surgi, an eighteen-year-old from Louisiana, watched the battle aboard the USS *Yorktown*. He had a ringside seat for the Japanese attack on his ship—and the aftermath.

◻ ◻ ◻

AVIATION MECHANIC BILL SURGI, USN
Aboard the USS *Yorktown*
Coral Sea
7–8 May 1942

On 6 May the *Neosho* refueled us. But then she left us with the *Sims*. On the next day our planes were out searching for the Japanese fleet and they found the *Sims* and the *Neosho* right after they had been attacked. The *Sims* went down within minutes. Thirteen people survived out of two hundred fifty–odd people. But somehow the *Neosho* managed to stay afloat. It took four days for the crew to get rescued.

That night, several Japanese aircraft were trying to get back to their carriers and they mistakenly got into our landing pattern. And they're surveying our group, sending us blinker signals and we're not answering them. They're at the outer limits of the approach circling us when we start landing our Wildcats. Then someone saw an airplane coming in with fixed landing gear, which we didn't have. All our planes had retractable landing gear, so we knew it wasn't ours. That's when Captain Elliott Buckmaster broadcast over the ship's address system, "Stand by to repel!" And the guns cut loose. It was a Japanese dive-bomber. We shot him down.

The next day, 8 May, I was standing up forward of the island, in the catwalk, when the Japanese attacked. They came at us with torpedoes and dive-bombers. One bomb went right beside us and exploded in the water. And the shrapnel came up and did some minor damage to the ship. It was a near miss for me but it killed my buddy, P. C. Meyers. He was the first person I'd ever seen killed. We were ordnance men; we worked together.

Then, a little while later, another bomb went through the flight deck, through the hangar deck, mess deck, living spaces deck, and exploded in the supply deck. We have compartments in there that we lived in and when that bomb went off we had a space the size of a theater. There were fifty-four people in there; only four people got out alive. We had other near misses on the port side that perforated the hull and gave us an oil leak. But we still made out better than the *Lexington*. She took at least four bombs and two torpedoes. For a while it looked like she might be able to make it, but then a gasoline leak set her afire and they had to abandon ship. It was a terrible sight watching her burn and all those men trying to make it over the side and down the lines into the water. She stayed afloat, burning, and then after they had everybody alive off, one of our destroyers had to sink her with torpedoes.

✪ STATION HYPO
PAC FLEET SIGNALS INTELLIGENCE CENTER
OAHU, HAWAII
20 MAY 1942

As Admiral Fletcher limped back toward Hawaii with the damaged *Yorktown* and her escorts, he couldn't tell who had won the Battle of the Coral Sea. He didn't know until he arrived back in Pearl Harbor that in Rabaul, Admiral Inouye, having lost the element of surprise, had already recalled the Port Moresby invasion force for fear that the transports might still be engaged by a surface force or attacked by land-based aircraft.

The consequences of the fight were clearer to those who had monitored the battle from Hawaii. Tactically, Nimitz judged the outcome to be a modest Japanese victory. Though the Japanese had lost far more aircraft and suffered many more casualties, the loss of the 30,000-ton *Lexington* was far more serious than the sinking of the 12,000-ton *Shoho*. And the small Japanese destroyer-transport and barges sunk at Tulagi hardly equaled the loss of the *Neosho* and the *Sims,* as far as the U.S. Navy was concerned.

But from a strategic perspective, Nimitz considered this first engagement, in which the opposing ships never saw each other, as a victory for the Americans. For the first time since the war began, the Japanese had been forced to turn back an invasion force. He and his commanders had validated the use of Station Hypo intercepts in "near-real" time—meaning that the intelligence was useful in the midst of a battle, not just in planning one.

Now, on 9 May, as dawn was breaking in Hawaii, Nimitz had even bigger concerns. On 5 May, just before the battle was joined in the Coral Sea, Station Hypo had intercepted a message from Imperial Fleet headquarters in Kure to the Combined Fleet. The message, now almost totally decrypted by Rochefort's code-breakers, ordered the invasion of a place designated as "AF" to commence on 4 June.

Nimitz was now down to two undamaged carriers. He had only the *Enterprise* and the *Hornet*, which had not yet engaged in anything except the Doolittle Raid. Now he needed them to stop a major Japanese invasion of a place called AF. And as of 9 May, he didn't even know where AF was. He decided to press Rochefort and Layton a little bit harder to come up with the answer before it was too late.

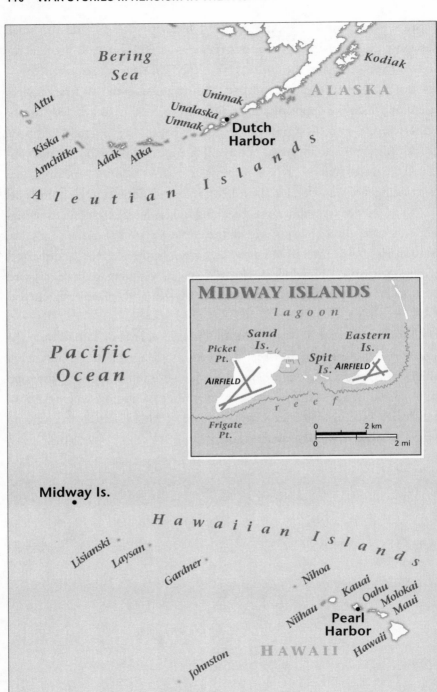

CHAPTER 6
TURNING POINT:
THE BATTLE OF MIDWAY
(JUNE 1942)

✪ **MIDWAY ATOLL**
   1,137 MILES NORTHWEST OF HAWAII
   10 MAY 1942

Midway—1,100 miles west-northwest of Hawaii, an atoll of two tiny islands, is just 2.4 square miles of land barely above water. The highest terrain features are radio pylons on Sand Island and the control tower at the airfield on Eastern Island. Before the war Midway had been a weather station and refueling stop for the Pan American Airways Flying Clippers—the first trans-Pacific air service. In 1935, the U.S. Navy had worked a secret deal with Pan Am to significantly increase aviation fuel storage on Eastern Island and to have Pan Am service Navy PBYs that landed at the big seaplane ramp.

Before 7 December 1941, Midway had been practically defenseless. But it wasn't anymore. At the very moment Fuchida's aircraft were lifting off for Pearl Harbor, the *Lexington* had been delivering planes to the Marines assigned to protect Midway. Immediately afterward, the Navy took over the island and began to beef up its defenses.

By New Year's Day, 1942, and for the next five months, Midway had a strong garrison of Marines equipped with anti-aircraft and coastal defense guns, a fighter squadron, and a scout-bomber squadron. Admiral Nimitz had given Midway all the troops, guns, and aircraft the atoll could hold until the runways and aprons were expanded and more barracks built.

Yamamoto tested the island's defenses in late January, when one of his submarines surfaced and tried to take out Midway's radio station with its deck gun. A Marine three-inch battery opened up and forced the sub to make a panicked dive just minutes after it had surfaced. There were two more sub attacks on the island during the next two weeks, with the same results.

On 1 March the two Marine air squadrons were melded into a new unit, dubbed Marine Air Group 22, and brought up to a full complement of sixty-four aircraft. The new group was formed from Fighter Squadron 221, flying antiquated, Navy cast-off F2A-3s, and Marine Scout Bombing Squadron 241, with hand-me-down Navy SB2U-3 Vindicators the Marines nicknamed "Vibrators" because the ancient engines were so ragged. Unfortunately, the Marine pilots assigned to fly the SB2s were fresh out of flight school and untrained in dive-bombing. So when they arrived on Midway they began practicing shallow-glide bombing attacks—a tactic that would prove to be lethal.

Naval Historical Center

Airfield at Midway.

By 18 May 1942, Admiral Nimitz had done all he could with what he had available to improve Midway's defenses. For more than a week, in the aftermath of the shootout in the Coral Sea, Commanders Edwin Layton and Joseph Rochefort had been telling him that they were "fairly sure" that the entire Imperial Combined Fleet was about to invade the place.

✪ STATION HYPO
PAC FLEET SIGNALS INTELLIGENCE CENTER
OAHU, HAWAII
20 MAY 1942

On 5 May, as the battle in the Coral Sea was developing, an Australian radio intercept site—part of Rochefort's "Magic" network—picked up and transcribed a long message in JN-25. The message was passed to Station Hypo still encrypted, but within two days, Rochefort's code-breakers determined that it was an operations plan issued by Combined Fleet headquarters in Kure ordering an invasion of two widely separated U.S. installations.

By 10 May the team at Station Hypo had determined that the lightly defended U.S. bases on Adak, Attu, and Kiska in Alaska's Aleutian Islands chain had been targeted for invasion.

A second target identified in the intercepted message was designated by the letters "AF" in the Japanese code. But the code books being so painstakingly assembled by Commanders Rochefort and Layton, Lt. Commander T. H. Dyer, and others in the Hypo bunker had no reference for "AF." They simply did not know where it was—and yet, according to the Combined Fleet message, AF was to be attacked a day after the Aleutians. And what an attack it was planned to be!

From the 5 May intercept and subsequent messages, the code-breakers determined that AF was to be struck by six heavy carriers, the *Akagi*, *Kaga*, *Hiryu*, *Soryu*, *Shokaku*, and *Zuikaku*, and the light carriers *Hosho* and

Courtesy Janet Elerding

Commander
Joseph Rochefort

Zuiho. Accompanying them were to be more than forty destroyers, fifteen submarines, seaplane tenders, and dozens of transports and support ships. After surprise air strikes to destroy U.S. aircraft on the ground, three cruisers and seven battleships would then bombard AF, including the biggest battleship in the world, the *Yamato*, Admiral Yamamoto's flagship. After this "softening up," AF would be assaulted and occupied by a force of 5,000 troops.

By 15 May, Nimitz had learned through other intercepts that the carrier *Shokaku* wouldn't be at AF. She was at Truk undergoing extensive repairs from the damage sustained during the Coral Sea battle. And his intelligence officer had other intelligence that the *Zuikaku* wouldn't make it to AF—wherever it was—because the carrier had lost most of its air group in the same battle.

But to Nimitz, the lack of these two carriers hardly mattered. The Japanese force headed for AF was the biggest naval armada ever assembled—145 ships—and he still didn't know where they were going.

By 19 May, Layton and Rochefort were convinced that AF was Midway. But others, including many on his staff, thought it could be Darwin, Australia, mainland Alaska, or even Hawaii itself. Nimitz had to know. His only two operational carriers, the *Hornet* and the *Enterprise*, were in the South

FNC *War Stories*

Commander Edward Layton

Pacific, east of Australia. The badly battered *Yorktown* had limped to Tonga near the Fiji Islands and was now headed slowly back to Pearl Harbor—with estimates that repairs from the damage sustained in the Coral Sea would take three months. Nimitz knew that if he put his carriers in the wrong place he could precipitate a disaster worse than the Day of Infamy.

That night, aware of his commander's desperation, Rochefort devised a brilliant and devious scheme to trap the Japanese into revealing their target. Using the secure underwater cable between Oahu and Midway, he sent instructions to Marine Air Group 22 on Midway to broadcast a routine radio message "in the clear"—meaning unencrypted—that they were running short of fresh water. The Marines complied, broadcasting the innocuous message over their standard high-frequency "administrative & logistics" radio.

Fewer than twelve hours later, early on the morning of 20 May, an Australian intercept site transcribed a Combined Fleet coded message to Yamamoto informing him that a Japanese submarine had reported hearing a radio call: "The aviation unit on AF is running short of fresh water."

Thanks to Station Hypo, Nimitz finally knew the target. And later that day, Rochefort's code-breakers gave him another piece of vital but frightening information: the attacks were scheduled for 3 June in the Aleutians, and for 4 June on Midway.

Nimitz now knew the targets and the dates of attack. He correctly judged that the Aleutian invasion for the third was a deception designed by Yamamoto to draw U.S. forces away from Hawaii and Midway. And while Nimitz didn't want to lose even another inch of American territory to the Japanese, the tiny islands of Adak, Attu, and Kiska were expendable compared with the strategically valuable Midway. If Yamamoto managed to seize the little atoll, Hawaii itself would be vulnerable, and with Japanese long-range land-based patrol aircraft and submarines operating from the Aleutians in the north Pacific and from Midway in the central Pacific, he would have only one way of striking back—through the narrow channels of the South Pacific islands. By the morning of 21 May there was no doubt in the mind of Chester Nimitz: He had to hold Midway. The only questions now were: How? And with what?

Japanese codebooks

The commander of the Pacific Fleet wasn't one to waste time worrying. Nimitz ordered the Midway harbor and beaches mined and barbed wire emplaced. Seventeen Army Air Force B-17s—all he had to spare—were ordered to Midway. On 25 May, the seaplane tender *Kitty Hawk* delivered additional fighter planes and dive-bombers to the island, bringing the little airstrip up to a complement of sixty old Navy and Marine fighters and dive-bombers that had been taken off carrier duty, along with six new TBD torpedo planes—the first to reach the Pacific—twenty-three land-based bombers, and thirty-two of the new but untested Catalina PBY bombers.

He ordered the *Hornet* and the *Enterprise* to steam at flank speed back to Hawaii to refuel and re-arm so that they could get in position northeast of Midway to meet the onslaught. He dispatched every available submarine in the Pacific Fleet—nineteen in all—to screen the island's western approaches. To ensure that the Japanese wouldn't have a free ride in the Aleutians, he ordered several smaller bases evacuated and sent a surface force of five cruisers, fourteen destroyers, and six submarines under the command of Rear Admiral Robert A. Theobald to do their best at disrupting the Japanese landings in Alaska.

Meanwhile, as the Japanese Combined Fleet headed east, the battle-damaged USS *Yorktown* was making her way from Tonga to Pearl Harbor. Navy Aviation Mechanic Bill Surgi was still aboard.

▯ ▯ ▯

AVIATION MECHANIC BILL SURGI, USN
Aboard the USS *Yorktown*
Pearl Harbor, Hawaii
27 May 1942

We went from the Coral Sea to Tonga to survey the damage. The *Yorktown* was pretty well shot up. We had near misses on the port side, which gave us an oil leak. After patching her up as well as we could with all hands working around the clock, we headed for Pearl. It took us over a week to get back, and the damage-control people and the engineers they flew down to Tonga estimated, "It's gonna take ninety days to fix her."

Well, we got to Pearl Harbor, working on her the whole way, and when we pulled into port, they never really repaired it. For all the shrapnel holes in the hull and the fuel and water tanks, they drilled wooden pegs of different sizes and shapes that would fit the holes and we drove them in with sledgehammers to make her watertight. In the spaces below decks where the bombs had gone off, they put in big timbers and welded beams across to shore up the decks and bulkheads. Nobody got shore leave like we usually did when we came into port. We had shipyard workers on board, and our working parties were going around the clock. Nobody slept.

To fix the holes that the bombs had made in the flight deck, they hoisted aboard big metal plates and we fastened them down with four big metal spikes, one in each corner. Then, after just three days, we got the word that we were going back out.

The ship was not what we call seaworthy, but the flight deck was operational. The *Yorktown*'s air group was still intact; the squadrons were brought up to full strength and everybody was on board. As we were leaving Pearl Harbor, the skipper comes over the ship's address system and says, "We're going to help out at Midway."

○ PEARL HARBOR SHIPYARDS
OAHU, HAWAII
28 MAY 1942

Admiral "Bull" Halsey's Task Force 16, composed of the USS *Enterprise* and USS *Hornet* and their escorts, arrived at Pearl Harbor on 26 May. The next day Task Force 17, with Admiral Fletcher shepherding the crippled USS *Yorktown*—trailing a miles-long oil slick—limped into Pearl for repairs. The damage assessment for fixing the *Yorktown* was ninety days. Halsey ordered them to make her ready for sea in three days. Working night and day, yard workers and the crew made repairs so that the carrier could launch and land aircraft again. They did it, and Nimitz came aboard to pronounce the vessel "ready for action" even though repairs continued as the ship sailed.

But when the *Enterprise*, the *Hornet*, and their screen of five heavy cruisers, one light cruiser, and nine destroyers constituting Task Force 16, sortied from Pearl Harbor en route to Midway on 28 May, Halsey wasn't aboard. He had been taken to a hospital in Hawaii for a severe case of dermatitis—seemingly not a serious condition, but after months of combat at sea, it had become a problem for the hard-nosed admiral, keeping him from sleeping. The doctors ordered the tenacious commander to bed rest, and Rear Admiral Raymond A. Spruance took command of the two-carrier Task Force 16, while overall command was handed to Admiral Fletcher aboard the battered but bandaged *Yorktown* with Task Force 17.

The *Yorktown* left Pearl Harbor with Fletcher aboard on 29 May and rendezvoused with the *Hornet* and the *Enterprise* 150 miles northeast of Midway on 2 June.

The timing of the Americans' departure from Pearl Harbor was impeccable. Though Yamamoto was fairly certain that *Enterprise* and *Hornet* were in the South Pacific, he had ordered Japanese submarines to be positioned in Hawaiian waters by 1 June to intercept any other carriers or major combatants that might have arrived from the U.S. mainland. If they couldn't sink them, they were to at least warn the rest of the Combined Fleet if the Americans sailed when the Aleutians were attacked on 3 June. He also dispatched seaplanes from the Japanese-held Marshall Islands on 1, 2, and 3 June to scout Hawaii and carry out the same task. But neither the subs nor the scout planes arrived until well after the two American carrier task

Naval Historical Center

USS *YORKTOWN*

forces had already sailed. The Japanese, believing that they had sunk both the *Yorktown* and the *Lexington* in the Coral Sea battle—and now more convinced than ever that Halsey was still in the South Pacific with the *Hornet* and the *Enterprise*—thought they had nothing to fear as they closed in for a surprise attack on Midway.

Meanwhile, Station Hypo was in high gear. Layton and Rochefort's team went two days straight without sleep, taking catnaps at their radio sets. Having provided the strategic intelligence Nimitz needed, they now wanted to give the commanders at sea good information on the tactical situation.

✪ STATION HYPO
PAC FLEET SIGNALS INTELLIGENCE CENTER
OAHU, HAWAII
2 JUNE 1942

On 2 June, Rochefort's code-breakers had cracked enough JN-25 messages that he was able to tell Layton the dispositions of the enormous Japanese fleet as it closed on Midway—including the intended sequence of attack from the seven different subordinate commands that Yamamoto had established for the operation. And as if the Navy at sea and the Marines at Midway needed any more motivation, the Station Hypo crew let the Americans lying in wait know that the first attack aimed at the atoll would be commanded by Admiral Chuichi Nagumo, heading the First Carrier Strike Force, the very man and unit that had devastated Pearl Harbor on 7 December.

But neither Yamamoto nor Nagumo had considered two important factors: One, they no longer held the element of surprise—American code-breakers had seen to that. And second, they misjudged the Americans' response, thinking that Nimitz would race to defend the Aleutians with everything he had available out of some sense of "military honor."

✪ JNS YAMOTO, IMPERIAL COMBINED FLEET FLAGSHIP
700 MILES NORTHWEST OF MIDWAY ATOLL
3 JUNE 1942
1930 HOURS LOCAL

The Japanese struck the Aleutians right on the schedule that Rochefort's code-breakers had predicted. Bombers from the Imperial Navy's Second Carrier Strike Force attacked Dutch Harbor, the biggest target off the Alaskan mainland, and two Japanese invasion forces captured the tiny uninhabited islands of Attu and Kiska. Dutch Harbor suffered only moderate damage.

Yamamoto received word of Admiral Kakuta's successful attack against Dutch Harbor and cautioned his forces to be on alert, certain that the

Americans would deploy to protect their territory and that the "decisive engagement to destroy U.S. naval power in the Pacific" was just ahead in the waters around Midway. And, Yamamoto reasoned, once that battle was over, no one in Japan—not the emperor, not the politicians—need ever fear another embarrassment like the Doolittle Raid in April.

It was this event, more than anything else, that had led Tokyo to approve Yamamoto's audacious plan. The desire to avenge the Doolittle attack—and ensure that nothing like it would ever happen again—had also clouded the Japanese High Command's otherwise successful strategic and tactical judgment.

Until the Battle of the Coral Sea, the Japanese had applied sound strategic and tactical doctrine in their naval engagements. They had insisted on gathering good intelligence before committing to action, required the use of overwhelming force against their enemy, operated from relatively simple, understandable, and straightforward plans, concentrated their forces at the main point of attack, and mandated strict radio discipline to preserve the element of surprise.

But in the Coral Sea fight, the Japanese had split their forces—and suffered losses as a consequence. And now, as the Combined Fleet closed on Midway, Yamamoto had constructed an elaborate plan, splitting his force into seven separate groups with two objectives: the Aleutians and Midway. Either from arrogance or from fatigue, they had little good intelligence, a very complicated plan, and no radio discipline whatsoever.

Yet with all this, the sheer number of ships—145 in total, all with experienced crews and pilots, still gave him a powerful advantage over the U.S. Pacific Fleet. To carry out the mission of destroying the U.S. Navy in Japan's ocean, Yamamoto had personally chosen the First Carrier Strike Force—*Kido Butai*—the same force that had led the attack on Pearl Harbor. These were the same indomitable Bushido warriors who had led the attack on the American base, the very same commanders and pilots who had been victorious in every encounter with Japan's enemies, from the Hawaiian Islands to the Indian Ocean: Vice Admiral Chuichi Nagumo and Air Officer Mitsuo Fuchida.

Against all this, Nimitz could only muster the Marines on the ground at Midway and the Army, Navy, and Marine pilots based on the atoll; nineteen submarines with defective torpedoes; eight cruisers; eighteen destroyers; two battle-untested carriers—the *Hornet* and the *Enterprise*—and the battered hull and patched flight deck of the USS *Yorktown*. And, of course, the American pilots who would fly from those carrier decks.

✪ USS ENTERPRISE
155 NAUTICAL MILES NORTH-NORTHEAST OF MIDWAY ATOLL
4 JUNE 1942
1045 HOURS LOCAL

At 0415 on 4 June 1942, the Marine air base on Eastern Island was still covered in predawn darkness but alive with the roar of PBY Catalina and Army Air Corps B-17 aircraft engines. The patrol pilots were given their orders: find the Japanese fleet some 200 to 250 miles northwest of Midway, just across the International Date Line, somewhere near 180° longitude and 39° latitude, and report their exact position. The B-17s were told to hit any capital ships they could find west of Midway.

Fifteen minutes later, 108 strike aircraft were launched from four of Admiral Nagumo's First Strike Force carriers hiding in the fog banks 150 miles northwest of Midway—where the PBYs were heading. Nagumo gave the order for his carriers to close on Midway so that his pilots wouldn't have to fly so far when they returned from destroying the sleeping Americans and their airfield.

At about the time Nagumo launched his first strike, the Midway-based B-17s, flown by inexperienced pilots and crews, spotted a group of Japanese support vessels and dropped their bombs, failing to score a single hit. Four of the Catalinas drew first blood in the fight by sinking a Japanese oiler, though. Hearing the report of the attack, Admiral Fletcher ordered search planes aloft from the *Yorktown*, hoping to pinpoint the rest of the Japanese fleet and get the word back to the American carriers.

Nearly two hours after the B-17s, Catalina bombers, and PBY search planes launched from Midway, the Japanese attackers arrived over the atoll, hoping to catch the Americans with their aircraft on the parking aprons, as they had at Pearl Harbor. But most of the U.S. Marine fighters, dive-bombers, and torpedo bombers of Marine Air Group 22 were already aloft.

The Japanese air attack was fierce, but the Marines on the ground were ready and responded with a furious anti-aircraft barrage. The Marines of VMF-221, however, flying combat air patrol in the old Brewster Buffalos, were cut to pieces by the far superior Japanese carrier-based planes. Two-thirds of the squadron was gone in five minutes of air-to-air combat. At 0645, ten minutes after it started, it was over. Only six Japanese aircraft had been downed, but when the leader of the Japanese strike made one last pass over the air base in the gathering daylight, he saw that their bombs had started a fuel tank fire and destroyed a hangar. It was what he didn't see that alarmed him. There were only a few burning American airplanes on the ground—and worse, the runways were still intact. It would require another bombing attack. He headed back to his carrier to inform Admiral Nagumo to prepare another bombing run against Midway.

Meanwhile, a Midway-launched PBY spotted the Japanese carriers. Almost simultaneously, a Japanese scout plane found the *Hornet* and the *Enterprise*. Both pilots radioed back the locations to their respective fleets, and both the Japanese and American admirals prepared to attack each other's ships.

With half his aircraft heading back from attacking Midway, Nagumo was beginning to fuel and arm his remaining planes with torpedoes and high-explosive bombs fused for an anti-shipping attack. Suddenly, two waves of Marine dive-bombers and torpedo bombers that had launched from Midway before the Japanese assault arrived overhead.

Though the Marine attacks were totally unsuccessful—no Japanese ships were hit—the attack by land-based aircraft convinced Nagumo that he first had to deal with the aircraft and runways on Midway before taking on the American carriers. He therefore ordered the armament on his planes changed back to ordnance for a ground attack. For almost an hour, there was chaos on the Japanese flight decks as pilots, plane crews, ordnance men, and deck handlers—already shaken by the violent maneuvers to avoid the American torpedo attacks—tried to comply with Nagumo's order.

In the midst of this confusion on the Japanese carriers, a second strike launched from Midway arrived overhead. Marine Major Lofton Henderson, with a flight of brand new Dauntless SBD dive-bombers, led the way, followed by Army Air Corps B-17s and

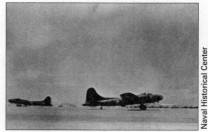

B-17s at Midway

more of the ancient Vindicators. The experienced Japanese gunners and fighter pilots made short work of this raid, but as the *Akagi, Soryu, Hiryu,* and *Kaga* jinked and turned, leaving snakelike wakes in the Pacific—maneuvering to avoid the Marine attackers and the U.S. Army B-17s—it was impossible for the Japanese crewmen on the flight and hangar decks to complete the ordnance changeover that Nagumo had ordered.

And then, to compound the problem Nagumo had created by ordering the ordnance change for a second strike at Midway, his combat air patrol aircraft and the planes he had sent on the first Midway attack showed up overhead, urgently needing to land before they ran out of fuel.

Once again Nagumo ordered the aircraft preparing to launch to be shuffled out of the way to clear his carrier decks. For the second time that morning, fatigued and confused Japanese crewmen started shutting down aircraft, pushing them aside, and lowering them, fully fueled and armed, into the hangar decks of his carriers.

At 0830, in the midst of this new round of turmoil and disorder on the Japanese carriers, the USS *Nautilus* stuck up her periscope and fired off two torpedoes, which did no damage but did instigate a furious half hour, as Japanese destroyers churned around, tossing depth charges while Nagumo's carriers zigged and zagged—still making it impossible to launch or recover aircraft. Then the first of 155 U.S. Navy carrier aircraft appeared over

Nagumo's head. Spruance had launched every bomber from the *Hornet* and the *Enterprise*—holding back just the three dozen fighters of the Task Force 16 combat air patrol. Half an hour later, Fletcher had sent up six Wildcats, sixteen Devastators, and seventeen Dauntlesses from the *Yorktown*. Despite withering anti-aircraft fire and the swirling Zeros, the Navy Devastator torpedo pilots attacked first, skimming over the whitecaps in three waves, aiming for the Japanese carriers.

As they had with the Marine raiders from Midway, the Japanese gunners and pilots in their more maneuverable Zeros blasted plane after plane out of the sky. Not one of the Devastators' "fish" found their mark. All fifteen of the *Hornet*'s TBDs of "Torpedo 8" were downed, as were ten of the fourteen launched by *Enterprise*. But the bravery of the torpedo bomber pilots was not wasted. Their low-level attack drew the Japanese combat air patrols down to the wave tops—making it impossible for their fighters to gain enough altitude to engage the *Enterprise*'s Dauntless dive-bombers, led by Lt. Commander Clarence McClusky, Jr., when they appeared over the *Akagi* and the *Kaga* at 1025.

At almost the same moment, the *Yorktown*'s aircraft found the *Soryu*. The *Yorktown*'s torpedo bombers fared no better than those of the *Enterprise* or the *Hornet*, but the American dive-bombers scored hits on the decks of all three ships among the clutter of Japanese planes that were being fueled and re-armed. Not one of the U.S. Navy dive-bombers was engaged by a Japanese fighter until after it had dropped its bombs. In under six minutes, all three of the Japanese carriers were hit and awash in burning fuel, an inferno that spread as aircraft with live ordnance caught fire and exploded on the flight and hangar decks.

By 1030 on 4 June, the entire balance of naval power in the Pacific had shifted dramatically. Three of Japan's biggest carriers were fiery wrecks heading for the ocean floor. Hundreds of the best pilots in the Japanese navy were perishing in the flames, and scores more would die before the day was done, for the battle was not yet over.

Lewis Hopkins was a twenty-three-year-old ensign from Georgia, flying a Douglas Dauntless SBD dive-bomber from the deck of the USS *Enterprise* during the Battle of Midway. To Hopkins and his squadron-mates, the initials SBD stood for "Slow But Deadly." He recalls hoping that the planes would live up to the second part of their name on 4 June 1942.

□   □   □

ENSIGN LEWIS HOPKINS, USN
Aboard the USS *Enterprise*
155 Miles Northeast of Midway
4 June 1942
1050 Hours Local

The best thing about the SBD was that it was built for its mission capability—meaning it could do the job for which it was designed. As far as I'm concerned, there never was a better dive-bomber designed or built than the SBD.

On the morning of 4 June, we got up at three o'clock in the morning, went to breakfast in the pilots' wardroom, and pushed the eggs around the plate.

We had been told the night before that we would be attacking the Japanese fleet in the morning, and I thought about this being the first time I'd ever carried a live bomb. We launched at about 0720 in the morning and headed southwest to where the Japanese carriers were reported sighted.

Well, we got to where they were supposed to be at about 0920, and they weren't there. So Lt. Commander McClusky, the flight leader, signals us that we'll continue to search for another fifteen minutes. All the other ensigns and I are looking at our navigation plotting boards in our cockpits and thinking, "Hey, I'm going to be short of fuel! How am I gonna get us back?"

We made a box-pattern search—a series of right-hand turns—and then we saw smoke off in the distance. It was from all the firing that they were doing against our torpedo bombers. At 1020 we arrived over the Japanese fleet and the signal was given to attack.

We dove at 300 miles an hour from 22,000 feet down to 2,500 feet in forty-two seconds. When each SBD was right overhead, it would release its bombs. The ship was the carrier *Akagi*, and by the time I made my run, she was on fire and dead in the water, with people abandoning ship and jumping into the water all around. That didn't stop us from dropping more bombs on it. This was one of the ships that had bombed Pearl Harbor.

As I pulled up from dropping my bomb, I was attacked by a Japanese fighter plane, so I had to take all the evasive maneuvers I ever learned. But after I shook the Zero, I looked back and could see three carriers—all of them with explosions on their decks and burning from bow to stern. It was all over in just minutes.

None of us could look for long, though. We were all really low on fuel and had to think about getting back to the *Enterprise*.

⊛ ABOARD USS YORKTOWN
175 MILES NORTH OF MIDWAY
4 JUNE 1942
1205 HOURS LOCAL

The hair-raising battle wasn't over yet. The USS *Yorktown* was the farthest from the Japanese fleet and the last of the three carriers to launch its strikes. It was only because the *Yorktown*'s squadrons flew a more direct route to their targets that they had hit the *Soryu* at the same time that Ensign Lewis Hopkins and his shipmates from the *Enterprise* were attacking the *Kaga* and the *Akagi*. And unfortunately for Rear Admiral Jack Fletcher and the *Yorktown*, his were the last aircraft to leave the area where the three Japanese carriers were on fire.

As his aircraft returned with stories of three Japanese carriers sunk, Admiral Fletcher had cause for concern. He knew from Station Hypo intercepts that there were four big carriers in Admiral Nagumo's force—so there was a very strong likelihood that aircraft from the surviving carrier might have followed his aircraft home. If that was the case, the *Yorktown* was in trouble. She and her Task Force 17 escorts were closer now to the *Hornet* and the *Enterprise*, but if they had to run for it, *Yorktown*, with her Coral Sea damage, wouldn't be able to keep up.

Fletcher's concerns were valid. At 1000—while the American aircraft were en route to attack the *Akagi*, the *Soryu*, and the *Kaga*—the undamaged *Hiryu* had launched eighteen bombers escorted by six fighters. At 1100, while her three sister carriers were burning, the *Hiryu* also launched ten torpedo bombers and six more fighters. The bombers must have seen the *Yorktown*'s SBDs heading back to the east, for at 1205, while Fletcher was refueling the *Yorktown*'s combat air patrol, the ship's radar detected the *Hiryu*'s planes fifty miles out and closing.

While the *Yorktown* hastily launched the planes on deck and waved away the bombers returning from the attack on the *Soryu*, Fletcher called for help. Fighters from the *Enterprise* and the *Hornet* joined his—making a twenty-eight-plane combat air patrol—and they headed west to intercept the attackers. Only eight of the Japanese aircraft succeeded in getting through to the *Yorktown*, but three of their bombs hit home. One blew another hole in her patched flight deck, a second detonated deep inside, causing flooding, and the third knocked out her boilers.

Despite the new damage, the *Yorktown* was under way again, making twenty knots, when the *Hiryu* torpedo bombers came skimming over the waves at 1425. Two of the Japanese torpedoes struck her amidships on the port side, and she immediately lost power and took a twenty-degree list to port. With fires raging belowdecks and without power for her pumps or generators, her list increased to twenty-six degrees, and the ship was in imminent danger of capsizing. Her skipper, Captain Elliott Buckmaster, ordered abandon ship.

Admiral Fletcher shifted his flag to the cruiser *Astoria* and turned over tactical command of the two task forces to Admiral Spruance. Many of *Yorktown*'s aircraft were able to make it to Midway or to the deck of one of the other two American carriers.

As for the crew of the *Yorktown*, it was the second time in a month that their ship had taken a terrible beating from the Japanese. To Bill Surgi, it felt like déjà vu.

AVIATION MECHANIC BILL SURGI, USN
USS *Yorktown*
150 Miles North of Midway
4 June 1942
1500 Hours Local

The first attack came at about noon, from Japanese dive-bombers. The anti-aircraft fire was fierce but a few planes got through and they hit us with three bombs. The first one hit on the flight deck and blew a big hole in it. A second bomb went through the flight deck and started a small fire belowdecks, but the third bomb went down the stack and exploded in the same vicinity where we'd been hit before. This one did the most damage; it blew down bulkheads and opened up a space inside about the size of a stadium.

But as bad as we were hit, we had her back in business in under two hours. The fires belowdeck were mostly out, and we patched the flight deck again and then got the fires in the boilers going. We were under way and launching and recovering aircraft when the second Japanese attack came in about 1430. This time it was torpedoes and they both hit right under me.

The detonation was so big it threw me straight up into the overhead. If I hadn't been wearing my steel helmet, it would have splattered me all over the overhead. But even so, it knocked me unconscious and when I came to I was covered with water and oil—I guess from some ruptured pipes.

By the time I'm able to get up and move around, the ship has a really bad list and is dead in the water. A few minutes later, the captain passes the word to abandon ship. Even though there were lots of guys hurt, it went much better than I thought it would. It was all very orderly. I put on a life jacket and went down the side on a rope—or maybe it was a rope ladder—and grabbed hold of a net on a life raft. I was only in the water a little while when a destroyer came up beside us and threw a net over the

side for us to climb up. So I grabbed that net and there was no way I was
going to let go.

⊙ ABOARD USS ENTERPRISE
45 MILES EAST OF MIDWAY
4 JUNE 1942
2030 HOURS LOCAL

At 1700 hours, twenty-four dive-bombers from the *Enterprise* and the *York-town* found the *Hiryu* about a hundred nautical miles west-northwest of
the two remaining American carriers. The crew of the Japanese carrier,
exhausted from a full day's fighting, had just started to eat when the first of
four Dauntless bombs struck the carrier, instantly igniting an aviation gasoline tank on the hangar deck. The ship went up like a torch. By 1930 the
Kaga and the *Soryu* were on the bottom.

Aboard the *Enterprise*, Admiral Spruance ordered the *Yorktown*'s escorts
to join the screen for the *Enterprise* and the *Hornet*, and then headed east
to avoid a surface engagement with Yamamoto's battleships and cruisers.

AFTERMATH

As darkness fell on 4 June, as Admiral Spruance withdrew to the east,
Yamamoto canceled the order to take Midway and turned toward Japan
with the entire Japanese Combined Fleet, taking advantage of the few
remaining hours of darkness.

When dawn broke on 5 June, the
severely damaged *Yorktown* was still
afloat. But Japanese destroyers sank
their own *Akagi* and *Hiryu* with torpedoes just after first light. Admiral
Nimitz, hopeful that *Yorktown* could
make it back to Pearl Harbor's dry

Japanese aircraft carrier *Akagi*

Naval Historical Center

dock for repairs, ordered the vessel taken under tow.

Later that day, two Japanese cruisers, the *Mikuma* and the *Mogami*, collided, trying to avoid torpedoes fired from an American submarine. On 6 June, aircraft from the *Enterprise* and the *Hornet* attacked these same two cruisers, still dead in the water. The *Mikuma* was sunk, but the *Mogami* managed to stay afloat and escape to Japan for repairs.

That same day the Japanese submarine I-168 found the *Yorktown* as she was being towed slowly toward Hawaii. The destroyer *Hammann* had been lashed to the carrier's starboard bow to provide power and firefighting foam for damage-control parties struggling to save the vessel. When the I-168 fired a spread of four torpedoes at the damaged carrier, one of them struck the *Hammann* and she sank at once, taking most of her crew down with her.

The *Yorktown* stayed afloat until early on 7 June, when she finally succumbed and went down. When Yamamoto and Nimitz added up their gains and losses, the score looked like this:

Japanese Losses	*U.S. Losses*
4 carriers	1 carrier
1 heavy cruiser	1 destroyer
322 aircraft	147 aircraft
3,500 lives	307 lives

CHAPTER 7
THE FLYING TIGERS
(1937–1945)

Long before the successful battles of the Coral Sea and Midway—when the tide of war began to change for the Allies—Americans had been fighting Japanese imperialism without the glare of the media spotlight. A small group of U.S. volunteers—an air force called the Flying Tigers—had been helping the Chinese in their skirmishes with the Japanese since 1938. Few Americans knew very much about them until five months after Pearl Harbor, following the Doolittle Raid.

When Jimmy Doolittle planned that first American air raid against Japan, he hoped that his sixteen B-25 aircrews would be able to land safely in China on airfields controlled by Chiang Kai-shek's National Chinese Army. It was a logical assumption. Chiang was an American ally in the war against Japan and had been fighting the Imperial Army since soldiers marching beneath the banner of the Rising Sun had invaded his homeland

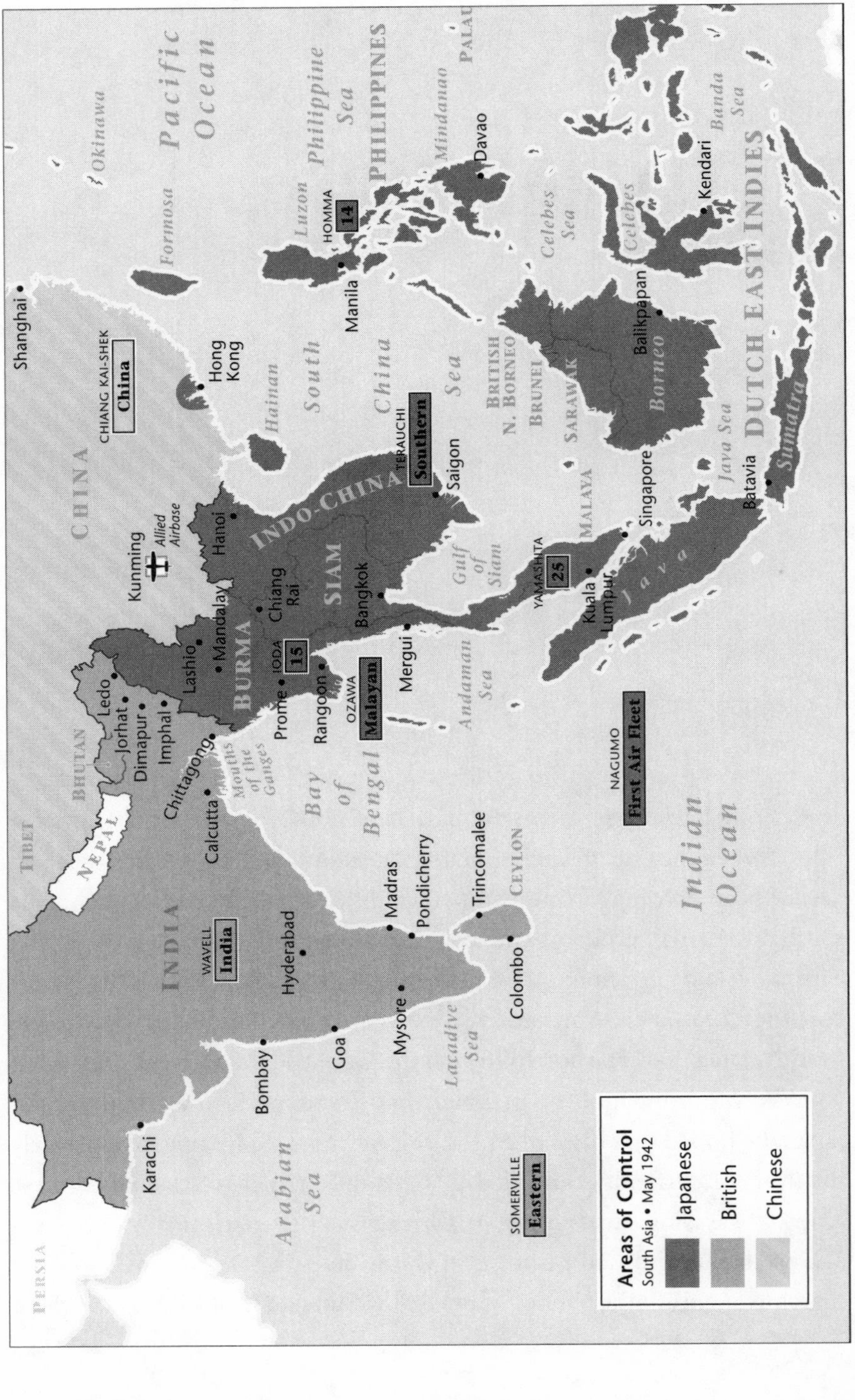

Areas of Control
South Asia • May 1942
Japanese
British
Chinese
PERSIA
TIBET
NEPAL
BHUTAN
INDIA
WAVELL
India
CHINA
CHIANG KAI-SHEK
China
BURMA
SIAM
INDO-CHINA
MALAYA
PHILIPPINES
PALAU
BRITISH N. BORNEO
BRUNEI
SARAWAK
DUTCH EAST INDIES
CEYLON
Karachi
Bombay
Goa
Mysore
Hyderabad
Madras
Pondicherry
Trincomalee
Colombo
Calcutta
Chittagong
Imphal
Dimapur
Jorhat
Ledo
Lashio
Mandalay
Prome
Rangoon
Mergui
Chiang Rai
Bangkok
Hanoi
Kunming
Allied Airbase
Shanghai
Hong Kong
Saigon
Manila
Davao
Kuala Lumpur
Singapore
Batavia
Balikpapan
Kendari
IODA
15
OZAWA
Malayan
TERAUCHI
Southern
YAMASHITA
25
HOMMA
14
NAGUMO
First Air Fleet
SOMERVILLE
Eastern
Arabian Sea
Lacadive Sea
Bay of Bengal
Mouths of the Ganges
Andaman Sea
Gulf of Siam
Indian Ocean
South China Sea
Hainan
Formosa
Okinawa
Pacific Ocean
Philippine Sea
Luzon
Mindanao
Celebes Sea
Celebes
Banda Sea
Borneo
Java Sea
Java
Sumatra

in 1931. Better still from Doolittle's perspective, a good number of American "advisors" were also in China—and many of them had been there for years.

Most histories mark the start of World War II as 1 September 1939, when Adolf Hitler's legions invaded Poland, but Chiang and the Chinese people knew better. For them, the bloodiest conflict in history began in September 1931, when the Japanese Imperial Army marched into coal- and iron-rich Manchuria and occupied Mukden, the provincial capital, on the pretext that the troops had come to protect a Japanese-built railroad.

The Chinese government in Peking (now Beijing), a signatory to the League of Nations charter, protested the Japanese incursion and called on the international community for help. Distracted by the global economic disruptions of the Great Depression, the League took the matter "under consideration." Tokyo's response to this vacillation was a demand that "all Chinese associations of an anti-Japanese nature" be disbanded. On 28 January 1932, when the Chinese government refused, Japanese troops landed at Shanghai.

Though lacking aircraft or tanks, the Chinese put up a spirited defense—and again appealed to the League of Nations. While the diplomats dithered, Tokyo set up a puppet regime in Mukden, renamed the entire territory "Manchukuo," and claimed that Japanese troops would remain at the request of the government of this new and "independent" state. The League of Nations responded by censuring Tokyo and demanding the withdrawal of Japanese troops. Japan promptly withdrew from the League.

Realizing that they could act in China with virtual impunity, unhindered by intervention from the rest of the world, the Japanese began a methodical troop buildup on the Chinese mainland. By March 1933, they had annexed the Chinese province of Jehol and Japanese troops had penetrated all the way to the Great Wall.

For the next four years, much of what Americans knew about events in China came less from newspapers or radio than it did from their churches. American missionaries of every Christian denomination had been flooding into China and building churches, schools, hospitals, and orphanages for decades. Now the correspondence between those religious institutions in China and their counterparts in the United States coupled spiritual matters with what was happening to the Chinese people, caught in the crossfire of a civil war and menaced by the increasingly hostile Japanese.

Many letters and telegrams from China in the early 1930s describe the fight between the revolutionaries led by Mao Tse-tung and the Nationalist followers of Generalissimo Chiang Kai-shek as a struggle between godless Communism and the future of Christianity in the world's most populous country. It was a description that Chiang sought to exploit as he looked for help contending with Mao and the Japanese.

In this effort, the Nationalist leader had a formidable ally. His beautiful wife, Soong Mei-ling, known to the rest of the world as Madame Chiang, was the American-educated daughter of a Christian missionary. A graduate of Wellesley College, fluent in English, with considerable connections in Washington, she dispatched a constant stream of letters and telegrams to friends in the United States begging for help against the Communists and the Japanese.

General Chiang Kai-shek

By the summer of 1937, Chiang and Mao had negotiated an uneasy truce between the Nationalists and the Communists. The military government in Tokyo, believing that a "united China" posed a threat to their plans for a "Greater East Asia Co-Prosperity Sphere," decided it was time to act. On 7 July, they ordered a full-scale invasion, claiming that Japanese nationals in Peking were at risk in the continuing civil disorder.

Just days before the assault, Madam Chiang and the Generalissimo had met with Claire Chennault, a recently retired American airman. The forty-five-year-old Chennault had been medically retired for chronic bronchitis and deafness from flying in open-cockpit fighters. Arriving in May, via a stop in Japan, he had come to China at the suggestion of a friend who wanted advice on how to help the Chinese build a decent air force.

Chennault was appalled by what he found. Though the Chinese showed more than 500 fighters, transports, and bombers on their rolls, in reality they had only ninety-one aging, second-rate aircraft. With characteristic bluntness, he told the Nationalist leader and his wife that they needed his help—and that of the United States. They hired him on the spot to provide that assistance. But before he could even begin, the Japanese invaded.

The next five months were a fury of activity for Chennault as he tried to build an air force worthy of taking on the Japanese invaders. As Chinese troops gave

Madame Chiang Kai-shek

ground grudgingly, the new American advisor to the Nationalist government tried to mold the chaotic Chinese air arm into a real fighting force. Lacking everything from repair facilities to spare parts to decent flight instructors, Chennault reached out to colleagues he had known for years in the Army Air Corps. Some were already in China. Others, responding to the call of an old friend, came from the States—even though FDR had signed the Neutrality Act into law in May, just about the time Chennault arrived in China.

By 23 August, when the Japanese began large-scale bombing raids on Nanking, Chennault had two partially trained Chinese fighter squadrons and an air group made up of Russian expatriates. Flying outmoded Curtiss Hawks and old Boeing P-26s, they scored well against the unescorted land-based bombers that the Japanese launched from Formosa. But when the Japanese responded by sending fighter escorts with the bombers, the scales again tipped against the young Chinese pilots.

Despite Chennault's best efforts—and those of his expatriate pilots, mechanics, and technicians—there was a limited amount that could be done without modern aircraft. In a letter handwritten by Madame Chiang and signed by the Generalissimo, they made an emotional appeal directly to President Roosevelt, begging for aid.

On 7 October, without reference to the letter, Roosevelt announced that he would not invoke the new Neutrality Act against China. But he didn't promise aid either. Instead he "condemned" the Japanese invasion and called for an international conference in Geneva to discuss "the deteriorating situation in China."

The Generalissimo, Madame Chiang, and Chennault now realized that whatever help the Chinese air force might get from the United States wasn't going to come soon. And they were right. When the Japanese finally broke through Chinese lines and invaded Nanking, the Nationalist capital, in mid-

National Archives

Claire Chennault

December, the Chinese air force had fewer than fifty planes left. As the invaders commenced an orgy of rape, murder, and plunder in Nanking, Chennault was trying to reconstitute a fighting force in Hankow, 300 miles farther up the Yangtze.

Photographs and films of the "Rape of Nanking" stunned the civilized world. Now Madame Chiang's correspondence to her friends in the States—and countless other letters from missionaries to congregations across America—contained graphic images showing and describing stacks of dead Chinese women and children; Chinese men being shot, bayoneted, disemboweled, and beheaded; and countless other Japanese atrocities. It was genocide on an enormous, very visible scale, and yet the rest of the world looked on and officially did nothing to intervene.

But "unofficially," Roosevelt did intervene. In January 1938, the White House very quietly authorized American companies to start selling used or outdated aircraft, arms, and military equipment to the Nationalist government by transacting the sales through entities like the Universal Trading Corporation, the Central Aircraft Manufacturing Company (known as CAMCO) and the China National Aviation Corporation. But the trickle of planes, parts, and aviation support equipment that started to arrive in China during the spring of 1938 wasn't enough to slow the Japanese advance. By August, the capital had to be moved again—this time well into the Chinese interior, to Chungking. Chennault packed up and moved the

Chinese Air Force Training Command to Kunming, in western Yunnan Province, practically in the foothills of the Himalayas.

Ensconced on the sprawling base at Kunming, Chennault spent the balance of 1938 and nearly the whole of 1939 and 1940 doing what he did best: teaching others how to fly and fight. When the lack of planes, parts, or pilots grounded his students, he used the time to construct outlying airfields. He also built an early warning network to warn of Japanese air raids and a primitive but effective radio and telegraph communications system linking the Chinese air bases. Chennault also devised plans for recovering downed aviators and returning them to safety. During this period he wrote home frequently, commenting to friends and family about the courage of the Chinese soldiers, the bravery of the Chinese people, and the daring of his Chinese pilots—and reminded them of the one thing that was most needed: decent planes to take on the Japanese.

By the summer of 1940, the Chinese had given up more than half a million square miles of territory and nearly 200 million people to Japanese domination. Americans reading about the plight of the Chinese in their church bulletins didn't hesitate to remind their congressmen that this was an election year. In September 1940, Congress approved a loan of $25 million to the Chinese government for "economic support." But it was too little, too late. It was clear to the Generalissimo, Madame Chiang, and Chennault that courage was no longer enough. Unless the Chinese got some modern arms and aircraft—and quickly—the Japanese were going to succeed in conquering *all* of China. Chiang decided that Chennault should return to the United States and make a personal effort to get planes and—if possible—pilots.

Chennault arrived in Washington on 1 November, on the eve of the presidential election. There, Chennault drew up a wish list of all that the Chinese air force needed in order to fight the Japanese. At the top of the long list of planes, parts, ammunition, and the machinery of war, he wrote: "Time."

The only way to buy time for the Chinese pilots, aircrews, mechanics, and repair personnel would be to have someone else do the fighting for them. So Chennault prepared a separate list: "350 pursuit aircraft; 150 bombers; Americans to fly them."

The November election made it clear that the American people wanted to avoid war if possible, but that they also wanted to support the Chinese. In December, FDR got another $100 million loan for Chiang. Chennault promptly arranged for the purchase of a hundred Curtiss-Wright P-40C fighters.

Once he had decided that the P-40 was what they needed, Chennault wanted to make sure that the Chinese supported his decision. A group of visiting Chinese officials gave him that opportunity. Chennault took them to nearby Bolling Field, just across the Anacostia River from the Capitol, to demonstrate the Curtiss P-40. When the flight demonstration was over, the Chinese were considerably excited. One of them told Channault, "We need a hundred of those airplanes!"

Chennault shook his head. "No," he said, tapping the chest of one of his pilots, "you need a hundred of these."

The aviator who piloted the P-40 for Chennault and the Chinese officials that day was a young Army Air Corps first lieutenant named John Alison.

 ▯   ▯   ▯

FIRST LIEUTENANT JOHN ALISON, USAAF
Bolling Air Force Base
Washington, D.C.
December 1940

I reported to the commander's office, where Claire Chennault, several Chinese, and two representatives from the Curtiss-Wright Company had already arrived. The commander said, "We want you to demonstrate the airplane for the Chinese."

The Curtiss salesman had one of their test pilots there. He said, "Can our pilot fly the airplane?" Well, the commander at Bolling didn't want to do that. And finally, the salesman just threw up his hands and says, "Well, go on out and use your judgment to demonstrate the airplane."

I knew the airplane very well by this time; I lined the airplane up right into the wind. The Chinese all went out to the middle of the field. And I put the throttle up to 980 horsepower and ran down the runway. Just as soon as I got it off the ground, I started the wheels up, pushed it up to full throttle, and let it go.

Now, this airplane wasn't one that was ready for combat. It had no bulletproof fuel tanks, guns, or armor plate. And it didn't have tactical radios, so it was a very light aircraft, and it just *soared* skyward. I did a loop right off the runway. And then I came down at low altitude, below a hundred feet, and put the tip of the wing right over the group, made a number of circles at max power, did a chandelle, and landed.

When I got into the hangar, I could tell by the smile on the face of the Curtiss salesman that he liked the demonstration. And the Chinese were excited.

After that, Chennault went back to China. Little did I know that I'd be flying for him later in the war.

✪ KUNMING AIR BASE
1ST AIR COMMANDOS
SOUTHWESTERN CHINA
11 MAY 1942

Now that he had the planes the Chinese needed, Chennault set to work making arrangements to have them packed and shipped. He was about to gain an unlikely ally in his quest for American pilots to fly them.

Navy Commander Edward O. McDonnell was a member of a military assessment team dispatched to China by the White House. Shortly after the new year began, McDonnell returned with the recommendation that an American Volunteer Group (AVG) of aviators be immediately formed and dispatched to help the Chinese. McDonnell urged that the AVG be formed from officers and enlisted aviators "recently retired' or "loaned" from the Army, Navy, and Marine Corps—and that they be allowed to "return to their service" in the event of war. To head the AVG, McDonnell suggested "an experienced American aviation officer accountable only to Chiang Kai-shek…Chennault is the best available officer."

Roosevelt agreed, and the AVG officially came into existence on 15 April 1941. Chennault plunged into his new assignment, dispatching recruiters to Army, Navy, and Marine air bases to find volunteers. He charged around Washington and New York with characteristic bravado, calling on friends and contacts, trying to find a ship to carry his newly acquired aircraft and personnel to China via Burma.

In total, 112 American military pilots "resigned" from their U.S. military units with the understanding from their president that they could return to their respective branches of service when their job was done.

In July 1941, the first of the AVG planes and personnel finally arrived in Rangoon. But to Chennault's frustration, it would take nearly five more months to unpack the planes, assemble and test them, and whip his volunteer pilots into effective fighter pilots who could fly and fight as a team.

The first AVG planes and pilots didn't get over "the hump" to China until 18 December—ten days after Pearl Harbor was attacked. Two of the three AVG squadrons saw their first action two days later, when the early warning network Chennault had installed two years earlier alerted them to an incoming raid by ten Japanese aircraft. For months, while Chennault was away in the United States, the Japanese had been sending their twin-engine Mitsubishi bombers over Kunming virtually unopposed.

Today would be different. Chennault sent up one squadron over the airfield as bait and told the other to swing west—anticipating that when the Japanese pilots saw the "bait" P-40s they would drop their bombs in the jungle and run for home. He was planning an aerial ambush—and that's what he got. In the wild melee that followed, the Americans destroyed six of the bombers and sent the other four back to their base in Hanoi smoking and full of holes. Only one P-40 was damaged—when the pilot ran out of gas and had to put his fighter down in a rice paddy.

Chennault had left his third squadron in Rangoon, anticipating that the Japanese would be attacking there, too, since every other part of the Far East appeared to be under Japanese assault. The 3rd Squadron didn't have long to wait. On 21 December, fifteen AVG P-40s, accompanied by eleven RAF Brewsters, ambushed a flight of fifty-four Japanese bombers, escorted by a dozen Nakajima I-97 fighters. Though the AVG lost two aircraft and a pilot, the RAF reported thirty-two confirmed wrecks of Japanese planes in the jungles and rice paddies around Rangoon. Chennault tallied the battles more conservatively and claimed Japanese losses as fourteen bombers and thirteen fighters against two AVG pilots lost, four planes destroyed, and seven damaged.

Over the course of the next month, the AVG continued to run up scores like this and better. By the end of January 1942, Chennault and his pilots were front-page news. And by February, stories about the Americans who flew planes with menacing sharks' teeth painted on their noses were describing the AVG as the Flying Tigers. Asked where the name came from, Chennault told a reporter, "It wasn't me—it was one of you guys."

By March 1942, the AVG had racked up an extraordinary record. Chennault and his colorful aviators were destroying Japanese formations in every engagement. Though plagued with the familiar problems of insufficient spare parts and too few mechanics, Chennault had a better "up" record than any aviation unit in China, Burma, or India. And in a way, he became a victim of his own success. The Doolittle Raid was a case in point.

Flying Tiger P-40 fighter

When planning the raid, Doolittle assumed, incorrectly, that Washington would use Chennault's early warning network and his AVG resources to help recover any of his B-25 crews that went down in China. But because Chennault was not "officially" an American officer, in an excess of secrecy, Washington decided not to inform him of the raid. He was therefore unable to put any AVG people in position to help.

In spring 1942, the U.S.-British Joint Staff decided that China, Burma, and India (CBI) deserved to have their own "theater of war." And in the new CBI theater, there was no need for a group of cocky, mercenary pilots fighting their own war against the Japanese.

On 25 April 1942, Chennault was informed that effective 4 July, the AVG would be dissolved and reconstituted as the 23rd Pursuit Group, U.S. Army Air Corps, reporting to the 14th Air Force in India. Any Navy or Marine pilots who wished to return to their services could do so and all others would be accepted into the U.S. Army Air Corps—or returned to the United States as civilians.

Neither the Japanese nor the weather cared what the men of the AVG called themselves. As the pilots and mechanics were deciding what they wanted to do, the Japanese ground offensive continued unabated. In May, the monsoon began, turning the ground into a quagmire and filling the air with dense clouds that made the hazardous flying even more dangerous.

By the time Lieutenant General Joseph ("Vinegar Joe") Stilwell arrived to assume responsibilities as the senior American officer in the CBI theater, seventy of Chennault's men had decided to stay with him and fight on against the Japanese as members of the U.S. Army Air Corps.

Chennault's pilots liked to say, "We lived like dogs and flew like fiends." It wasn't a boast—it was true. They shot down more than 200 enemy planes while losing only six of their own aircraft.

But it wasn't enough. Tojo's infantry in Burma was far more effective than anything the Allies could cobble together on the ground. Three months after invading Burma, the Japanese captured Rangoon and drove General Stilwell's Anglo-American troops back into India. It was a terrible defeat. Stilwell summed it up: "We got a hell of a beating. We got run out of Burma and it is as humiliating as hell. I think we ought to find out what caused it, go back, and retake the place."

After Burma fell on 11 May 1942, every bean and bullet needed to fight the Japanese in China had to be flown over the most inhospitable terrain in the world, the Himalayas. Chennault's pilots called it "flying over the hump," and crammed C-46 transports and B-25 Mitchell bombers with up to four tons of supplies for the 525-mile trip across the roof of the world. Flying in terrible weather at very high altitudes, without rescue beacons, communications, or decent charts, they were at the mercy of treacherous updrafts and downdrafts, blinding blizzards and intense monsoon storms.

A sign on the hangar at the Kunming air base said it all when the pilots got back: "You made it again."

The flight was so perilous that they nicknamed it the "aluminum trail," because the ground below was littered with the remains of 1,000 men and some 600 planes—many more were lost to the unforgiving weather than to the Japanese. One of those who made it over the hump to fly with Chennault was John Alison—the pilot who had demonstrated the P-40 at Bolling Field for the Chinese officials in late 1940.

▯ ▯ ▯

FIRST LIEUTENANT JOHN ALISON, USAAF
23rd Pursuit Group
Kunming, China
July 1942

After Pearl Harbor and America's entrance into World War II, I sat down and wrote a letter to General Arnold that simply said, "Dear Chief, Please send me to a combat assignment."

And I got this wire, just one line: "Report to China." We flew across India and landed at Dinjan, which was the Indian terminus, for the flight over the "hump" to China. Our airplanes were so old and decrepit I couldn't get enough altitude to clear the clouds and the first mountain range. So I called the squadron commander and said, "Look, I can't keep up. I'll find a way and meet you in Kunming, China." I flew south until I found a break between two big thunderheads, and I got over the first mountain range and headed for China.

July 1942 was when the U.S. Army Air Corps took over the American Volunteer Group that included some of the great characters of aviation, like the great Marine pilot "Pappy" Boyington, who later put together the famous Black Sheep Squadron. They had been fighting the Japanese since December 1941 and were a really experienced bunch.

My first fight was at night in late July. When I got to Kunming air base in China, Chennault assigned me to the 75th Fighter Squadron. Tex

Hill had been commander of that squadron, and Chennault put me in as his deputy.

It was hard to get through to the Japanese bombers, particularly when they had an overwhelming number of fighters as escorts. You'd get involved in a fight with the Zeros before you got to the bombers, and pretty soon the bombers were gone. But we still shot down a lot of bombers.

One night with a full moon the radio calls me and says, "John, we can hear 'em. There are bombers approaching the airport. Now they're right overhead."

I said, "I can't see 'em." Then, all of a sudden, I see these flickering exhausts, about 3,000 feet above me. So I start after them; they're headed north, away from the airport. I'm going full-throttle, climbing to meet them. They make a 180-degree turn, back into their bombing run. So I cut them off, turn into them, but at night you have no depth perception. I'm going so fast that I realize I'm going right into them! So I pull the throttle back, lift the nose, sideslip the plane, and suddenly I'm the fourth man in their formation.

And they begin shooting at me. The first burst from the turret machine gun from the airplane on the right started hitting the front of my airplane, went right on back along the fuselage. They put several slugs through the cockpit—I got one right through the parachute. My radio's in the cockpit; they took that out. I got grazed on my left arm. I had a five-inch hole through the crankcase of the engine, but didn't know it at the time. Of course the oil ran out, and later my airplane caught fire. But not before I kicked it around and hit the first Japanese airplane. It didn't explode but I think I killed everyone aboard. The other two bombers exploded when they were hit.

But now I'm in big trouble. My engine is running badly and I'm 15,000 feet above the airport. So I start down, hoping to slide the airplane in on its belly if I can't get the wheels down. That's when my airplane catches fire, and fire in an airplane is kind of terrifying. Fortunately this wasn't a gasoline fire, just the oil from the crankcase. Still, flames are coming out of both sides of the engine and this is enough to frighten me.

I misjudge the airport approach. There's no way I can pull the nose up. The engine is still running, but poorly. Fortunately, the Lord put a river about two miles ahead. And the airplane barely made the river. It was a relatively soft landing in the water, and soon the airplane's under fourteen feet of water. But it did put the fire out. I had hit my head on the gun sight and received lacerations. I had no doctor, no medical corpsman. I don't believe we even had a first aid kit. Fortunately there was a missionary in this little town. And he had a suture needle. So I finally got a rowboat; it took me across and through to our lines. The doctor wouldn't let me out of the hospital. I wanted to get right back to the air base, because I knew we were going to be attacked the next morning. So I went to the roof of the hospital and watched the air battle. I'd been in my first combat and we had five airplanes; there were forty-five Japanese planes. I guess we did all right.

If the Japanese had taken Kunming air base, I'm convinced that China would have fallen. But Chennault wasn't going to let that happen.

✪ ✪ ✪

Thanks to the skill and daring of the Flying Tigers, Kunming didn't fall— and the Chinese stayed in the war, effectively tying up more than twenty-five Japanese divisions that wouldn't be used elsewhere against the Americans. And Claire Chennault, the man who had gone to China as a retired Army Air Corps captain in 1937, returned to the United States in 1945 as a major general.

Pacific Ocean

Okinawa

Formosa

Philippine Sea

PHILIPPINES

Luzon

HOMMA 14

Mindanao

PALAU

Davao

Banda Sea

Kendari

Celebes Sea

Celebes

Shanghai

Hong Kong

Hainan

South China Sea

China

Manila

CHIANG KAI-SHEK
China

CHINA

Allied Airbase

Kunming

Hanoi

INDO-CHINA

TERAUCHI
Southern

Saigon

BRITISH N. BORNEO
BRUNEI

SARAWAK

Borneo

Balikpapan

Batavia

DUTCH EAST INDIES

Sumatra

Mandalay

Lashio

BURMA

Chiang Rai

SIAM

Bangkok

Gulf of Siam

YAMASHITA 25

MALAYA

Kuala Lumpur

Singapore

Java Sea

Java

TIBET

BHUTAN

Ledo

Jorhat

Dimapur

Imphal

Chittagong

NEPAL

Mouths of the Ganges

Calcutta

IODA 15

Prome

OZAWA

Rangoon

Malayan

Mergui

Andaman Sea

Bay of Bengal

NAGUMO
First Air Fleet

INDIA

WAVELL
India

Madras

Pondicherry

Trincomalee

CEYLON

Hyderabad

Mysore

Colombo

Indian Ocean

Bombay

Goa

Lacadive Sea

Karachi

Arabian Sea

PERSIA

SOMERVILLE • Eastern

Areas of Control
South Asia • May 1942

Japanese

British

Chinese

CHAPTER 8
THE FORGOTTEN FRONT
CHINA-BURMA-INDIA THEATER (1937–1945)

⊗ **BRITISH BASE AREA**
LALAGHAT, INDIA
JUNE 1943

The decision to dissolve Claire Chennault's American Volunteer Group and reconstitute it as a regular U.S. Army Air Corps unit wasn't the result of petty jealousies or a "power grab" by the 14th Air Force, as some claimed at the time. Rather, it was the consequence of a major reorganization in the Allied war effort that British prime minister Winston Churchill had been advocating since shortly after Pearl Harbor.

With England struggling against Hitler in Europe and Africa, the warlords in Tokyo decided that the time was right to "liberate the Asian people" in Burma. Churchill had initially believed that Britain could defend her empire alone, but he soon realized that American help would be essential if the crown were to hold on to its most prized possession in the Far East: India.

By April 1942, the U.S.-British Joint General Staff had hammered out a compromise command arrangement for what they called the

China-Burma-India theater. The British would have overall command and the mantle was given to Field Marshal Harold Alexander. General William Slim was the British ground forces commander, and his American counterpart, "Vinegar Joe" Stilwell, Chiang Kai-shek's senior American advisor, was designated the chief U.S. officer in the region. Even though Stilwell had his headquarters with Chiang Kai-shek in China, both British and U.S. combat forces were intended to operate independently, relying on the combined staff in India for coordination and support.

Though the command-and-control arrangement was less than ideal, it was far from the greatest challenge the new CBI commanders faced. They were all aware that Churchill and Roosevelt had decided that the European campaign was to have first priority for all ships, planes, tanks, troops, and war-fighting matériel. Stilwell also knew that MacArthur, smarting in Australia and anxious to avenge his humiliating withdrawal from the Philippines, would receive the second-highest allocation of those scarce resources. These realities meant that a constant shortage of men and matériel would characterize the entire Allied campaign in the CBI theater.

The new command measures had little effect on the Imperial Army's relentless advance into Burma. The Japanese 15th Army, commanded by General Shojiro Iida, had four well-supplied, combat-hardened divisions, the 18th, 33rd, 55th, and 56th, supported by more than 400 aircraft. The demoralized British colonial troops and the two understrength Chinese divisions led by Stilwell lacked almost everything and had virtually no air support other than Chennault's AVG.

By 21 April, as the Japanese were preparing for their final offensive in the Philippines, the outnumbered and out-

National Archives

General Joseph Stilwell

gunned British forces in Burma were in full retreat, hacking their way 600 miles through mountainous jungle back into India. Stilwell's Chinese troops commenced a retreat of their own, fighting their way back into China, arriving emaciated and exhausted after more than a month in the jungle.

By mid-May 1942, the Japanese held all of Burma, were on the attack against Chiang in China, and were threatening India. From this point onward, the Allies' shortages of conventional combat forces and extraordinary logistics challenges would dictate their strategy and tactics in the region. Their paucity of combat power made it necessary for both the British and the Americans to employ highly irregular warfare techniques and made the CBI theater the venue for some of the most spectacular unconventional operations of World War II.

By their very nature, unconventional operations require leaders with imagination who can "think outside the box" and motivate those they lead to undertake daring action deep in enemy territory against numerically superior adversaries. The British had such a man in Major General Orde C. Wingate. For the Americans it was Major Frank Merrill on the ground and Claire Chennault in the air. The forces that these three men commanded were outnumbered 700 to 1 by the Japanese. Yet between spring 1942 and late 1944, these three leaders and the men they commanded succeeded in inflicting enough damage on the Japanese 15th Army in Burma that it were unable to exploit its initial advantage and launch successful offensives against India to the west or northward against Chiang.

✪ ✪ ✪

Major General Orde C. Wingate was a maverick in every sense of the word. He had been serving in Palestine when the War Office assigned him to the British campaign to liberate Ethiopia from Mussolini's Italian Occupation Army in early 1941. Wingate organized a unit of irregulars mounted on horses and camels that he called the Gideon Force. Though his troops made only a modest contribution to the success of the five-month fight, on 5 May Wingate was accorded the honor of riding beside Haile Selassie, the "Lion of Judah," when the Ethiopian emperor made his triumphal entry into Addis Ababa.

The positive press coverage of Wingate's Ethiopian escapade convinced Churchill's senior officers to overlook the man's considerable eccentricities and grant his wish to try his Long-Range Penetration (LRP) concepts against the Japanese in Burma. As soon as he arrived in India, Wingate set about recruiting a force of more than 2,500 Burmese and Indian troops led by British officers and NCOs to start operating deep inside Burma. He called them Chindits—and worked them mercilessly, marching them up and down the mountains and teaching them to fight in the jungle and live off the land with minimal supplies.

FNC War Stories

Major General Orde Wingate led Britain's Special Forces in Burma.

By February 1943, Wingate believed his men were ready. British HQ gave the green light for 2,800 Chindits to launch an LRP attack into the trackless mountains along the Indo–Burmese border frontier. In a break with traditional warfare doctrine, Wingate sent RAF officers with each of his units to help maintain contact with British aircraft that would parachute supplies to his troops.

For four months, the Chindits, operating hundreds of miles deep inside Burma, cut Japanese communications and supply lines, destroyed railroads, and thoroughly disrupted General Iida's plans for an attack into India. By the end of April, with the weather deteriorating and his outnumbered, exhausted men suffering from malaria and prolonged exposure in the mountainous jungle, Wingate decided to break contact and hastily withdraw to India before they were surrounded by the Japanese. Though they were closely pursued by the Imperial 15th Army, the withdrawal of the Chindits proceeded in relatively good order, unlike the British rout less than a year before.

When Wingate's men arrived back in India in June 1943, the LRP operation was deemed to have been a great success—though it had come at the cost of more than 800 British and colonial soldiers killed or missing. But during the course of their hurried withdrawal, Wingate had been compelled to make some agonizing decisions. Lacking any means of evacuating his wounded, he had no choice but to leave them behind rather than slow his entire column and put them all at risk of death or capture.

On several occasions, rather than sacrifice 2,000 still able-bodied men, Wingate gave the sick and wounded extra ammunition, some grenades, water, and a Bible—and left them beside the trail as the others marched away. Often, before the departing troops were out of earshot, they heard the explosions or gunshots from the place where they had left wounded comrades who had chosen not to wait for the Japanese troops to arrive and use them for bayonet practice. Distraught over the inability to evacuate his casualties, Wingate spent the balance of 1943 training replacements, refitting and repairing his battered LRP force, and trying to solve the demoralizing medical evacuation problem.

Wingate wasn't the only one using the interval to rebuild in India. Stilwell was also utilizing bases along the Indian plain to train Chinese troops. U.S. Army engineers were busy trying to reopen the Burma Road so that Chiang's forces would no longer have to rely solely on American pilots flying over the Himalayas for resupply. By the winter of 1943–44, with Admiral Louis Mountbatten now in command of the Allied effort in the CBI theater, the British in India and the Americans in China were finally preparing to go on the offensive.

Unfortunately, so were the Japanese. Having consolidated its positions and established puppet regimes in Indochina, Malaya, and the Philippines, Tokyo ordered the commander in Burma, General Renya Mutaguchi, to launch a fresh offensive against India.

The Japanese set a start date of 17 April 1944 for the campaign, codenamed Operation Ichi-Go, to commence. British code-breakers intercepted the message, and Mountbatten decided to disrupt Mutaguchi's plans by sending two LRP columns into Burma. Wingate's Chindits were to enter from the west and Merrill's Marauders from the north. For the first time in the CBI theater, gliders and paratroopers would be used to insert forces deep behind enemy lines and Claire Chennault's Flying Tigers—now part of the 14th Air Force and equipped with more than 300 bombers, transports, and fighters—would support the British with "air commando" operations.

The daring plan, approved by Admiral Mountbatten, also solved Wingate's dilemma of how to evacuate the sick and wounded from deep behind enemy lines. American "air commandos" would bring in equipment to cut landing strips in the jungle from which light aircraft could operate and fly out casualties to hospitals in China or India.

Such cooperation was relatively rare in the CBI theater. It was no secret that Chiang Kai-shek and the acerbic "Vinegar Joe" Stilwell all but hated each other. Nor did Stilwell make any pretense of getting along with Chennault. Nonetheless, after being pressured by General Hap Arnold in Washington, he gave his grudging approval to Mountbatten's plan. The concept of using gliders and light aircraft to support LRP operations was the brainchild of two brilliant young aviators, Lieutenant Colonels Phil Cochran and John Alison. Because heavy transport aircraft would never be able to take off from the rough-cut airstrips carved out of the jungle, Cochran and Alison proposed using American-built CG-4A Waco gliders to ferry men and matériel behind enemy lines. Thousands of the CG-4A gliders were being built for use in World War II. Designed for a one-way trip into combat, the plywood and fabric craft were inexpensive to construct, could be towed to the vicinity of their landing sites by conventional transports, and required only a clearing in which to land. But they also needed incredibly daring pilots and crews to fly missions in them.

The Waco CG-4A glider

Cochran and Alison also convinced Hap Arnold that the air commandos would need an allocation of tiny, single-engine, Stinson L-5 aircraft to use as air ambulances. They had run some tests and confirmed that the little planes could carry one ambulatory patient and one litter patient from the bare-bones landing strips built by the air commandos.

General Arnold approved the Cochran-Alison air support plan and convinced Stilwell to go along with it. Alison recalled Arnold's admiration for Wingate: "This man walks into Burma, and it takes him six weeks to get into position to where he can really hurt the Japanese. When he gets there, his men are tired, many of them have malaria, and a lot of them are sick. Some of them are wounded—some killed." The plan Wingate's subordinates had developed would move the irregular troops into place in just a few hours by air. Arnold then told the two young officers, "I don't want them to walk. I'm going to give you everything you need to do it. Now...which one of you is gonna go?"

After briefly thinking about it, Arnold dispatched both Alison and Cochran as "co-commanders" to India to oversee the delivery of equipment, the assembly of the Waco gliders, and the training of the 523 American pilots and aircrews who volunteered to join the 1st Air Commandos. The two men were uniquely suited to the task.

Alison had already proven himself a skilled pilot, a gifted flight instructor, and a resourceful staff officer. He was already an ace, having shot down more than five enemy aircraft while flying with British and Russian pilots that he'd helped train.

Alison's close friend Lt. Colonel Phil Cochran was the epitome of the suave and daring fighter pilot. Milton Caniff, creator of the *Terry and the Pirates* comic strip, fashioned Terry's flight instructor after Cochran. He wasn't just a great fighter pilot; he was also a charismatic leader who instilled confidence in the men he led.

Charles Turner served with Alison and Cochran as one of the Waco glider pilots in the 1st Air Commandos. Sergeant Raymond Bluthardt was an Army engineer who helped cut airstrips and build roads deep inside Burma during Operation Thursday—the largest unconventional warfare campaign in the CBI theater.

⬜ ⬜ ⬜

LIEUTENANT COLONEL JOHN ALISON, USAAF
Forward HQ 1st Air Commandos
Allied Expeditionary Air Base
250 Miles Inside Japanese-Controlled Burma
5 March 1944

Phil Cochran and I started out as co-commanders, but after about a month, it was so confusing I said, "Look, Phil, let's just go back and be regular soldiers. You're the ranking officer; I'm your deputy, let's get this job done." So then we considered what tools were available. We had the option of using either gliders or paratroopers. We used paratroopers as

pathfinders to mark landing sites, but needed a way to take in an airborne engineer company, scrapers, and carry-alls. So we decided that we should use gliders, to get the troops and heavier equipment in so they could then make airfields for transports that could deliver the rest of the troops and their

C-47 towing two Waco gliders

equipment. General Arnold gave us thirty P-51s, fifteen B-25s, thirty C-47s, a hundred L-5s to use as ambulance planes, and almost a hundred cargo gliders.

Somebody suggested that we try snatching the glider's tether with a moving C-47. American Aviation of Wilmington, Delaware, had developed the technique for picking up mail sacks in the West Virginia mountains. They had devised a level-winding reel that had an automatic brake and you could adjust the tension. At the end of this line we put a loop of nylon rope that had a catch just like a big fishhook.

We decided to try it and set up poles to hold the glider's tether up off the ground. The C-47 would skim overhead trailing its hook, grab the tether, and snatch that glider right off the ground. For anyone sitting in the glider, it was quite an experience. The C-47 pilot would open the throttles, the winding reel would play out, and gradually the tension would tighten and the glider is off like it was shot off a catapult!

The night we went in, 250 miles behind the lines, we couldn't use one of the two landing sites, so all the gliders had to land at the same zone. Because we had twice as many gliders landing as we'd planned for, some of the gliders on the second wave crashed into gliders from the first wave that were still on the zone. We had a number of dead and injured—we didn't know the exact count then, but in the dark things looked bad.

I was lucky; my glider didn't hit a log or a ditch or anything. We had eight assault gliders [in our unit], and I think that my glider was the fourth to hit the field. The men got out, and started to fan across the landing area to see if there was any enemy opposition. Thank God there wasn't. Anyway, we got all our people in.

The next morning we got up and looked out at all the wrecked gliders and learned that our commander and some airborne engineers had been killed in the landing.

Well, that didn't stop these soldiers. In about twelve hours we had cleared a runway. We had lights, we had a generator. We set up a control tower on top of one of the wrecked gliders.

By radio Phil Cochran asked, "When can you take your first airplanes?"

I said, "Just as soon as it gets dark. But send them in one at a time, slowly at first." I looked up just at dark, and here are five or six airplanes. We got 'em in, and we got 'em out—about 500 men and I don't even know how many mules—that first night. The next morning, they were on their way through the jungle to fight the Japanese.

□   □   □

LIEUTENANT CHARLES TURNER, US ARMY GLIDER PILOT
Expeditionary Air Base
250 Miles Inside Japanese-Controlled Burma
5 March 1944

In the glider program they sent us through, we were flying Piper Cubs. We were trained to kill the engine and make dead-stick landings. They taught us to do that in both daylight and night. And we did that for hours on end. And then they moved us into the big transport gliders.

These cargo gliders that we trained on in India had an eighty-three-foot wingspread, carried fifteen to seventeen troops, and weighed approximately 3,600 pounds. Our payload was about the same. At that weight they flew well but the landing speed was fast, around seventy to seventy-five miles an hour or more.

They were stunning to sit in and to think you were expected to fly 'em. But after a few takeoffs and landings, and a few flights, they flew very well. It was easy to control, and was not a tricky airplane to fly at all. The tricky part of it was your judgment, in anticipating your altitude and your airspeed to the point of the landing. You have to arrive at the proper altitude and the proper speed at the proper point, every time, or you're a casualty. A glider pilot has only his decision-making process. I think the idea that a glider was named the "flying coffin" emanated from the fact that there were numerous accidents, early on.

We had to assemble all of our gliders, a hundred of them, in India. And all the pilots pitched in, along with the mechanics, to put those gliders together.

Operation Thursday relied on the gliders to penetrate behind enemy lines and put the men and matériel into position. They dropped the pathfinders in by parachute. But they wouldn't have equipment to build a landing strip capable of taking transports by hand. That would have been impossible. With the gliders we were able to bring in jeeps, mules, horses, anti-tank guns, bulldozers, tractors, and scrapers. And with that equipment we built a strip on which we could land eighty or ninety C-47s a night. Now, paratroopers couldn't have done that in months—if ever. So the gliders were the only way to get men and matériel in to the right spot, at the same time, in reasonable safety with minimal losses. They calculated that our losses might be as high as 40 percent. Thankfully, they were not nearly that high.

Twenty-four hours before the mission was launched, we were called into a meeting and given photographs of the landing sites, and told where they were, and the tow plane pilots were briefed. The gliders were all ready, the towropes—or tethers as they were called—were laid out. We stood by for the troops to be loaded. We were going into Burma.

They used a double tow to enable one airplane to tow two gliders and get twice the load to the target. It was very difficult on the airplane and on the glider pilots. At night it was particularly hard because we glider pilots couldn't see each other, the tow plane, or the towrope.

The tow plane flew over at about twenty to thirty feet off the ground and snatched the glider off the ground. The glider ran about 150 to 200 feet, max, on the ground before it was airborne. The reel on the tow plane would pay out the cable like a fishing reel, so that the G-force would not break the cable. For those of us in the glider it was like being shot out of a cannon. We went from zero to 120 miles per hour, in about 200 feet.

The visibility at night is bad. It's not like landing at an airport. We were totally at the mercy of what's in front of us. There could be enemy troops all around the landing field. Anything can happen, and most everything that can happen is bad.

The landing was normal, for a glider overloaded 20 or 30 percent. I estimate that my landing speed was somewhere in the neighborhood of ninety miles an hour. And when landing a glider, in order to stop it fast, we put the nose over on the ground by pushing the stick forward. Then, if there's uneven ground, the nose breaks and dirt comes boiling into the cockpit with you. We landed fast and hard. I ran the length of the field, and I was next-to-the-last glider in. I put my glider in between two gliders that landed ahead of me. The last glider came over me, very fast; he had cut loose way too late and he made a 180-degree turn. His wing caught a big tree and he went straight into the ground with the equipment, the engineers, and the bulldozer. It killed them instantly.

We knew the danger that was there. But I think most glider pilots would agree that while glider flying was dangerous, in the total analysis, it was worthwhile.

◻   ◻   ◻

SERGEANT RAYMOND BLUTHARDT, US ARMY
Expeditionary Air Base
250 Miles Inside Japanese-Controlled Burma
5 March 1944

I was drafted into the Army and reported to Fort Leavenworth, Kansas. That was the induction center. Then I was assigned to the 1877th Airborne Engineers, Company C, at Westover Field in Massachusetts. They said we were going to be an airborne unit. I asked, "What's an airborne unit?"

It was cold when we got to Massachusetts, and when they issued our gear they gave us parachutes. We hung them over the foot of our beds and every one of us, for three months, had to take it down to the hangar, unfold it, hang it up, and dry it for three days. Then we would have to repack it. The funny thing is, after we got to India, we never saw another parachute.

After Massachusetts, they took us for more training in New Jersey, and from there we made a twenty-eight-day trip on the USS *America*, sailing first to Rio de Janeiro, where we stayed one night and took on supplies. Then we took off for Cape Town, South Africa.

Eventually we arrived at Lalaghat, India, a British air base not far from the border with Burma. It was a grass-field landing strip. They put us on the backside of this base, and that's where we learned how to make runways. When we finished that training, they picked Company C of the 1877th and made us the 900th Expeditionary Engineers and told us we would be involved in some special project and that we would be over there probably a year. We were there for three years.

After a while, they brought in a whole bunch of Waco gliders—and lined them up, two gliders behind each C-47. Inside some gliders were Clark bulldozers. They had six-inch tracks and thirty-seven-inch blades, and were gasoline-operated. The only men on my glider were the pilot, copilot Paul Johnson, a bulldozer, and me.

About an hour out, the window on my side just blew out and it got pretty cold. We didn't realize until we got over the Himalayas that the Japanese had control of that area. You could see their campfires all along the way. And every once in a while we could see a tracer bullet go past. But we never got hit.

Then the C-47 pilot cut us loose. We circled the landing site a few times and then came down. My CO was killed there. His glider didn't make it past the trees. He, the pilot, and seventeen British troops were on that glider, and all were killed. When my glider came in, we hit the grass and the wheels washed out from under us. We slid toward the jungle and dove right into it.

There were two big trees there and the fuselage of our glider went right between them. Our wings stopped us, and the ropes on the bulldozer broke and it ripped the front of the glider open. The pilot and I ended up upside down but we were okay.

Since we were there to get a runway built, we just got to work on that grassy, bumpy field. We had started out with four bulldozers, three graders, two carry-alls, scrapers, and two jeeps. All we had were the two jeeps, one Clark bulldozer, one carry-all trailer, and a scraper to skim that grass off, level the field, and push it out of the way. There was buffalo grass out in the middle of it, probably six or eight inches deep.

We used air-driven chain saws to cut down the trees at one end of the runway for a better approach. Then we cleared the dead timber and took our little Clark bulldozer, picked up the dirt in the carry-all, and dragged it behind the tractor to take the debris away. Then we had the men tramp the dirt down good and tight so it wouldn't be a problem for the transports when they landed and took off.

It wasn't too difficult, except where crashed gliders had to be pushed off the runway and into the jungle. That was about the worst. It took a lot of time for our equipment to get that stuff out of there. And we had just one day, working as soon as daylight broke till dusk, before the first plane came in. Everything worked fine, even though there were just a few of us to get the runway done.

We just had that one day but we had trained for it. And when you've got a bunch of guys who know what to do, you just do it. It's something we had to do and we did it.

I wouldn't take a million dollars for the experience, and I wouldn't give ten cents to go through it again.

✪ ALLIED AIR BASE
1ST AIR COMMANDOS
LALAGHAT, INDIA
5 AUGUST 1944

By nightfall on 6 March 1944, at the end of just twenty-four hours on the ground, the 1st Air Commandos had succeeded in establishing an advanced air base deep inside enemy-held territory in the Burmese highlands. Back in India, at Hailakand, they had fighter planes and ambulance aircraft standing by. Ten miles away, at Lalaghat, were the C-47s that had towed the sixty-three gliders—two at a time—into Burma. Both sets of aircraft were designated for direct support of Wingate's troops on the ground in Japanese-held territory.

By penetrating 250 miles deep into Japanese-held territory in a matter of hours, Wingate had achieved tactical surprise. Though the high-risk venture had resulted in fifty-seven casualties, the transports that then landed at Broadway—and other Expeditionary airfields like Blackpool and Aberdeen—made it possible to insert nearly 9,000 men and a remarkable amount of matériel deep behind enemy lines. Those who arrived by glider that first night survived what amounted to a crash landing, and yet, the men of the 1st Air Commandos were still able to construct the first of several airstrips, which would serve as logistics bases and medical evacuation sites for Chindit casualties.

Though the overall effort was successful, not everything went according to plan. Wingate had wanted to build two airstrips that he had dubbed Broadway and Picadilly. But on 4 March, the day before the operation was to commence, reconnaissance photos of the proposed landing sites showed that the enemy had strewn huge teak logs all across the field code-named Picadilly. The glider pilots were concerned that none of the gliders could make it in safely. After reviewing the options, it was decided at the last minute to abandon a landing at Picadilly.

There were no visible obstacles at the Broadway site, so all sixty-three gliders employed the night of 5 March were ordered to land there. This decision doubled the number of Wacos landing at Broadway and caused the problems that Alison and Turner experienced with gliders landing on top of one another. The result was that only thirty-seven of the sixty-three gliders attempting to land made it intact. Twenty-four men were killed and another thirty-three were injured, many seriously.

Despite the casualties, men, mules, and tiny bulldozers went to work. When darkness fell on 6 March, Broadway had *a usable runway!* Later that night, there were also lights, provided by a generator. The first C-47 transports—flying ammunition, anti-aircraft batteries, and security troops to protect the base from Japanese attack—landed without incident after dark.

By dawn of the second day, more than 500 additional troops had been delivered and all the injured from the glider crashes had been evacuated.

Within the first week, C-47s were able to deliver aviation fuel in fifty-five-gallon drums to Broadway, and P-40 fighters soon followed. Positioning fighters forward in Burma permitted the P-40s to provide fighter escort for the B-25s launched out of India. The effect was almost instantaneous. With fighter cover from Broadway, B-25s could now go after the big Japanese airbase at Shwebo, which was immediately targeted. The first American raid on the base—by B-25s escorted by Broadway-based P-40s—caught the Japanese air force completely by surprise. Sixty enemy planes were destroyed on the ground. Another mission by Allied planes did even more damage to the Japanese air base two days later.

Wingate's Chindits, supported by the 1st Air Commandos and Chennault's Flying Tigers, were able to pursue a far more aggressive campaign in 1944 than they had a year earlier. With Broadway secured as a "rear" base, the Air Commandos and Chindits forged deeper into the Burmese jungle, hacking out additional airstrips as they advanced through the inhospitable terrain.

Wingate's deep penetration operation was certainly not the decisive factor in the eventual defeat of Mutaguchi's campaign to invade India—that credit surely goes to General William Slim and his 14th Army. They bore the brunt of the Japanese attack along the border and withstood Mutaguchi's offensive against Imphal and Kohima, two of the biggest engagements in the CBI theater.

But it is also evident from postwar records of the Japanese 15th Army that Wingate's LRP force, along with the proper air support, became just what the Allies had hoped it would be—a disruptive thorn in Mutaguchi's side. Within two weeks they succeeded in cutting the Mandalay-to-Myitkyina railroad—the main Japanese logistics route that the Imperial Army had built with POW slave labor.

Wingate was well aware that the railroad his irregulars had seized was one of several in Burma that the Japanese were constructing with slave labor provided by Allied prisoners of war. When he was planning the March 1944 Chindit operation into Burma, one of the missions he assigned his officers was to be prepared to use their LRP units to rescue any Allied prisoners within their zone of action. Unfortunately for men like Private Kyle Thompson, a Texas National Guardsman captured in the opening days of the war, Wingate's Chindits never got close enough to rescue him or his long-suffering mates toiling and dying in the Burmese jungle building railroads for the Japanese military.

◻ ◻ ◻

PRIVATE KYLE THOMPSON, TEXAS NATIONAL GUARD
Japanese POW Work Camp Kilo 80, Burma
Autumn 1944

In October 1940, my National Guard unit in Wichita Falls, Texas, started training to go overseas. In November 1941, my battalion was sent to the West Coast and we sailed out of San Francisco the day after Thanksgiving. We went through Pearl Harbor on Sunday, a week before it was bombed on 7 December. We were supposed to go to the Philippines but got sent to Java instead, because Manila was already under attack.

After Singapore fell to the Japanese on 15 February 1942, we pretty well figured Java was next, because they were invading Borneo, Sumatra, Bali, and the other islands around us. During the night of 28 February and the early hours of 1 March they landed on Java with at least 50,000 very experienced, well-equipped, first-class soldiers. The Japanese army was a tremendous fighting force. It was their duty to fight to the death and it was against their principles to be captured.

We were badly outnumbered and had been retreating for several days when we dug in around a big bamboo grove. The next morning a Dutch officer drove up and talked to our commanding officer, Lt. Colonel Thorpe, and informed him that the Dutch government had surrendered to the Japanese, and that we were all prisoners of war. I don't know, how do you describe something like that? We were stunned, frightened, and had no concept of what lay ahead.

We just disappeared when the Japanese captured Java. Back home they started referring to us as the Lost Battalion. Once the Dutch surrendered we had no way to communicate with anyone.

The Japanese came and loaded us on a train, and they started screaming, poking at us with bayonets and loaded rifles. It was something out of a nightmare. And it went downhill from there. The Japanese beat us and punished us excessively. I have no idea of the total number of times I was beaten by the Japanese guards—sometimes by rifle butt, sometimes with a bamboo pole. But maybe they were trying to toughen us up for what was coming.

In early March 1943, we got to our first work camp in Burma, at the end of a rail line. They made us start working from there, southeastward, through the Burma jungles.

We were taken out in work parties of 100 or 200 men. A few weeks later, 368 survivors of the USS *Houston*, an American cruiser that had been sunk off of the Java coast, joined us. The Japanese rounded up the sailors who made it to shore. When the *Houston* survivors joined us, it brought us to about 900 American POWs. All of us were put to work on building this railroad through the jungle.

We called it the Siam Death Railway. Now, where we were made to work, it was a 260-mile stretch of total jungle. There were no towns, villages, or people.

I was put to work on the crew that was preparing the rail bed. Our job was to make a railroad bed level by filling, digging, breaching streams, and carrying dirt and rock.

The only tools we had to build this railroad were picks and shovels, and bamboo baskets and poles for carrying dirt. There was no machinery, nothing like a bulldozer. We didn't even have wheelbarrows.

They gave us each a quota of one cubic meter of dirt to be moved each day. Later, because we got behind schedule, they upped that to *two* cubic meters of dirt daily.

The Japanese needed this railroad because they were mired down in northern Burma fighting the British. The Japanese were in dire need of an overland route to bring up troops and supplies.

We heard about British troops out there in the jungle. And we kept hoping that they would come to get us.

We never had enough food; we were always just on the verge of starving to death. We had to work up to eighteen hours a day, in rain, in mud and muck, and after a few months, the tropical diseases began to take hold of us.

I had a huge ulcer on my right leg and the leg bone was exposed in two places. I was flat on my back for nearly six months. All of my friends thought I was going to die. I got sent back to Kilo 80 Camp, and was there about two or three months.

It was a miserable, miserable existence. I'd get up before daylight, have a little cup of rice for breakfast, march out to the work site under the Japanese guards, where I'd work all day long until dark. And then, if we hadn't completed the task that the Japanese thought that we should have, we'd have to build bonfires so we could have light to work in the dark.

It was an excruciatingly hard, cruel work; it was slave labor. Death became more common than life, and for many of the guys who didn't make it, death was more or less the route that they chose. It was easier to die than it was to live. But I had faith in my country and my God. I started out in a section crew of thirty-six guys. In less than a year, thirty-four of 'em were dead.

It all ended on 16 August 1945, the day after Japan surrendered. They had just moved me again—this time from Tarakan to another railroad work camp. The Japanese camp commander ordered all prisoners to assemble in front of our compounds. He got up on a box and in broken English announced to us that the war was over, that Japan had surrendered.

✪ AFTER ACTION REPORT
1ST AIR COMMANDOS
14 AUGUST 2004

It was tragic that Wingate's Chindits were never assigned a specific rescue mission for POW slaves consigned to work on the Japanese military rail system in Burma. There were times when LRP units were fewer than twenty-five miles from some of the 60,000 enslaved Allied prisoners of war building that infamous 260-mile-long railroad. In addition to the American, British, and Dutch POWs, the Japanese also conscripted 200,000 young Burmese men to work on the rail line—making the ratio simple: 1,000 slaves for every mile of track. At the completion of this particular rail line, 16,000 Allied POWs and 100,000 civilians were dead. Four hundred and forty-six men died on every mile of the Imperial Army's Railway of Death from every conceivable cause: malnutrition, overwork, disease, dehydration, torture, and in some cases, brutal execution.

Former POW Kyle Thompson survived, but he cannot forget. He says, "I was nineteen when we were captured, I had my twentieth, twenty-first, twenty-second, and twenty-third birthdays as a prisoner. So a pretty good part of my young life was sacrificed on the altar of the Japanese Imperial Army.

"After the war, many who survived being POW slave laborers of the Japanese asked for compensation from Japan because the Germans were paying reparations to their slave laborers. Our group included survivors from the Philippine Islands and the Bataan Death March and civilian internees, and we got together and filed lawsuits against the Japanese industries that used us as slave laborers without compensation during World War II. Interestingly enough, some of the big Japanese industries that exist today were involved in it. Yet our own government opposes this. The State Department, when the suit was heard in federal court, came out and sided with the Japanese. It's disappointing."

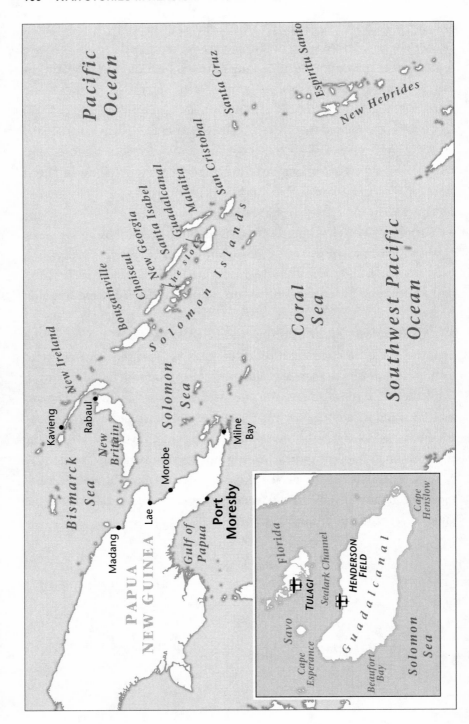

CHAPTER 9
DEATH BY INCHES: GUADALCANAL
(AUGUST 1942–FEBRUARY 1943)

✪ **GUADALCANAL, SOLOMON ISLANDS**
1ST MARINE DIVISION COMMAND POST
7 AUGUST 1942
1740 HOURS LOCAL

As far as Major General Archer Vandegrift, the fifty-five-year-old commanding general of the 1st Marine Division, could tell, the first American ground offensive of World War II—Operation Watchtower—was going better than expected. After an air and naval gunfire "prep" of the landing beaches, his Marines had come ashore at 0910 on the northwest coast of Guadalcanal. The Japanese had not opposed the Marine landing craft when they hit the narrow beach. Now, though the offload of supplies and equipment was proceeding slowly, it was the best that could be expected considering the thick jungle, lack of roads, and minimal cleared space ashore.

Contact with the enemy had been light and sporadic in the eight and a half hours since the assault waves touched down in their new Higgins boats. By late in the afternoon, 10,000 of his 14,000 Marines were ashore on Guadalcanal and U.S. carrier-based aircraft had beaten off an attack by high-altitude bombers from the Japanese base at Rabaul.

Nineteen miles to the north, across the body of water soon to be known as Ironbottom Sound for the number of Allied and Japanese ships sunk there, the occupation of lightly defended Florida Island at 0740 had gone well, but Tulagi and Gavutu-Tanambogo had been a different matter. Though the Tulagi landing at 0800 had been uncontested, Vandegrift had received reports of stiff resistance as the Marines moved to seize the high ground.

At Gavutu-Tanambogo, two islets connected by a causeway, the 0810 assault waves had been met with significant opposition from Japanese troops defending their seaplane base, despite strikes by U.S. Navy aircraft from the *Saratoga*, *Enterprise*, and *Wasp*. At 1200, Vandegrift had requested and received permission to commit his only reserves from Rear Admiral Richmond Kelly Turner, commanding the amphibious forces, and Vice Admiral Jack Fletcher, the tactical commander of the expeditionary forces. Shortly after 1300, the 1st Marine Parachute Battalion was landed under heavy fire to help secure Gavutu-Tanambogo.

National Archives

Major General Archer Vandegrift commanded the Marines at Guadalcanal.

Intelligence had indicated the presence of more than 7,000 Japanese troops on Guadalcanal, and several thousand more on the surrounding islands. Though that estimate would prove to be much too high, it appeared to Vandegrift and his Navy superiors that they had taken the Japanese completely by surprise. By 1700, Vandegrift began to hope that his hastily assembled, untested Marines would be able to quickly secure the airfield the Japanese were constructing on the Lunga plain in the northwest quadrant of Guadalcanal. Then, if all went according to plan, the island could serve as a jumping-off point for the Marines' "island-hopping" offensive up the Solomons toward the big Japanese base at Rabaul on the northern tip of New Britain. It was not to be.

Though Vandegrift's optimism in those first few hours of Operation Watchtower would soon be dashed, his initial confidence was well-founded. The appearance of a formidable eighty-three-ship U.S. naval armada in the waters of the Coral Sea—including three carriers, a cruiser-battleship surface action force, and the amphibious shipping for an entire Marine division—had caught the Japanese totally unprepared. But the Marine landings on the morning of 7 August had succeeded mostly because there were fewer than 2,500 unwary defenders on Guadalcanal and about the same number dug in on the nearby islands.

Ever since the disaster at Midway, the Japanese high command had been preoccupied with efforts to complete their outer defense perimeter. To consolidate their toehold on New Guinea, a step they deemed essential to protecting Rabaul, the Japanese army began pouring troops and aircraft originally intended for Midway into the fight to capture Port Moresby.

At the end of June, the Japanese army quietly landed infantry and construction troops on Guadalcanal with orders to build an airfield on the relatively flat plain along the northwest quadrant of the island.

On 21 July 1942, as construction of the air base on Guadalcanal neared completion, the Japanese army quietly landed 1,800 troops at Gona and Buna on the north coast of New Guinea. Their orders were to proceed over the Owen Stanley Range—the island's spine—and attack Port Moresby. By 29 July, more than 13,000 Imperial troops had succeeded in hacking their way up the Kokoda Trail—despite the stubborn resistance by an outnumbered Australian brigade, supported by Papuan natives—and were within forty miles of their goal. From Australia, MacArthur rushed Australian and U.S. Army reinforcements into Port Moresby in an effort to hold the vital port and its airfields.

Once on New Guinea, the green American troops soon realized that the Japanese weren't the only enemy they faced. The island's yearly rainfall of ten feet or more, impenetrable, snake-infested jungles, malaria-bearing mosquitoes, and tropical diseases soon felled more soldiers than Japanese suicide attacks. These same conditions would soon start to claim Marines on Guadalcanal.

✪ ✪ ✪

Guadalcanal was an unlikely objective for America's first offensive operation in World War II. Had the Japanese not decided to build an airstrip on
the island's northwestern plain, it might well have been avoided altogether.
Operation Watchtower—as developed by the Joint Chiefs of Staff—had
been a compromise in a campaign to eliminate the threat posed by the
Japanese base at Rabaul. Both MacArthur, the southwestern Pacific area
commander—and Nimitz, commander of the Pacific Ocean areas—recognized the strategic necessity of destroying Rabaul before retaking the Philippines. The question was how.

MacArthur favored a direct, carrier-supported assault by U.S. Army
troops from Australia and Marines from New Zealand, where they had been
training in amphibious operations. Nimitz, unwilling to risk his few carriers or surrender control of his Marines, preferred to use his amphibious
forces to seize "unsinkable carriers"—small islands—from which land-
based aircraft could pound Rabaul to rubble before any troops had to set
foot ashore.

On 2 July, the Joint Chiefs in Washington—after lengthy discussions
between General Marshall and Admiral King—resolved the acrimonious
debate by placing Nimitz in charge of the first phase of the Rabaul campaign, ordering him to seize advance bases in the 900-mile-long Solomon
Islands chain. Though none too happy with the decision, MacArthur would
soon have his hands full simply trying to hold on to Port Moresby.

Things didn't quite go as Nimitz had planned either. When a long-range
patrol aircraft and Australian coast watchers reported that Japanese construction troops were building an airstrip on Guadalcanal, Nimitz had to
quickly adapt to the changed situation. In addition to the known Japanese
bases on Tulagi, Florida Island, and Gavutu-Tanambogo, he now had to
allocate Marines, transports, and support ships to seize and secure an additional island.

Though the Joint Chiefs had insisted that Operation Watchtower commence on 1 August, the requirement to seize the airfield being built on

Guadalcanal bought Nimitz an additional week of planning. He scrapped plans to secure Savo Island, which didn't appear to have a Japanese garrison, but there was no way to increase the number of ships, planes, or troops dedicated to the endeavor. MacArthur had nothing to spare, and every other combatant vessel, transport ship, landing craft, aircraft, and soldier available in the U.S. was already committed to the invasion of North Africa in November. Nimitz would have to make do with what he had.

Scarce resources weren't the only problem for Nimitz. In the aftermath of the victory at Midway, the *Chicago Tribune*, owned and published by FDR's political adversary, Colonel Robert McCormick, ran a story on how the U.S. had broken the Japanese JN-25 code. It became front-page news across America, and Tokyo quickly replaced the compromised codes—leaving Nimitz and his forces in the dark regarding Japanese intentions. Roosevelt was fit to be tied and ordered Attorney General Francis Biddle to arrest McCormick, a World War I hero, and put him on trial for treason—a wartime crime punishable by death.

In Washington, Admiral King tried to calm things down, believing that a sensational trial would reveal even more classified information—particularly the U.S.–British "Ultra" project that was busily breaking German war codes. He succeeded in convincing FDR that the best damage control for Station Hypo and other cryptological efforts would be to let the story die.

Newspaper stories about Midway weren't a problem in Japan. There, the

Henderson Field

stunning defeat at Midway had been carefully covered up. Prime Minister Tojo had ordered that there be no news of their humiliation and no one involved was to even talk about it. Wounded sailors hospitalized in Japan were isolated so no one could ask them questions about what had taken place at Midway. Instead of news about the catastrophe, Japanese newspapers printed glowing reports about "fantastic Japanese victories" in the northern Pacific, where they'd bombed the islands of Attu and Kiska, two barren, icy dots in the long chain of Aleutian Islands off the coast of Alaska.

✪ HQ 1ST MARINE DIVISION
LUNGA POINT, GUADALCANAL
8 AUGUST 1942
2000 HOURS LOCAL

By the afternoon of 8 August, General Vandegrift was satisfied that all his 1st Marine Division needed for success was to complete the offload of supplies from the transports lying at anchor offshore. On Guadalcanal, the uncompleted airfield was already in U.S. hands and renamed Henderson Field in honor of Major Lofton Henderson, who had been killed leading his bombing squadron during the Battle of Midway.

Naval Historical Center

Admiral Richard K. Turner

Nineteen miles north, across the water, Brigadier General William Rupertus reported that his Leathernecks had finally secured Tulagi—though it had required killing nearly all of the entrenched Japanese defenders. The Marines had withstood several determined banzai charges and desperate hand-to-hand combat over a period of thirty-one hours, but the Americans finally prevailed. Rupertus had lost 115 Marines and seven Navy medical corpsmen in the fight, but the Americans had killed ten enemy soldiers to every one of their own.

Earlier in the day, a second Japanese aerial attack—this time by torpedo bombers—had been met first by U.S. carrier aircraft and then by overwhelming anti-aircraft fire from the fifty-five American transports, cruisers, and destroyers in the waters south of Savo Island. Though nearly all of the attackers were eventually downed, by the time the air battle was over, eighteen of Admiral Turner's carrier aircraft had been lost, the transport *USS Elliot* had been sunk, and two destroyers were badly damaged. One of them—the *USS Jarvis*—headed for Noumea but sank en route. Though these losses weren't insignificant, Vandegrift was more concerned that the two attacks had seriously disrupted the offload of supplies and equipment urgently needed by his Marines ashore.

As darkness fell on 8 August, few of the transports had landed more than 30 percent of their cargo. Vandegrift importuned Admiral Turner to have the transports remain in the anchorage for another forty-eight hours. Shortly after Turner approved, Admiral Fletcher informed him that he would have to take *Saratoga*, *Enterprise*, and *Wasp* well south of Guadalcanal to refuel, since the loss of eighteen aircraft that morning made replenishing his carriers that far north too risky. Just hours later, MacArthur's headquarters belatedly informed Turner that an Australian patrol plane had spotted several Japanese ships, "probable seaplane tenders" headed toward Guadalcanal from Rabaul.

Lacking the kind of intelligence Station Hypo had provided at Midway, Turner and Vandegrift didn't know that the Japanese group bearing down on them was actually a formidable surface action force comprising seven cruisers and a destroyer—all commanded by Vice Admiral Gunichi Mikawa. Operation Watchtower was about to come unraveled—and would soon live up to the nickname the Marines ashore had already given it— Operation Shoestring.

✪ **IMPERIAL JAPANESE NAVY FLAGSHIP CHOKAI**
NORTH OF SAVO ISLAND, SOLOMON ISLANDS
9 AUGUST 1942
0530 HOURS LOCAL

The senior Japanese naval commander in the South Pacific, Vice Admiral Gunichi Mikawa, was bent on vengeance. He had been humiliated by the losses at Midway, and within hours of being informed of the Marine landings on Tulagi and Guadalcanal immediately decided to counter-attack. On the afternoon of 7 August, he ordered every available combatant at Rabaul to sortie after dark and follow him south in his flagship, the heavy cruiser *Chokai*, to engage the American ships at Guadalcanal.

A few minutes after 0100 on 9 August, Mikawa's ships exited the southern end of the slot—the narrow passage between New Georgia and Santa Isabel islands—and entered Savo Island Sound north of Cape Esperance on Guadalcanal. The Americans, completely unprepared, first learned of Mikawa's presence when his cruisers opened fire at close range with guns and torpedoes. The USS *Chicago* and HMAS *Canberra* were struck in the first volley and put out of action. Mikawa then split his force into two columns and swung north to engage the *Vincennes*, *Astoria*, and *Quincy*. Within minutes all three heavy cruisers were dead in the water, afire and listing heavily.

Naval Historical Center

Gunichi Mikawa. His ships were dubbed the Tokyo Express.

At 0220, Mikawa, fearing an air attack, ordered his force to withdraw without engaging the now defenseless transports. As the Japanese cruisers passed north of Savo Island and raced back up the slot, they nearly collided with the U.S. destroyer *Talbot*. Without slowing down, every passing cruiser pumped heavy shells into the hapless picket ship—killing scores of sailors and wrecking her superstructure.

The engagement had lasted little more than an hour, but it had cost the Allies dearly. The U.S. heavy cruisers *Vincennes* and *Quincy* were on the bottom before dawn. The crippled Australian heavy cruiser *Canberra* was abandoned and had to be sunk by an American destroyer at 0800. The USS *Astoria* finally went down at 1145.

The *Chokai* had taken a single hit from an eight-inch gun—likely the *Astoria*'s—and Admiral Mikawa celebrated his victory. The engagement had cost the Japanese fifty-eight dead and fifty-three wounded. Though Mikawa didn't know the full magnitude of the U.S. and Australian losses—1,023 dead and 709 wounded—he was certain that he had struck back hard at those who had inflicted such losses on the emperor's fleet at Midway.

The Battle of Savo Island also convinced Mikawa that Japanese sailors were superior at night fighting. This impression would govern his tactics in the months to come as he sought to wrest control of Guadalcanal from the Marines. The Americans might have more carriers and the ability to control the skies in daylight. But he was determined that the Japanese—with years of night gunnery training—could dominate the seas in darkness.

✪ 1ST MARINE DIVISION COMMAND POST
GUADALCANAL, SOLOMON ISLANDS
21 AUGUST 1942
1600 HOURS LOCAL

For General Vandegrift and his Marines on Guadalcanal, Tulagi, Florida, and Gavutu-Tanambogo, the days after the Battle of Savo Island were a matter of making do with less and less. On the afternoon of 9 August, Admiral Turner, fearing another night attack by Mikawa's cruisers, had ordered the transports to withdraw to the south toward Noumea, carrying with them more than half the supplies and equipment as well as 2,000 of the division's Marines.

On Guadalcanal and Tulagi, Vandegrift's troops, already on half rations, cut food consumption by half again. Living in the jungle without shelter or the prospect of medical evacuation for the wounded, and compelled to conserve ammunition in every engagement, they nonetheless managed to finish the runway and parking aprons on Henderson Field. By 11 August they had also succeeded in eliminating most of the Japanese from the jungle surrounding the airfield. The Leathernecks were soon boasting, "We have done so much, with so little, for so long, that we now can do anything, with nothing, forever."

But for Nimitz and the Marine planners in Hawaii, it was no laughing matter. Though a U.S. submarine had managed to sink one of Mikawa's cruisers, the *Kako*, on 10 August, there was grave concern at Pearl Harbor that a determined counter-attack could spell disaster for the first American offensive of World War II.

On 12 August, in an effort to alleviate the crucial supply problems for the Marines on Guadalcanal, Admiral Turner was ordered to land the division's remaining troops and supplies on Espiritu Santo in the New Hebrides islands. That afternoon, a Marine C-46 transport aircraft flew from the Espiritu Santo airstrip to Henderson Field, delivering urgently needed medical supplies and evacuating a dozen seriously wounded Marines. On the night of 15 August, four little destroyer-transports raced into Ironbottom Sound and offloaded Marine aviation ground crews, ammunition, bombs, and aviation fuel in fifty-five gallon drums—but no food.

Unfortunately for the hungry Marines, the Japanese weren't just waiting for them to die of starvation. On the night of 17 August, four Japanese destroyers anchored off Taivu Point and landed 900 Imperial Army soldiers. Their mission: recapture Henderson Field.

National Archives

Admiral Robert Ghormley, in charge of the Guadalcanal invasion, was replaced with Admiral "Bull" Halsey by Nimitz.

The Japanese might well have succeeded but for Vandegrift's remarkable ability to persevere in the face of overwhelming adversity. Wary of Navy promises to protect Guadalcanal with carrier-based aircraft, and despite his gnawing hunger and fatigue, the Marine general bombarded Admiral Robert Ghormley in Noumea and Nimitz in Hawaii with radio messages insisting that they send Marine squadrons to "Cactus"—the code word for Guadalcanal—to protect his troops. He pulled his defenses tight around the airfield to demonstrate that aircraft would be safe on the ground. His persistence was rewarded on 20 August when nineteen Grumman Wildcat F4F fighters and twelve Douglas Dauntless SBD dive-bombers landed at Henderson Field, flown in from the deck of an escort carrier dispatched from Espiritu Santo.

The planes arrived just in time. That night, just before dawn, the 900 Japanese troops launched a banzai attack across the Tenaru River in hopes of overrunning the airfield. The battle lasted for more than eight hours and was, for the Japanese, an unmitigated disaster. More than 800 of the attackers were killed in the assault and subsequent counter-attack—at a cost of 44 killed and 71 wounded from the Marines. Vandegrift's line had held—and "Cactus" finally had its own air force. In the days ahead, both would be sorely tested.

✪ BATTLE FOR THE EASTERN SOLOMONS
NORTH OF MALAITA AND GUADALCANAL
25 AUGUST 1942
1030 HOURS LOCAL

The horrific losses on the banks of the Tenaru persuaded Admiral Yamamoto that Guadalcanal could be retaken if Japanese reinforcements delivered to the island were sufficiently supported by adequate naval forces. To that end, he ordered Rear Admiral Raizo Tanaka to take his flagship, the light cruiser *Jintsu*, three slow transports escorted by four patrol boats, and land 1,300 Imperial Army troops and marines on Guadalcanal. To support Tanaka, Yamamoto dispatched the entire Combined Fleet, under Vice Admiral Nobutake Kondo, from Truk to destroy the aircraft on Henderson Field, attack any U.S. ships in the area, and support the landing.

Naval Historical Center

Kondo's fleet included two heavy carriers, *Shokaku*—now repaired from damage suffered on 8 May in the Coral Sea—and *Zuikaku*. He also had a light carrier, *Ryujo*, which he sent in advance to destroy the Marine and Army Air Corps aircraft on Henderson Field.

Vice Admiral Nobutake Kondo commanded the Japanese Second Fleet at Guadalcanal.

Early on the afternoon of 24 August, a long-range patrol plane out of Henderson Field spotted the *Ryujo* about 100 miles due north of Malaita

Island. When he received the report, Admiral Fletcher was holding station 150 miles east of Guadalcanal with *Enterprise* and *Saratoga*. Though he had sent the *Wasp* carrier group south to refuel earlier in the day, Fletcher nonetheless ordered an immediate attack on the Japanese carrier by thirty dive-bombers and eight torpedo planes.

Ryujo was practically defenseless, having launched all her aircraft for the attack on Henderson Field. A well-coordinated bomb and torpedo attack sent her to the bottom in less than an hour. Her bombing raid on Henderson fared little better. Marine fighters, vectored by radar to intercept the attackers, downed several. Those who survived turned around but found only an oil slick where their carrier had been.

While the "Cactus Air Force" was beating off the Henderson Field raid,

FNC *War Stories*

Admiral Raizo Tanaka was a brilliant naval strategist who escaped many Allied traps in the seas off Guadalcanal.

Wildcats from *Enterprise* and *Saratoga* were doing the same. In the gathering dusk, Kondo's dive-bombers and torpedo planes from *Shokaku* and *Zuikaku* didn't spot *Saratoga*, so they came in three fast waves against *Enterprise*. American fighters high overhead decimated the attackers, who then flew into a hail of anti-aircraft fire. The battle lasted fewer than ten minutes. When it was over, *Saratoga* had taken three bombs on her flight deck that damage control parties promptly dealt with—allowing her to recover her air wing and continue under way at twenty-four knots.

Fletcher's dive-bombers and torpedo planes, unable to find Kondo's two remaining carriers in the dark, attacked and sank the *Chitose*, a large seaplane tender, on their way back to the U.S. carriers. By midnight, Kondo, having lost a light carrier and more than ninety planes and pilots, turned around and headed back to Truk.

But the battle wasn't over. Early on the morning of 25 August, the dawn patrol out of Henderson Field found Tanaka's little group of transports preparing to disembark troops and supplies on Guadalcanal. The Marines scrambled their dive-bombers, and after a five-minute flight from Henderson Field, sank a troop transport and blasted the *Jintsu*—very nearly killing Tanaka. An hour later, Army Air Corps B-17s from Espiritu Santo arrived overhead and sank a destroyer.

This was enough for even the indomitable Tanaka. Taking advantage of a tropical downpour, he turned the remnants of his battered force back to the north and headed up the slot, staying beneath the clouds to avoid pursuit.

✪ ✪ ✪

Unfortunately for Tanaka, he didn't go far enough. Late on 27 August, Tanaka held up in an anchorage in the Shortland Islands, off the south coast of Bougainville. Assuming that he was beyond the range of any U.S. aircraft, he started repairs on *Jintsu*, the two surviving transports, and a destroyer, all of which had been damaged two days earlier. An Australian coast watcher reported the Japanese presence to Admiral Ghormley in Noumea, who in turn relayed the information to the Marines. At dusk on 28 August, a flight of six SBD dive-bombers from Henderson Field, having carefully conserved fuel on the 275-mile-long flight, appeared overhead and proceeded to sink one armed transport and damage two others. By the time the Marine aircraft landed back on Guadalcanal they claimed they were "flying on fumes."

The "Battle of the Eastern Solomons," as the engagement of 24–25 August came to be known, finally convinced Yamamoto that daylight reinforcement and resupply for the Japanese troops on Guadalcanal was too costly. From then on, it became Combined Fleet policy to have fast destroyer-transports, sometimes escorted by cruisers, loiter in the slot until dark and then dash south to disgorge their troops and cargo off the north or west coast of the island. After offloading their payload, the Japanese would swing around Cape Esperance into Ironbottom Sound, fire several salvos at Henderson Field, and race back up the slot before first light.

By early September the pattern became so regular that the Marines took to calling the nightly deliveries and attacks the Tokyo Express. Despite pleas from Vandegrift for night-fighters to interdict these nocturnal forays, there was little that Ghormley or Nimitz could do to help. On 31 August, a Japanese submarine sent a torpedo into the *Saratoga*'s side—sending her into the repair yards for three months. Nobody in Hawaii wanted to risk the *Hornet* and the *Wasp*—the only two undamaged carriers left in the Pacific—on a night engagement with the Japanese. The Marines would just have to dig their holes a little deeper and pray that some supplies could get through.

✪ 1ST MARINE DIVISION FORWARD COMMAND POST
BLOODY RIDGE, GUADALCANAL
13 SEPTEMBER 1942
0530 HOURS LOCAL

The effectiveness of the new Japanese night reinforcement strategy was felt almost immediately. Sustained contact with Japanese infantry patrols operating around the airfield increased significantly. On 3 September, Brigadier General Roy Geiger flew in from Espiritu Santo to take command of the Marine squadrons operating from Henderson Field and the nearby auxiliary strip known as "Fighter One." That night, the newly arrived commander of the 1st Marine Air Wing was treated to a naval gunfire barrage by a Japanese destroyer, a strafing attack by a Mitsubishi Zero seaplane nicknamed "Louie the Louse," a high-altitude bombing raid by a solo long-range bomber the Marines had dubbed "Washing Machine Charlie," and, finally, a probe of the airfield's perimeter defenses by Japanese infantry. The following morning Geiger discovered that only eleven of the fifty Wildcats delivered to the island were still flyable, due to the nightly bombardments.

Things were no better for the ground troops, who were literally rotting in their foxholes on less than half rations. On the night of 4–5 September, a Japanese destroyer in Ironbottom Sound sank two U.S. ships attempting to deliver food, fuel, and ammunition to the beleaguered Leathernecks.

By 10 September, the Tokyo Express runs had brought Japanese troop strength on Guadalcanal up to more than 6,000. The next day, the naval gunfire and regular nightly air raids by land-based bombers from Rabaul, Bougainville, and the Bonin Islands forced General Vandegrift to move his command post, repair facilities, and hospital away from the beach to a high ridge leading upwards from the south to its crest, directly overlooking Henderson Field.

The Leathernecks had nicknamed the ridge after the 1st Marine Parachute Battalion commander, Merritt "Red Mike" Edson. "Red Mike" was

Edson's radio call sign and his troops used the name affectionately. Since his tough, parachute-trained Marines were protecting the division command post on the side of the mountain, the name Edson's Ridge stuck.

By 12 September, General Kiyotaki Kawaguchi, the senior Japanese officer on Guadalcanal, had concluded that the 6,600 troops he had ashore were sufficient to dislodge the Marines protecting Henderson Field and to retake the airstrip. His reconnaissance patrols had pinpointed the relocated Marine command post on Edson's Ridge. Kawaguchi reasoned that if he overran the post, confusion would ensue in the Marine ranks and the battle would be decided in his favor. But when he launched his attack that evening to force the Marines off the ridge, Edson's Raiders were ready with massed machine gun, mortar, and artillery fire.

The battle along the ridgeline—some of it hand-to-hand—raged for more than twenty-four hours. When it was over—just after dark on 13 September—more than 1,500 of Kawaguchi's troops were dead. The Marines had 40 killed in action and 103 wounded. From then on, they would call the scene of the battle "Bloody Ridge."

For those in this and numerous other battles on the high ground overlooking Henderson Field, the suicidal enemy charges were horrific. There was nothing in the experience of these young Americans to prepare them for the carnage of massed bayonet charges by waves of Japanese soldiers, attacking through minefields and throwing themselves against machine guns. Captain John Sweeney, of Columbus, Ohio, was one of those who fought with Edson on Bloody Ridge, where he and his fellow Marines were outnumbered 600 to 1.

▯   ▯   ▯

CAPTAIN JOHN SWEENEY, USMC
Edson's Ridge, Guadalcanal
13 September 1942
1900 Hours Local

The Japanese held a toehold on our side of the Matanikou River. They were dug in very well, with lots of machine guns.

I found out I was the only officer left in the company. Red Mike said, "You're now the CO. Take over. I'll meet you back along the ridge to give you the orders for tonight and the next day." I went back to the new position with the troops that we had. We're out in front, knowing the jungle on each side could hold the enemy.

Henderson Field was located in the area just behind where the artillery was established, about a thousand yards away. On this particular night, some 600 Marine Raiders and 300 paratroopers defended this particular portion of the airfield

One of the fears that I had was knowing that something was going to happen right after dark, and steeling my own backbone to come up with the sort of leadership that was expected of me. And one of the things that kept running through my mind was a prayer or two that I wouldn't fail my men.

Right in front of us, until that point, it was quiet. But we knew they were there and ready for the attack. It'd sweep up to the main ridge itself.

About two o'clock in the morning, the Japanese commander decided he was going to make a break for it and attack A Company's flank.

Then it was hell, with screams—hollering from both Japanese and Marines. Flares are flying in the air, and fired over the ridge by the Japanese in order to illuminate the target as our wounded were evacuated by corpsmen. The banzai charge was a lot of yelling—and enough to scare anybody, except the people who were able to keep their cool, and keep their ammunition going.

We heard a rattle of a BAR [Browning Automatic Rifle], and rifle shots. And fortunately Van Ness, the BAR man, finished off the others that were with the gun crew of a Japanese machine gun. After that, the tide turned, and although we were bloodied up a couple of times, the Japanese in the area were picked off.

We had a few in our ranks who were killed that night, and they are the real heroes. Henderson Field was right behind us, and had the Japanese broken through our lines, they would've had the airfield. And if they'd seized the airfield, they might have won the war in this part of the Pacific.

I'm very proud of the citation. [Sweeney was awarded the Navy Cross for that night.] But the men who were killed that night are the real heroes. I participated in what is one of the shining moments of the Marine Corps. And that in itself was my satisfaction.

✪ ✪ ✪

When it was over, Edson and his Marines had somehow managed to hold their ground. Their raw courage in the face of overwhelming odds saved Henderson Field. "Red Mike" Edson was awarded the Medal of Honor for his efforts, and Captain John Sweeney was awarded the Navy Cross.

A day after "Bloody Ridge," the carrier *Wasp*, the brand-new battleship *North Carolina*, and the destroyer *O'Brien* were all torpedoed by Japanese subs. The *North Carolina* managed to limp back to Pearl Harbor for repairs, but the *Wasp* and *O'Brien* both went down—fortunately after most of their crews managed to abandon ship. These losses left only one operational carrier, the *Hornet*, and one battleship, the USS *Washington*, at sea in the Pacific—and made Admiral Chester Nimitz wonder if Guadalcanal could be saved. Within a month he would have even more reason to doubt the outcome.

✪ BATTLE OF CAPE ESPERANCE
ABOARD USS SAN FRANCISCO
12 OCTOBER 1942
0100 HOURS LOCAL

The loss of half his operational carriers and battleships on 15 September stunned Nimitz and his staff in Hawaii. Ashore on Guadalcanal, the Marines were, however, heartened by the safe arrival of 4,200 more Marines from Samoa. These new arrivals were immediately fed into the narrow perimeter around Henderson Field and Fighter One. More than 1,000 of Vandegrift's sickest and most seriously wounded casualties were evacuated.

Unfortunately, the Japanese were also adding to their forces. On 18 September the Imperial General Staff ordered that retaking Guadalcanal be given strategic priority over the effort to seize Port Moresby. From that point on, the Tokyo Express landed between 500 and 1,000 fresh troops and supplies nightly on Guadalcanal. By 10 October, the Japanese had nearly 12,000 Imperial Army soldiers on the island—roughly the strength available to Vandegrift.

The reinforcements General Kawaguchi received convinced him that he had sufficient strength to overwhelm the Henderson Field defenses—providing the Imperial Fleet could deliver enough fire to support his advance and keep the "Cactus Air Force" from launching against his troops. The attack was carefully planned for the night of 11–12 October, and a surface action group of three heavy cruisers and two destroyers commanded by Rear Admiral Aritomo Goto was dispatched from Rabaul. Once the cruisers opened fire on Henderson Field and Vandegrift's command post on Bloody Ridge, Kawaguchi would launch his ground assault.

Fortunately, in Hawaii, Station Hypo had succeeded in breaking enough of the new Japanese naval code to warn Admiral Ghormley of the impending attack. Ghormley immediately dispatched the only forces he had available—a cruiser-destroyer flotilla commanded by Rear Admiral Norman Scott—and ordered him to interdict the Japanese before they could open fire on the Marines.

At 2305 on 11 October, Scott, aboard his flagship *San Francisco* and accompanied by the cruisers *Helena*, *Salt Lake City*, and *Boise*, and the destroyers *Farenholt*, *Duncan*, *Laffey*, *Buchanan*, and *McCalla*, practically bumped into the oncoming Japanese northwest of Cape Esperance. Scott's force succeeded in "capping the 'T'" of Goto's little armada and immediately sank a Japanese cruiser and a destroyer and set a second cruiser afire. Within the hour, the Americans severely damaged the third cruiser, Goto's flagship *Aoba*, as it fled north up the slot.

The Americans weren't completely unscathed. The USS *Duncan*, hit by both Japanese and American gunfire, sank shortly after the melee. The destroyer *Farenholt* and the cruiser *Boise*, damaged by Japanese shells, had to be taken out of action for repairs. But the attack had been turned away. Ashore, Kawaguchi cancelled his ground assault and the Marines around

Henderson Field enjoyed their first night in over a month without Japanese naval gunfire or ground attacks. On the morning of 13 October their spirits were further buoyed by the arrival of a convoy from New Caledonia delivering new aircraft, food, ammunition—and, best of all, 3,200 fresh troops from the U.S. Army's American Division.

Unfortunately, the respite was all too brief. That night, the new arrivals were subjected to a brutal, ninety-minute barrage from two Japanese battleships that wrecked the "Cactus Air Force" aircraft, destroyed a bomb dump, some fresh food stores, a fuel dump, and blasted holes in the Henderson Field and Fighter One runways and aprons. The damage was so severe that heavy air raids by land-based bombers from Rabaul were practically unopposed the next day. Encouraged, Goto returned with two new cruisers and did more damage.

By 15 October, there were fewer than a dozen flyable U.S. aircraft left on Guadalcanal. When Australian coast watchers reported that six Japanese transports were sneaking down the slot to deliver 4,500 troops to Kawaguchi that night, there were too few planes to mount a raid. By the morning of 16 October, when fifteen replacement Wildcats and Dauntlesses were flown in, the Seabees and Marines had patched the airfields but the Americans on Guadalcanal were once again outnumbered, scarce on ammunition, and living on half rations.

✪ ✪ ✪

With so few fleet assets available, Nimitz knew that the only way to hold Guadalcanal was to keep the fighters, bombers, and torpedo planes based at Henderson Field and the nearby Fighter One auxiliary strip flying. That required the infantry to protect the airfields—and the constant delivery of planes, parts, bombs, ammunition, fuel, and pilots.

One of those pilots was a South Dakota farm boy named Joe Foss. He had become part of the "Cactus Air Force" on 9 October. At the ripe age of twenty-seven, Foss was one of the oldest pilots flying in the Pacific. Just four days after his arrival, he led sixteen Wildcats from Henderson Field to intercept thirty-two Japanese planes.

□   □   □

CAPTAIN JOE FOSS, USMC
Henderson Field
Guadalcanal, Solomon Islands
16 October 1942
1400 Hours Local

We would try to get off early. The coast watchers up the line told us how many airplanes were headed our way. And they'd give the numbers of the dive-bombers and Zeros. We had a pretty good idea about the time that they'd hit Guadalcanal.

I went up with a flight of eight Wildcats and there were two flights of eight up there—sixteen airplanes. We'd start climbing up to get altitude. I was always aiming for 25,000 feet.

Zeros were always sneaking around there. You never knew whether they came off a carrier or where they came from. They just swarmed down on us. They could gain altitude in a hurry and come back because the one thing they had was speed. Where we got our speed was to nose over at full throttle—you picked up speed with our heavier airplanes. The Wildcat weighed 8,900 pounds and the Zero weighed 5,900.

In this case, I was right in the middle of a lot of Zeros and there were Zeros off to the right. Four airplanes were off to my left.

I thought that I'd go for number one, because, old hunter that I am, in shooting down a goose or duck, if you get the leader, it sort of confuses the flock. In this case I got number one but somebody had "sprinkled" me with machine gun fire before I got there and evidently my radio went out. Well, I got this guy and swung wide, figuring that I'd get another one. But, these guys cut across and started giving me a good blast. So when I dived, that's when *pow!* The son-of-a-gun hit the oil cooler, and it doesn't take long for that engine to seize. When it did, the engine was running full throttle so that sudden stop caused by the seized engine twisted off the reduction gear and that caused a tremendous scream and vibration.

When I leveled out I went to make a right turn around the field, then I came around to land toward the sea on Fighter One. And the Zeros were blasting me as I'm slowing down. I drop the gear the last minute just before I hit the ground. I just punched the handle to release the ratchet and then the whole thing goes *plowing!*

The flaps didn't work and the speed is above 140 knots. I was trying to preserve the airplane and applied as much brake as I could without going "end over appetite."

I was just sailing on that coral runway and the end of it was coming up. I went up between the palm trees in the only row where there were no trucks or anything stored and stopped. I thought, "Well, the score's tied right now. I got one, they got one."

They fixed my plane and most of the others. In the four times I got shot down, three times I landed on the field. So I always liked to stay right out there between the Henderson Field and Cape Esperance and fight.

I personally shot down twenty-six planes and I had some smokers, too. Our squadron probably had as many smokers as confirmed kills. I just was happy to knock one off so he won't be back to bother you tomorrow. After all, you're fighting for your life. The idea was to get rid of them. I fight for keeps.

Joe Foss on LIFE magazine.

FNC War Stories

✪ ✪ ✪

Joe Foss's "Flying Circus" holds the record of 208 aerial victories—a feat that is unlikely to ever be broken. He personally achieved twenty-six kills and tied Eddie Rickenbacker's World War I record. Foss was awarded the Congressional Medal of Honor for his achievements at Guadalcanal.

✪ 1ST MARINE DIVISION FORWARD PERIMETER
BLOODY RIDGE, GUADALCANAL
26 OCTOBER 1942
2230 HOURS LOCAL

On 18 October, Nimitz flew to Noumea to see Admiral Ghormley and learned that his deputy—though responsible for the Guadalcanal campaign—had never gotten within 1,000 miles of the battle. Dissatisfied with Ghormley's explanations for not doing more to curtail the Tokyo Express or providing sufficient support for Vandegrift, Nimitz replaced his friend with a man who had a reputation for "going into harm's way"—Vice Admiral William "Bull" Halsey.

"The Bull," as the Marines and sailors called him behind his back, flew immediately to Henderson Field to meet with General Vandegrift. The Marine commander was blunt, telling Halsey that his Marines could hold Henderson Field, but that the Navy wasn't doing enough to support them.

Stung by those straightforward words, Halsey promised Vandegrift that from now on he would get what he needed from the Navy. Before leaving Henderson Field, he decorated more than fifty of Vandegrift's Marines.

But the Bull didn't stop at handing out medals. When he returned to Noumea, the code-breakers at Station Hypo informed him that Yamamoto was planning a major Combined Fleet operation to support another Imperial Army assault on the Guadalcanal airfields. Halsey directed the battleship *Washington* and its escorts to step up patrols north of Guadalcanal to interdict the Tokyo Express. He also ordered Vice Admiral Thomas Kinkaid to take the *Hornet* and the hastily repaired *Enterprise* and head northeast of Guadalcanal to intercept a Japanese carrier-battleship fleet headed south from Truk.

On the island, the Marines prepared for the onslaught. On the rainy night of 25 October, a platoon led by Platoon Sergeant Mitch Paige was sent to cover a part of the perimeter on Bloody Ridge. Paige's platoon consisted of just thirty-three men manning a line of water-cooled machine guns. He had no other troops because so many Marines from his battalion were tied up defending the line at the mouth of the Matanikou River or in sickbay, suffering from wounds, malaria, or other tropical diseases.

Though Sergeant Paige couldn't know it as he put his men in position, General Kawaguchi had more than 2,500 of his troops hiding below in the rain-soaked jungle, preparing to overrun the airfield closer than 1,000 yards away.

□   □   □

SERGEANT MITCH PAIGE, USMC
Second Battle of Bloody Ridge, Guadalcanal
25 October 1942
2230 Hours Local

Every weapon that the Marines landed with on Guadalcanal in August 1942 was valuable, even if they were World War I surplus. Most had a 1903 Springfield five-round bolt-action rifle. But I felt that I probably had the best machine gun platoon in the Marine Corps.

Everyone in my platoon could take apart, field strip, and put together a water-cooled machine gun, a .30-caliber light machine gun, a 1903 Springfield rifle, and a 1911-model .45-caliber pistol.

By 25 October we had about 25,000 Marines, soldiers, and sailors on Guadalcanal. And the Japanese had about the same. On the island, these people were fighting for the little airstrip called Henderson Field. Every platoon leader was called down to Marine headquarters and the word I got was, "Sergeant Paige, this is all the ammo we have for your machine guns. And this is all the C-rations."

We were on the west side of the Bloody Ridge perimeter, on a finger that sloped down into Japanese territory. Twenty-four hours a day something was going on somewhere along that perimeter. As we moved into position it was raining and we were under artillery fire. Major Connelley came to my platoon and said, "Mitch, I want you to take your machine gun platoon to the ridge up there."

My platoon was sent to hold the high ground for the entire division. I told 'em, "Look, we're going to fight this thing till we whip every one of them. There's nobody in the world that can beat this platoon. Nobody! You're the best machine gunners in the world."

We had eight water-cooled and eight light machine guns. We had worked on them to where we'd built up the rate of fire from 550 rounds a minute to 1,300 rounds a minute.

This water-cooled machine gun sits on a fifty-one-pound steel tripod. Now the gun itself weighs forty-two pounds, plus seven pints of water. And each ammo belt is twenty-two pounds. This is a lot of weight.

Every one of our machine guns were 1917 or 1918 model A-1 machine guns. All of our light machine guns were .30-calibers and air-cooled. These were used as a backup weapon for the water-cooled guns.

You could stack fifteen sandbags on the water-cooled guns, and it would still vibrate a little bit.

Marines would crawl and control the day, and the Japanese would do everything they could to control the night. Every man knew he had to kill or be killed. The Japs were battle hardened. They'd been fighting in China for almost ten years. Many of them were Mongolians over six feet tall, and weighing over 200 pounds.

And I reminded my men, "They love to run bayonets through you first and then shoot you."

I lined up my machine guns as quietly as I could and warned the men that they couldn't have anything rattling. "If there's anything rattling, you wrap it with something. Don't let 'em hear the machine guns, setting the gun on the tripod—nothing, you're going to have to be very quiet."

I crawled from man to man and encouraged them. I told them, "Major Connelley says if there's going to be an attack, they're not going to attack G Company. You can expect an attack here."

And I said, "When they come at our line, don't fire because if you fire too soon they'll pull back and wait, let you expend all your ammunition, and then charge when you run out. But when they start their attack, and they hit our line, they're committed. They're not going to turn around and run back."

There was a Jap patrol right within twenty yards of us. We didn't want to give away the machine guns' position so we threw hand grenades.

We heard all this screaming and hollering and figured we got about eighteen or nineteen of 'em with the hand grenades.

I always carried a long line with me, rolled up in a bag. And I had some empty C-ration cans that were blackened in the fire. I tied 'em just ten feet in front of my whole line of guns. I put one empty .30-caliber cartridge in each one of 'em—as a noise-making trip wire. They'd have to go through me first to get to Henderson Field.

Suddenly flares lit up and we saw nothing but bayonets coming at us. They would scream "Banzai!" and "Blood for the Emperor!" It was horrible.

Meanwhile mortars are going off, and 105s that they were firing over us into the jungle. Soon, they were coming up, elbow to elbow. When we first heard those trip wire cans, I screamed out, "Fire, fire, fire! All machine guns fire!"

They hit my line and dove right into the guns and we just literally wiped out a whole batch of them, right there. They were scattered all over the place, and I was tripping over them. I recall vividly one of 'em impaling Sam Liepardt—ran a bayonet right through him—on their first banzai assault.

I had a .45-caliber pistol, which I fired until it was empty. As I threw it down, I saw this bayonet coming towards me, aimed for my neck. And all I had left was my K-bar [knife]. I reached for it and stuck my other hand out, and his bayonet went right through my hand, and just split everything—my finger and all. Everything happened so fast and he lost his balance. I did too, but I got my K-bar and put it in his left side.

So then I took off down the line, to see how the rest of the platoon was holding up. As I saw Liepardt, I knew he was dead. I ran over to the next gun just as Charlie Locke was killed by a Jap gunner who fired point-blank and hit him. Charlie was hit right in the front as this guy splattered him with his submachine gun. Blood was flying all over the place. I was just covered with blood, and I learned later that one of his bullets went through my pistol belt, and through my side, where it took a chunk out.

Men were trying to come up with ammunition, crawling up from George Company. Fox Company was taking casualties. I sent two men back there to tell them, "Hold the line, but don't shoot straight ahead because you'll be killing us!"

Scarp and Pulawski from my platoon were both killed, and there were hundreds of enemy soldiers coming up and charging over the hill. You just couldn't kill them fast enough.

Gaston was down, and this Jap was whacking at him with his samurai sword. Gaston's a big Marine, about 210 pounds. With his foot that *wasn't* being whacked on, he kicked the Japanese under his chin, broke his neck, and killed him.

I was literally walking into some of these Japanese, and they were bumping into me. I thought they'd overrun us.

Our entire position would soon be isolated, and they could just knock off and annihilate the entire division. They stopped right on the crest of the hill, and began going down toward Connelley.

I grabbed a gun from George Company and it was just about the first good break of my day. I just sprayed that whole area, and all these guys never knew what hit them. The next morning, Connelley and I looked at them; they had holes in the back of their heads, in their backs, the soles of their feet, and every Japanese was dead.

I don't know how many attacks there were, it just seemed like it was constant. There was wave after wave. And we're fighting and shooting. I was running from gun to gun and the first thing I knew, nobody was on the guns. I was the only one alive on the guns.

And at that precise moment, up from the jungle, about ten yards away from the edge of our perimeter, I saw a place where somebody could crawl up and fire. If they got up that close, we could knock them off with either hand grenades or swing a gun over that way. But when I look again, there's a Japanese with a light machine gun there. He'd plunked his gun down to my left. I grabbed hold of one of our machine guns, and there was no ammunition in it. And this guy is sitting there, aiming at my head. He's ready to pull the trigger.

But when I looked down, somebody had brought some more ammo up so I reached down, picked up a belt of ammunition, and fed the 250 rounds into the gun. I pulled the cover down, pulled the cocking handle twice to lock and load the gun. Then all I had to do was put my finger on the trigger.

But while I was loading, a Jap gunner has me in his sights from my left, and he's got me cold. Before I could swing my gun around he fired all thirty rounds from his light machine gun at me and missed. I could feel the warmth of the bullets going past. I immediately fired one burst, and he was gone.

I got ready to go down the hill and a guy jumps up, an officer. He had his revolver out, and I ran toward him, bouncing and running down the hill, firing. He and sixteen or seventeen guys came out of the *kuni* grass, and with one big burst, I just mowed them down. The officer, firing at me, hit my helmet twice. He threw his revolver down and reached for his samurai sword, and as he started to pull it out, I was on top of him. I gave him a burst, and later, I thought, "That's exactly what poor Charlie Locke got."

The hand-to-hand combat lasted probably four or five hours. I looked around, and nobody was moving. And it was as quiet as a cemetery. All our machine guns were still hot—absolutely red hot and steaming. But they were still able to fire. They'd fired beautifully, with no stoppages.

No writer has ever written about it because nobody knows anything about it except my platoon, but we were the first and closest to the enemy, and we killed over 1,000 Japanese that night.

A few nights later I watched five Jap ships come in. They were going to land their troops right near my platoon on the beach, fourteen miles inside enemy territory.

They started down the beach but something had told me to put my machine guns on the beach, in an echelon, instead of lining up four guns. When they hit the surf, we were supposed to kill them all as they came ashore.

I told my platoon, "We're here, and we're going to hold this ground. I know our machine guns are going to work well. We've got the best weapons in the world."

Meanwhile, "Chesty" Puller's outfit had 800 Marines on his line. Nimitz had sent us 1,400 men of the Army's 164th Infantry Division. They did a fabulous job.

When it was all over the colonel came through and said, "Sergeant Paige, you're now Lieutenant Paige."

☐ ☐ ☐

Mitch Paige never mentioned it, but one of the decorations he received for the action that night was the Purple Heart. The other was the Congressional Medal of Honor.

✪ NORTHEAST OF SANTA CRUZ ISLAND
NEAR 165° LATITUDE, SOUTH PACIFIC
26 OCTOBER 1942
2130 HOURS LOCAL

A few hours after Mitch Paige and his desperately outnumbered Marines had prevailed in fighting for their lives to hold Bloody Ridge, Admiral Kinkaid and the sailors and airmen of the *Enterprise* and *Hornet* battle groups found themselves engaged in a battle of their own—with about the same odds. Admiral Nobutake Kondo had departed Truk with an armada of four aircraft carriers, five battleships, fourteen cruisers, and forty-four destroyers, intending to support General Kawaguchi's ground offensive.

Naval Historical Center

Admiral Thomas Kinkaid commanded the USS *Enterprise* task force and later commanded MacArthur's 7th Fleet.

But he arrived too late. At about 0300 on the morning of 26 October, a PBY out of Espiritu Santo detected Kondo's carriers shortly after he had turned north after receiving word that Kawaguchi's ground attack had failed.

Halsey, hearing the patrol plane's report and looking at his plotting board in Noumea, sent a three-word "flash" precedence message to Kinkaid: "ATTACK. REPEAT—ATTACK."

At dawn on 26 October, aircraft from the *Enterprise* found Kondo's fleet northeast of the Santa Cruz Islands and promptly holed the flight deck of the light carrier *Zuiho*. But the Japanese counter-attacked immediately, pounding *Hornet* with bombs and torpedoes, leaving the carrier dead in the water, afire and listing.

By midday the Battle of the Santa Cruz Islands was over. U.S. bomb and torpedo attacks had crippled the heavy cruiser *Chikuma* and seriously damaged the carrier *Shokaku*. The American pilots and anti-aircraft gunners—particularly those on the battleship *South Dakota*—had killed 102 of Kondo's airmen. But a Japanese sub managed to slam a torpedo into the side of the destroyer *Porter*, and the final air raid of the engagement had put three bombs into the flight deck of the *Enterprise*.

The *Porter* had to be scuttled and *Hornet* went down after dark—joining the remains of seventy-four U.S. Navy pilots who had been downed in the fight. As the *Enterprise* and her escorts limped back to the south as Kondo retired toward Truk, for the first time since the war began, the U.S. Navy had no operational carriers in the Pacific Ocean.

✪ NAVAL BATTLE OF GUADALCANAL
NEAR GUADALCANAL, SOLOMON ISLANDS
13 NOVEMBER 1942
2330 HOURS LOCAL

The stunning Japanese losses ashore on Guadalcanal—roughly ten killed for every American casualty—did nothing to diminish Tokyo's insistence that the island be recaptured. By 12 November the Tokyo Express had brought Kawaguchi's ground forces up to nearly 30,000 troops—more than the Americans had ashore. The Japanese continued their persistent probes and contact patrols, creating casualties on both sides every day and night. But they never again mounted another major ground offensive against the airfields.

At sea, however, it was a different story. For the remainder of October and up through the first days of November, the Tokyo Express continued an established pattern of nighttime deliveries of troops and supplies—then blasting away with naval guns at the U.S. Marines and Army troops ashore—before scooting back up the slot to safety. But on 5 November, Station Hypo code-breakers deciphered a lengthy message ordering another major attack. Cruisers, carriers, battleships, and eleven transports escorted by an equal number of destroyers were directed to deliver 13,500 fresh Japanese troops to Kawaguchi.

After seeing this intelligence, Nimitz called for help. Bombers and fighters were flown out from Hawaii. A regiment of Marines from the 2nd Marine Division and 6,000 more soldiers from the Americal Division recently arrived from the U.S. were rushed to shore up Vandegrift's defenses. Repairs to the *Enterprise* were hastily completed and she was dispatched with the battleships *Washington* and *South Dakota* in company to seek out and destroy the enemy counter-invasion force.

On the afternoon of 12 November, a hastily assembled U.S. cruiser-destroyer force, designated as Task Force 65 and commanded by Rear Admiral Dan Callaghan, took up station at the southern end of the slot to intercept the Japanese Combined Fleet. Task Force 65 consisted of two heavy cruisers: the USS *San Francisco* (Callaghan's flagship, damaged when a Japanese pilot crashed his flaming plane into her) and USS *Portland*; three light cruisers: *Atlanta* (Admiral Scott's flagship), *Helena*, and *Juneau*; and eight destroyers: *Barton*, *Monssen*, *O'Bannon*, *Cushing*, *Laffey*, *Sterett*, *Aaron Ward*, and *Fletcher*—thirteen ships in all. They were no match for the two battleships, heavy cruiser, and fourteen destroyers under the command of Admiral Hiroaki Abe.

It was clear but moonless at 0200 on 13 November when the two forces met at close range in the waters between Guadalcanal and Savo Island. In a furious thirty-minute melee, which the Marines watched from ashore, both Admirals Callaghan and Scott were killed, four American destroyers were sunk, and the cruiser *Atlanta* was set afire from bow to stern and had to be scuttled. The cruiser *Portland* and another U.S. destroyer were left dead in the water and the cruiser *Juneau*, struck by a torpedo, was forced to retire to the south.

But the Japanese didn't fare that well, either. Two of Abe's destroyers, *Akatsuki* and *Yudachi*, were sunk outright and three more of his destroyers were seriously damaged. And his flagship, the battleship *Hiei*, was so badly damaged that she became a crippled, defenseless target for bombers from Henderson Field, who sent her to the bottom.

By dawn of 13 November, the remnants of Abe's force were fleeing north, pursued by aircraft from Henderson Field and B-17s from Espiritu

Santo. The violent encounter might have escaped notice in the U.S. press but for the fate of the *Juneau*. As the damaged heavy cruiser limped south thorough Ironbottom Sound, she was torpedoed by a Japanese submarine and went to the bottom with more than 700 aboard—including the five Sullivan brothers from

The five Sullivan brothers killed in the sinking of the *Juneau*.

Waterloo, Iowa. They had all enlisted in December 1941 to avenge the death of their friend Bill Ball, who was killed at Pearl Harbor.

Seaman Frank Holmgren was a nineteen-year-old captain's orderly aboard the *Juneau* and was with his high school buddy Charlie Hayes when the Japanese torpedo hit the ship's number-one engine room.

▢   ▢   ▢

SEAMAN SECOND CLASS
FRANK HOLMGREN, USN
Near Guadalcanal, Solomon Islands
13 November 1942
0330 Hours Local

In November, we were assigned to a group that was going to take more Marines and supplies to Guadalcanal. Around one o'clock in the morning I could hear this *boom, boom, boom*. I thought they were planes dropping bombs. I had no idea that the Jap fleet was coming in. And here we are, right in the middle of them.

I got to my station and in five minutes or so we were hit in the number-one fire room. And the firemen were trying to keep the bulkhead from collapsing and trying to get men out of there. Then all the lights went out. I'm not a very good swimmer. I was scared to death.

I got up to the second deck and I didn't know until we got topside that we were really in among the ships of the Jap fleet. And I could see they were still firing.

The *San Francisco* got hit at the stern, right through the fantail. They must have been right in the middle of it, too. We saw what was left of the thirteen ships that went in, and I remember seeing the *Helena*. The *Portland* was hurt. And the *San Francisco*. I didn't even see the destroyers because they were out. After we got hit I was thinking that we'd have to go back to Pearl Harbor for repairs. While Charlie and I were sitting there, we noticed three life rafts tied down to the deck. So since we'd been hit and in bad shape and didn't want to "go down with the ship," we untied them.

It was just about then, when everything seemed quiet, that we were hit by another torpedo. The ship blew up in my face. And the next thing I know I'm in the air. When I come back down on the ship my hand hit a life jacket so I wrapped it around me, got up on my feet, and held on to a gun mount.

I looked back at the fantail and there was nothing there! And then all of a sudden I heard the roar of the ocean and I said, "I'm gonna die!"

I went down with the ship. How far down I went, I don't know. But I thought I was dead at the time. And the next thing I know, I'm coming up out of that water. And I could see light. The life jacket was bringing me back up, and when I popped to the surface there was fuel oil, all over.

I looked around and saw some guys on a raft, so I made my way over to them. They were the three rafts that Charlie and I untied on the deck of the ship just before we were hit. They were the only rafts that got off the ship.

I remember someone saying, "The ships are leaving us!"

They kept on going; they didn't come back and pick us up.

I think it was the second day that an Army plane came down low and dropped a rubber raft but no supplies. All the guys were really hurt badly and passing out. I remember somebody taking the dog tags off of someone before they rolled him off into the ocean. The sharks came then and after they got one, they went after more. People were dying, left and right.

As the days went by, we didn't have anything to eat and we had sharks all around us. Every so often it would rain, so we'd get some water to drink. But some of the guys were going out of their heads from drinking salt water. Others went out of their heads and jumped off the raft even though the sharks were waiting for them.

On the fourth day somebody else jumped off, and as he did I saw a shark take him. That left just five of us.

That afternoon things were getting bad. Then we heard this seaplane coming in. The pilot landed in the water and they finally pulled us in. The first thing I said to the pilot was, "Did you find those cork nets out there?" I knew my buddy Charlie Hayes was on one, but he said no. That's how I learned Charlie never made it. That's when I passed out.

They took us back to Guadalcanal. How many survivors? After that torpedo hit it was seventy-five, or maybe a hundred. Now there were just five of us.

I just had confidence that I was gonna make it.

❏   ❏   ❏

✪ NAVAL BATTLE OF GUADALCANAL
NEAR GUADALCANAL, SOLOMON ISLANDS
14 NOVEMBER 1942
2330 HOURS LOCAL

While Frank Holmgren was floating in the waters of Ironbottom Sound awaiting rescue, thousands of his countrymen were fighting to save Guadalcanal.

In the early morning hours of 14 November, Admiral Mikawa's bombardment force cruisers arrived offshore and proceeded to pound the airfield and the Marine positions around it. At dawn, "Cactus Air Force" planes and bombers from *Enterprise* found Mikawa's cruisers, sinking one and damaging three others. Then U.S. planes pounced on Tanaka's troop transports, sending seven to the bottom, carrying more than 7,000 Japanese soldiers with them.

While U.S. aircraft were pounding Tanaka's transports and escorts, Halsey ordered the battleships *South Dakota* and *Washington* to detach from *Enterprise* and proceed at flank speed to intercept a new threat: Admiral Nobutake Kondo was heading back into the fight with the battleship *Kirishima*, four cruisers, and nine destroyers.

At 2315 on 14 November, the two American battlewagons, accompanied by four destroyers—all under the command of Rear Admiral Willis Lee aboard *Washington*—were on station south of Savo Island when Kondo's force emerged from the radar "shadow" of Savo Island. The Japanese struck the first blow, sinking two of Lee's destroyers with Long Lance torpedoes and so severely damaging the *South Dakota* with naval gunfire that she retired to the west escorted by the two surviving U.S. destroyers. Lee, aboard *Washington*, now faced Kondo's entire force alone. The battleship's crew, responding to their commander's courageous order to open fire and close with the enemy, rose to the occasion and hit the *Kirishima* more than fifty times with five- and sixteen-inch radar-directed shells—all in under seven minutes.

The barrage wrecked the Japanese flagship and Kondo decided he'd had enough. He ordered the *Kirishima* and a disabled destroyer scuttled and quickly fled north, providing a sufficient distraction for the tenacious Tanaka to beach his four remaining, badly damaged transports on the Guadalcanal coast. There he succeeded in disembarking 2,000 surviving Imperial Army soldiers—but not their supplies—before the ships were pounded to pieces by the "Cactus Air Force."

By the end of the three days' battle, only 2,000 of the nearly 11,000 Japanese troops on the transport ships made it ashore, but with none of their necessities—ammunition, rations, and other supplies and equipment.

The two opposing forces withdrew and counted the costs. The Japanese had sunk eight American ships and damaged seven more. Almost 2,000 American sailors lost their lives—including 720 from the *Juneau* alone. Of the 725 men thrown into the sea when their ship went down, just five sailors survived.

The Americans sank five Japanese ships and damaged three others. But the loss in Japanese lives was horrific. More than 11,000 soldiers and sailors had died in the waters around Guadalcanal.

There would be one more major battle—the Battle of Tassafaronga—on 29–30 November. By then the Japanese had given up trying to retake Guadalcanal and concentrated on getting their troops off the island. They repeated their strategy of sending transports down the slot in Ironbottom Sound, but this time the eight Japanese ships were met by nine superior ships of the U.S. Navy. After the battle, each U.S. ship had sunk one Japanese ship, and the Americans suffered damage to three others.

The Japanese were on the run both physically and psychologically. Still, they eventually managed to evacuate 13,000 troops from Guadalcanal. Thousands of Japanese soldiers were left on the island to fend for themselves. Rather than surrender, they fought to the death, committed suicide, or died of starvation or disease before it all finally ended in early February 1943.

After the six-month series of battles for Guadalcanal, Rear Admiral Kelly Turner was promoted to vice admiral, and Vice Admiral "Bull" Halsey was promoted to full admiral. When he put on his fourth star, Halsey credited it to the Marines and the courageous actions of Admirals Dan Callaghan and Norman Scott—both awarded posthumous Medals of Honor.

The final Japanese toll for Guadalcanal was catastrophic: 25,000 lives lost; more than two dozen ships sunk—including irreplaceable carriers and battleships—and the loss of at least 600 planes. The Japanese defeat at Guadalcanal also spelled the end of their efforts to take Port Moresby and the rest of New Guinea.

The Americans lost 1,600 lives in the land, sea, and air battles for Guadalcanal. U.S. ship and aircraft losses equaled Japan's twenty-four ships and 600 aircraft. For those who fought on Tulagi and Guadalcanal, it was indeed a tropical hell. The grisly hand-to-hand combat would become the blueprint for action in later Pacific island battles. But Admiral Halsey best summed up the overall result of the fight: "Before Guadalcanal, the enemy advanced at his pleasure. After Guadalcanal, he retreated at ours."

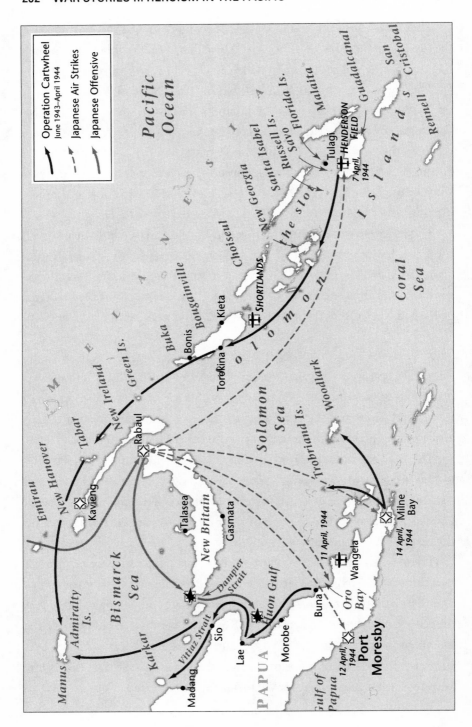

CHAPTER 10
THE BLACK SHEEP SQUADRON
(AUGUST 1943–JANUARY 1944)

✪ **MARINE FIGHTER SQUADRON VMF-214**
ESPIRITU SANTO, NEW HEBRIDES
22 JULY 1943
1130 HOURS LOCAL

The failure of the Japanese efforts to retake Guadalcanal was paralleled by their collapse on New Guinea's Papuan Peninsula. By mid-January, MacArthur had more than 30,000 Australian and American troops committed to overrunning 12,000 Japanese in the "Buna Pocket." At the end of the month, just before Guadalcanal was finally secured, the last surviving Japanese defender was killed or captured—at a cost of more than 3,000 Allied lives—nearly double the U.S. losses to take Guadalcanal.

In Washington, the Joint Chiefs seized on the moment to establish priorities for the next offensive steps against Japan. Recognizing that the European theater was still the main war effort, they nonetheless developed what they called the "Strategic Plan for the Defeat of Japan." It called for:

- Cutting the flow of oil and resources to Japan with intensive submarine attacks

- Sustained aerial bombing of Japanese-held territory
- Retaking the Aleutian islands seized by Japan
- A central pacific attack from Hawaii west toward the Home Islands
- A two-pronged attack north from New Guinea and the Solomons
  to capture Rabaul.

Nimitz wasted no time in implementing his part of the grand design. On 26 March, before the Strategic Plan even received its final approval, he launched an attack aimed at ejecting the Japanese from Attu and Kiska—the two Aleutian islands seized in June 1942 during the Battle of Midway. By 30 May 1943, the U.S. Army's 7th Infantry Division had retaken Attu—but not before the Japanese killed scores of wounded American soldiers in a final banzai charge on the hospital. Before the Americans could invade Kiska in August, the Japanese succeeded in evacuating their garrison—undetected by the Americans—who unwittingly proceeded to conduct an uncontested full-scale amphibious assault against the island.

While the warlords in Tokyo were willing to write off the territory in the Aleutians, that was certainly not the case in the South Pacific. While Nimitz and MacArthur paused to build up their forces for their dual drives on Rabaul, Yamamoto was busy shoring up its outer defenses. But despite his best efforts, the tide had turned.

In early March, during the three-day Battle of the Bismarck Sea, his once vaunted fleet lost seven of eight transports and four of eight destroyers—along with 3,650 men and twenty-five aircraft—during an attempt to reinforce the Japanese garrison at Lea on the north coast of New Guinea. A subsequent bombing raid in late March against Guadalcanal—already becoming a major American and Allied naval and air base—by more than 300 aircraftcost him forty aircraft and their experienced pilots. Now, increasingly concerned about the state of readiness for an anticipated American offensive against Bougainville, Yamamoto decided to see for himself how prepared his forces really were. It was a deadly mistake.

The coded radio message with Yamamoto's detailed itinerary was intercepted and passed to Station Hypo code-breakers. With President Roosevelt's personal authorization, U.S. Army Air Force P-38s launched from Henderson Field to intercept and kill the mastermind of Japan's naval strategy. At 0935 on 18 April 1943, one year to the day since Jimmy Doolittle's daring raid on Tokyo, the man who planned the surprise attack on Pearl Harbor was himself surprised. As the "Betty" bomber in which he was a passenger approached Bougainville at 4,500 feet, sixteen P-38s pounced out of the sun. According to postwar reports, Yamamoto was dead before his flaming plane hit the ground.

Yamamoto's successor as head of the Combined Fleet, Admiral Mine-ichi Koga, quickly devoted himself to the same task as his deceased prede-cessor: protecting Rabaul. He clearly understood that the heavily defended base on the north coast of New Britain—with its 100,000 battle-tested Japanese troops and 600 aircraft spread over five different airfields and naval facilities—was the primary American objective in the South Pacific. He set out to do everything in his power to keep the Americans from real-izing their goal—or failing that, to make it as costly as possible.

His first steps were to continue reinforcing the islands between Guadal-canal and Rabaul—and to slow MacArthur's advance to the east on New Guinea as much as possible. He reinvigorated nighttime deliveries by the Tokyo Express, even relying on submarines to deliver supplies and rein-forcements when necessary. By mid-June Koga convinced his reluctant staff to try a major air raid against Guadalcanal—even though the once-contested island now had five air bases, more than 300 aircraft, scores of anti-aircraft batteries, and a major port operation with U.S., Australian, and New Zealand combatants in the roadstead, all with alert anti-aircraft gunners.

The raid by seventy Zekes—the latest version of the infamous Zero—and twenty-four heavy bombers was a disaster. All but one of Koga's planes was downed—at a cost of four American and two New Zealand fighters.

The disastrous June air raid on Guadalcanal had another unanticipated adverse consequence for Admiral Koga besides the loss of his planes and pilots. It convinced Halsey that it was time to get moving north—up the Solomons—to wrest the fortress of Bougainville from Japanese control. But first he had to eliminate two enemy air bases that threatened his advance: one at Munda on New Georgia Island and the other at Vila on nearby Kolombangara Island.

On 30 June, Admiral Turner, commanding the 3rd Amphibious Force, landed 6,000 Marines and soldiers on New Georgia and promptly seized the Munda airstrip. The Seabees followed immediately to patch the runway, and the first American aircraft prepared to land on the captured airstrip within seventy-two hours of the landing. But it didn't go as planned.

The plan called for a quick clearing operation and then an attack to seize the airstrip at Vila, on Kolombangara, less than ten miles away across the Kula Gulf. But just as on Guadalcanal, the bottom fell out of Turner's timetable.

The 4,500 well-entrenched Japanese troops on New Georgia might have lost their airstrip, but they weren't about to give up. The dogged defenders held on for more than a month—requiring the commitment of 32,000 soldiers and 1,700 Marines. And, as was becoming the custom, those Japanese troops who couldn't be evacuated by the Tokyo Express fought to the last man.

That was enough to convince Halsey that he should skip the heavily defended Vila airdrome and seize the lightly held Japanese island of Vella Lavella, fifty miles to the north. On 14 August, 6,000 troops from New Georgia were backloaded onto waiting amphibious ships and landed the following morning on the southwest coast of Vella Lavella. Once again the Seabees rushed ashore and in a matter of forty-eight hours constructed a rough but functional fighter strip. As soon as they finished, Marine, Army and Navy aircraft came winging in to protect the troops ashore and the ships of the amphibious force.

The Americans were finally on the move toward Rabaul. Though Nimitz, MacArthur, and Halsey realized that there were long and difficult battles ahead, there was no longer any doubt that U.S. superiority on the sea and in the air were essential ingredients for successful operations on the ground.

By the summer of 1943, U.S. air superiority could be measured in both quantity and quality. Army, Navy, and Marine air training commands had quadrupled the output of pilots, navigators, gunners, bombardiers, mechanics, and air crewmen from the levels achieved in 1942. In that same time frame, the production of new and better aircraft had increased seven-fold. The quantitative and qualitative edge the Japanese had enjoyed the previous year was now gone.

For the first months of the war, the Mitsubishi A6M *Reisen*, or "Zero," ruled the skies over the Pacific. These planes were light, fast, and were also equipped with heavy armament—two 20 mm cannons and a pair of 7.7 mm nose-mounted machine guns.

The Zero was a proven plane, having been battle-tested in China for more than a year before the first ones appeared in the skies over Pearl Harbor on 7 December 1941. It had proven itself superior to any other aircraft in China, Burma, the Philippines, and the Dutch East Indies.

So too had most of the Japanese pilots, many of whom had ten years of combat experience. The age of the average American pilot was nineteen.

A typical Zero pilot wore a parachute and a harness and carried a small pistol—not for personal protection but as a "suicide weapon." In the Japanese warrior tradition it was dishonorable to be captured or to surrender—suicide was preferable to the dishonor of defeat or surrender.

But the Japanese no longer ruled the skies. By the spring of 1943 Army P-38s and Marine Chance-Vought F4U Corsairs were being delivered in significant numbers. The Marines inherited the powerful, gull-winged fighters from the Navy when a landing gear problem caused the F4U to fail its aircraft carrier qualification. Though the Corsair was not as maneuverable as the Zero, the Marines loved it for its powerful rate of climb and firepower. Corsair pilots called it "Hog Nose" for its massive front cowling. It was powered by a 2,000-horsepower supercharged radial engine—nearly twice

The *Reisen* or "Zero."

the horsepower of the Zero. And with six .50-caliber machine guns in the wings, the Corsair was also better armed.

As Halsey started island-hopping up the Solomons in the summer of 1943, Marine Fighter Squadron VMF-214—flying their new Corsairs—

became a key component in the successful drive. The squadron was commanded by a scrappy, thirty-one-year-old Marine combat pilot named Gregory Boyington. Born in Coeur d'Alene, Idaho, Boyington had received his commission and as an aviation cadet served in the Marines. But in August of 1941 he resigned his commission to join Claire Chennault's Air Volunteer Group in China, the Flying Tigers. The pay was good and the pilots got a $500 bonus for every confirmed kill.

In his autobiography, *Baa Baa Black Sheep*, Boyington claimed to have shot down six aircraft while with the Flying Tigers. But the official records state that he had only two aerial victories that could be documented. Boyington argued that he should have been paid for the four enemy planes he had destroyed while they were sitting on the tarmac at a Japanese-held air base in China.

Pappy Boyington led the Black Sheep Squadron.

It may have been after his stint with the Flying Tigers that someone came up with the nickname "Pappy." At thirty-one, he was one of the "old" men of the unit. But he also had another nickname— "Black Sheep"—which he earned with the Flying Tigers. General John Alison said, "He was a liability. He lost airplanes; he got lost, landed wheels up . . . and, well, you know what Pappy's problem was? He drank too much. Chennault sent him back to the United States. He got a commission as a Marine major in the reserves, and was sent overseas in January of 1943."

The decision on who should command the newly constituted VMF-214 Marine squadron fell to the assistant commanding general of the 1st Marine Air Wing, Brigadier General James "Nuts" Moore. Major Boyington landed on Espiritu Santo about when General Moore was trying to make that decision. Perhaps more on the basis of his tenure as a combat pilot than for his spotty record with the Flying Tigers, Major Boyington was picked as CO of VMF-214.

Now the squadron needed a new name. The men in the squadron submitted all kinds of names, including a few that were outright profane. The Marine public information office did their best to discourage those, reminding the men that it would prevent them from sending news releases to hometown newspapers publicizing their exploits. How could they do that with a squadron name they couldn't print in a family newspaper?

Eventually common sense took over and the name of VMF-214 became the "Black Sheep Squadron." The pilots of VMF-214 were combat-trained by Pappy Boyington. What his green pilots lacked in seat time they made up in strategies, taught to them by their leader in colorful sessions on the ground. In earthy, blunt terms, he preached to them, "Whenever you see a Japanese plane, kill it. That's our mission. Pick one out and kill it."

The Black Sheep Squadron did just as they were ordered. Their first mission was to fly escort for twelve B-24s on a bombing run to Kahili.

The flight turned into a pitched battle with Japanese Zeros, covering some 200 miles of sea and airspace during a brief forty-five minutes. When it was over, sixteen of the twenty-four Black Sheep fighter pilots had seen combat action for the very first time.

The squadron claimed eleven Japanese planes downed in the battle that day, with Pappy getting the credit for five of those kills. In their first month of combat, the Black Sheep Squadron was credited with fifty-seven kills and nineteen "probables," and their fame grew. And so did the pressure on Pappy Boyington to get even more victories. During the next three months under Boyington, the unit claimed ninety-four enemy aircraft shot down.

On 15 August, Halsey's amphibious forces, aided by the Black Sheep Squadron flying cover, landed on small Vella Lavella Island, where the Seabees immediately went to work building the airstrip that would become the newest forward air base for VMF-214.

Lieutenant John "Jack" Bolt, a twenty-three-year-old aviator and instructor from Florida, had been flying combat missions over the

Solomons since May. Two Marine aviators, Lieutenants Henry "Hank" McCartney and Henry "Boo" Bourgeois, just a year younger than Bolt, arrived about the same time.

〰 〰 〰

LIEUTENANT HENRY MCCARTNEY, USMC
Solomon Islands
18 September 1943
1530 Hours Local

Guadalcanal was no fun. Munda was no fun either. Living on Munda was miserable. There was no place to take a shower or a bath. The guys would go down to a creek close by. The only tour in which I thought we had halfway decent living conditions was the tour I spent on the Russell Islands.

Our friends in the Marine artillery had a 105 right up in back of my tent. And they'd do harassing fire against the Japs. Of course, every time they'd fire that thing off, we'd come up out of the sack. And it was difficult to get a good night's sleep.

So one of the very first mutinies at Guadalcanal was the fighter pilots going down to Operations. They said, "Get that artillery gun out, or you won't have any fighter pilots." They moved it.

I came into the squadron January of '43, with four kills to my credit. I may have had more than Pappy at that time. All together, I'm credited with five and a half, and three probables.

Our first combat tour with 214 was relatively quiet. When they came back from the second tour, that's when they developed the concept of the fighter sweeps and there were more enemy aircraft challenging us. That's when our scores went up.

〰 〰 〰

LIEUTENANT HENRY BOURGEOIS, USMC
Vella Lavella Island
21 September 1943
1500 Hours Local

I always wanted to be an aviator. And when a recruiting bunch came through, they got me. I'd already made up my mind I wanted to be a Marine.

I got to Guadalcanal in January 1943. I was assigned to VMF-122, flew two combat missions with them, and went with Boyington when he organized 214.

Since some of the other guys and I had combat experience, he selected eight of us as division leaders. The rest from the fighter pool would be new pilots. I flew my first mission with 214 out of the Russell Islands.

On this one mission, I remember the bombers were to go after the shipping in the harbor. And, they were probably at 9,000 or 10,000 feet.

We had sixteen Corsairs, closely covering the bombers, and above that some P-38s beyond sight, high up. We got up there, and saw that the whole harbor was covered with a thunderstorm.

And the bombers pushed over early because they had to get down below. By the time they pushed over, a whole sky full of Japanese airplanes appeared, going after everybody.

It quickly broke into an air-to-air dogfight. And, pretty soon, they're all over the sky. I had somebody shooting at me. I'd go into a cloud, mill around a little, come out, and shoot at a Japanese airplane, get shot at again, go into a cloud, and come out and still try to stick with the bombers if we could.

That was the typical type of gunfight. We lost two SBDs and two Corsairs that time. One of our SBD rear gunners claimed one Zero kill. And I think we claimed five or six.

So I decided to head back to base, and I'm not paying too much attention to what I'm doing. I'm just flying along at about 5,000 to 7,000 feet and see tracers coming by. I look in the rearview mirror, and there's a Zero back there, shooting at me. So, I two-blocked the throttle, and headed downhill as fast as I could. But the Zero was sticking with me.

And this guy kept sneaking up and firing, sneaking up and firing—getting closer. Then I discovered I was headed in the wrong direction and running low on fuel. So I'm going to have to turn and fight this guy.

I knew he was going out-turn me unless I did it first. I was just about ready to do that when he turned back to his base.

We did a lot of escort missions for B-24s, dive-bombers and torpedo bombers, and did a lot of strafing missions. Or we'd be protecting destroyers that had been hit, backing down a slot.

Pappy Boyington was thirty-one years old then, at least seven years older than the rest of us. Major Boyington, in the air as a pilot, was a superior leader.

If you talk about his accomplishments in the air as a flight leader, you can't fault him. He was excellent. In two combat tours, we lost eleven pilots out of a total of fifty-four. And Pappy Boyington asked Bailey, Case, Beggart, and me to stay for a fourth combat tour. I said, "Pappy, I think my time's running out. I'd better go back home."

◻ ◻ ◻

FIRST LIEUTENANT
JOHN F. "JACK" BOLT, USMC
Vella Lavella Island
28 September 1943
0730 Hours Local

From the beginning, we were facing pilots who had been in the Zero for several years. They probably had 500 or 600 flight hours. Our typical pilot in Joe Foss's squadron or my squadron would have had maybe 150 or 200 flight hours.

But we were finally getting experienced pilots who had been fighting the Zeros for three combat tours. Joe Foss was one of them. They were instructing us on the advantages and the disadvantages of fighting them.

Boyington had acquired a tremendous amount of knowledge in his experiences in China, far more than anybody else had. And he could rev up the guys to do the best they could. He was a scoundrel, and charming, but we had a real good esprit de corps by the time we went into combat.

I got my first kill on 16 September. It was my first escort mission to Bougainville. The Zeros were probably about 10,000 or 12,000 feet, and I'd come down from maybe twenty and gotten in behind them, trying to remain in their blind spot. I got two on that flight.

I got back at the base at Turtle Bay and went to the scrap heap for some parts of wrecked planes, and got a .50-caliber machine gun and shot different rounds into this debris. The common belting for our machine guns was one armor-piercing shell, one incendiary, and a tracer.

The armor-piercing shell was something you didn't need on the Zero. The Zero didn't have armor. And you just need tracers initially to see where your guns are hitting. The thing that would torch off the Zero was the incendiary. It would scatter phosphorous around the small area [inside the cockpit] so that it was almost solid phosphorous for maybe a foot in diameter where the incendiary went off.

So, I got Boyington out to the scrap heap and showed him what the rounds were capable of. After that we immediately went to a belting of a much larger number of incendiaries. And we got real good results from it, too. The Zeros were blowing up noticeably faster.

✪ MARINE FIGHTER SQUADRON VMF-214 READY TENT
MUNDA POINT, NEW GEORGIA
17 OCTOBER 1943
0400 HOURS LOCAL

Like the rest of the Allied air bases springing up on the Solomon Island chain and the others to the northwest, Munda Point, on the island of New Georgia, was a terrible place with a reputation as a "malarial hell-hole."

Each night the Black Sheep Squadron had visitors who made life miserable for them. Their first night at Munda, the Japanese welcomed them with a bombing raid at one o'clock in the morning. They kept up that routine, visiting the base up to three times a night, making it impossible for the pilots to get a full night's sleep.

When the air raid alarm went off, the men found cover, waited for the Japanese bombers to leave, then went back to bed, only to be awakened a few hours later with the same routine. By 0400 the pilots were roused again—but on 17 October 1943 the last call wasn't the air raid alarm. It was the duty officer getting them to the flight line for another day's mission. This day, the Black Sheep Squadron was on another bombing run against the Japanese air base at Kahili.

Spurred on by his sense of competition, Major Boyington tried a new tactic with his pilots. Now, instead of waiting for Japanese aircraft to attack, he began flying over their bases and taunting them to respond. He even used his radio to let them know he was coming and told them that he was the guy who shot down all their planes. The tactic worked—the enemy picked up the gauntlet and fought back with a vengeance. And as the Black Sheep moved ever closer to the Japanese stronghold of Rabaul, those fights over enemy airspace got increasingly hotter.

It's always riskier getting into a dogfight over an enemy's airspace. If your plane got hit and you had to bail out, there was a good chance you would survive if you were in your own airspace. But over enemy territory, the odds were in favor of your dying there. If you bailed, there was every chance that a Zero pilot would try to gun you down in your parachute. If you were lucky enough to survive the parachute drop, chances were that enemy soldiers on the ground would kill you when you landed.

Boyington had first challenged the Japanese to aerial battles when they were dogfighting over Bougainville. With its strong Japanese presence, sweeps over Bougainville were always high-risk.

Boyington continued to goad the enemy until he received a cable from Admiral Halsey. It read: YOUR STEEPLECHASE IS OVER. YOU ARE RETIRED TO STUD.

Actually, Halsey was saying that their first tour of air combat duty was over and he was granting the squadron some well-deserved R & R in Australia.

Two other members of the Black Sheep Squadron who went with Boyington to Australia were just twenty-two when they landed in the South Pacific.

□　□　□

LIEUTENANT ED HARPER, USMC
Vella Lavella Island
29 October 1943
1100 Hours Local

The first time I saw an F4U Corsair was on an air station before I went overseas, before I got to the South Pacific. Espiritu Santo is the first time I saw one up close. At Espiritu Santo we got assigned to 214 as part of the replacement pool.

I wasn't even aware who Boyington was for the first few days. We only knew he'd been in the Flying Tigers when we started training as a squadron.

Initially I was very aggressive, and had no fear at all, until suddenly I was on the receiving end instead of the delivering end. And that's very sobering. It never got easier, when you were on the receiving end. Zeros were hard to shoot down. I fired a whole load of ammunition into one, almost point-blank, as he dove away. And he barely burned. But he obviously was done for. He was no longer fighting and was crashing into the sea. But he didn't blow up for me. In fact, he didn't burn easily at all.

Zeros were flown by very skilled pilots and were hard to shoot down. Most Zeros that were shot down were targeted by pilots that didn't let the Zeros see them coming.

I got hit a couple of times with Zeros that I never saw, too. And that was pretty typical. I was just a kid trying to do some good. I only got one confirmed, and a couple of probables, and a few more I just shot up.

The intelligence officer took your word for it. If I'd have been inclined to exaggerate, I could've been an ace. I really shot that guy down that went in the ocean and I shot up a couple more until they were riddled with holes, but I didn't see them burn or crash. So you didn't count them.

Boyington gave me the nickname "the sleeve" after I got shot up the first time. A "sleeve" is the target sleeve that's towed behind another plane to offer fighters gunnery practice.

It was my first tour and I hadn't shot down anything. Other guys were having a little luck. But I was trailing and I was getting anxious.

I got off by myself and found a Zero down below me. I started making runs on him. That's when I discovered how maneuverable they were. Every time I got close to him, he'd do a split S underneath me. I'd do a wing over, and come back. And he'd do another split S. We were working ourselves down over the harbor, right off the end of their runway. And my thought was, that little bugger can't split S forever. He'll do a split S into the ocean. But what I didn't realize, all the way down, he must have been hollering for help on his radio.

Suddenly I had a lot of extra company. And instead of being on the offense, I suddenly was on the defense, trying to stay alive. There was a small cumulus cloud, a mile or so away. I jinked left and right, and up and down, and I finally made it into the clouds. And of course you felt like you were playing tag. I popped in and out, ended up getting some pretty good shots at several Zeros.

After playing that game for a while, I dove out the bottom of the cloud and headed home. Nothing fatal was hit—the engine wasn't hit. I wasn't hit. The landing gear wouldn't come down so I had to make a belly landing. But, otherwise it was a non-event.

It didn't seem to be a big deal, except I had over a hundred holes in my airplane when I got back. Boyington took a look at the airplane and said, "You were a target sleeve today."

We had no idea we were setting records. And we were having reasonable success. But we didn't expect the attention that we received along the way. You didn't want to think about it.

3 January 1944, Boyington was shot down. We were coming out of Bougainville, and when he didn't come home, we asked to go on a search

The USS *Arizona* explodes just minutes after the initial Japanese Pearl Harbor air attack on 7 December that devastated the American fleet, killed 2,388, and wounded 1,200. (Chapter 1)

Of the ninety-six ships at anchor in the harbor, eighteen were sunk or damaged. More than 700 U.S. aircraft were damaged or destroyed. (Chapter 1)

General Edwin P. King (third from left) surrendering Bataan and 78,000 troops (66,000 Filipinos and 12,000 U.S.) against MacArthur's orders to hold Bataan at all costs. It was the largest contingent of U.S. Army troops ever to surrender in history. (Chapter 2)

Japanese soldiers savagely killed civilians along with Filipino and U.S. troops during the infamous sixty-five-mile horror of the Bataan Death March. (Chapter 3)

Eighty American fliers in sixteen B-25 two-engine bombers launched from the USS *Hornet*, led by Colonel Jimmy Doolittle (standing above center), flew over 700 miles to Tokyo in a daring daylight raid. (Chapter 4)

The B-25s took off from the 470-foot *Hornet* deck, found their targets and dropped their bombs, then escaped to the coast of China. The mission's success created fear and panic in Japan but lifted Americans' spirits. (Chapter 4)

U.S. sailors abandon ship just before the USS *Lexington* sinks during the Battle of the Coral Sea on 7–8 May 1942. (Chapter 5)

U.S. Marines first tasted the bloody hand-to-hand combat of the Pacific islands war at Guadalcanal in the Battle of Bloody Ridge. (Chapter 9)

The Americans had an edge in the Battle of Midway when Navy code-breakers of "Station Hypo" cracked the vaunted JN-25 code and confirmed that the Japanese were planning to attack Midway. (Chapter 6)

A battle for the tiny dot of Midway Island helped to turn the tide of the naval war in favor of the U.S. Navy and stunned the Japanese. (Chapter 9)

In September 1944, hundreds of landing craft of the 1st Marine Division head toward the beaches of Peleliu in September 1944, still smoking from the offshore U.S. naval bombardment. (Chapter 13)

Colorful and flamboyant Marine air ace Gregory "Pappy" Boyington led the famous Black Sheep Squadron in raids until he was shot down and captured by the Japanese. He was a POW until the end of the war. (Chapter 10)

Every tree, bush, and blade of grass was destroyed at the violent struggle to take the tiny island of Tarawa, where 6,000 died in a seventy-six-hour battle. (Chapter 11)

On 1 November 1943, 23,000 men of the 2nd Marine Division boarded ships in New Zealand for their transport to Tarawa. On D-Day for the Battle of Tarawa, the beaches were littered with the bodies of Marines. (Chapter 11)

A Japanese combatant surrenders on Peleliu Island, one of a small number of enemy soldiers who defied the *bushido* code forbidding surrender and expecting the Japanese fighting men to fight to the death. (Chapter 13)

Raising the American flag on the island of Guam after the U.S. recaptured it from the Japanese, who had seized Guam in the early days of the war. (Chapter 12)

The Japanese, after experiencing great losses of men, ships, and aircraft, began using suicide attacks in desperation to save what was left of their fleet. Here a kamikaze plane attacks a U.S. ship in the Battle of Leyte. (Chapter 14)

"I have returned." General Douglas MacArthur wades ashore at Leyte, fulfilling his promise to return to the Philippines. (Chapter 14)

A U.S. Army Ranger carries an emaciated American POW after liberating Camp Cabanatuan and rescuing over 500 other prisoners in the largest prison break in U.S. military history at the time. (Chapter 15)

National Archives

In perhaps what is the most memorable photo of the war, Marines hoist the stars and stripes atop Mt. Suribachi on Iwo Jima, where nearly 7,000 Americans were killed—a third of all their casualties in the war. (Chapter 16)

AP/Wide World Photos

On 2 September 1945, General Douglas MacArthur reviews the surrender documents signed by the Japanese in ceremonies aboard the USS *Missouri*. (Chapter 18)

party. And they wouldn't let us. The following morning, they let four of us take off and go look for him, providing we got back in time for our regular mission. If the Japanese sub hadn't come along and picked him up early that morning, we would've found him.

I said then, and I still say sixty years later, Pappy made me feel secure. He made me feel aggressive. He gave me confidence. He was a leader. Sure, he got in trouble on the ground from time to time, and liked to drink and fight. But he was terrific in the air. And he made us young fighter pilots brave. And that's leadership.

▯ ▯ ▯

LIEUTENANT W. THOMAS EMRICH, USMC
Vella Lavella Island
29 October 1943
1315 Hours Local

I remember vividly that first time. We didn't see any enemy airplanes at first, on my first mission. And suddenly about sixty Zeros appear. There's probably thirty or so of us from various squadrons. So airplanes are all around. You look off to the left, there's airplanes going down in flames. There are airplanes crossing twenty feet in front of you. And I think, what am I doing here? I'm scared to death. My mouth was so dry, if you'd have called me on the radio, I couldn't have answered you. That's how scared I was.

On October 17 I shot down two Zeros—two on the same day. You have to remember that the Zero had no armor plate and no self-sealing fuel tanks. Their fuel tank was behind the cockpit. And both the airplanes I shot down, I came in from behind. They never saw me. And when I fired, the Zero just exploded because my bullets were incendiary and the gas tank behind the pilot blew up. You never saw them again. It's obvious when they're on fire that they're finished.

In such fights, you're not only flying the airplane, you're shooting six guns. It isn't just flying skill that counts. It was also marksmanship.

The next tour after that, we were flying along in an overcast of 800 feet after we'd come back from an aborted mission. We were flying at about 500 feet and you can imagine what these Japanese thought, with eight Corsairs, passing 300 to 400 feet over them.

About a minute or two later, my engine quit. I tried to turn on the other fuel pump and check the tanks. Before that time, I'd always thought, *If something happens, do I want to make a water landing or bail out?* Well, at 500 feet I didn't have any choice about bailing out. So it was going to be a water landing. But the engine quit and the airplane slowed down, and when I hit the ocean, water gets right up to my windshield. Naturally I try to get out. I climb onto the wing, jump off into the water, and the airplane disappears. That's how fast it was.

And my friend Ed Harper starts circling to see that his buddy was okay, and calls for some assistance. In about an hour a boat came out, picked me up, and took me to shore. There was an auxiliary field there, and another Army plane came and flew me back to base.

✪ MARINE FIGHTER SQUADRON VMF-214
CAPE TOROKINA BEACHHEAD
EMPRESS AUGUSTA BAY, BOUGAINVILLE
27 DECEMBER 1943
0940 HOURS LOCAL

In mid-November, U.S. Marine Raiders from the 3rd Infantry Division finally landed at Bougainville, where the Japanese least expected. They were followed by 34,000 Marines and Army troops, who, having bypassed the enemy garrisons on the south coast, sailed halfway up the western side of the island before going ashore just north of Empress Augusta Bay at Cape Torokina.

The bulk of the Japanese forces in Rabaul, far to the south, needed time to move troops and equipment across the island to hold back the Americans. By that time, the Seabees—with the help of an engineer brigade from New Zealand—had finished two airstrips while the infantry established a

The Black Sheep Squadron in front of a Corsair on Vella Lavella.

secure beachhead. The Allies were actually making some headway when the Japanese finally came up from the south.

Combat on Bougainville was terrible, with the jungle and terrain even worse and more unforgiving than those on Guadalcanal.

By the time Bougainville was partially secured, Major Boyington and the squadron had returned from R & R to the forward base at Vella Lavella. There, Boyington learned that he had nineteen new men to train. But Pappy wanted a more challenging target than Bougainville and suggested the fortified Japanese base at Rabaul. His old friend General "Nuts" Moore gave him the go-ahead.

On 17 December 1943, Boyington led the first single-engine fighter sweep across Rabaul. The Japanese forces at Rabaul had been steadily worn down by Allied bombing and strafing attacks, by both MacArthur's air force and the Black Sheep Squadron. This day Pappy Boyington's pilots would be up against more than two hundred Zeros and their pilots, who knew how to fight the Marine Corsairs.

The Japanese shot down six Black Sheep pilots on their first two runs on Rabaul. But at the end of the day Boyington alone had a total of twenty kills to his credit—just six fewer than the American record held by Joe Foss and Eddie Rickenbacker. On 23 December he knocked down four more, closing the gap even more.

A press corps interviewer asked Pappy if any Japanese planes showed up to attack the Black Sheep Squadron. He replied, "Yes, there were a number of Japanese planes that came up over there . . . and we got all we could in dogfights. And I saw eight other planes destroyed besides the four I destroyed myself."

The next night, at a base Christmas party, he boasted, "They can't kill me. If you ever see me with thirty Zeros on my tail, don't worry. I'll be all right. I'll meet you six months after the war in a bar in San Diego and we'll all have a drink for old time's sake."

Ten days later, Major Gregory "Pappy" Boyington was shot down in a running gun battle in the skies just off the coast of Rabaul. But he didn't go quietly. Before his plane disappeared into the sea, he was seen burning another enemy Zero—his twenty-fifth—one short of the all-time record.

Boyington's disappearance created a press and public relations frenzy. Rumors were rampant. The *New York Times* reported that Major Boyington was alive on an island, hidden by natives and waiting to rejoin the squadron. There were other guesses as to what happened. None of the stories about his disappearance were true.

No one but the Japanese knew that Pappy Boyington had been shot down and picked up in the water by a Japanese sub. He was taken to Japan and only resurfaced at the war's end, when his name showed up on a list of American POWs.

The Marine Black Sheep Squadron fell apart after its leader had been missing in action for several months. VMF-214 was officially disbanded in March 1944. The men of the formerly tight-knit squadron went their separate ways. Some returned home to the U.S. for duty while others were reassigned to other units in the Pacific.

MacArthur and Halsey—with the help of the Black Sheep—had effectively isolated the Japanese on Rabaul. Cut off from supplies or evacuation and virtually abandoned by their leaders, Rabaul's garrison of more than 100,000 Imperial troops were allowed—in the words of Admiral Halsey—to "wither on the vine." From early 1944 to the end of the war in August 1945 the garrison received no food, supplies, or reinforcements.

When Japanese commanders surrendered Rabaul after the war, among the 101,000 troops still on the island fortress were five divisions commanded by nineteen army generals and eleven admirals of the Imperial Navy contingent.

Makin

Gilbert

Marakei

Abaiang

Tarawa

Maiana

Apamama

Kuria

Nonouti

Beru

Nikunau

Tabiteuea

Tanyah

Tamana

Islands

Arorae

Buariki

Taratai

Abaokoro

Marenanuka

LAGOON

Nabeina

Tabiteuea

Abatao

Buota

Bikeman

Betio

Bonriki

Tarawa

Eita

Bikenibeu

Bairiki

Teaoraereke

Naanikai

TARAWA ATOLL

HILL
II
MARINES

20 Nov., 1943

CENTRAL PIER

20 Nov., 1943

LANDING BEACHES

21 Nov., 1943

23 Nov., 1943

BETIO ISLAND

CHAPTER 11
BLOODY TARAWA
(NOVEMBER 1943)

✪ **USS MARYLAND, FLAGSHIP, U.S. 5TH AMPHIBIOUS FORCE**
TARAWA, BETIO ISLAND
20 NOVEMBER 1943
0800 HOURS LOCAL

As Rear Admiral Harry Hill watched from the bridge of his flagship, the largest amphibious assault yet tried in the Pacific was finally under way. Called Operation Galvanic, it aimed to capture the Gilbert Islands in the first phase of a new central Pacific offensive—a strategy long advocated by Admiral Chester Nimitz and bitterly opposed by General Douglas MacArthur.

The long struggle to isolate and neutralize Rabaul had built support in Washington for Nimitz's plan. And though MacArthur believed that the road to Tokyo had to go through the Philippines, everyone else was looking for a way to avoid more of the long, bloody battles like those fought in the steaming, mountainous jungles of New Guinea and Guadalcanal.

Operation Cartwheel, the two-pronged Allied approach toward Rabaul launched in the aftermath of Yamamoto's demise, had been a difficult but resounding success. By the end of October 1943, troops from MacArthur's southwest Pacific command had moved well up the northeast coast of New Guinea and were preparing to land at Cape Gloucester on New Britain. Halsey's South Pacific forces had made parallel progress up through the Russell Islands, Munda, Vella Lavella and Choiseul. On 1 November, the 3rd Marine Division and the Army's 37th Division landed on Bougainville.

These engagements were fought as conventional land battles, supported by Navy cruiser/destroyer surface action groups and land-based Army, Navy, and Marine aircraft. While Halsey was slugging his way to the northwest, his lack of carriers forced him to seize and build little island airstrips.

Admiral Harry Hill

General George Kenney, commanding MacArthur's 5th Air Force, was building a virtual air armada of first-rate, land-based Army Air Force fighters and bombers supported by hundreds of transport aircraft. By the fall of 1943, Kenney's airmen were ranging hundreds of miles from Australia and Papua, attacking Japanese ships, bases, troop concentrations, and supply depots at will. On 2 November, Kenney sent seventy-five B-25 Mitchell bombers and eighty P-38 Lightnings to raid Rabaul itself, sinking more than a dozen Japanese ships, damaging twenty others, and destroying ninety-four of the emperor's planes in the air. On the ground, American losses totaled eight B-25s and nine P-38s.

That same night, in the Battle of Empress Augusta Bay, U.S. cruisers commanded by Admiral Stanton Merrill and a destroyer division led by Captain Arleigh Burke turned away a Japanese counter-invasion force of cruisers, destroyers, and transports attempting to interdict General Vandegrift's amphibious landing on Bougainville. The following day, Admiral Halsey sent carrier aircraft from *Saratoga* and the light carrier USS *Princeton* to bomb the Japanese fleet anchored at Rabaul. On 11 November, he did it again—adding the carriers *Essex, Independence,* and *Bunker Hill*—a five-carrier raid that lasted for hours, wrecking the Japanese base.

These engagements were little noted by an American press corps focused on the bloody Allied campaign in Italy. But for the Joint Chiefs, the operations demonstrated how dramatically the balance of power had shifted in the South Pacific since the beginning of the year. Even though the war in Europe was still the first priority, with Rabaul effectively neutralized, it was finally time to start a new drive toward Japan—this time in the central Pacific.

While Halsey and MacArthur were battling their way north, determined to isolate Rabaul as they aimed for the Philippines, Nimitz had been slowly building up his forces in Hawaii. By November 1943, American industry was churning out hundreds of airplanes a day, bigger and faster ships, thousands of landing craft, and hundreds of thousands of fresh soldiers, sailors, airmen, Coast Guardsmen, and Marines.

Over MacArthur's vehement objections, Nimitz convinced the Joint Chiefs that a new drive through the central Pacific should become the main axis of attack against Japan. For MacArthur, holding tight to his goal to liberate the Philippines, it was a bitter pill to swallow. But once the Chiefs decided, they made sure that Nimitz got what he needed, particularly the new *Essex*-class fleet carriers capable of carrying more than a hundred of the latest Navy aircraft: Grumman F6F "Hellcat" fighters, Curtiss SB2C "Helldiver" bombers, and F4U "Corsairs," which the Japanese had taken to calling "Whistling Death." Nimitz also got better submarines, now equipped with new torpedoes and commanded by bolder skippers who were decimating the Japanese merchant marine fleet. By November 1943, at fleet anchorages in Pearl Harbor, Midway, and the Ellice Islands, he had nineteen carriers—light, medium, and heavy—twelve battleships, fourteen cruisers, and fifty-six destroyers.

To support and supply them—and to land his Marine and Army assault troops—Nimitz also assembled more than 200 other vessels: twenty-nine fast attack transports, scores of new LST and LSD amphibious assault ships, dozens of fleet oilers, repair ships, ocean-going tugs towing fuel barges, hospital ships, tenders, and hundreds of smaller PT boats, landing craft, and tracked amphibious assault vehicles.

With all this combat power, Nimitz was ready for Operation Galvanic. The plan called for his 5th Amphibious Force to seize three tiny atolls in the Gilberts 2,600 miles west of Hawaii, near the intersection of the equator and the International Date Line. Some described these little spits of land as "the first stop past the middle of nowhere," and they all had, like so many other places in the vast Pacific, strange-sounding names: Abemama, Makin, and Tarawa.

✪ ✪ ✪

The plan of attack approved by Nimitz was fairly simple: Fast carrier forces would isolate the three atolls from the threat of any Japanese reaction coming from Truk or the Marshalls. They would then conduct pre–D-day aerial attacks to destroy any Japanese aircraft at their seaplane base on Makin and the airfield being built on Betio Island in the Tarawa atoll.

After the battleships "softened up" fortifications ashore, Admiral Kelly Turner's 5th Amphibious Force would simultaneously storm Makin and Tarawa. The ground force, designated as the 5th Amphibious Corps, commanded by Marine Major General Holland M. Smith, consisted of the 18,000-man, reinforced 2nd Marine Division for the Tarawa assault and 6,700 soldiers of the Army's 27th Infantry Division to secure Makin, 100

National Archives

Major General Holland M. Smith

miles to the north. The U.S. submarine *Nautilus* would land a Marine rifle company on lightly defended Abemama. It would be the only part of Operation Galvanic that went according to plan.

On 13 November, B-24 Liberators of the 7th Air Force began a weeklong series of bombing raids to "soften up" both Makin and Tarawa. Then, the night before the landings, seven battleships and nine cruisers began pounding both Makin and Betio in a pre-assault bombardment unlike anything ever tried before by the U.S. Navy. Everyone, including the Marines watching offshore, assumed that it would be enough to pulverize the defenses ashore. They were wrong.

The man Tokyo entrusted to defend the Gilbert Islands, forty-nine-year-old Rear Admiral Keiji Shibasaki, commanded a mixed force of 2,900 elite naval infantrymen (similar to our Marines), about 1,500 armed construction troops (like the U.S. Navy's Seabees), and 1,500 conscripted Korean laborers. He dispatched 284 of the naval infantry and about 500 of the construction troops and laborers to Makin. The rest, about 4,000 in all, were packed into bunkers and revetments on the narrow two-mile spit of land called Betio Island at the south end of Tarawa atoll—where the British had started an airstrip before Japan seized the Gilberts on 7 December 1941.

By the time Admiral Hill and his Marines arrived offshore, Shibasaki and his troops had been working on the Betio defenses and airstrip for months. He had once asserted that his troops could "hold Tarawa against a million Americans for a hundred years." They built massive concrete blockhouses, bunkers covered with six feet of coconut logs and sand, dug sheltered trench lines

Admiral Keiji Shibasaki

and tank traps, and constructed more than 400 mutually supporting bombproof gun emplacements and machine gun positions. His shore-based artillery, manned by instructors from the Imperial Artillery School, boasted eight-inch, five-inch, and smaller caliber naval guns and mortars—all with pre-registered targets on the coral reef surrounding Betio.

And Shibasaki knew what the Americans did not: The coral reef was itself a formidable natural barrier that would prevent almost any landing craft from crossing at any time other than a very high tide. To make matters worse for the Americans, the naval planners in Pearl Harbor decided to conduct Operation Galvanic during a "neap tide"—the time of month when the alignment of the sun, moon, and Earth create lower than usual tides. For the Marines going ashore on Betio, it would prove to be a very costly error.

✪ U.S. 5TH AMPHIBIOUS FORCE
BETIO ISLAND, TARAWA ATOLL
20 NOVEMBER 1943
1800 HOURS LOCAL

Major General Julian C. Smith, the 2nd Marine Division's commander, had insisted on a massive pre-invasion bombardment before his troops hit Betio's narrow beach. He got what he asked for. His Marines, many of them veterans of the Guadalcanal campaign, had been treated to a pre-dawn breakfast of steak and eggs and were circling outside the reef in their landing craft and LVTs when the sixteen-inch guns of the battleships and the cruisers' eight-inch guns had opened up at 0500. The ear-shattering barrage

Major General Julian C. Smith

went on for more than an hour as more than 2,500 tons of high-explosive shells rained down on the little island. Then, at 0610, the naval gunfire lifted so the carrier aircraft could deliver another 900 tons of bombs and strafe the landing beaches. After the dive-bombers and fighters finished their work, the naval gunfire resumed again until 0845, when Admiral Hill ordered a cease-fire for fear of hitting the LVTs and Higgins boats as the men of the assault wave headed for their landing beaches.

To the Marines headed toward the beach and the pilots flying overhead, it looked as if the entire island was on fire. The wooden barracks, equipment sheds, and Shibasaki's headquarters building were blasted into splinters and burning. Huge billows of black smoke and suspended particles of sand were blasted into the air by the shells and bombs, and the cloud drifted a mile into the sky.

Unfortunately, the first three assault waves—using 125 LVTs—took much longer than expected to make it across the coral reef. As soon as the destroyers stopped firing, the Japanese defenders rushed back to their guns, raking the tracked amphibians as they crawled up onto and across the reef where the water was only two or three feet deep. Few of them made it to the beach unscathed. Worse still, all the LCMs and LCVPs carrying the fourth, fifth, and sixth waves for Red Beaches One and Two ground to a halt 600 to 1,000 yards offshore, forcing the Marines to disembark and wade through chest-high water under heavy machine gun and mortar fire. In many places, the water was even deeper. At Red Beach Three, those who made it to the beach were exposed to withering fire from Japanese gunners hidden in the pilings of the long pier jutting out into the lagoon.

For the Marines who had watched the pre-landing bombardment and finally made it to the beach, the results of that volume of enemy fire was unbelievable. It seemed like the only thing those thousands of tons of munitions had done was to push a little sand around and cut down a few palm trees.

Twelve miles offshore, General Smith and Rear Admiral Hill waited for a situation report aboard the flagship USS *Maryland*. But most of the radios that the assault waves had taken with them had been soaked during the reef crossing and were now useless. It was only after Colonel David M. Shoup, the assault commander, managed to get up to the seawall and find a dry radio did they realize the magnitude of the carnage on the beach. Smith immediately committed the division's reserves to the fight, sending in another 1,100 Marines. By 1800, nearly 5,200 exhausted troops were ashore—most of them in two widely separated pockets—and almost a third of them casualties. One of those who had made it was Lieutenant Don Lillibridge from Mitchell, South Dakota.

□   □   □

SECOND LIEUTENANT DON LILLIBRIDGE, USMC
Betio Island, Tarawa Atoll
20 November 1943
2300 Hours Local

I was a lieutenant in A Company, 1st Battalion, 2nd Marines. I was the youngest officer in the battalion, just turned twenty-two, but I had thirty-nine men in my rifle platoon who were seventeen, eighteen, and nineteen years old, so they were a lot younger. I'd never been away from home in my life and I was very inexperienced.

We loaded up, and after we were on board, we were told where we were going. Nobody had ever heard of Tarawa or knew where it was. I saw the stuff on the map and it was just little dots in the middle of the Pacific Ocean. A captain assigned all of us replacement officers to different units.

Tarawa was my first battle. In the dark you could see the naval shells streaking red through the sky onto the island. And following all the explosions after the aerial and naval bombardment of the island, we assumed that there would probably be nothing left. It just didn't seem possible that there could be anybody left alive on the place.

National Archives

Marines at Tarawa

When we hit the reef and started to go up over it, we were hit by machine gun fire. I remember a bullet came through the Amtrac because it wasn't armored. It passed between my dungarees and my backpack. I could feel the heat as it went through. And I thought, *Maybe I've been hit!* But it was a fraction off—if it hadn't been, it would've shattered my spine—so I was lucky.

We hit the beach and all leaped out. I jumped out first, by the seawall, and on the very narrow beach were bodies everywhere—in the water, floating on the water, and on the little beach. My guys were jammed up against the seawall for protection against enemy fire.

I leaped up over the seawall and I just took off inland. And they all came after me. But the Marines who followed us, about two or three minutes later, all got shot, just wiped out. I ran inland until I came to this large, twenty-by-twenty-foot depression in the sand, about two or three feet deep. And there were guys in there, and facing me with his back to the wall was Lieutenant Seeley.

He looked at me and said, "Lilly...I faced death eleven times today."

One of the curious things about Tarawa was, you almost never saw the enemy. They were in the bunkers, and they were firing at you and you were firing at them. The only way to get them out—as it turned out—was when a handful of Sherman tanks got ashore.

There was this big structure built with coconut palms and concrete. It must've been thick because it was very solid. It hadn't been destroyed by the naval bombardment and I saw it had a huge aperture about a foot high and about four feet long. This tank came up and I pointed to it. He rolled right up to it, stuck the muzzle right up into the opening, and fired a couple rounds. That's the kind of thing, plus the flame-throwers that the combat engineers, the flame-thrower demolition outfit, used on the bunkers. The flame-throwers didn't just burn people; they also sucked all the oxygen out of these structures, and the people inside suffocated.

Marines using a flame-thrower on Betio.

Since many of the Japanese were killed in their bunkers, most of the bodies all over the island by the end of the battle were Marines. So many were killed just trying to get on the beach. And that held true for the second day as well.

That experience was a devastating shock. It was the single most traumatic event I've ever experienced in my life. I lost twenty-six of the thirty-nine men in my platoon. By the third night, I was the only officer left in the company, which was about the size of my original platoon

Tarawa was so small that you could stand on one side and see over to the other side, from the lagoon to the ocean. It was 800 yards wide at the widest point, and then tapered down to about four feet at the east end. It was about two and a half miles long. That's what made the battle so unusual—its tiny size and all this concentrated fury.

I didn't get across the island until the morning of the third day. Bodies were everywhere: a hand here, an arm there, a leg, a shattered torso. A head, even.

Well, even though I had another battle ahead of me, Tarawa was the first one, and it's the impact of losing so many guys that I think really lasted throughout my whole life. None of this occurs at the time of the battle, you understand. This effect and the impact of it all comes after the battle is over.

✪ HQ 2ND MARINE DIVISION
USS MARYLAND
5 MILES WEST OF BETIO ISLAND, TARAWA ATOLL
20 NOVEMBER 1943
1830 HOURS LOCAL

With four battalions of his 2nd Division ashore, General Julian Smith and his staff sought ways to break the bloody deadlock. Once darkness fell, the shooting stopped almost entirely. An expected Japanese counter-attack never materialized because the communications wires connecting Admiral Shibasaki with his subordinate commanders had all been cut by the furious bombardment and the gunfights earlier in the day.

Exhausted Marines from intermingled units held onto their positions in three-to-five-man foxholes dug in the soft sand or in shell holes and bomb craters created by the pre-landing bombardment. On the beach, Navy medical corpsmen continued to load wounded into LVTs, shuttling them back out to the ships. On their return trips to the beach the Amtracs brought in 75 mm howitzers, mortars, ammunition, fresh working radios, and water for the terribly dehydrated Marines.

As the night wore on, LCVPs and LCMs that had made it across the reef at high tide were policing up bodies and equipment floating in the lagoon. Among the salvage officers engaged in this grisly task was movie star Eddie Albert. Now a lieutenant (jg), he had volunteered for the Navy after Pearl Harbor and was serving as a small boat officer on the USS *Sheridan*, a transport anchored offshore.

At thirty-three, Albert was likely one of the oldest lieutenants in the Navy. He could have been in Hollywood making training movies. Instead, he went to Officers' Candidate School, got his commission, and was assigned as a salvage officer off Betio.

During the operation he made twenty-six trips bringing back the wounded from Betio. On one of his forays into the seawall, he picked up a wounded Japanese officer. He told how it happened: "There were piles of dead and wounded and I was in the mess . . . and a Japanese was among the wounded . . . standing up. And I thought, 'Well, he's the only Japanese that knows what is going on. Maybe I could get him up to our ship.' He's the only Japanese that the interrogators had to talk to—the rest of them were dead."

Eddie Albert said that the multiple trips to the beach were just part of "doing his job." But he was awarded the Bronze Star for valor. One of those who believe he deserved it is Dean Ladd, a rifle platoon commander who spent much of the night of 20 November circling offshore in the lagoon, waiting to get ashore and help his pinned-down comrades. Ladd was only twenty-two but already a combat veteran of Guadalcanal by the time he reached Tarawa.

▯ ▯ ▯

LIEUTENANT DEAN LADD, USMC
Betio Island, Tarawa Atoll
21 November 1943
0845 Hours Local

We knew we were moving out; we didn't know where until about the first of October 1942. We were put into the line battalions and started training as a unit against snipers and the things that we'd learned from what was going on in Guadalcanal. In the process, I went to Officers' School, which they did with a lot of us who had combat experience to see if we had the necessary leadership ability in high-stress situations. Many of the NCOs became officers. I was one of those. As corporal I got a field commission and a week or two later we got the mission to go to Guadalcanal.

I joined a green unit that hadn't been in combat. We were there on Guadalcanal three months. We made our last drive to shove the Japanese off the island as they started to withdraw. They fought a real rear guard action. We were just continually being whittled down. A lot of it was from sickness, malaria. I had four men killed and three wounded on Guadalcanal. When we finally drove the Japanese off the island, we had no idea what our next mission was going to be.

I was twenty-two, almost twenty-three. I was leading guys who were seventeen, eighteen. Some had joined the Marine Corps when they were sixteen, having lied about their age.

The Japanese decided that Tarawa was going to be defended. They brought in a lot of concrete, cut down coconut trees, and put in some of the thickest-walled bunkers you can imagine. They put in eight-inch naval turret guns. They had rifle pits and a seawall all the way around made of coconut logs that were about four feet high. And then, spaced between the riflemen in the pits, were hundreds of machine guns. Well, we were led to believe that our naval gunfire would pretty well obliterate that place. But it didn't.

As we got into our LCVPs, each holding a platoon—roughly thirty men—we didn't have any communication. Because of the disruption, we didn't get the final word of where we were to land until our battalion commander came by in his LCVP and said, "We're landing on Red Beach Two," which turns out was the worst one—it was right in the crossfire.

I was the first one out when we got to the reef, yelling, "Come on, let's go, follow me." And I start wading as fast as I could. I looked back and the men were kind of slow getting out, a little reluctant. I said, "Come on, let's go," a couple more times and then the next thing I know, I'm hit. The Japanese got me with a machine gun, firing at us from the right flank. I was around 600 yards out in the water when I was hit very seriously in the abdomen. And course nobody's supposed to stop for the wounded. Everybody's got to keep going. But one of my men, Private Sullivan, started to drag me over to one of these landing craft where the ramp was down. Eddie Albert, the famous movie actor, had brought one of the LCVPs to pick up the wounded. There were about twenty or more of us already hit.

Guys still in the water shoved us up over the ramp, and we rolled down inside, and I was in agony by that time. And someone says, "You're gonna make it."

I was the first one on the operating table on the *Sheridan*. There were two surgeons, and the one who operated on me had been an abdominal specialist at the Mayo Clinic. What a fortunate chain of events: One of my men disobeyed orders and dragged me to safety, Eddie Albert was there to take me to the ship, and a surgeon who was an abdominal specialist at the Mayo Clinic was there to treat me. Amazing!

□ □ □

✪ 2ND MARINE DIVISION
BETIO ISLAND, TARAWA ATOLL
21 NOVEMBER 1943
0900 HOURS LOCAL

By dawn on D+1, the full magnitude of the D-Day carnage was evident. More than 1,500 U.S. Marines were either dead, wounded, or MIA.

On the morning of D+1, the Corps reserve, which had been circling in the lagoon for most of the night, landed to reinforce the beachhead. The troops were fatigued, seasick, and most hadn't eaten. Nevertheless, they waded on to the beach while taking tremendous casualties. The new battalions used the 500-yard-long pier between Red Beaches Two and Three as cover to ward off at least some of the enemy rifle and machine gun fire.

Among those reinforcements was Marine Reservist Harry Niehoff from Portland, Oregon, who had trained on the use of a flame-thrower. He would put that training to the test on Tarawa. Lieutenant Michael Ryan had grown up in St. Vincent's Orphanage in Kansas, joined the Marine Corps Reserves, gone to Guadalcanal, and at age twenty-seven was known as "the old man" by his buddies. By the time he reached New Zealand to prepare for the Tarawa invasion, he was the commander of L Company.

□ □ □

CORPORAL HARRY NIEHOFF, USMC
Betio Island, Tarawa Atoll
22 November 1943
1120 Hours Local

When I was at Tarawa I was considered a combat engineer, attached to a line company with the 8th Marines. I had a flame-throwing demolition team of five members. We were to do whatever the 8th Marines wanted us to take care of.

My primary job was demolition but I also trained on the flame-thrower. We used diesel fuel as the main fuel instead of gasoline. Then you had the igniter, just like a cigarette lighter. When you pressed that igniter, the air pressure in the middle tank forced the diesel fuel through and you had ignition. A huge flame bellowed out.

Later in the war, when they developed napalm, they took that and mixed fuel with the napalm gelatin, and that's where you got the straight shots coming out rather than the billowing flame. But at Tarawa, we used strictly the diesel.

I had never heard of Tarawa before. It was something brand-new to me. It was just another atoll in the Pacific Islands.

When we arose on D-Day, we heard the bombardment already taking place. As time went on and daylight came, it was quite clear, and then the big battleships started to let go. We could really hear them—they made a noise all their own. It was quite impressive.

When we approached, we all looked at what we could see of the island. All you could see was just a little dark streak on the horizon. And you'd see all the smoke coming up and the bombs and shells hitting it. Someone said, "Boy, they're really getting it! There won't be anybody left. They'll sink the island."

Then all of a sudden we started to hear the whine of the shells coming toward us.

We had a job on our hands. I think everybody must have thought, "I don't know about this trip. This is going to be a tough one." And when we got there almost all of the Marines who had landed earlier were killed, and we were killing Japanese in hand-to-hand combat.

I was originally assigned to F Company. But the Amtrac landed at the wrong place and I ended up with E Company. I tried to find F Company, but they had all been shot. There was no unit there!

All the officers had already been killed. I was told, "When you come ashore, you'll be assigned to this platoon. Your job is to take care of that bunker."

We found out later that "that bunker" provided the electricity for the island. So I thought that was going to be my team's job, so we went right to it and tried to figure out what to do. Well you couldn't go around the right side or the left side.

There was only one way and that was to go straight up. The bunker was twenty-five or thirty feet high. And it was covered with sand, so if you tried to climb up the side of the bunker, which we were trying, the sand would just cascade out from under you and you'd start sliding down.

Lieutenant Alex Bonnyman, who led the Pioneer Platoon, had been there since the day before. He rallied us and tried to help us. He knew what we were trying to do. He said that they needed to get that bunker taken. But it was still a barrier. No one could get over or around it.

Behind the bunker was a Japanese command post. So there was a lot of manpower and a lot of rifles. So any move you made around there, somebody was sure to pick you off. And then Lieutenant Bonnyman yelled out for everybody to go over to the top. He was next to me and turned around to yell to get more demolitions. At that moment he was hit, and he fell dead. I expected to be hit next because we were side by side.

I was out of ammunition and demolitions. So I came back down, went over to the supply point, picked up some TNT, and came back to the bunker. I was prepared to charge and a major said, "I want you to be careful, that Jap's already killed five men."

My hair stood straight up on the back of my neck. I got down alongside the pillbox and we made our charges with four blocks of TNT. Each block was just about two and a half inches square by five inches long, so I had a five-inch square package of TNT taped together.

I lit the fuse. When I reached around to push it through the rifle slot, I found out the rifle slot was only about three inches wide. But I had a package that was five inches square and I didn't know what to do with it except drop it and take cover. The charge didn't kill the man in the bunker, but it opened up the slot. And before I knew it, one of my men came up beside me and put another charge in. That took care of it.

The devastation on Tarawa was quite horrific. Crossfire went in every direction. Troops who went in got shot at from the front and from the side. The men were just dying by the hundreds. We had dead and wounded Marines in the water. We had the wounded on the beaches that we couldn't get to. There was no way to get them. If you went out to try to help them, which many of the Marines did, you might wind up being shot yourself. But the guys did it anyway. They would try to get anybody they could.

Tarawa was really the worst.

□   □   □

MAJOR MICHAEL RYAN, USMC
Betio Island, Tarawa Atoll
22 November 1943
1650 Hours Local

I came on active duty as a Marine second lieutenant, a platoon leader, and we were sent out to join the 1st Marine Division.

We didn't land on Guadalcanal. We landed to the north on two small islands—Gavutu-Tanambogo—that formed the Japanese seaplane base. That was my introduction to operations and to combat.

The Japanese had made a counter-attack and overran the Marines there. When I got there you could see Japanese bodies all over the ground. None of our guys had seen combat but they did well.

I was promoted to first lieutenant. Within a couple of months I was promoted to captain and made a company commander. After a while we were ordered to Guadalcanal itself, and participated in a number of operations there. We moved from Guadalcanal and were on our way to Fiji when we heard that we were going to a place called Tarawa.

I was hoping that Tarawa would be a short operation. We thought that it would be relatively easy, because we were told the tonnage of bombs that were going to be used and how much the ships were going to fire. We heard that the bombardment would go on for four or five hours. We were to land in boats, form in the center of the beach, and await orders. Our orders were to go as far as we could in the boats, and if we couldn't get over the reef, to wait for the tractors to come back and then go in.

Well, from where we were sitting it didn't look like any tractors would get back out again. Implied in the order was, "Get in the best way you can." And that's what we planned to do.

The tractor right in front of my boat was on fire. But all the Marines were out—I thought—until two Marines climbed up on the side with their clothing on fire. I could see when they fell that they'd probably died before they hit the water.

We got out and started to walk in, and it's about 1,300 yards to the beach. By the time we got there, K Company was ashore. And so was what was left of I Company. When we got out and started in, other casualties were in the water. You didn't know whether they were dead or wounded.

When I and K Companies landed, they moved behind the seawall. When I got over the parapet, Captain Crane came over and said, "Captain Tatem was killed. Lieutenant Turner has taken over I Company. That was the one that got so shot up over there."

If the Japanese didn't kick us off the island, they were going to lose it. We fully expected the battalion headquarters to come in with more troops, but they didn't show up, and so I became the battalion commander.

Regimental headquarters now consisted of a major—me—and a runner. Everyone else was dead or wounded and there were no radios. We could see that the 2nd Battalion was advancing on Red Beach Two. But we had no way of knowing how far they got in or how many of them were there. Nor did we know where regimental headquarters or battalion headquarters were. We couldn't get in touch with them. It was late in the afternoon that it suddenly dawned on us that the battalion commander wasn't going to get in. We thought he must've been killed. We called "fire!" only once, when we were certain that we had a place that they could fire without hitting friendlies.

The tanks came in late afternoon. As I recall, there were two tanks. But one tank had a disabled main gun. Gradually people turned to me for orders, simply because I was the senior person there. I formed a defensive position inward from the point, and we waited out the night. Our only radio had gotten wet and no longer worked. Out on board our ships they probably wondered what was happening over on the island. But they didn't know how they could get anything to me.

Troops came in from the One and Six. They had cover for their landing and spent the night on the beach with us, then moved out the next day. They took their tanks with them and started reducing the rest of Green Beach.

Many NCOs were okay. Some had been killed, of course. Now each platoon was checking its own rosters.

A wounded sergeant came up and saluted. You're not supposed to salute in combat. But that was one salute I was going to return, no matter what.

I told him where the aid station was; he didn't leave. He kept getting his people into position. He wasn't from our unit. I think he might have come from another battalion on our left.

Whether he lived through the operation, I don't know. I never saw him again.

Watching the men trying to get in, under that heavy fire, that was the worst. It's difficult to sit there and watch people being cut up

Did we learn anything in the Battle of Tarawa? Yeah, I think we did, because at the next operation, they had a greater, longer bombardment. And they did it methodically. They checked to see if there was a position, and then they would fire their big guns. And they did it for a couple of days.

And they had more tractors so that the landing was easier, unlike ours. I think that those changes came from what we saw at Tarawa.

✪ 2ND MARINE DIVISION COMMAND POST
BETIO ISLAND, TARAWA ATOLL
23 NOVEMBER 1943
1730 HOURS LOCAL

Mike Ryan assembled the remnants of two battalions and organized a charge that effectively eliminated Japanese resistance on the western end of the island. General Julian Smith came ashore and established his command post in what had been one of Admiral Shibasaki's command bunkers. Unbeknownst to the Marines, the Japanese commander was already dead. When he and his staff had moved to a secondary command post on the south side of the island, a sharp-eyed Marine had spotted them. With a radio finally dried out and working, the Marine had alerted a destroyer just outside the reef. The Navy responded instantly, firing salvo after salvo over the heads of Marines in the open. They scored a direct hit, killing Shibasaki, his chief of staff, his gunnery officers, and his operations officer. It probably changed the course of the battle.

On the night of 22–23 November, the now leaderless Japanese launched three futile and uncoordinated counter-attacks. The Marines, now better supplied, mowed them down. As the battle entered its third day of fighting, additional troops were landed across Green Beach and came ashore without opposition.

With most of the airfield now in Marine hands, General Smith ordered his weary troops to clear the Japanese pocket that still held between Red Beaches Two and Three and to conduct a sweep east down the narrow length of the island. As they were preparing to do so, a message to Tokyo from the remaining Japanese defenders was intercepted by Navy codebreakers: OUR WEAPONS ARE DESTROYED. FROM NOW ON EVERYONE WILL ATTEMPT A FINAL CHARGE. MAY JAPAN EXIST FOR TEN THOUSAND YEARS.

Only thirteen Japanese were captured, most of them wounded or unconscious, and about a hundred Korean slave laborers gave themselves up. That afternoon, shortly after 1300 on 23 November 1943, General Smith declared that organized resistance had ended on Tarawa atoll.

But the Battle for the Gilbert Islands wasn't quite over. On Makin atoll, a hundred miles north of Tarawa, the poorly prepared soldiers of the 27th Division had taken two days longer than expected to secure tiny Butaritari Island. Though there were fewer than 400 enemy combatants on the little spit of sand, the 6,000 American soldiers had suffered sixty-four killed and 152 wounded. Another forty-three U.S. sailors had been killed and nineteen wounded in the pre–H-Hour bombardment when a turret exploded on the battleship *Mississippi*. By the afternoon of 23 November all but one of the Japanese defenders were dead and 104 construction workers and Korean laborers were captives. Unfortunately, things were about to get worse for the Americans.

Early on 24 November, while the Navy waited impatiently for the Army to backload onto their waiting transports, a Japanese submarine slipped through the destroyer screen around Makin atoll and sent a torpedo into the side of the carrier escort *Liscome Bay*. She blew up immediately, taking 650 of her 900 men to the bottom.

The following day, American and British flags were raised and flown over Tarawa. However, there was still the grim task of burying the dead. Some 6,000 men—5,000 of them Japanese defenders—lay dead on this tiny island atoll on the equator, their corpses strewn across an area smaller than the Pentagon and its parking lots. More than 1,000 Marines had been killed and about 1,500 wounded.

Later, when Admiral Nimitz toured the island he remarked that it was the first time that he had actually smelled death. He was likewise astounded that most of the Japanese bunkers, pillboxes, and gun emplacements seemed to be only lightly damaged despite the initial furious naval and aerial bombardments.

Nimitz directed that detailed architectural drawings of all the fortifications be made and had exact replicas of the Japanese defenses constructed on the naval gunnery range at Kailavi. He then insisted that every destroyer, cruiser, and battleship heading into the western Pacific pass a test of destroying these fortifications.

Marine Corps combat cameraman Sergeant Norman Hatch had a ring-side seat for the battle and documented it through the lens of his motion picture camera.

▢   ▢   ▢

SERGEANT NORMAN HATCH, USMC
Betio Island, Tarawa Atoll
24 November 1943
1745 Hours Local

My position on Tarawa was that of a combat motion picture cameraman. My responsibility was to document what went on in the course of the battle as best I could. And that's said with some reservation, because at that time, what we were doing was brand spanking new. No one had ever photographed an amphibious landing against a well-fortified enemy. Realizing that, I knew that I had a great deal of responsibility.

The only thing that I didn't know was that I was going to be the only motion picture cameraman on the beach for the first day and a half. All the rest of them were stuck in the boats and couldn't get ashore.

There was so much going on that I didn't have any difficulty finding subjects to shoot. The way that the Japanese had zeroed in on the reef was the big obstacle for the boats. It was devastating. It seemed like every time a boat would come in that morning and drop its ramp on the reef, a shell would land right in the middle of the boat, which would hit just about everybody and sink the boat.

The commanding officer of the battalion that I was accompanying, Major Jim Crowe, wasn't due to go in until the fourth, fifth, and sixth waves of troops were in. But there was a machine gunner shooting at the amphibious tractors as they were coming in, forcing them to go to the right. They could only go so far because there was a pier there.

The Marines were bunched up, and when Major Crowe saw this, he said, "I don't like it. I'm losing my beachhead." That meant it would be difficult for other boats or Amtracs to get in.

So he said, "Put this damn boat in right now!" Well, the coxswain gunned it, and we went in and hit the reef 600 yards off shore, and stopped cold. Then the ramp wouldn't go down in the front. That meant everybody in the boat, some thirty or forty guys, had to get up over the sides of the boat. The sides of the boat were about shoulder height for a six-foot-tall man.

With sixty or seventy pounds of gear it was difficult to get up over that, much less drop into the water up to your chest, and keep your equilibrium.

Well, it was done. I had an assistant with me, Bill "Kelly" Kelleher. He carried two canisters of film and I carried two. We couldn't fall into the water, because it would have ruined the equipment.

The men who had gone out ahead of us were now dog-paddling in the water, and all you could see were their helmets.

There were snipers under the pier, and that had me really worried, because I had to stay upright. I was probably too good a target. But neither Kelleher nor I got hit.

It's difficult to walk in water; there's too much resistance. The only thing that enabled us to do it was the fact that we had so much weight on our bodies that we were able to stay upright and keep walking.

When we got in we were exhausted. We fell into a shell hole for a few minutes and right above me, to my left, was a guy who got his right buttock shot off and was unconscious. Shock had set in. The corpsman had taken care of him, and I realized then that this was a very dangerous situation.

There wasn't much chaos on the beach at that time. Everybody was digging in, trying to make sure that they had themselves protected.

Kelly and I shared a shell hole. We dug it out, and the division chaplain came along and asked me if I'd dig a hole for him because he was busy ministering to people.

The Japanese went for the amphibious tractors that were stuck out on the reef. They just swam out there in the night and got in. In the morning, they shot at us from our backside.

Early on I figured out that I could not carry a weapon over my shoulder and a camera at the same time. Lieutenant Colonel Tom Colly, the intelligence officer, agreed with us and he got the quartermaster to issue pistols to the photo section.

Before the landing Major Crowe said, "I don't want any damn Hollywood cameramen with me."

I said, "I'm not Hollywood. I've been in the Marine Corps for five years now and I've been fully trained, and I'm a sharpshooter." I told him, "I've had plenty of training, and I can bend down and pick up a rifle any time I need it."

He finally said, "All right, just don't get in my way." And from that time on, I was practically glued to him.

Major Bill Chamberlain, the battalion commander, came into Major Crowe's command post on the morning of the third day and said, "I'm ready to take that command post now." Chamberlain came to me and said, "Sergeant, would you like to photograph our attack on the command post?"

I said, "Yes, sir!" We had to crawl to get to this command post because the shells that our Navy was firing from the ships just sort of bounced off and we didn't want to get killed by our own navy.

We looked at it and figured that we'd more or less have to go over the top of it as well as around the sides. So we did.

The photography of those efforts and the other things that went on helped later in the training of new Marines. They had a good opportunity to see what it was really like. That was one of the major benefits of the film.

Wherever I looked, there was something to shoot. By the end of the battle, which lasted seventy-six hours, I'd only shot a little over 2,000 feet of film.

Attacking places that are well equipped for protection, like a pillbox, is very difficult. It's a two- or three-man operation. Sometimes you have to sneak up on the pillbox, crawl up to the entrance, and toss a grenade inside, or a flame-thrower will come up and put an inferno inside.

When you're taking pictures and looking through the viewfinder, you divorce yourself from everything else. The picture you're taking is the only thing of importance.

So when it was time to bring all of that film back to Washington, Frank Capra, then a major in the Army, was stationed at the Army Pictorial Center in Long Island. The Joint Chiefs of Staff asked him to come down to look at the film of Tarawa and make a film out of it.

My footage was used in the film produced for public exhibition by Warner Brothers and distributed by Universal. It was called *With the Marines at Tarawa*, and it received the Academy Award for the Most Outstanding Short Documentary for 1944.

✪ THE WHITE HOUSE
WASHINGTON, D.C.
17 DECEMBER 1943
1100 HOURS LOCAL

Norm Hatch's award-winning documentary might never have been made except for an inadvertent release of some of the footage he and his assistant, Bill "Kelly" Kelleher, had shot during those four furious days. Their 16mm negatives, rushed back to the States by zealous public affairs officers, were supposed to be subject to clearance by military censors in Washington. But

National Archives

U.S. Marine casualties at Tarawa.

when the film reached San Francisco, instead of sending it directly on for clearance, black-and-white prints several minutes long were made selectively from Hatch's black-and-white reels and from Kelleher's color footage. Fox Movietone News then distributed hundreds of these black-and-white celluloid prints to local movie theaters. The agency was never told that government censors hadn't cleared the footage.

Roosevelt was furious. The American people were stunned. On the eve of the holiday season, local movie screens were showing American war dead—not one or two, but hundreds. The Movietone narrator succinctly summed up the graphic images: "The battle of Tarawa is officially described as the most ferocious fight the Marines have ever been in. Each hour was terrifying with violence and gunfire and the hurling of grenades."

Nimitz and Vandegrift—now the senior Marine in the Pacific—importuned Admiral King, the chief of naval operations, that they had nothing to cover up and that the American people deserved to know the bitter truth about how difficult it was going to be to beat the Japanese. Roosevelt agreed, and the footage shot by Norm Hatch and Bill Kelleher was edited to produce the Academy Award–winning documentary *With the Marines at Tarawa*. And though enlistment in the Marines dropped by 35 percent for a few months, war bond sales increased dramatically.

The lessons learned in seventy-six hours at Tarawa were almost all technical and resulted in changes that would make future amphibious assaults less costly, including the biggest one in Europe: Normandy. As a result of the losses at Tarawa, the Marines received hundreds of improved LVTs equipped with heavy guns and armor. The Navy developed LCMRs—landing craft equipped with rocket launchers to provide heavy suppression fire just before the assault waves hit the beach. Better long-range waterproof radios were developed and fielded. Naval gunnery improved with new training, ammunition, and fuses. Marine and Navy carrier pilots were provided with better training and more lethal bombs—like napalm—for dealing with well-prepared defenses.

And for the Marines who would have to do it again and again and again all the way across the Pacific, the survivors of the 2nd Division's assault on Tarawa were sent as cadre to other Marine units to teach others the "lessons learned." And wherever they went, those who fought at Tarawa were greeted with awe. As one survivor said, "Every participant became a hero in spite of himself."

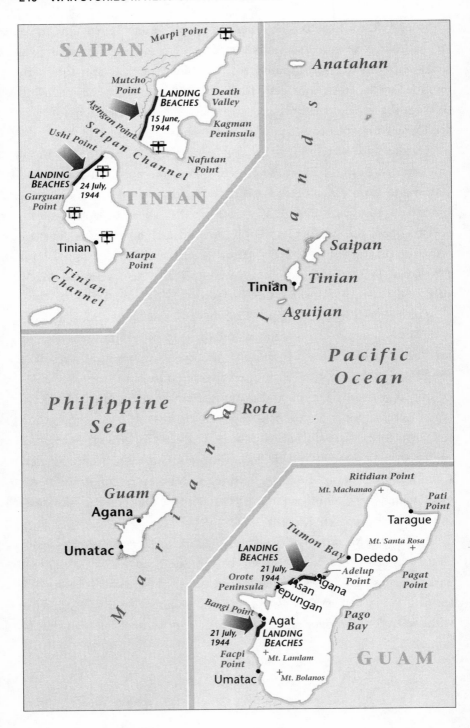

CHAPTER 12
ASSAULT ON THE MARIANAS
(JUNE–AUGUST 1944)

✪ **HQ CENTRAL PACIFIC**
PEARL HARBOR, HAWAII
11 JUNE 1944

After the horrific bloodletting on Tarawa, Major General Holland M. Smith urged Nimitz to reconsider Operation Flintlock—the invasion of the Marshall Islands—scheduled for 1 February. The plan Nimitz had approved called for simultaneous landings on Maloelap, Wotje, and Kwajalein atolls. Smith, joined by Admirals Spruance and Turner, insisted that the central Pacific forces were inadequate to seize all three Japanese bases at the same time and that a protracted period of "softening up" the three targets—with sequential assaults—would yield the same results with fewer American casualties.

Navy code-breakers and occasional long-range reconnaissance flights by PBYs flying from the Ellices, Tarawa, and Pearl Harbor confirmed what Smith, Turner, and Spruance feared. The Japanese had held the Marshalls since 1935 and were now hastily improving the defenses on all three atolls and their other outlying bases in the Marshalls: Jaluit, Mili, and Majuro. By January, there were already 5,500 Japanese troops on Kwajalein atoll and more were on the way from the Marianas and the Home Islands. Tokyo apparently believed that the Americans intended to seize the Marshalls next—and the Japanese planned to make any U.S. invasion as expensive as possible.

Nimitz was already under pressure from Washington to advance his timetable for seizing the Marianas. The Joint Chiefs wanted to use the islands as a base for a new generation of long-range bombers now coming off production lines in the U.S. The big Boeing B-29 "Superfortresses," with a 20,000-pound destructive potential that had no other rival in the air, could make the trip to Tokyo from the Marianas in under six hours.

Realizing that he would have to take the Marshalls before moving on to the Marianas, Nimitz countered his critics with a concept of operations that was even bolder than his original plan. The increasingly powerful 5th Fleet would simply bomb and isolate the Japanese garrisons on Wotje, Maloelap, Jaluit, and Mili and go straight for lightly defended Majuro and heavily protected Kwajalein atoll. Once these two bases were secured, the 5th Amphibious Force would seize Eniwetok.

This daring strategy notwithstanding, Operation Flintlock succeeded beyond anyone's expectations, save perhaps those of Nimitz himself. Starting in early January, Admiral John Hoover's land-based bombers, flying from the Ellice Islands and Tarawa, began systematic raids on all the Japanese bases in the Marshalls. Well before the end of the month, no Japanese aircraft remained east of the Marianas.

Meanwhile, Admiral Ray Spruance's 5th Fleet—more than 350 ships, 700 carrier-based aircraft, and 53,000 assault ships—was deployed to conduct the invasion. A small Marine combat team would secure the lightly defended Majuro. The Army's 7th Infantry Division was tasked with taking Kwajalein, and the new, untested 4th Marine Division was assigned to seize Roi and Namur at the northern end of the Kwajalein atoll.

The Marines remembered the lessons learned at Tarawa: The islands of Roi, Namur, and Kwajalein were hit with more than 15,000 tons of bombs.

Then, for three days before the assault forces went ashore on 1 February, battleships and heavy cruisers battered the landing beaches and anything above ground on the target islands.

Hastily deployed Navy underwater demolition teams (UDTs) reconnoitered every beach. New armored amphibians equipped with 37 mm howitzers and machine guns took the assault waves across the coral reef and then ashore. LCMRs equipped with rockets and 40 mm cannons raked the landing beaches under covering fire from close-in destroyers. The USS *Appalachian* and USS *Rocky Mount*, recently arrived amphibious command ships standing close offshore, coordinated the landings and the delivery of supporting fire over new, more capable, waterproof radios used by the assault commanders.

Though inadequate training and rehearsal marred the Marine landings on Roi and Namur, the Army assault on Kwajalein was flawlessly executed. And because nearly half the Japanese defenders were already dead from the massive pre–H-Hour bombardment and shelling, all of the objectives were secured by 4 February. More than 5,000 Japanese were dead at a cost of 177 American lives and fewer than 900 wounded. Before the assault troops were completely backloaded, Seabee bulldozers and graders had the runways, taxiways, and aprons on Roi and Kwajalein fully operational.

The victory was so swift and lopsided that Nimitz urged Spruance to press his attack on Eniwetok without returning to Pearl Harbor for refit, rest, and replenishment. Spruance agreed and raised Nimitz one by dispatching Marc Mitscher and his Task Force 58 fast carrier groups to destroy the Japanese naval and air bases on Truk, the forward headquarters of the Imperial Combined Fleet. Spruance himself joined in the attack with his flagship, the brand new battleship *Iowa*, and her sister, *New Jersey*, accompanied only by two heavy cruisers, four destroyers, and ten submarines.

In thirty hours of coordinated nonstop air, surface, and underwater attacks starting at dawn on 17 February, the Americans sank fifteen Imperial Navy combatants and sent nineteen Japanese military cargo ships, five tankers, and more than fifty smaller vessels to the bottom. Mitscher's pilots, flying new radar-guided TBM-1C Avengers, Helldivers, Hellcats, and

Corsairs, destroyed over 230 Japanese aircraft at a cost of twenty-five U.S. planes. The carrier *Intrepid*, hit by a Japanese torpedo launched from a Nakajima B6N "Jill," was the only American ship damaged, and she managed to limp back to Majuro for repairs.

While Truk—the Gibraltar of the Pacific—was being pummeled, Turner's 5th Amphibious Force assaulted Eniwetok atoll. The 22nd Marine Regiment quickly cleared its two objectives—Engebi and Parry islands—and then crossed the lagoon to assist the lesser-trained regiment of the 27th Infantry Division, which had become bogged down on Eniwetok Island. The entire atoll was declared secure on the afternoon of 20 February. Nimitz was now ready to take on a much tougher target 1,000 miles to the west, in the Emperor's back yard: the Marianas.

✪ ✪ ✪

Though the Joint Chiefs in Washington were more than pleased with the pace Nimitz was setting across the central Pacific, Douglas MacArthur was not. Declaring the Gilbert and Marshall Islands operations "diversions," he urged that more forces be allocated to his southwest Pacific drive and all but demanded that his advance on the Philippines be given priority as the main attack against Japan.

The Joint Chiefs, deeply engaged in the final preparations for Operation Overlord—the invasion of France—responded by curtly reaffirming the "dual advance" strategy advocated by Nimitz and ordering MacArthur to be ready for an assault on the Philippine island of Mindanao by November. Nimitz was directed to seize Saipan, Tinian, and Guam in the summer, secure the Palau Islands in September, and be prepared to support MacArthur's return to the Philippines when needed. The decision satisfied both strong-willed leaders—particularly since their respective commands were promised the men and matériel necessary to accomplish their difficult tasks.

One of the reasons that Washington could make such a commitment was the overwhelming response of American industry. By the spring of 1944, despite having more than ten million men already in uniform, American shipyards, airplane plants, and arsenals were churning out sufficient ships, planes, tanks, and weapons to fight a two-front war. There was no way for the Japanese to keep pace.

The statistics were staggering. In 1942, America produced 214 warships; Japan built 37. In 1943, America launched 414 ships to Japan's 57. The same disparity was evident in every other category of war matériel. And worse, from the Japanese perspective, American submarines were choking off their flow of oil and strategic materials from Southeast Asia and the East Indies, even coal and steel from Manchuria. By the time Nimitz was ready to send his 5th Fleet against the Marianas, U.S. submarines were sinking Japanese merchant ships faster than they could be replaced.

Admiral Soemu Toyoda succeeded Admiral Mineichi Koga after Koga was killed in action.

MacArthur, anxious to take advantage of the Japanese shortages and impatient to wrap up operations on New Guinea, started a series of rapid advances west on the island's northern coast. On 22 April, with support from Marc Mitscher's fast carriers, his 84,000 troops at Hollandia and Aitape bypassed Japanese garrisons at Wewak and Madang. Tens of thousands of Japanese troops were killed or left to starve to death in the fetid jungles of New Guinea. In each case, MacArthur's engineers built or improved existing airstrips for his growing fleet of 5th Air Force fighters and bombers.

While MacArthur marshaled strength for his next leap up the New Guinea coast—and while Nimitz was finalizing plans for the Marianas campaign—the strategic picture changed. In early May, their Imperial Japanese opponent—Admiral Mineichi Koga—was killed in a plane crash en route to inspect the construction of naval facilities in the Palau Islands designed to replace the bases on Rabaul and Truk. His replacement, Admiral Soemu Toyoda, was far more aggressive and assured the General Staff in Tokyo that he would "hold the line" and prevent the loss of the Philippines or the Marianas. He set out to surprise the Americans with a plan that he called *A-Go*.

MacArthur was the first to see and feel the effects of Toyoda's leadership. On 17 May he invested Sarmi against relatively light opposition. But on 27 May, his 7th Fleet Amphibious Force landed on the island fortress of Biak. Toyoda, anticipating the move, had reinforced the island garrison and its strength now stood at 11,000. With MacArthur's landing force heavily engaged ashore, Toyoda called for a surface raid by Japan's two largest battleships, *Yamato* and *Musashi*. Escorted by cruisers and destroyers, the battleships were to knock out MacArthur's transports and then decimate the American invaders from the rear with their heavy-caliber guns while the Japanese garrison counter-attacked.

But on 11 June, as Toyoda's battle group prepared to sortie from the Moluccan Islands, Nimitz began his attack on Saipan. Learning of it, Toyoda called off the *Yamato/Musashi* counter-offensive and sent the battleships north to defend the approaches to the Philippines. MacArthur's invasion of Biak was saved by the move he hadn't wanted Nimitz to make.

✪ USS INDIANAPOLIS, 5TH FLEET FLAGSHIP
25 MILES NORTHWEST OF SAIPAN
SOUTHERN MARIANA ISLANDS
18 JUNE 1944

Saipan, the first American objective in the Marianas, is roughly the size of Manhattan Island and had been seized by the Japanese the same day they bombed Pearl Harbor. But by the spring of 1944, Tokyo had declared it to be part of their "National Defense Zone" and posted General Hideyoshi Obata and a 27,000-man garrison to hold it "at all costs."

To wrest control of the island from Obata's troops, Admiral Spruance had assembled an armada of nearly 550 ships. It included 30 aircraft carriers, 1,000 aircraft, 14 battleships, more than 120 destroyers, and the amphibious shipping to carry the 2nd and 4th Marine Divisions and the 27th Infantry Division, totaling over 100,000 men.

Spruance embarked in the 5th Fleet flagship, the cruiser *Indianapolis*, and had departed the Marshalls on 6 June as 150,000 young Americans were storming the beaches of Normandy, France, half a world away. On 11 June, he sent Marc Mitscher's carrier aircraft on ahead to knock out any Japanese aircraft they could find in the southern Marianas. Once the Japanese air threat was eliminated, three battleships joined in pounding known and suspected targets on Saipan and stayed at it through the arrival of the amphibious force.

On 14 June, in an effort to further isolate the Marianas, Spruance dispatched two of Mitscher's fast carrier groups to the north to work over enemy airfields on Iwo Jima and Chichi Jima. That same afternoon, the rest of the battleships and heavy cruisers of his amphibious force arrived off Saipan and began blasting the fourteen-mile-long island with more heavy guns.

But the naval aviators dropping the bombs and the gunners pumping their sixteen-inch and eight-inch shells at targets ashore quickly learned that not all the lessons learned at Tarawa were still applicable. Unlike the flat atolls of the Gilbert and Marshall islands, Saipan and the rest of the Marianas were jungle-covered, mountainous coral islands, honeycombed with natural and man-made caves. The Japanese made good use of all the cover, concealment, and protection the island offered against the American onslaught.

While the bombers and large-caliber guns did their work, Navy UDTs confirmed that there were no mines on or off the landing beaches that Admiral Turner and General Smith had chosen on the southwest side of the island. Any celebration of this good news was quickly dampened by the impact of high-caliber rounds fired from Saipan that struck the USS *California* and one of her destroyer escorts, causing casualties on both. Clearly the pre–D-Day bombardment hadn't been as effective as hoped.

Among those watching the awesome pre-landing bombardment was Corporal Don Swindle. He had enlisted from Indiana and was still a teenager when he headed off to recruit training in San Diego. On 15 June 1944, he was a rifleman in the 4th Marine Division, preparing to invade Saipan.

□   □   □

CORPORAL DON SWINDLE, USMC
4th Marine Division
Off Saipan, Mariana Islands
15 June 1944

It's noisy as heck. And if you ever get the battlewagons in front of you or close to you, when those sixteen-inchers go off, it feels like it's pulling your Amtrac right out of the water. You can actually see a sixteen-inch shell go by if you're behind it.

After they fired for three days, you look to see, and you say, "Surely there can't be too many left." They hit what looks like everything. But most of the time the Japs really dug in and they had good bunkers.

We got about halfway in and our second battalion wave was hit. I was in the second or third wave, I think. We were receiving small arms and machine gun fire, but we were only able to take out one light machine gun.

I had two Bangalore torpedoes at the bottom of my Amtrac and I had a grenade box. I was supposed to blow barbed wire in case we ran into it. But we didn't.

And although the others got knocked out on each side of us, our Amtrac got through. It was a rough ride and we bailed out as soon as we got to the beach.

Then a sniper cut loose on us, evidently with a rifle, because he was firing single shots. He fired about five times at us.

I was scared all the time. But that thought never entered my mind then. We had talked about this quite a bit before. None of us ever thought we were going to die. But a lot of us did.

□   □   □

At dawn on 15 June, more than 8,000 Marines of the 2nd and 4th Divisions embarked in armored amphibians and armed LVTs. They were landed in under twenty minutes after a massive final bombardment. It wasn't enough.

The assault waves were greeted on the beach by furious artillery, mortar, and machine gun fire from the dug-in and well-prepared defenders. By dark, the 20,000 Marines who had come ashore were well short of their intended objectives and more than 10 percent of them were already casualties.

The next morning, General Smith committed a portion of his reserve, a reinforced regimental combat team of the Army's 27th Infantry division. Soon, they too found themselves having to fight for every inch of ground against 20,000 tenacious Japanese defenders who had pledged to the emperor that they would "push the Americans into the sea."

One of those the Japanese tried to push back into the sea was an eighteen-year-old Marine PFC, Rick Spooner, a native of California. For the next three and a half weeks he would experience a particular kind of hell.

▯   ▯   ▯

PRIVATE FIRST CLASS RICK SPOONER, USMC
Saipan, Mariana Islands
Pacific Ocean
17 June 1944

We'd heard of Guam, but we didn't know where the Mariana Islands were. When our lieutenant briefed us, he said, "You're going to land on Saipan." Navy and Marine aircraft had pounded Saipan for days. So we were surprised the next day, when we went ashore, that the shelling hadn't really bothered the Japs too much.

I was in Fox Company. We headed in toward the island; there was a lagoon and a barrier reef around it. The Japanese had registered their artillery, anti-boat guns, and heavy mortars on the barrier reef. Going into the beach, we lost twenty Amtracs and there were some bodies and body parts floating in the water.

We were on the first wave and had to get off at the first beach. But there were too many people there already.

There were a lot of dead Japs on the beaches, and a lot of dead Marines, too, with more and more as we went along.

The problem was that the Navy had laid down a heavy smoke screen, for which we were delighted at first, because that would mask our landing. But it also blinded all the landing craft drivers. So we wound up on the wrong beach.

I was a young PFC and I was scared to death, but I hoped no one around me knew it.

After leaving the beach, we were supposed to take a little Japanese fighter airstrip, secure it, and then dig in and wait. We managed to get across, but not everyone made it. There was no cover, no concealment. You had to run like hell and there was some fire, but we got across.

Our next objective was to be at Lake Susupe. We all knew where it was—we'd seen it on the maps, but sometimes maps are very deceiving. Lake Susupe turned out not to be a lake, but a swamp. And it was bristling with Japs.

We got up to the edges and took some casualties. Later on that same day we had to fall back to straighten out the regiment's lines. You know, Marines don't like to fall back when they've spilled blood. They don't like to give terrain up, but whoever made the decision was smart. They did the right thing because pulling back probably saved a lot of lives.

We were almost back to the beach but away from the swamp. There were places on that island that were coral, and the little entrenching tools we had were not really designed to go through coral; we needed jackhammers. But you know, when you're scared, and someone's shooting at you, it's amazing how powerful you can be and what you can do with an entrenching tool.

The first night there was a lot of artillery and we got some of our 10th Marines in. I heard 1,786 as the number that we lost those first twenty-four hours. By the time the campaign was over, we had more than 3,100 dead Americans just on Saipan.

The second night was the most horrific night of the campaign, I think. We could hear all that noise, and of course we were scared of what was coming at us. The Japs had forty-eight tanks, with infantry, and came down toward the beaches. At that point, we had a new weapon—the bazooka—the little 2.36 rocket launcher. Colonel Willy K. Jones picked one up from a scared private that was our bazooka man, told the assistant gunner to load him, and he fired at a tank at very close range, right into the belly of that tank. He made his men believers in the bazooka.

The next day, after that horrible attack, we counted twenty-four hulks of tanks knocked out by those Marines. Along with the tanks, there were about 1,200 enemy infantry troops killed. The Japanese had devastating losses.

There's no way anyone who's ever been in combat can glorify war. It's the most horrible experience and one of the worst things that a human being can live through. The sounds are bad—like an amphibious landing covering fire—and the smells are worse.

✪ ✪ ✪

While the Marines and Army were thus engaged, U.S. submarines patrolling far to the west detected two large Japanese naval formations passing through the Philippine Sea, headed east. Concerned that he would be unable to protect transports offloading in two locations, Admiral Spruance postponed the assault on Guam scheduled for 17 June and ordered Mitscher's carriers and the battleships to form up west of the Marianas and head off

Captured Marianas airfield

the anticipated counter-attack. Spruance, aboard *Indianapolis*, departed Saipan to direct the battle.

On the morning of 18 June, while his 103-ship armada, deployed in five task groups, raced west to engage Admiral Toyoda's mobile fleet, Spruance received word that the Marines had taken the southern portion of Saipan and had seized the airfield. That evening, code-breakers and radio intercept operators in Pearl Harbor pinpointed his opponent 350 miles west of his position. Spruance went to his sea cabin that night knowing that 19 June was going to be a very busy day.

At 0500 the following morning, Spruance had his seven battleships, fifteen aircraft carriers, and 900 aircraft ready to face Admiral Jisaburo Ozawa's nine carriers and 430 aircraft, which had linked up with Admiral Matome Ugaki's five battleships. Though Ozawa knew that he was out-

National Archives

Vice Admiral Jisaburo Ozawa, Japanese commander in the "Great Marianas Turkey Shoot."

numbered, he anticipated help from land-based Japanese aircraft flying out from Rota and Guam, not knowing that Hoover's land-based bombers and Mitscher's carrier pilots had all but eliminated the aircraft on those two islands and so badly cratered the runways in both places that the airfields were virtually unusable.

What few aircraft that could launch from Guam were quickly dispatched by Mitscher's fighters, and when reinforcements from Truk were detected by U.S. radar, they too were all shot down. Before noon, the only planes available to attack the American fleet were those flown by inadequately trained aviators aboard the Japanese carriers.

The resulting battle was so one-sided that it quickly became known as the "Great Marianas Turkey Shoot." U.S. aircraft and submarines ranged over and under the Japanese fleet. Ozawa's flagship, the carrier *Taiho*, blew up and sank with 1,600 of his sailors when it was hit by a spread of torpedoes from the USS *Albacore*. Another American sub, the *Cavalla*, sank the carrier *Shokaku*. Of the 335 Japanese fighters, bombers, and torpedo planes launched against the Americans, 242 of them were downed.

Twenty-three-year-old Chicago native Alex Vraciu was flying that day from the deck of the USS *Lexington*. He already had thirteen kills over the Pacific waters, and in the "Great Marianas Turkey Shoot" he got eight more.

LIEUTENANT ALEX VRACIU, USN
Aboard USS *Lexington*
Central Pacific Ocean
20 June 1944

While we were at the Marianas, I was on one of the hops, where a couple planes were shot down. We learned what they had done to some of our pilots: The Japs gouged their eyes out, cut off their ears, and worse. A lot of us had made up our minds what we were going to do.

I had a mission "beyond darkness" on 20 June, the next day. Because it was late in the afternoon, some of our search planes discovered where their fleet was. It was beyond the safe range and it wasn't till 1620 that we knew that we would be hitting them about dusk.

Most of the guys out there weren't qualified for night landings on carriers. We knew it was going to be tragic. But they launched over 200 of us. I was part of the squadron of nine fighter planes, nine torpedo aircraft, and fifteen bombers that were sent over to meet the Jap fleet. We knew that some of the planes would likely be half out of fuel before they got there.

On that mission I lost my wingman, Homer Brockmeier, over the Jap fleet. We were struck by a group of enemy fighters and we had to fight for our lives. But I got the plane that got Brock. I haven't forgotten that.

They called the Marianas "the great turkey shoot." We were shooting a bunch of planes that you had to hurry up and eliminate before they got your carriers.

We weren't attacking Saipan alone. We were about a hundred miles or so from the islands, waiting to see what the Japanese would be coming to do.

The Japanese not only had their nine carriers, but they were using their army land-based aircraft and maybe some navy types. They were shooting down planes at Guam. Our radar found a huge group coming in and they called us: "Come back from Guam, because the action is starting!" And if we'd known that the action was going be there, we would have already been up in the air.

In dogfights, we learned from the early guys that you can't fight them at low altitudes. When I got to 20,000 feet, I couldn't shift into high blower. So that meant 20,000 was my limit.

But as it turned out we were in perfect position. There was a motley group of them, not in any particular formation, that had come over 300 miles by that time. They were at 2,000 feet, below us, headed in the opposite direction—a perfect position.

We tried to keep them together because if they started scattering, we could miss the bombers in their formation. That day they had torpedo planes, dive-bombers, and some fighters in that group. There were a good fifty of them, so I pulled up on the other side and started my run.

I came down on one and burned him. Using my dive to maintain my speed, I pulled up in the position for the next round, and then I made a run on two planes in a loose formation.

I burned the first one, and as he was going down, I lowered my wing, got in position for the second one, and got him. So that made three.

Then I worked back in and brought down a fourth one. I must have hit his controls at the same time that he was on fire, because he did a wild gyration and went on down. And then I looked up ahead and saw a string of three of them.

So when I got the fifth one, another was still behind. I had to race to get that one, who'd started his dive already. I got that one and he blew up. I must have hit his bomb.

A battleship AA gun must've blown up the one ahead of him, because he just suddenly went up in flames.

All of a sudden, it was over as fast as it started.

Depending on which historian you ask, something like 300 planes were shot down that day as part of the "turkey shoot."

I headed back to the fleet and felt good. I considered this my payback for Pearl Harbor.

I was told afterwards that the whole battle took eight minutes. They said I used up only 360 rounds of .50-caliber ammo. We had 2,400 in the gun. But because I was going in so close, it was only ten rounds per plane, per gun. I had seventeen kills, and eighteen when I got one the next day.

We lost a good hundred planes, for various reasons: out of fuel, battle damage, not being able to land aboard the carrier. You couldn't believe the madness of it.

◻   ◻   ◻

As the remnants of the Japanese fleet fled toward Okinawa, Mitscher's pilots sank the carrier *Hiyo* and severely damaged two others, *Chiyoda* and *Zuikaku*. On their final sortie of the day, they plastered the battleship *Haruna*—killing more than 500 of her crew. By sunset on 20 June, the Imperial Fleet had lost all but thirty-six of its airplanes—to only nineteen American aircraft downed.

That night, risking attack by Japanese submarines, Mitscher courageously ordered his fleet to turn on their lights so that the returning aircraft—low on fuel and exhausted from two days of near nonstop fighting—could make it back to their carriers. Even so, more than eighty U.S. planes were lost in this night recovery than had been brought down by the Japanese. When the battle was over, forty-nine of Mitscher's pilots had been killed.

✪ ✪ ✪

By 24 June, Spruance and his fleet were back, standing off the Marianas and devoting their full attention to supporting the land battle on Saipan while other ships "softened up" Guam and nearby Tinian for invasion. On 9 July, the Americans pushed the remaining Japanese on Saipan into a pocket along some cliffs on the north coast of the island. There, more than 1,000 of them—including women and children—hurled themselves to their deaths rather than surrender or be taken prisoner. It was a terrible end to a brutal battle. More than 29,000 Japanese were dead, but 3,400 Americans had also been killed and another 13,000 wounded.

Just twelve days later, on 21 July, after pounding Guam for as many days with air and naval gunfire, the 3rd Amphibious Corps—composed of the

3rd Marine Division, the 1st Provisional Marine Brigade, and the U.S. Army's 77th Infantry Division—landed on Guam, the largest island in the Marianas chain. The Marine and Army units, relying heavily on naval gunfire from the fleet surrounding the island, moved slowly across the island from west to east. They met determined resistance from 8,000 Japanese, who holed up in caves while preparing for banzai charges every night until the island was secured.

Sergeant Cyril "Obie" O'Brien had enlisted in the Marines after being turned down for Officers' Candidate School because he was half an inch too short. He had seen action as a rifleman on Bougainville, but thereafter he served as a war correspondent. When the Marines invaded Guam, he went with them, filing reports from the front for American newspapers and wire services.

□   □   □

SERGEANT CYRIL "OBIE" O'BRIEN, USMC
2nd and 4th Marine Divisions
Guam, Mariana Islands
21 July 1944

While we were on the ships headed for Guam, Tokyo Rose announced on the radio, "Boys, we've got some surprises for you on the beach on Guam."

We all wondered, "How did she know we're going to Guam?"

Most of the Marines had been already in combat. More than half were already veterans of Bougainville.

The night we arrived off Guam I remember looking over the rail in the pitch darkness, two o'clock in the morning, as they started shelling. I remember thinking, "I'm gonna be in there tomorrow morning!"

In the morning I landed with the third assault wave. Those of us in the assault waves had one advantage. The later waves came in by Higgins boats. We came in on Amtracs. They took you right up and put you on the beach.

Nobody knows war like the guy on the front line, nobody. I was a correspondent on Guam. I don't think even the people back in battalion HQ had the same exposure as the men on the front line.

It's funny how the Japanese knew who was in charge. A Marine NCO came up to me and said, "Leave your pack in the shell hole, nobody's gonna steal it." So I left the pack there as he told me and he went and gave some orders to some other Marines.

Next thing I know, *boom,* right through the head. The Japs had observed us on the beach, guessed correctly that he was in charge, and a sniper killed him.

One time four or five little Japanese women came out of a cave. So the Marines went up and got them and brought them to safety. We had to cross a stream, and these Marines picked these little women up in their arms so they wouldn't have to walk through the water. They carried them over, probably thinking of their mother, their sisters, their daughters. Isn't that something?

I had a photographer with me, Herb Ball, and during a lull he said, "Obie, we're gonna have to cut each other's hair." And I said okay. So he cut my hair and did a good job. Then I cut his hair. He looked in the mirror, laughed, and said, "Now I don't care if get killed."

Most of the time all I had was a pistol, a .45, and of course, my typewriter. I figured it was the Marines' job to shoot the enemy and it was my job to write about it.

I'll never forget the first day. I had this Hermes portable typewriter on my lap and I'm typing away and all of a sudden mortars start to come in. I got mad—not that I almost got killed, but because they were interfering with my writing!

I'm writing, and I think I'm Ernest Hemingway!

I wrote that story back in the field, took it back to division, and Ray Henry got it back to the States in about a week. It went to AP, UPI, and the like. Everybody picked it up because we were the only ones on the spot doing the story.

We celebrated Christmas of '44 on Guam. Right afterwards, Bill Ross grabbed me and said, "Obie, you better go get ready and pack." I asked, "What for?"

He said, "You're leaving for the States in the morning."

But I didn't get to go home; instead, they sent me to Washington. When I got there, Colonel Bill McAhill said, "O'Brien, the reason we brought you here is that we're going to attack Japan around next Christmas (1945). I want you to volunteer to cover it."

So I said I would. But when I got home for a few days, my mother said, "Oh, you're safe, the war's over for you!"

I didn't tell her I was going back to Japan!

Thankfully, I didn't have to because Harry Truman had the courage to drop the bombs that ended the war. The planes that did it came from the airfields we had captured in the Marianas.

☐   ☐   ☐

✪ 4TH MARINE DIVISION
TINIAN, MARIANA ISLANDS
28 JULY 1944

On 24 July, while the battle for Guam was still being fought, the 4th Marine Division assaulted Tinian. Since so many of the Navy's heavy guns were engaged in supporting operations on Guam 110 miles to the south, the Marines on Tinian relied on the continuous fire from more than 200 artillery pieces lined up on the south coast of Saipan. Using napalm for the first time in direct support of the infantry, Marine and Navy pilots flying from Saipan's captured airfield flew nonstop missions against 10,000 Japanese defenders.

It took seven days to secure Tinian, at a cost of 385 Marine casualties. Guam, much larger and with a significant civilian population, took two weeks and cost 1,500 American deaths. On 10 August, Guam was declared secure. But even then, it wasn't: The last Japanese defender on Guam didn't give himself up until 1972.

Within a matter of days, the smaller airfields on all three islands were in operation as advance air bases, and Seabees were working to build the much larger air bases required for the B-29 "Superfortress" bombers that would soon start wreaking havoc on Japan's Home Islands. Guam's Apra Harbor and Magicienne Bay on Saipan were converted to fleet anchorages, fuel depots, and repair facilities for use by the combatants and support ships Nimitz would need to support the invasion of the Philippines and the Home Islands.

Prime Minister Tojo, seeing the inevitable, resigned on 18 September. By November, the B-29s that had precipitated the landings were launching raids over Tokyo and other Japanese cities from air bases in the Marianas. In August 1945, the two planes carrying the atomic bombs that ended the war—perhaps saving over a million lives—launched from blood-soaked Tinian. The sacrifices of the soldiers, sailors, airmen, and Marines who had captured the islands had not been in vain.

✪ U.S. NAVY 5TH FLEET
MARIANA ISLANDS
10 AUGUST 1944

Seizing Saipan, Guam, and Tinian was costly for the Americans. The U.S. tallied some 27,000 Marines, sailors, and soldiers as casualties. Nearly 5,000 were killed in action or died of wounds. The rest were wounded or MIA and presumed dead. The battles for control of all three islands lasted sixty days. But when it was over, America owned them and their incredibly valuable airfields. They immediately began converting existing 4,700-foot and 5,000-foot airfields into 8,500-foot runways needed for the B-29s.

It was a strategic victory in other ways. America had severed the main flow of Japanese raw materials, reinforcements, and matériel from the Home Islands bound for the south.

The U.S. was now in a position to move on the Palau Islands, the Philippines, or even northwest toward Iwo Jima or the cost of China.

In August 1944, the entire Mariana Islands chain was back in American hands. Later in the war, Nimitz would move his headquarters from Hawaii to Guam. Three months later, the first B-29s would take off from the Marianas to bomb the Japanese mainland. The bombers hit Honshu, striking Japan for the first time since the Doolittle raid in 1942.

Losing the Marianas' "absolute defense zone" was devastating for the Japanese. Once Nimitz seized these islands, American B-29s could hit the Home Islands of Japan. The war leaders in Tokyo were forced to begin serious preparations for handling casualties, evacuating cities, and the possibility of an American invasion.

Tojo, who had been Japanese premier and war minister, resigned three days after the landing at Saipan, even as the Battle of the Philippine Sea was ongoing. One of the members of the Japanese royal family is said to have lamented, "Hell is upon us, with the loss of Saipan." Tojo, before he was executed for war crimes, said that he felt in his heart that Japan could never win after losing Saipan.

American military leaders began to prepare for the conclusion of the war. For Admiral Nimitz, the prospect of leading even his massive forces into the homeland of Japan was daunting, not only because of the casualties that America would have to expect, but after witnessing how even Japanese civilians seemed bound by the Bushido code and might commit mass suicide, he could see the possible destruction of an entire civilization.

Nimitz was convinced that the plans for a proposed Allied invasion in 1945 or 1946 meant that the Americans would not be fighting the Japanese Imperial Army and Navy when they came ashore in Japan, but would have to battle every civilian old enough to walk and to throw a rock or carry a club.

The cultural brainwashing of the Japanese Bushido code meant tens of millions—perhaps most of the population—would have died. Nimitz had no doubts that many others would have been caught in the crossfire and bombing raids, while millions of others would die in suicide attacks against the American and Allied forces.

Later, after Roosevelt's death, Harry Truman was forced to consider Nimitz's concerns. His Joint Chiefs of Staff had told him to expect 60,000 to 80,000 American casualties at the first landing in Kaishu. They also fore-cast more than a million Japanese fatalities, including the entire garrison of 600,000, and 500,000 Japanese civilians. Once the Americans pushed onto other Japanese Home Islands they estimated that millions more would die.

Those staggering numbers became part of Truman's equation in decid-ing to use the atomic bombs to hasten the end of the war.

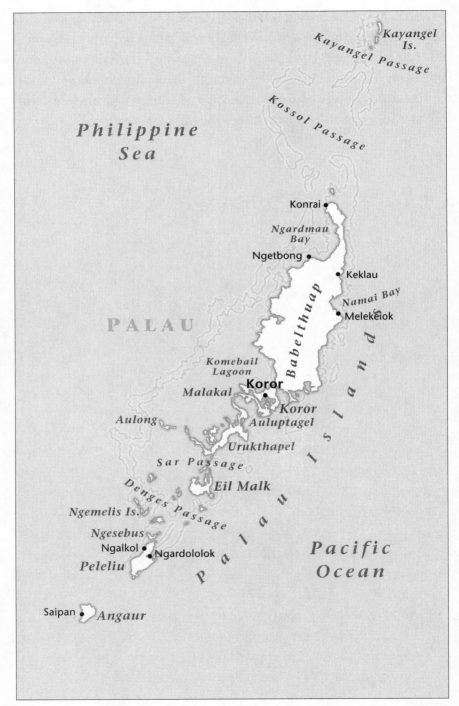

CHAPTER 13
FORGOTTEN PELELIU
(SEPTEMBER 1944)

✪ **HQ U.S. PACIFIC COMMAND**
PEARL HARBOR, HAWAII
26 JULY 1944

While the bloody battles for Saipan, Tinian, and Guam were still being fought, the bitter debate over Pacific strategy between MacArthur and Nimitz boiled up once again. MacArthur, having nearly completed operations in New Guinea, had effectively isolated Rabaul. Truk, the only other major Japanese naval and air base east of the Philippines, had been rendered useless by regular air raids and submarine attacks against Japanese vessels entering and leaving the anchorage.

With the Marianas all but secured, MacArthur once again insisted that it was time to make the invasion of the Philippines the main attack in the Pacific—and demanded that he be given the necessary fleet, air, and ground forces to make his "I shall return" promise a reality. Nimitz, in equally strong terms, asserted that continuing his central Pacific "island-hopping" strategy was the most effective way to beat the Japanese. Long an advocate of using his fast carriers, battleship heavy surface action groups, and amphibious forces for rapid leaps across broad expanses of open ocean, Nimitz once more advocated an assault on Formosa.

In Washington, Admiral King, General Marshall, and the Joint Chiefs tried, as they had in the past, to mediate a compromise between Nimitz and MacArthur. When their efforts failed, they threw the matter to the president. FDR, seeking a fourth term in office, and seeing political advantage in meeting with his two famous commanders, told them to join him for a conference of war in Hawaii. The two men did as ordered, and aboard the USS *Baltimore* in Pearl Harbor—during the only meetings the three wartime leaders would ever have—they hammered out a strategy for defeating Japan.

After listening to Nimitz and MacArthur, FDR decided that the Philippines were to be the next major offensive. Then, if the Japanese didn't surrender unconditionally, the Home Islands would be invaded. MacArthur was assigned to be the principal commander for the task. Nimitz would support him with carriers, battleships, cruisers, submarines, and troops, and would protect MacArthur's right flank by ensuring that the Japanese could not counter-attack from the Palau Islands 600 miles to the east.

MacArthur's first objective was Mindanao, then Leyte, and finally Luzon and the liberation of Manila. As soon as possible, new B-29 Superfortresses would start reducing Japanese factories, shipyards, military facilities, and cities to rubble. About the only issue left undecided was who would command the invasion of the Japanese Home Islands when it came time.

Immediately after the Hawaii conference, MacArthur and Nimitz went to work completing detailed plans for their respective missions. For Nimitz, disappointment at being directed to support the main attack through the Philippines was tempered by the assignment to secure the Palau Islands. That task meant that the 1st Marine Division—which had been "loaned" to MacArthur for operations in New Guinea and New Britain—would be returned to his control.

By 10 August, with "mopping-up" operations underway in the Marianas, Pacific Fleet planners were able to brief Nimitz on their proposal to "secure" the Palau Islands in plenty of time to release assets—particularly carriers, battleships, and cruisers—to support General MacArthur's three invasions in the Philippines.

Little was known about the Palau Islands—because they had been ceded to Japan after World War I. The American command believed that the only islands that needed to be taken were Ngulu, Ulithi, and Peleliu. The first two, smaller, and, according to U.S. intelligence, less defended, were to be assaulted by the 81st Infantry Division. The battle-hardened 1st Marine Division veterans of Guadalcanal, New Guinea, and New Britain were assigned to take Peleliu.

Just six miles long, two miles wide, and shaped like a lobster claw, Peleliu featured jungle-covered coral ridges and steep draws that revealed little. Numerous reconnaissance photographs were taken by PBYs, long-range land-based aircraft, and planes launched by the carriers—some by George H. W. Bush, the future president of the United States. Yet, despite all the photo missions, radio intercepts, and debriefings from the coast-watching native islanders, there was very little "hard intelligence" about Japanese strength or preparations on Peleliu.

Bombing missions had cratered the island's only major airfield, and ever since the "Great Marianas Turkey Shoot" the Japanese had abandoned their Palau fleet anchorages. From a desk in Pearl Harbor, it appeared that Peleliu was vulnerable to a good, heavy pre-assault bombardment followed by a quick attack by the 1st Marine Division—now resting and refitting on Pavuvu in the Russell Islands. By 1 September, the division, commanded by Major General William H. Rupertus, was expected to be back to its full complement of 19,000 Marines and ready for D-Day on 15 September 1944.

By the time the troops began to embark aboard their amphibious ships during the first week of September, what the Americans didn't know about Peleliu was far greater than what they did. Those who planned the operation, called "Stalemate," knew that the island had no rivers or streams. They didn't know, however, that there was no fresh water whatsoever.

U.S. pilots, naval gunfire officers, and Marine intelligence officers knew that early in the war some 3,000 Japanese troops and 500 press-ganged

Korean laborers had improved the fleet anchorage and had built an airfield. The Americans didn't know that the Japanese had constructed hundreds of sophisticated, interconnected caves and tunnels and mutually supporting, hardened fighting positions on the island.

The Marines going ashore knew from past experience that when pressed, Japanese officers would often order their men to conduct suicidal banzai attacks, hastening the defenders' inevitable collapse. But no one knew that Colonel Kunio Nakagawa, commanding the 10,000 tough Japanese troops on Peleliu, had ordered them to stay hidden in their tunnels and caves and "Make the American Marines come to you—and when they do, kill them." There would be no banzai attacks on Peleliu.

✪ HQ 1ST MARINE DIVISION, AFLOAT
PELELIU, PALAU ISLANDS
1130 15 SEPTEMBER 1944

It was still early on D-Day, but from his vantage point aboard the amphibious command ship General Rupertus could already tell things were not going according to plan. Four days ago, while making the 2,100-mile voyage from Pavuvu to Peleliu, he had told his regimental commanders that he expected this part of Operation Stalemate to be "tough but quick," and that it would all be over in "two or three days." Given the three days of continuous pounding by carrier aircraft and the battleships' eighteen-inch guns and the cruisers' eight-inch volleys, there was good reason for optimism.

But now, just three hours after H-Hour, more than twenty-five of his LVTs and landing craft, having taken direct hits from Japanese guns hidden in the coral cliffs, were wrecked or burning between the barrier reef and the shore. Another sixty had been damaged en route to or from the beach and were now useless. His communicators were receiving frantic radio calls from shattered units trapped on the narrow shelf between the water and the jungle, taking heavy casualties. It was obvious that Peleliu was going to be anything but a "quick" battle.

Just prior to the assault waves crossing the line of departure and heading to the beach, Rupertus and his staff had watched the final moments of the pre-assault bombardment. All the lessons learned at Tarawa and since were being applied here. Just before the first wave hit the beach, rocket-firing LCIs and Hellcats sprayed the beaches with 40 mm and machine gun rounds. Rear Admiral Jesse Oldendorf, commanding the bombardment force, had gone so far as to claim, "There are no more targets. I have destroyed everything."

But he was wrong. The shells, bombs, and rockets had not hit many of the targets at all. Or if they had, they had bounced right off the reinforced concrete and coral. Admiral Oldendorf's gunners had missed most of the hidden tunnels and caves—mainly because they couldn't be seen.

Further, the naval shelling of the relatively small island wasn't quite as devastating as it appeared. The number of rounds fired at the island before the assault had been governed by two factors: known targets ashore on Peleliu, and the requirement to have Oldendorf's battleships and cruisers provide the same kind of assault preparation for MacArthur's troops going ashore in the Philippines.

Since there were few known targets visible on Peleliu, Oldendorf's gunnery officers made the assumption that whatever needed to be hit had been. Therefore, they reasoned, firing more rounds both wasted ammunition that would be needed for the Philippines and created more wear and tear on the barrels and breeches. Either condition—a shortage of ammunition in the magazines or worn barrels on the guns—could delay MacArthur's invasion plans. And given all the attention "Dugout Doug" was getting from Washington and the press, nobody wanted to be responsible for delaying his return to the Philippines.

To make matters worse, MacArthur decided to bypass Mindanao and proceed directly with an assault on Leyte, advancing the timetable for when Oldendorf's bombardment group would be needed. That decided the matter: Instead of five days' pre-assault bombardment requested by the Marines landing on Peleliu, the island would be treated to three days of bombing and shelling unless new targets were identified. By the morning of 15 September, no new targets had been found, and Oldendorf departed to link up with MacArthur's Philippine invasion force.

For the veterans of the 1st Marine Division, 15 September 1944 began well before dawn with a traditional breakfast of steak and eggs. After returning to their troop compartments to draw ammunition and grenades from the armorers, they donned their field transport packs and proceeded up to the weather decks of their ships for a hasty prayer service led by unit chaplains. As dawn was breaking, those assigned to the assault waves went over the side, climbing down cargo nets into the waiting LVTs and landing craft bobbing in a gentle swell beside the assault ships. Churning toward shore, the troops could hear the sound of the battleships' sixteen-inch shells ripping through the air above them. Those who could look over the gunwales of their boats could see the flash and smoke of the big shells as they exploded ashore.

The survivors of that first assault wave recall that there was no sign of life on the island until the naval gunfire had ceased and the LVTs and armored amphibians reached the coral reef some 600 to 700 yards from shore. Then all hell broke loose.

Japanese gunners, protected from the U.S. barrage by their deep caves and tunnels high above the landing beaches, rolled their artillery, mortars, and even German 88 mm guns out as soon as the naval gunfire stopped raining down on the island. Strafing by carrier aircraft and rockets fired from the LCIs, both delivering suppression fire on the beach, did nothing to deter the Japanese gunners who were, in most cases, 800 to 1,000 meters back from the water's edge. The delivery of a last-minute smokescreen by the rocket ships didn't protect the Marines either, since the Japanese didn't need to see their targets. Their aiming points had all been pre-registered.

Most of the first wave of LVTs that did manage to make it ashore at 0832 were promptly struck by fire plunging from the cliffs above. The assault beach quickly took on the appearance of a junkyard. Scores of Marines exiting their Amtracs were felled by flying shrapnel as they tried to press forward out of the killing zone and into the scarce cover. As the second assault wave hit the beach five minutes later, they piled in atop the wreckage of the first wave. The Marines rushing out of their vehicles were greeted by Japanese shellfire and screams of "Corpsman up!"

For Marines in combat, the courage and skill of their Navy medical corpsmen are often the determining factors in who crosses that thin line between life and death on the battlefield. For those in B Company, 1st Battalion, 1st Marine Regiment that terrible morning on Peleliu, one of those who answered the call was eighteen-year-old Pharmacist Mate Third Class John Hayes. It was his baptism by fire.

❑   ❑   ❑

PHARMACIST MATE THIRD CLASS
JOHN HAYES, USN
B Company, 1st Battalion, 1st Marines
Peleliu, Palau Islands
15 September 1944

We went to the galley and had our first decent meal, steak and eggs—the last meal until we got off of the island. About seven o'clock, we started climbing down the cargo nets into the landing craft. I climbed over the side with all of my medical gear and six rounds of 60 mm mortar ammunition.

As we headed into the beach, it was apparent that things weren't going as planned. We got hung up on the reef and had to go into the water well off the beach. It was bad when we went over the side of the landing craft. I'm six-foot-seven and the water was over my head. I went right to the bottom and finally got up so that my head was above water and we all walked to shore as fast as we could. But when we waded out of the surf, everybody was backed up. Bodies were floating in the surf and body parts were everywhere. It was real carnage.

The first wave of shelled Amtracs were burning on the beach. Some had gotten hung up on the reef and others were shot on the way in.

Every soldier, airman, sailor, and Marine thinks that his battle is the worst and that's what we were thinking when we got on to Peleliu.

I guess, of course, in every serious episode of life there's a little humor. One of my platoon members had called for a corpsman, so I picked up my bag and I ran to him. And he says, "Doc, I'm hit."

I said, "Where are you hit?" He says, "I'm hit in the butt." And so I looked him over and I couldn't see any blood. He said, "I feel the blood running down my butt."

I said, "Well I don't see any blood."

A sniper had put a round through his canteen, and the hot water was running down the cheeks of his butt, so he thought he was hit.

So I told him, "You're not getting out of here that easy."

Peleliu was a battle of inches. They stopped us on the beach and we had to fight for every inch after we got there.

A platoon sergeant was near me and I said, "You know, I'm scared." He said, "So am I."

I said, "You can't be scared, you're a veteran of Guadalcanal. He said, "You're gonna be a veteran in five minutes." And I was.

That first night ashore we expected banzai attacks but there weren't any. Still, nobody got any sleep. We dug in the sand, threw flares up all night long, and exchanged fire. It was a long night, but we didn't have the heavy casualties we'd had during the day.

We had a lot of wounded. We'd do what we could for them, keep them from going into shock, bandage their wounds, and evacuate them out to the hospital ship. Our battalion surgeon, Dr. Robert Haggerty, did a masterful job under those circumstances.

We were told to attack up Bloody Nose Ridge, but got kicked back every day. We just couldn't seem to get a foothold because we didn't have enough artillery support to get into those caves. The Japanese had German 88 mm guns mounted in those caves on tracks with armor protecting the entrance. They'd roll back that armor door and roll the eighty-eights out and fire at any group of more than two Marines. Those guns took a heavy toll. Then they'd pull the gun back in and close the door. It was only after we were able to get some flame-throwers and have napalm dropped that we were able to make any headway at all.

Our biggest problems were the Japanese fire and heat exhaustion.

Bloody Nose Ridge was a coral escarpment honeycombed with caves. The naval gunfire and bombs had blown most of the leaves off the trees, so every time we moved we were always out in the open.

In the course of the six days that the 1st Marine Regiment was there, we had about 315 killed and we had over 1,400 wounded. That means we suffered 54 percent casualties, the worst casualty rate to that point of any regiment in World War II.

I got hit with shrapnel in the back on the third day but stayed until the sixth day, when they evacuated me to the hospital ship.

The corpsman is always vulnerable. And the Marines all knew that. They protected us. And as a result, there is a very close bond between the Marines and their Navy corpsmen.

One of my friends bandaged me and we just stayed there and toughed it out. On the hospital ship, they didn't take the shrapnel out. They said it wasn't impairing anything so they left it in. They sewed me right up over the hole.

I spent six weeks on "light duty," and then back on Pavuvu we started training for the invasion of Okinawa.

One of the things that I've always been very proud of is that I served as a medical corpsman with the Marines. In our military, the group that has the highest number of citations for bravery are the Navy corpsmen assigned to the Marines.

✪ OPERATION STALEMATE
1ST MARINE DIVISION
PELELIU, PALAU ISLANDS
16 SEPTEMBER 1944

By nightfall on D-Day there were slightly more than 7,000 Marines ashore on Peleliu. The 1st and 5th Marine Regiments were hunkered down just a few hundred yards inland from White and Orange Beaches, unable to press inland because of withering fire from Japanese machine guns. Efforts to penetrate further inland during the night were repulsed and at dawn of D+1 their positions were little changed.

Late on D-Day, General Rupertus committed most of the 7th Marines—his reserve—and landed them in the vicinity of "the point." But by the morning of D+1, they too were being held up by a series of well-fortified pillboxes on the ridge above them. With nearly the entire division now engaged, Rupertus sought a breakthrough.

He ordered the 7th Marines to shift the orientation of their attack and seize the airfield. Major Gordon Gayle was acting commander of the 1st Battalion, 7th Marines during the assault on the airfield. It would turn into a "run and gun" tank-infantry battle—a first for the Marines.

◻ ◻ ◻

MAJOR GORDON GAYLE, USMC
1st Battalion, 7th Marines
Peleliu, Palau Islands
21 September 1944

When I joined the Marine Corps, it was the size of the New York City police force. When the war was over, the Corps was half a million strong.

We went to Guadalcanal in '42, came out of New Guinea in '43. We landed in New Britain and came out in May of '44. It was hot, but not as hot as Peleliu.

After we left New Britain and went down to Pavuvu, a ship came in with replacements. I went down to watch our people leave and watch the new people come off the ship, and the contrast was just mind-boggling. The veterans who were leaving to become the cadre of new units forming up were all thin, lean, sharp-eyed, and walked on their toes, and they were tan.

The new guys coming off the ship were relatively white and heavy, walking on their heels. It was really one of the more impressive experiences that I had during the war. It wasn't anything you could talk about, because you didn't want to tell the troops that they didn't look ready, but it made a terrific personal impression.

My battalion landed on Peleliu in support of the two assault battalions of the 5th Regiment. The 5th Regiment was to land with the 1st Marines on their left and 7th Marines on the right.

It didn't surprise me that we were going to have bitter resistance. Some of the naval officers seemed to think that their bombardment had destroyed everything there and, Colonel Puller was told by the captain of his ship, "I'll see you back here for dinner."

I went ashore in an Amtrac. And as we went in, you could see other LVTs burning on the beach. You could see Marines lying on the beach, and a lot of pandemonium.

There were a lot of mines, and the Japanese had attempted to rig up log obstacles. The tetrahedrons were down on other beaches, but they weren't on our beach. The obstacles didn't create any particular problem of moving the tractors in or getting out of them and running to shore. It's just that there was a fair amount of fire.

I ordered my troops to move out as fast as they could. Our mission was to go through the two assault battalions and cross the airfield. And I told everybody, "Understand that the nice, comfortable trench that the Japanese dug alongside the airfield will be well registered by their guns, so don't go there."

We expected the airfield to be defended in depth. And all of those expectations came true. We had been warned that they had tanks, and about mid-afternoon, the Japanese launched a tank and infantry attack across the airfield.

I was in a bomb crater with my intelligence officer. I said, "Send our tanks after them." I had a platoon of five Sherman tanks, and I sent them into the fight. And they just knocked the Japanese tanks apart, literally.

We had to move as hard and fast as we could in the initial stages. As long as they were up on top of those ridges and looking down on us, we had to keep going.

The significant tactical mistake that was made there, in my judgment, is that the character of the battle changed from a maneuver battle to a siege. General Rupertus never recognized that.

He wanted us to hurry and finish it off. But we needed reserves, and we didn't have them.

You couldn't see those caves. The Japanese were in them on both sides, shooting down. You had to go in there with tanks and shoot them up, and that's what we finally wound up doing.

It became pretty clear that before we landed at Peleliu, somebody at the highest levels in Japan had made the decision to change their tactics. Instead of banzai attacks, they wanted their troops on Peleliu to dig in, hang tough, extract the maximum price, and get the best results that they could.

We captured thirteen Japanese military people out of 10,000. It was partially because of their stubbornness and how hard they resisted. They were tough fighters, and they obviously had a healthy respect for the Marines.

When we went up north, we ran into a hill that had been a mine and was full of Japanese. We had to capture that hill.

We had to get around it on the bottom and were being stopped by all the fire coming out of there. I prevailed upon Colonel Walt, who was executive officer of the regiment, to get a 155 mm gun, which we fired point-blank at 250 yards. We just pulverized the side of that hill and then we went in. That was the kind of fighting that had to be done. Fortunately, my regimental commander knew that. I never got pressured into charging some place where we weren't ready to go.

My battalion landed, covered, and then took the length of the airfield in two days. It took us a day to get across the causeway, which was 200 or 300 yards. Once we were on the other side, we advanced and covered that whole peninsula in the next two days with no opposition. But then when we got up to the north of the pocket, and started working down, if you made fifty yards in a day, you had a good day.

The final cleanup assignment took until 16 October, when they relieved us. My 1st Battalion of the 7th Marines was the last battalion engaged. The island was actually secured, in my judgment, as soon as we captured the north end. After that, the enemy had no more reinforcement capability. Somebody suggested that we should simply run barbed wire, and designate "the pocket" as a POW enclosure. There was still the thought that the Marines ought to clean it out. And that's why the campaign continued for another ten days.

The debate over whether or not we needed to go to Peleliu is a very difficult one for me. I lost half my men and 60 percent of my officers there, so it's hard to think that maybe we didn't need to take the island.

✪ OPERATION STALEMATE
1ST MARINE DIVISION
PELELIU, PALAU ISLANDS
19 SEPTEMBER 1944

Major Gayle's tank-infantry-tank battle at the airfield inflicted fifty-nine casualties on the Marines, but it proved fatal for nearly 900 Japanese.

On D-Day, an F4F had belly-landed on the Japanese-held airfield while the Marines were landing. When Gayle's Marines swept across the runways on 16 October, the body of the American pilot was still in the plane, slumped over the controls, dead. The pilot had evidently done a dead-stick landing and a sniper had shot him in the temple as his plane slid to a stop. By the fourth day, Marine Sherman tanks were operating well beyond the airstrip.

After losing fifteen tanks in the "run and gun" battle at the airfield, the Japanese changed tactics and dug in their remaining tanks, using them like pillboxes at roadblocks. Even that didn't change the outcome in a tank-to-tank fight. The Japanese light tanks on Peleliu had only half-inch armor and weighed three tons. The Sherman tank weighed ten times that much.

The shells from the Marines' Shermans were at first ineffective. One tank operator said he was using the standard anti-tank ammo, but the armor-piercing shells were going right through both sides of the Japanese tanks without detonating or causing much damage. Then he changed to high-explosive ammo that detonated much easier and got a "kill" with every hit. The same thing applied to the 2.75-inch bazookas the Marines brought up to the line.

An SBD dive-bomber, returning from another mission, still had a 500-pound bomb while the tank battle was going on. The pilot dove on one of these tanks, plopped the 500-pound bomb right on top of the Japanese tank, and vaporized it. The handful of Marine Sherman tanks wiped out a baker's dozen of Japanese tanks.

The outcome of the battle for the airfield did little to ease the pressure on the 1st Marines. Their regimental commander, Colonel Lewis "Chesty" Puller, pushed his Marines to move inland even though they were taking horrific casualties. Puller was already a legend—much in the mold of his cousin, General George Patton. His reputation for fearlessly engaging the enemy had grown on Guadalcanal, where he had been seriously wounded. Because his wounds hadn't healed fully, he probably shouldn't have been at Peleliu.

Puller's men paid a terrible price for his aggressiveness and Oldendorf's erroneous assumption that the Navy guns had already destroyed all of the Japanese targets on Peleliu. One of the many targets Oldendorf had missed was a large concrete blockhouse in the center of Puller's zone of action. Puller lost thirty-five of his Marines, killed or wounded trying to take this hardened fortification.

U.S. tanks on Peleliu.

National Archives

Finally, Major Ray Davis, the commander of Puller's 1st Battalion, was able to call in fire from the USS *Mississippi*. The venerable battleship's fourteen-inch guns quickly damaged the blockhouse enough that Davis's men could kill the occupants with grenades, demolitions, and flame-throwers.

The men who carried the explosives and flame-throwers were essential to victory for the Marines who fought their way ashore and across Peleliu's steep coral escarpments. Eighteen-year-old PFC Fred Fox didn't start out in the Marine Corps as a demolitions expert or as a flame-thrower man. But on Peleliu he learned just how valuable those skills could be.

□   □   □

PRIVATE FIRST CLASS FRED FOX, USMC
1st Marine Division
Peleliu, Palau Islands
22 September 1944

I was seventeen when I joined the Marines in New Orleans. We got on a train to San Diego for boot camp.

At that time, the Battle of Tarawa was in the news. Everybody wanted to do something. I wanted to be a Marine.

I'd taken machine gun training at Camp Elliott in San Diego, but company commander George Hunt said, "We are getting a new weapon called a flame-thrower, and you seem like you're pretty good at things, so you're going to take over and run the flame-throwers in my company."

The flame-throwers and bazookas were two special weapons that they were just getting into a rifle company. While we were aboard an LST, Captain Hunt said, "We're going to an island called Peleliu." He had a map and explained to us what we were going to do. "This is 'the point,'" he said, "and there's a little cliff about thirty feet high. They can sit inside that cliff and shoot down on our units, so we have take this from the Japs."

A few people had feelings they were going to get killed at Peleliu. I didn't ever have that, but a strange thing about it, a good percentage of the people who say those things do get killed. I had a sergeant that was in the tent with me. He had been at Guadalcanal and New Britain. He said, "I know I'm gonna get killed this time. I don't wanna go—I don't wanna go."

We got an order: "All personnel that have special equipment—machine guns, flame-throwers—go down to your Amtracs in the hull of the ship."

We were in the first wave. As soon as we got ashore, I had the flame-thrower on, and the assistant flame-thrower had a shotgun, and we ran down the beach to the left.

He shot a couple of times with his shotgun, and I tried to shoot the flame-thrower, but it wouldn't light, so we went back.

The first thing I saw was the platoon commander, and he had blood coming out of his shoulder, so I ran over to him and started to bandage up his shoulder, and a Japanese machine gun started shooting at us.

He said, "Don't worry about me, just throw me a pistol." I had a .45 automatic in a scabbard with the flame-thrower, so I took it and tossed it to him with two magazines. He gave me his Thompson submachine gun and some full magazines.

The place they called "the point" was a cliff about thirty feet high with Japanese gun emplacements in it. We almost took the point on the first day, but we lost thirty men when the Japanese counter-attacked. That counter-attack wouldn't have succeeded if our flame-thrower had been working.

If you wanted to get somebody with your flame-thrower, you had to get close, but you could almost always throw hand grenades at 'em.

We were getting dehydrated the first afternoon. I crawled out to where two Jap officers were, or where their bodies were, and they had canteens on 'em. So I cut off the two canteens, and brought 'em back, and drank nice, clear water. Later everybody was getting canteens off a dead Jap to get water.

The second day the CO said, "We have to know if the Japanese are gonna do a banzai charge." I told him, "I've been out there to cut the canteens off those two Jap officers, so I can crawl out there."

So as soon as it got dark, I got rid of everything I had that would make noise, took only a new .45 pistol. I'm on the edge of the cliff, on top of it well past the point.

Just before dawn I could hear Japs trying to get around us out in the water. So I had to get back and report. I climbed down the cliff and took about three steps and there were Japs right under me. As soon as I turned, a bayonet hit me right in the chest. I grabbed the bayonet where it's attached to the rifle, and I had this pistol cocked, loaded, and all I had to do was pull the trigger. I just slammed it right in his face, as hard as I could. I didn't shoot, but he dropped everything, and I dropped the pistol, grabbed his rifle, and jabbed its bayonet into him.

Then I got a hit several times with a saber, which cut me up real bad so I fell to the ground and played dead.

While all this was going on, our guys picked up a machine gun and started shooting at the Japanese who had attacked me. While the Japanese were dodging the fire from our machine gun, I jumped into the water. As soon as I got down to where I figured our lines were, I yelled for a corpsman. A voice said, "I'll come and get you." I found out later on it was Andy Byrnes, the guy who had the machine gun, and he came into the surf and pulled me out of the water. By now it was daylight and as Andy carried me up to our lines, the Japs started shooting at us. Thankfully, Andy got me back safely. He was awarded the Silver Star for this act of valor.

I had a big cut across my back from the saber. I remember lying there on my stomach as the corpsman bandaged me up.

Later that afternoon they brought an Amtrac in and picked up all the wounded. They took me out to a ship called *Tryon,* not a hospital ship but rigged like one. Five or six days later we got to the Admiralty Islands, where there was a naval hospital. We went from there to a hospital on Guadalcanal and then they put me on a ship back to the United States.

✪ OPERATION STALEMATE
1ST MARINE DIVISION
PELELIU, PALAU ISLANDS
26 SEPTEMBER 1944

The Japanese weren't the only enemy on Peleliu. The steamy island offered no respite from the sun. By noon every day the temperature would rise to between 110 and 120 degrees.

And in this heat, water was precious. It was also scarce. Forced to bring in their own water supplies, the Marines pumped a whole lot of it into fifty-five-gallon gasoline drums. But the drums hadn't been washed out and the water was so contaminated that only the most desperate Marines drank it. Instead, they looked for canteens on the bodies of the dead, or for stagnant pools as they moved forward. They scraped the green scum from the surface of the water in a swampy area and drank that, carefully coaxing as much of the filthy water as possible into their canteens.

Along with the heat and thirst, Peleliu's terrain was yet another nightmare for the Marines. The Japanese took every advantage of every wrinkle in the earth, each furrow, rock, and cave. Some of the caves and tunnels were four or five stories deep, and many had electric lights, furniture, cots, and supplies to help the defenders outlast the Americans. The Japanese were dug in so well that it was impossible to see them or even where their machine gun fire was coming from as it laced into the Marines.

To the attackers, it seemed as though every bunker or fighting position had been laid out so that others could support the one being assaulted. If the Marines got close enough to engage a bunker, cave, or blockhouse, at least two more emplacements opened up from the flanks.

The most difficult terrain to maneuver through on Peleliu was a hilly region called the Umurbrogols, a series of high, zigzagging coral ridges, full of natural caves and dangerous cliffs. The drive was halted for a month in the Umurbrogol area, which the Americans came to call Bloody Nose Ridge.

Twenty-five-year-old Captain Everett Pope from Milton, Massachusetts, came to know the area well. Colonel Puller had ordered Pope, the C Company commander, to seize Hill 100, a strategic piece of terrain on Bloody Nose Ridge. Just after noon on 20 September, Captain Pope led ninety Marines—all that remained of his reinforced company that had numbered 235 on D-Day—into the attack on Hill 100. The temperature was already over 105 degrees as they started up the slope.

□   □   □

CAPTAIN EVERETT POPE, USMC
C Company, 1st Battalion, 1st Marines
Peleliu, Palau Islands
28 September 1944

We landed on Peleliu on 15 September 1944. We were told the operation would take two or three days to clean up a few Japanese. No one told us the Japanese had been there since 1930. Or that they knew what they were doing, and were very good at it.

I took over Charlie Company when we were getting ready for the Peleliu landing. We went in on an LVT. When we got to the reef, we ground to a halt and got pounded. There were twelve or more LVTs afire on the shore.

The first instinct is to get off the beach. The landing craft attracted a lot of unwanted attention. We got to the beach as fast as we could, but still got shot at wherever we moved. I lost my first Marine right there on the beach.

They didn't waste any of their people on banzai attacks on Peleliu. In fact, they had a very tactically serious defense.

The morning of the second day we were charged with taking Hill 100. We ran into this blockhouse that was not supposed to have been there, and we had to pull back until naval gunfire reached in and damaged it. Shortly thereafter, my company, Charlie Company, reached the first objective. It was supposed to have been reached within an hour of the landing. We only reached it the second night.

We were ordered to take that hill, and we moved forward through a swamp and met some very serious opposition—not from the top of the hill, but from the other side of the swampy area. We couldn't get through to get at the machine guns that were firing at us. We couldn't get a flame-thrower up, and we couldn't mount a charge.

Then the decision was made to cross that causeway. After a very tough fight, we managed to get across the causeway and up the slope, and by late that night we got to the top of the hill. We just barely managed to hang on while the Japanese threw everything they had at us. It got to be hand-to-hand combat and sharp raining fire by rifles and grenades.

We ended up at dawn the next morning with no ammunition. We could fight for a couple hours, no more. The Japanese sent in a company of troops as dawn broke, and we were assailed from high ground we couldn't even see. On our maps it showed Hill 100 to be the highest piece of terrain, but it wasn't. There was another hill, higher than ours, about 150 yards away. We didn't hold the key terrain—the Japanese did.

For twelve days and nights we fought, buried our dead, and waited. Nobody could get in there. Every day and night we took casualties, including two lieutenants killed in action. Everybody else was wounded. Our rifle company had taken 95 percent casualties counting killed and wounded.

I was wounded. When I went down to the battalion aid station, they pulled some shrapnel out and told me it wasn't serious. Only eight of us came off that hill. It was the closest I ever came to being killed.

✪ OPERATION STALEMATE
1ST MARINE DIVISION
PELELIU, PALAU ISLANDS
28 SEPTEMBER 1944

After Peleliu's airstrip was under American control, Marine Corsairs began to use the field. The aircraft would take off, bomb, strafe, or drop napalm and land again all in the space of five minutes. Many times the pilots wouldn't even bother to raise their landing gear.

After a week of furious battle, General Roy Geiger came ashore to assess the situation. By the time the amphibious assault force commander made his visit to Peleliu, Puller's 1st Marines had taken 2,300 casualties. Despite Puller's objections, Geiger decided that the depleted regiment had to be pulled off of the island. The 1st Battalion had suffered a horrific 70 percent dead or wounded. Ray Davis, its commander, would be awarded the Navy Cross.

General Geiger replaced the 1st Marines with a regimental combat team from the U.S. Army's 81st Infantry Division, the "Wildcats," at the end of that terrible first week. Using bazookas, tanks, and flame-throwers, the fresh troops broke the back of the Japanese defenses, though organized resistance didn't end until 13 October.

After seventy-two grueling days, the 5th and 7th Marine Regiments were finally withdrawn and rejoined the 1st Marines on Pavuvu.

Before committing ritual suicide at the end of October, Colonel Nakagawa sent a final message for Tokyo: "CHERRY BLOSSOM. CHERRY BLOSSOM. CHERRY BLOSSOM." The meaning: "Peleliu has fallen."

The victory had come at a ghastly cost. Nearly 600 soldiers, sailors, and Marines received awards for heroism. But the 1st Marine Division suffered a total of 6,500 casualties and the Army lost another 3,000. And for the Japanese it was even worse. Of the 10,000 troops of the original garrison, fewer than a hundred were alive at the end. In April of 1947, two and a half years after the battle for Peleliu ended, thirty-four Japanese soldiers surrendered. They still couldn't believe that the war was over.

Decades after the Battle of Peleliu, debate continues as to whether the United States really needed to fight the Japanese for the island. There are those who hold to the original premise that an unsecured Peleliu was a threat to MacArthur's flank and would have made the Allied thrust northward to Japan vulnerable.

National Archives

Others think it wasn't necessary. They believe that the U.S. had already driven the Japanese fleet from the island waters and that any air threat from Peleliu could have been ameliorated by regular bombing of the airfield. According to this argument, the 10,000 Japanese troops on Peleliu were no more of a threat than the 120,000 isolated Japanese troops rotting at Rabaul.

Major General Roy Geiger

Peleliu is sometimes called the "forgotten" battle of the Pacific war. But for those who fought there, it will always be remembered. Certainly no one questions the courage and determination of the Marines, soldiers, sailors, airmen, and Coast Guardsmen who fought in this battle and eventually seized this Japanese fortress. One Marine said it best about the bitter struggle: "All gave some; some gave all."

CHAPTER 14
"I HAVE RETURNED":
THE BATTLE OF LEYTE
(OCTOBER 1944)

✪ **U.S. 7TH FLEET**
VICINITY SURIGAO STRAIT
NEAR THE PHILIPPINE ISLANDS
15 OCTOBER 1944

The carnage in the Palau Islands did little to alter the short-term war plans for either the U.S. or Japan. Both sides were now locked into a bloody fight to the finish. For Tokyo there was only one choice: inflict as many casualties as possible on the Americans in hopes that the bloodletting might cause FDR to accept something less than unconditional surrender. It was a battle plan of utter desperation.

In Washington, the costly battles for Tarawa and Saipan had already tempered any pretense of euphoria. Now, the Peleliu casualty figures were cause for the Joint Chiefs to contemplate the long-range consequences of invading the Home Islands. To the small handful who were aware of its potential, Peleliu was a good reason to consider the as yet untested atomic bomb as a preferable alternative to assaulting the emperor's native soil.

But all that was well into the future. In the near term, no one was prepared to suggest that MacArthur revise his plans for returning to the Philippines. Even before the fighting was done on Peleliu, Nimitz began shifting his subs, carriers, and surface forces south from the central Pacific to support the invasion of Leyte.

In preparation for the operation, code-named King Two, American bombers struck Imperial air and naval bases on Formosa and Luzon repeatedly in order to minimize the effectiveness of any counter-attack against MacArthur's invasion forces. By 11 October, when the ships of the 3rd Amphibious Force were ordered to sortie from the Admiralty Islands, the Japanese had lost air superiority over much of the southern Philippines. Two days later, the 7th Amphibious Force deployed from bases MacArthur had seized on the north coast of New Guinea.

On 15 October, the two amphibious forces rendezvoused with the rest of the 3rd and 7th Fleets, just east of Leyte, at the north end of the Surigao Strait. The combined 738-ship armada included eight large aircraft carriers, twenty-four small carriers, a dozen battleships, two dozen cruisers, and 141 destroyers—making it the most powerful naval force ever assembled.

Among those engaged in this extraordinary endeavor were some of the most famous names in the history of the U.S. Navy: Admiral "Bull" Halsey, commanding an abbreviated 3rd Fleet aboard the battleship *New Jersey*; Admiral Marc Mitscher, on the carrier USS *Lexington*; Rear Admirals Frederick Sherman, Ralph Davison, and Gerald Bogan; and Vice Admiral John S. McCain, the grandfather of Senator John McCain.

Vice Admiral Thomas Kinkaid, commander of the 7th Fleet, was also designated as the overall commander of the invasion operation. MacArthur, deployed aboard the cruiser *Nashville*, was little more than a passenger until he got ashore—as he clearly intended to do as soon as possible. Halsey's 3rd Fleet, though not under Kinkaid's operational control, was nonetheless assigned the mission of providing cover for Kinkaid's 7th Fleet and the landings by the amphibious forces. It was a command arrangement that would come to haunt the invaders.

✪ HQ 6TH RANGERS ASSAULT
SULUAN AND DINAGAT ISLANDS
PHILIPPINE ISLANDS
18 OCTOBER 1944

Though D-Day for the invasion of Leyte had been set by the Joint Chiefs for 20 October, operations ashore actually commenced on 17 October when the 6th U.S. Army Ranger Battalion, commanded by Lieutenant Colonel Henry "Hank" Mucci, charged ashore on the islands of Suluan and Dinagat. Their mission: destroy the Japanese radar and communications facilities and anti-shipping artillery on the tiny spots of land that provided natural obstacles off Leyte's landing beaches.

Supported by carrier air strikes and naval gunfire, Mucci's 500 Rangers made short work of the Japanese garrisons on both islands. On Dinagat, in a fashion reminiscent of Peleliu, the enemy had installed heavy artillery that could roll out of caves and fire at the approaching U.S. Navy ships. The guns were spiked in short order and despite lingering Japanese resistance, the Rangers set up beacons to guide the ships of the main landing force to their beaches. After securing the islands, the Rangers planted an American flag— the first to fly in the Philippines since Japan had taken the islands from the United States almost three years earlier.

✪ ABOARD USS NASHVILLE
LEYTE GULF
PHILIPPINE ISLANDS
20 OCTOBER 1944

For the next forty-eight hours after Mucci's rangers seized the two little sentinel islands off Leyte, the landing beaches were pounded by the 7th Fleet's battleships. Carrier aircraft bombed and strafed the beaches. Employing lessons learned from the assaults on the Marianas and Palau Islands, naval gunfire spotters in small aircraft overhead and aboard close-in destroyers and LCIs adjusted the fire of the battleships and cruisers until they were sure that every known target ashore had been hit at least four times.

But the Americans weren't the only ones who had learned lessons at Peleliu. The Japanese didn't bother to return fire on the U.S. battleships and cruisers—they were too far out at sea. Instead, the surprised defenders hunkered down in their holes waiting for softer targets—the landing craft ferrying MacArthur's troops from ship to shore.

Despite a Philippine occupation force that numbered more than 270,000, the Japanese troops ashore, led by General Tomoyuki Yamashita, were woefully unprepared for MacArthur's invasion. On Leyte, the 16,000 men of the Imperial Army's 16th Division were short on supplies, ammunition, and fuel. American carrier aircraft had bombed their air force practically out of existence. And U.S. Navy submarines, operating from bases in New Guinea, New Britain, and the Marianas, were sinking Japanese merchant ships and crude oil carriers faster than they could be replaced.

Early on the morning of 20 October, MacArthur and Kinkaid agreed that the landing beaches had been sufficiently "prepared." When MacArthur was told that the headquarters of the 16th Division had likely been destroyed, he is said to have remarked, "Good, that's the outfit that did the dirty work on Bataan." Shortly before dawn on 20 October, Kinkaid gave the order: "Land the landing force."

The assault, led by the 96th and 24th Infantry Divisions, began after sunrise as the final fires from hundreds of heavy guns swept the beaches and more than 1,000 carrier aircraft crowded the skies. Well before noon, soldiers of the 96th Infantry Division had captured Hill 120, a key D-Day objective. On the other side of the waterfront town of Tanuan, the 24th Infantry Division moved smartly inland. Then, a little after noon, a Navy landing craft motored to within a few feet of the beach. It let down its ramp, and with bullets snapping through the air a few hundred meters away, General Douglas MacArthur strode through the shallow water to the shore. The old general had kept his promise: He had returned.

Once ashore, MacArthur headed to the 24th Infantry Division's command post. From there he broadcast a message to the Filipino people and to listeners in America: "This is the voice of freedom. People of the Philippines, I have returned." After informing them that Filipino president Sergio Osmeña, Manuel Quezon's successor, had returned with him, he concluded with "Let no heart be faint."

One of those who was there for this remarkable moment was twenty-two-year-old First Lieutenant Paul Austin from Ft. Worth, Texas, the commander of F Company, 2nd Battalion, 34th Infantry, 24th Infantry Division.

▫   ▫   ▫

FIRST LIEUTENANT PAUL AUSTIN, US ARMY
F Co, 2nd Bt, 34th Inf, 24th Inf Div
Northeast Coast of Leyte
21 October 1944

We were taken out to the transports, and more than 400 ships left New Guinea, headed for the Philippines. That last night aboard the ship, it was unusually quiet. There was some letter writing going on, some rifle cleaning. It was a serious time in our lives.

It was about six o'clock that morning when they dropped anchor. And then there was a loud explosion. The ship just trembled. We all looked at each other, and felt maybe we had been torpedoed. But someone said, "No, that's the beach bombardment beginning." Our battleships were firing with sixteen-inch shells.

About 9:15, we went over the side, down the cargo net, and into the boats. I was in the second wave. I could see Japanese artillery shells hitting the water, exploding, around the first wave, then around the second wave. I looked over to the left, and two LCIs had been hit and were on fire. I heard a loud explosion behind me, and I looked around. The boat that had been behind me wasn't there. All I could see was three or four helmets floating upside down in the water. About thirty men in the boat were killed within a split second.

Then I heard a loud voice to my left. He said, "Let's get off this beach! Follow me!"

General MacArthur came in the same area we did. He brought with him the president of the Philippines, Osmeña. When MacArthur waded ashore right behind our battalion, the word went just like wildfire. "MacArthur has landed!" kept going through the ranks. Everybody knew who he was, and it was uplifting.

We had heard that phrase "I shall return" over and over. It was kind of a motto, something for us to look forward to.

A tank came roaring up from the beach right after we got fifty yards inland. The tank rolled right on through F Company, up to K Company, and the battalion commander stepped over and started talking to the crew on the tank-infantry phone, giving the gunner the targets. Anything that looked like it could conceal an enemy soldier, he put a 75 mm shell in. He literally blasted his way through that jungle.

When they quit firing that tank, he turned and said to our battalion, "All right, you can go through now." When we got to a little town, we surrounded it and dug in. I went down the line out and told the men, "Dig 'em deep. You will get hit tonight for sure." And they did. At dark we got in those foxholes, and didn't come out until daylight. If you did, you were fair game for the Japanese, and you'd get shot.

About one o'clock that morning, a mortar shell exploded about twenty feet behind my foxhole. I felt like they used that one shell as a signal to begin their attack. Right after that, all hell broke loose. As it turned out, two of our platoons were caught in a banzai attack, and they hit G Company something awful. It was a full Jap battalion; two companies hit that roadblock, and they held it for two hours. The third Jap company swung out across this field in front of F Company and started coming toward us.

They began to lay a murderous fire on us. They knew exactly where we were. After about fifteen minutes, the bullets were coming over our foxhole so thick and fast that I had the distinct fear that if I stuck a finger up, it would be cut off. There was just a constant popping as the bullets came whizzing by.

After a bit, there was a steady roar of our M1s, a machine gun, and about four Browning automatic rifles.

The toughest part, personally, was lying on the ground in a dark jungle, where you can't see your hand before your face, and there was a man about six feet away from us who had been shot through the stomach. But we couldn't do anything for him. We're five or six miles from the road, it's pitch black, and we had no chance in the world to get him out. We did have a medic with us, and he was doing all he could for him. But the man woke up about every hour and called for his mother. That's hard.

I had about 180 guys in my rifle company when we landed on Leyte. When we left, there were fifty-five men left. But I think of it this way. If we hadn't done what we did, today it wouldn't be the United States of America. We'd be speaking Japanese west of the Mississippi River, and across the river they'd be speaking German.

That's what could have happened, and would have happened, if millions of us hadn't put on uniforms and decided it wasn't going to happen.

✪ JAPANESE FIRST STRIKING FORCE
IMPERIAL NAVAL BASE
BRUNEI, BORNEO
21 OCTOBER 1944

The Japanese army may not have been prepared for MacArthur's return to the Philippines, but the Imperial Navy was as ready as it could be given the shortages Japan was experiencing from the U.S. Navy's round-the-clock submarine attacks. Word of the Leyte landings was passed quickly and from Tokyo, Admiral Soemu Toyoda quickly put his Sho One plan into effect. *Sho* is the Japanese word for victory, and Toyoda intended to be victorious.

The Imperial Navy's Sho One plan was a last-ditch effort to engage the U.S. Navy in a decisive battle. Within hours of learning about the landings on Leyte, most of the remaining ships in the First Striking Force were under way, steaming toward the Philippines from their base in Brunei, on the island of Borneo. Admiral Soemu Toyoda had a complicated plan—but one goal: to engage and destroy a U.S. fleet that outnumbered him almost three to one.

Toyoda hoped to lure the American 3rd Fleet away from the invasion beaches and get it into a position where the Japanese could trap it and inflict mortal damage to the ships and men.

Knowing he was outnumbered—particularly in aircraft—Toyoda believed that his more experienced commanders could somehow prevail. His subordinates shared that belief in the Sho One plan, themselves, and their ships.

Admiral Takeo Kurita, aboard the heavy cruiser *Atago*, commanded the Japanese First Attack Force, consisting of five battleships—the *Kongo*, *Haruna*, and the "super battleships" *Nagato*, *Yamato*, and *Musashi*—nine other heavy cruisers, and thirteen destroyers. The three "supers" were the largest battleships ever built and the *Yamato* boasted eighteen-inch guns.

Admiral Jisaburo Ozawa, who had been humiliated at the "Great Marianas Turkey Shoot," led the Northern Force of carriers. Though Ozawa's primary mission was to act as a decoy for Halsey, he was placed in overall tactical command of the operation. A third Japanese naval task force called the Southern Force was split into two separate units, SF-1 and SF-2. Admiral Shoji Nishimura's battleships, cruisers, and destroyers were designated SF-1, and Admiral Kiyohide Shima led a similar surface action force called SF-2. They, along with Kurita's force, intended to enter the Leyte Gulf from opposite sides—Kurita from the north and Nishimura and Shima from the south—in an effort to box in the Americans. Admiral Toyoda calculated that if he could catch the Americans in this "pincer movement" he could trap, destroy, and sink the American ships.

And, like so many other Japanese naval operations, Toyoda's plan relied on deception. He hoped to use Ozawa's task force as a decoy to get Halsey's 3rd Fleet to leave the area around Leyte and go after Ozawa's carriers. Toyoda and Ozawa gambled that, if tempted with nailing four Japanese aircraft carriers, Halsey would leave his station at the east entrance to the San Bernardino Strait and go after the really "big fish."

If all worked as planned, then Ozawa would engage the 3rd Fleet while the other Japanese task forces moved in and decimated the landing forces and the covering ships of the 7th Fleet. Then, in withdrawal, Kurita's force could come to Ozawa's assistance in a decisive battle to destroy or at least severely cripple the U.S. 3rd Fleet. At least, that was the plan.

✪ ✪ ✪

✪ JAPANESE CENTER FORCE
PALAWAN PASSAGE ENCOUNTER
PHILIPPINE ISLANDS
23 OCTOBER 1944

Before dawn on 23 October, Toyoda's battle plan was coming to fruition. Kurita's First Attack Force, which sortied from Brunei, Borneo, was steaming parallel to Palawan Island toward the American invasion beaches. Nishimura's SF-1, which left the same anchorage, was taking a more easterly route toward Leyte. Meanwhile, Shima's battleships and cruisers were racing at flank speed south from Japan and Okinawa.

Admiral Takeo Kurita

Naval Historical Center

At Leyte, the Americans, busy offloading supplies for MacArthur's troops, were blissfully unaware of the pending battle. Then, at 0630 on 23 October, two American submarines, the USS *Darter* and USS *Dace*, observed Kurita's First Attack Force racing north off the west coast of Palawan Island. The *Darter* was able to torpedo the *Atago*, which sank twenty minutes later. The *Dace* torpedoed the *Maya*, causing it to sink just moments after the *Atago*. The *Dace* also seriously damaged the *Takao*, but somehow she was able to withdraw and make her way back to Brunei for repairs. After his flagship sank, the destroyer *Kishinami* rescued Admiral Kurita, who transferred his flag to the *Yamato* and continued on course toward the now-alerted Americans at Leyte. Despite his losses, Kurita made it clear that he expected all remaining ships from his First Attack Force to press on to the San Bernardino Straits.

✪ BATTLE OF THE SIBUYAN SEA
ABOARD 3RD FLEET FLAGSHIP
VICINITY OF LUZON ISLAND
24 OCTOBER 1944
1740 HOURS LOCAL

By dawn on the morning of 24 October, American recon planes, ignorant of Shima's onrushing fleet, were searching without success for Kurita's First Attack Force and Ozawa's carriers.

At about 0800, U.S. Navy scout planes located Kurita's battleships in the Sibuyan Sea, heading for the San Bernardino Strait. The ever-aggressive Halsey wasted no time ordering his 3rd Fleet carriers—now designated as Task Force 38—to launch an air strike. Admiral Frederick Sherman was the first to respond, launching his carrier planes off the USS *Princeton* to engage Kurita's battleships in the Sibuyan Sea. Meanwhile, his ships and carrier aircraft fended off Japanese bombers from Clark and Nichols Fields. The American carriers and their escorts threw up a furious anti-aircraft barrage. It wasn't enough.

At 0935, a single shore-based "Judy," launched from Clark Field, managed to penetrate the Hellcats and anti-aircraft fire and drop one bomb on the flight deck of the *Princeton*. The bomb started fires that raged out of control, causing a huge explosion in the carrier's torpedo storage deck. This explosion also damaged the cruiser *Birmingham*, which had come alongside to help fight fires and transfer wounded. *Princeton* went to the bottom less than an hour later.

Meanwhile, Navy carrier pilots from Bogan's, Davidson's, and Halsey's carriers were taking their revenge. Navy dive-bombers and torpedo planes put nineteen holes in the battleship *Musashi*, eventually sending her down—carrying more than 1,000 Japanese sailors to the bottom with her.

With all of his battleships damaged by at least one bomb or torpedo hit, Kuirita broke away and headed west to get out of range of the American planes.

Halsey's 3rd Fleet aircraft had launched some 260 sorties against the Japanese ships, losing only eighteen planes that day, though casualties aboard the *Princeton* and *Birmingham* were heavy. Briefed by his pilots, Halsey believed that the entire Japanese fleet had suffered heavy casualties, and that Kurita was withdrawing to Brunei.

✪ **USS NEW JERSEY**
OFF CAPE ENGAÑO, LUZON
PHILIPPINE ISLANDS
24 OCTOBER 1944
2000 HOURS LOCAL

Meanwhile, still hoping to get Halsey's attention, Ozawa's decoy force had launched all its planes to the south during the Battle of the Sibuyan Sea to attack the 3rd Fleet, leaving no aircraft to cover the Northern Force carriers. Ozawa desperately wanted the decoy plan to work. Unless he could draw Halsey's ships north, Kurita's First Attack Force would be unable to get through the San Bernardino Strait in sufficient time to engage the Japanese Southern Force before it could wreak havoc on Leyte.

Ozawa's decoy mission was a disaster for his pilots. Before the Battle of the Sibuyan Sea, Ozawa had 116 aircraft. By late afternoon of 24 October, when one of Halsey's scout planes finally spotted black smoke spewing intentionally from Ozawa's carriers, he had just twenty-nine remaining.

Halsey jumped at the bait. He ordered his 3rd Fleet to give chase—with the goal of launching a dawn attack on the Japanese flattops. That's when things began to unravel for the Americans.

As he sped north, Halsey thought that the 7th Fleet transports and their escorts at Leyte faced no serious threats because he'd accepted the exaggerated reports of his returning pilots that Kurita's force had been compelled to retire and head back to Brunei. This faulty information led him to presume that Kinkaid no longer needed the 3rd Fleet's covering force. The hard-charging "Bull" was wrong.

Kurita had turned toward Brunei, but then he reversed course and headed back east toward the San Bernardino Straits. At 2000 on 24 October, as he sped northward, Halsey was heading away, just as Ozawa and Kurita intended.

Halsey radioed Admirals Nimitz and Kinkaid with the message: "I AM PROCEEDING NORTH WITH THREE TASK GROUPS TO ATTACK ENEMY CARRIER FORCE AT DAWN."

✪ BATTLE OF SURIGAO STRAIT
7TH FLEET FLAGSHIP COMMAND
VICINITY OF LEYTE GULF
24 OCTOBER 1944
2020 HOURS LOCAL

Earlier that day, Halsey had sent a message indicating that he was going to create a new task force group by pulling ships from the other groups. This new force, to be called Task Force 34, was to consist of four battleships, six cruisers, and fourteen destroyers. Halsey had said that it would be used "to engage the enemy decisively at long ranges."

Admirals Nimitz and Kinkaid had each received Halsey's earlier radio message, but neither had any idea that creating Task Force 34 meant Halsey was not going to provide a covering force for the 7th Fleet's amphibious force, which still had 110,000 troops and 250,000 tons of ammunition, fuel, rations, and other supplies still to be put ashore.

When Nimitz and Kinkaid received Halsey's message at 2000 about heading north with three groups, they each assumed that he would use Task Force 34 to guard the San Bernardino Strait against Kurita's return and would be taking his only three carrier task groups to engage Ozawa's fleet.

As long as the 7th Fleet commanders were able to provide cover from their own ships in the south, and there was no interference from Kurita's Center Force or Ozawa's Northern Force, there was no need to worry. They could handle the Southern Force, and no one replied, questioning Halsey's order.

For his part, Halsey believed his intentions were clear. He said, "I am proceeding north," and had earlier reported that he would be with Task Force 34. No one questioned the fact that he was going north, nor did they think to inquire who was left to guard the San Bernardino Strait.

When the news came that afternoon about Kurita's losses and apparent withdrawal, Halsey changed his mind about creating Task Force 34. He reasoned that with Kurita so weakened and in retreat, Kinkaid could handle any other problems the Japanese navy might pose. So Halsey steamed north, to engage Ozawa, leaving no U.S. force to guard the San Bernardino Strait or provide cover for Kinkaid's 7th Fleet.

On the night of 24 October, believing that Halsey's Task Force 34 was guarding the San Bernardino Strait and the northern waters, Kinkaid concentrated on the south. He assigned Rear Admiral Jesse Oldendorf to "plug up" the Surigao Strait between Dinagat Island (taken by the 6th Ranger Battalion almost a week earlier) and the southern tip of Leyte Island. It would be the logical sea entrance for an attack by the Japanese Southern Force.

Kinkaid relied on more than logic, however. He'd received reports earlier in the day that the Southern Force had been sighted in the Sulu Sea—due west and opposite the invasion's landing beaches. By having Oldendorf cover the southern entrance to the Surigao Strait, and with Task Force 34 supposedly covering the waters north of the landing site, the U.S. invasion of Leyte could continue until completed without interference by the Japanese. All Kinkaid had to do was keep the Japanese Southern Force from getting through. Kinkaid and Oldendorf both reasoned that Task Force 34 would surely take care of Kurita's Center Force if and when it returned.

At 1900 hours on 24 October, Nishimura was already at the southern end of Surigao Strait and sailing north toward the American transports. At 2230, one of Oldendorf's thirty-nine torpedo boats sighted Nishimura's force in the strait and radioed its presence to Oldendorf and Kinkaid.

At fifteen minutes past midnight on 25 October, another U.S. torpedo boat encountered Nishimura's force and launched its torpedoes. Others joined in the fray; altogether they launched thirty-four torpedoes during the three-hour attack, but scored only one hit. Emboldened, Nishimura charged in. He thought he had somehow successfully maneuvered through the gauntlet of American torpedo boats on both sides of his line of ships.

But then Nishimura's luck ran out. He was confronted by Oldendorf's main force, positioned at the top of the strait. Waiting for the Japanese ships were six U.S. Navy battleships, four heavy cruisers, four light cruisers, and twenty-one destroyers. Oldendorf had positioned his ships to trap the Japanese force. It was a traditional old-fashioned naval battle, with extensive use of big guns and torpedoes.

At exactly 0300, Oldendorf's twenty-one destroyers caught the enemy from both sides near the southern tip of Leyte. The gauntlet began to close as Nishimura's ships moved closer to the transports.

In less than an hour Nishimura was confronted first by the destroyers, then by Oldendorf's cruisers and battleships, which proceeded to unleash their big guns. The brutal shelling took a terrible toll.

By the time the engagement was over, the U.S. 7th Fleet had put every one of Nishimura's ships out of commission. He and his crew perished when the Americans sank his flagship, the battleship *Yamashiro*.

Meanwhile Admiral Shima, with his half of the Southern Force, had entered the bottom end of the Surigao Strait. He'd arrived just in time to see the results of Oldendorf's awful destruction of Nishimura's flotilla.

Shima's flagship, *Nachi*, collided with the retreating and blazing *Mogami* of Nishimura's force, and *Nachi* was damaged in the incident. U.S. torpedo boats had already attacked Shima's force on the way in, knocking one of his light cruisers out of formation. Now Shima had a paltry force of three cruisers and four destroyers, and he could see that they didn't stand a chance. His ships made a quick U-turn and headed back to the safety of the Mindanao Sea.

As the battle of the Surigao Strait developed, Lieutenant (jg) Jim Halloway, a twenty-two-year-old gunnery officer from Charleston, South Carolina, was aboard the destroyer *Bennion*. Through his binoculars, he could see the approaching enemy vessels.

◻   ◻   ◻

LIEUTENANT (JG) JAMES HALLOWAY, USN
Aboard USS *Bennion*
Surigao Strait
24 October 1944
0004 Hours Local

I remember thinking at the time, "That looks just like a Japanese battleship!" We'd gotten reports from submarines that had seen this group coming into Surigao Strait. They first reported a battleship, then a second, and a third. Then they submerged and came up and reported, "Now we see a cruiser."

Their battleships turned out to be the *Fuso*, which had nine fourteen-inch guns, and each projectile is as tall as I am. That's a big hunk of explosive. And the *Yamashiro* had nine or maybe twelve sixteen-inch guns. The *Yamashiro* was followed by the *Mogami*. She was very heavily armed with eight-inch guns, torpedo tubes, and six-inch guns. And I think there were four or five destroyers with torpedoes. We had, in our group, nine destroyers that would be taking on this group as they came through.

The Japanese were coming in a column. And we were coming down on their bow. Our destroyers were at 300-foot intervals, and we were making thirty-two knots.

I was standing up with the binoculars. And there it was, clearly a Japanese battleship. At that point-blank range, we were given our target from the squadron commander of the destroyers. He said, "Your division will attack the second ship, the *Yamashiro*."

We could see two battleships now. And we cranked the director around, put the crosshairs right on the second battleship, and lowered the crosshairs to the waterline. I told the people in the plotting room, tracking *Yamashiro* by radar, to get her course and speed.

We received the orders to make the run in. That's when we increased speed to thirty-two knots, made smoke, and headed for our launch point for the best torpedo shot, 1,000 yards from the *Yamashiro*.

It sort of gave us comfort when our battleships started firing, six in a row, with their tracers. Looking through the lens, I could see them impacting on both the *Fuso* and the *Yamashiro*. Guns were being torn off and the superstructure began to collapse, and fires started. But the Japanese guns didn't slow down a bit.

One torpedo would not sink it. It would take three or four. We could launch ten, but were told to only launch five—our division would launch fifteen—so there would be fifteen torpedoes going against the *Yamashiro*.

We fired a spread to take care of the ship's maneuvering area. That way, between three and six torpedoes hit *Yamashiro*. And then she's in trouble.

We could also see where the projectiles from our ship were striking the Japanese ships. When one of those large armor-piercing shells hits, the first thing that happens is that the whole area of the armor where the shell hits turns pink. I guess it's just all that energy being dissipated, and then comes the explosion. It was quite a Fourth of July show because when it hit, the shell exploded, and then it set off ready ammunition topside, and that would also explode, and it was a pretty wild scene.

We were sent south again to sink the rest of the Japanese ships that were trying to escape. As we went again into the strait, it was really a scene out of Dante's *Inferno*. The seas were covered with oil, there was wreckage all over the place, and there were Japanese sailors hanging onto the wreckage as we went by.

That's when *Bennion* encountered the *Asagumo*, a Japanese destroyer about five miles away. It looked like it was badly hit and was limping away. But the commander of the 7th Fleet ordered us to destroy it.

"One of our destroyers, the *Grant*, was badly shot up and dead in the water, but she was able to get steam up and get under way again. I think *Grant* lost something like sixty people.

Early in the melee, just as we were beginning to withdraw, we saw a large shape on our starboard side. It started firing toward the *Grant*. We were only about 2,000 yards away but the cruiser hadn't seen us—it was shooting *over* us. The plotting room said, "We have her course and speed, and she looks like she's in a turn." The captain said, "Fire five torpedoes!"

So we swung the tubes out, ready to fire, hit the switch, and away they went. We sank the cruiser *Asagumo*.

We listened to the TBS, the VHF radio to "talk between ships." Normally, it wouldn't range that far, but we were getting some skip distance and we heard this voice say, "This is Taffy 2. I'm under fire by some sixteen-inch guns, and two battleships and three cruisers are bearing down on me."

Here we'd just finished this night action, and thought we'd destroyed the Japanese threat to the Leyte beachhead. Now, suddenly we find that aircraft carriers providing our air cover are under attack from Japanese surface ships in the vicinity.

I went from the elation of great victory to a feeling of, "This can't be happening." It was a tremendous reversal for all of us.

The only advantage we had was that, for a while, the Japanese ships were firing armor-piercing shells and they went in one side of the carrier and out the other before exploding. But then the Japanese caught on and began using 2,000-pound bombs.

☆ TASK UNIT TAFFY 3
BATTLE OFF SAMAR ISLAND
25 OCTOBER 1944
0815 HOURS LOCAL

Admiral Oldendorf's destroyers, cruisers, and battleships had set a trap for the Japanese Southern Force and it had worked. The crossing of the "T"—a classic maneuver taught at naval schools for centuries—had caught Admiral Nishimura off guard. His flagship, the *Yamashiro*, was sunk, taking its skipper to the bottom of the bloody, oily, fiery waters of the Surigao Strait.

For Oldendorf and his men, victory had been complete. But Halsey's move north was having devastating consequences. Admiral Kurita, having changed his mind about retreating, entered the San Bernardino Strait just after midnight and was surprised that the 3rd Fleet was nowhere in the vicinity. Four hours later, Kurita's ships slid unnoticed through the strait and headed south to Leyte Gulf.

Kurita planned to reposition his ships from a search and patrol night formation to the circle formation used for anti-aircraft defense. It was just about the time that the Battle of Surigao Strait was ending to his south. At 0415 Admiral Kinkaid radioed Halsey and asked about Task Force 34, inquiring whether it was still guarding San Bernardino Strait. Halsey didn't get the message until two and a half hours later.

At about 0720, Oldendorf recalled his ships from the Surigao Strait, and about that time, Halsey—a few hundred miles north of Leyte Gulf—was composing a radio message in response to Kinkaid's earlier query. This message should have informed Kinkaid that Task Force 34 had not been deployed and was not guarding the San Bernardino Strait. Instead, it merely informed the 7th Fleet commander that Task Force 38 was heading north in its entirety.

Ten minutes later, Oldendorf received an urgent radio message from an carrier escort with one of the 7th Fleet's task units. The 7th Fleet had eighteen carrier escorts, divided into three task units of six small carriers each, code-named "Taffy" 1, 2, and 3.

Task Units Taffy 1 and 2 were 120 miles out from Leyte on submarine and anti-aircraft patrol. Taffy 3's commander, Admiral Clifton Sprague, had launched twelve fighters and six planes of an anti-submarine patrol just after 0600 to provide cover for the ships in Leyte Gulf, to combat air patrol over the invasion beachhead, and to execute ground attacks on the enemy troops on Leyte. The Taffy task units and their aircraft weren't trained, or even equipped, to fight an enemy fleet.

Then, just after dawn on 25 October, Kurita's Center Force off Samar Island surprised the carrier escorts of Taffy 3. About 0700, a recon plane from Taffy 3 located the Japanese ships but Kurita reacted first, ordering a "general attack."

Kurita's order meant that each Japanese skipper would initiate independent action. When the shells from Kurita's battleships and cruisers began splashing in the ocean near his carriers, Sprague sent Kinkaid an urgent radio message that they were under heavy attack from Kurita's fleet, and that their own small force was no match for the Japanese. Sprague asked for immediate help from Task Force 34, which he assumed to be nearby, or from the rest of the 3rd Fleet somewhere north of his position.

The terrible news that the enemy fleet was already halfway into Leyte Gulf was passed up the line. The entire Leyte invasion operation was now in jeopardy.

When Halsey finally replied to Kinkaid's earlier radio inquiry, Kurita's big guns were already shelling the small escort carriers of Taffy 3. Admiral Sprague radioed that he was under fire from four battleships, eight heavy cruisers, and eight destroyers. All of his carriers were well within range of the big Japanese guns and the enemy ships were all out of range of his much smaller five-inch guns.

Suddenly, Sprague saw an avenue of delay, if not delivery: a bank of fog and rain. He ordered his carriers and destroyer escorts to enter the nearby rainsquall. It bought them about fifteen minutes of cover. As Sprague lay hidden, both he and Kinkaid were wondering what had happened. Where was Halsey's Task Force 34? Where was the rest of the 3rd Fleet?

Once the rainsquall no longer protected them from visual contact, Admiral Sprague knew he couldn't outrun or outgun the Japanese battlewagons or cruisers. Having already sent all his planes out on patrol, and desperate to save his carriers, at 0715 Sprague ordered his three escorts, USS *Hoel*, USS *Heermann*, and USS *Johnston*, to counter-attack the Japanese formation.

If the carriers were going to survive, the little destroyers were going to have to go up against battleships and cruisers four times their size, many with fourteen- to eighteen-inch guns. It was like a dog chasing a truck—the entire Taffy task unit was smaller than the *Yamamoto*.

The destroyer's confrontation with Kurita's powerful First Attack Force seemed like a suicide mission. Yet Sprague's order was carried out with extraordinary courage and determination. The gamble paid off and most of the carriers survived the first and only encounter between carriers and surface combatants.

Thirty-five minutes into the lopsided fight, Sprague sent his only remaining surface combatants, little destroyer escorts, to engage the battleship

Yamamoto, Kurita's flagship. After several exchanges, the *Yamamoto* fled to escape the American torpedoes. For the rest of the naval skirmish, Kurita remained off-balance and was unable to get back into action.

During the battle between Kurita's Center Force battleships and Sprague's Taffy units, Lieutenant Tom Stevenson, a twenty-two-year-old communications officer, had a ringside seat on the deck of one of Taffy 3's destroyer escorts, the USS *Samuel B. Roberts*.

□   □   □

LIEUTENANT THOMAS (TOM) STEVENSON, USN
Aboard USS *Samuel B. Roberts*
25 October 1944

As the communications officer and a deck officer, I stood eight hours of deck watch a day and decoded all the messages that came in. We were aboard the smallest of the major war vessels and I would have to prepare the messages for the appropriate officers on the ship and supervise the general operations of the radio room and the signal apparatus.

Taffy 3 screened for anti-submarine and for anti-aircraft purposes.

Planes were taking off from the carriers of Taffy 3 and were supposed to put up combat air patrol to protect the ships from air attack, and to launch strikes at the beach every morning at dawn to support the troops with bombing and strafing.

The planes would come back and re-arm, go back, and make a second strike during the day, and sometimes a third strike. Meanwhile, we'd keep a combat air patrol of six fighters above our own formation to try to ward off any attacking Japanese planes.

At night the radio for TBS signal skips, and you can hear it sometimes many miles away. So I heard the reports of the Battle of Surigao Strait during the night. We were aware that we had won a terrific victory.

Suddenly, the "general quarters" alarm rang for everybody to report to their battle stations. The Japanese ships had spotted us. We could only see the tops of the masts of the *Yamato*, the *Kongo*, and big battleships. They were over fourteen miles away. We didn't know they were coming after us until they opened fire.

Evidently, they were on their way to Leyte Gulf, where the troop transports were. They just stumbled on us.

Well, against the battleships, there was no defense because they were so far away and their guns could reach us, while we couldn't even shoot a quarter of the way at them. So our only defense was to lay smoke around the carriers

As they closed on us, we had hoped that we'd be able to fire on them, but it took a long time before they came within range. Then we could use our five-inch guns, which we did. But our main weapons to really cause some damage were our torpedoes. But unfortunately the destroyer escorts only carried three each, whereas the destroyers had ten. So as things got worse, the admiral ordered the "small boys" to form up for a torpedo attack. The "small boys" were the destroyers, and the "small, small boys" were the destroyer escorts.

The destroyers were the *Hoel*, the *Johnston*, and the *Heermann*. We saw the *Hoel* and the *Johnston* form up for a torpedo attack, but the *Heermann* had not yet shown up, so we just fell in behind the *Johnston* and the *Hoel*.

We saw the *Johnston* starting to get hit pretty badly. We were able to go all the way in to fire at about 6,000 yards. We were tracking a heavy cruiser. I don't know whether it was the *Tone* or the *Chikuma*, but we felt that we made a hit.

I was up on the signal bridge when we saw the *Johnston* the last time. She was really shot up, but she was still firing and still steaming along pretty well. But all of a sudden she got into the smoke and I never saw her again.

The captain came on the squawk box and indicated that our chances of surviving were not great, but we were going to do a lot of damage to the enemy. John McClair and I were good friends, so we were up on deck together, and we shook hands and said good luck to each other.

The first real hit that I could feel was when a cruiser shell went through the main deck and through the side of the CIC where we were and into the fire room, below the bridge structure.

It was a panic, because everything went out and you could hardly breathe. Everyone ran to get out. I had a talker's helmet and a voice megaphone in front of me. I had a hard job getting them to get out, so I got out there a little late myself. Thank God that I did, because as I looked down on the main deck I saw a lot of bodies strewn around.

First thing I had to do was to go back down into the radio room where the decoding machine was and get the decoding wheels and throw them overboard.

Then I was supposed to blow up the ECM, which was a top-secret coding machine. I didn't put the hand grenade in the side of it, as I was supposed to do, because I was afraid I'd set it off too soon and kill myself. One of the enlisted men had a submachine gun, and he shot the thing up for me. It was just as good a job as having the hand grenade do it, I guess.

There was a safe right outside my room with the secret documents and all the invasion plans. They were all in weighted bags, and we each got several bags and threw them overboard.

The last one I threw overboard didn't sink. I'd failed to put weights inside it. The captain said, "You'd better get that bag." So I retrieved the bag and took it with me.

They taught us in communication school that if you didn't destroy the electric coding machine and the wheels, you'd better go down with the ship, because you would be court-martialed and be in more trouble than if you died.

Then I decided to go up on the bridge. It was crowded up there because everybody had gathered there.

I went back to the signal bridge, right behind the navigating bridge. And then a big explosion hit aft, and the blast came forward and knocked us all down. The signal bag caught on fire from the shrapnel. But the ship was still steaming, although they only had one fire room and two engines running.

But then another big explosion struck aft on the port side, and with that, everything went out. The ship just stopped, a big hole in the side from the last explosion. After that there was no power and nothing much you could do.

The air ejection for the guns had failed and the aft gun exploded. A powder bag "cooked off" in the breech of the gun because there was no air-cooling coming through. So that gun was finished. And the forward five-inch gun had run out of ammunition.

The captain decided to carry out the destruction drill and abandon ship. That's when we started to get off. I knew if I got off that ship alive that I was going to live.

A group attached themselves to scaffolding that floated off the deck. I swam out to them, maybe 400 yards away, and tried to persuade them to get off that thing, and join us where we had a floater net.

We had some water and malted milk tablets. They had nothing. We thought that they'd be better with us, and we thought as a larger group we'd be noticed. But they didn't want to leave. They insisted on staying on that scaffolding. We took one man who was badly burned back to our group, but the rest of them refused to get off. They were never found. We learned later that they had been attacked by sharks. There were about sixteen of them.

In the beginning, everybody was delighted just to be alive, and thinking that we'd get picked up right away. Shortly after the ship sank, a plane came over us. He buzzed us two or three times, and then wiggled his wings to signal us. We felt sure that we were going to be rescued then.

Unfortunately he couldn't land on his carrier, and eventually landed in Tacloban where the airfield was semi-operational. By then he'd forgotten the exact coordinates of where we were. Evidently he was struggling to find a place to land and had nothing to write with.

As the second night approached, things really deteriorated, and it was every man for himself. We really started to lose hope, and didn't see any way we were going to be picked up. I thought, "I'd better make peace with the Almighty."

The oil slick helped us though. It kept the sharks away from us. We had shark scares, but that heavy oil, almost like tar, kept the sharks away and it coated you from the sun. We were right on the equator, and during the day the sun is brutal.

Well, we were about on our last legs, and then we saw these small vessels on the horizon, coming towards us. We were sure they were Japanese. But they were LCIs: American patrol craft. But they had their guns trained on *us,* because *we* looked like Japanese to them. We were screaming, "We're Americans, we're Americans!" That's when they turned their bullhorn on and asked about the World Series. Fortunately somebody knew who won.

So it was like a madhouse. They had to pull us out of the water. But it was great joy, I'll tell you.

I think that we prevented the Japanese from taking over the Gulf and isolating the troops ashore. If that had happened, I think the invasion would have been a flop. I mean, eventually it would have taken place, but I think that Taffy 3 kept things going so that the invasion was kept right on schedule.

✪ ✪ ✪

The battle against Kurita's Center Force lasted more than two hours. During that time the aircraft from all three Taffy units arrived on the scene to help out. Some of them had already spent their munitions on land-based targets, but although they had no bombs or ammunition for their guns, they still dove and swooped menacingly at the Japanese ships. It was an effective feint that caused the ships to swerve and retreat in evasive maneuvers.

Some of the planes still had armaments and were able to inflict mayhem on the enemy ships, bombing and strafing them with great success. The Taffy units' planes sank three Japanese heavy cruisers and damaged a number of other ships.

By the time the two-hour battle was over at 0945, the *Hoel* and *Johnston* and the destroyer escort *Samuel B. Roberts* had been sunk by gunfire from the Japanese ships. And though at least one torpedo struck one of the

Japanese ships, the Japanese finally succeeded in hitting the American carrier escort *Gambier Bay*. Hammered by enemy gunfire, the little carrier became dead in the water, and finally sank at 0907. And then, just minutes later, the little carrier escort *St. Lo* was struck four times in the first organized kamikaze attack of the war.

At 0925 one of the sailors aboard Sprague's flagship yelled, "They're getting away!" Unexpectedly, Kurita ordered his ships to break off action against the Americans and retire to the north. The destroyer escort torpedo attacks on the *Yamamoto* had effectively slowed Kurita's flagship, and it trailed sluggishly behind the other ships. Finally, it was so far back that Kurita couldn't plan a strategy. He was still confused, thinking that the little Taffy units were Halsey's Task Force 38.

Admiral Sprague was incredulous. Kurita's cruisers and destroyers—poised to destroy the American ships—turned and headed back out to the open ocean.

The sinking of the *Gambier Bay* carrier escort affected Lieutenant Dick Roby, a twenty-four-year-old pilot of Taffy 3. He'd flown cover for the 20 October landings at Leyte and had taken part in the Battle of Surigao Strait and other action of that week. He was assigned to a different mission when his Taffy unit came under attack.

⬚   ⬚   ⬚

LIEUTENANT RICHARD ROBY, USN
Battle of Leyte
25 October 1944

My plane was a Grumman FM2 built by General Motors, the successor to the original F4F. It had a single-row, nine-cylinder, 1,350 horsepower engine.

We'd provide combat air patrol either over the ships or over the island, and we'd also escort the bombers on bombing missions.

On 21, 22, and 23 October I led eight planes to predawn combat air patrol over the Tacloban airstrip on Leyte Island. On 24 October, I had been relieved at about 7:20 in the morning and started back to the ships. All of a sudden they said, "Hold up, we've got Japanese bombers coming in!"

When they radioed me that these planes were coming in, I was about probably 10,000 or 11,000 feet, and they were a little below me, so it was easy to pick up speed and go down and make a run.

I made what they call a semi-high side run and I shot the right wing off the first one. Then I pulled up and shot another one. I went after the third one and chased him from about 6,000 feet down to sea level. I got two plus a probable that day.

On the morning of 25 October they woke me up about one o'clock in the morning and we started loading five torpedoes.

We were going to go chase the survivors of the Battle of Surigao Strait, which was fought the night before south of Leyte. So they expected us to go down there and bomb the second group. The battleships and cruisers had started after them, too. But then they cancelled us.

Approximately ten minutes to seven the word came out that the Japanese fleet was twenty-five miles away. So Sykes, Dugan, a fellow named Rocky Phillips, and I got off. We were vectored northwest to take on two destroyers that were approximately twenty-five miles from the task force. We were over a thin overcast at about 2,000 feet, and they didn't have any radar fire control and didn't see us coming. And interestingly enough, you can sink a destroyer with .50-caliber machine guns, because every round we had was an armor-piercing round. In every three rounds, one was armor-piercing, one an armor-piercing tracer, and one an armor-piercing incendiary.

When the four of us went down in our first run, they didn't start to shoot at us until we were recovering because they couldn't see us coming. All four of us made two runs.

But when I came back up on top, I was above this 2,000-foot layer of clouds, and I couldn't find anybody. Not a soul. I knew where the Japanese fleet was supposed to be so, I headed in that general direction.

I ran into Fowler, the skipper of VC-5. He had about five torpedo bombers and a whole bunch of fighters. He was going to fly right by them;

he didn't see them. I finally got his attention and indicated, "They're over that way."

He then turned and we went over. I probably had 1,000 rounds of ammunition left, maybe 1,200, in my four guns. I made a lot of runs after I didn't have any more ammunition, because if I'd see one of our torpedo bombers, and he had his bomb bay doors open, I'd fly in front of him to give him cover—drawing fire to me rather than to him.

On a combat ship, you know the destroyer is armed, but they've got basically no armor. So, our fifties go right through them. But, on the cruisers and battleships, you're talking armor. They've also got a lot of guns on the flight decks. So you aim for those. By the time that day was over we had sunk three cruisers.

✪ USS NEW JERSEY
BATTLE OF CAPE ENGAÑO
25 OCTOBER 1944
0845 HOURS LOCAL

Halsey's race to the north wasn't a total waste. Though he had taken the bait and left his station to chase after Ozawa's flattops, he did manage to catch the Northern Force early in the morning of 25 October. At 0540, his dawn patrol found the Japanese carriers and their escorts about 200 miles east of Cape Engaño, on the northern coast of Luzon.

The first American aircraft appeared over Ozawa's fleet shortly after 0710. The Japanese admiral had no intention of trying to wage a serious battle against waves of American dive- and torpedo-bombers. But, in hopes of delaying Halsey as long as possible, he sent up his last twenty-nine fighters. In a matter of minutes they were all downed.

While the futile aerial battle was being waged, Ozawa, unaware that Kurita's badly battered First Attack Force had retired, desperately tried to summon help. There was no help available. The land-based Japanese air armada on Luzon had been all but destroyed in four full days of aerial combat with the U.S. Navy pilots.

At 0820, just as Halsey's pilots were lining up to make their first dive-bomb and torpedo runs on Ozawa's now undefended carriers, he received a message from Kinkaid informing that Kurita was at that moment engaging the Taffy carrier escorts. The crusty admiral was stunned. But before he could act, his pilots were engaging Ozawa's carriers.

They first clobbered the Japanese aircraft carrier *Chitose* with bombs and torpedoes and then went after the destroyer *Akatsuki*, which exploded and sank. Next, they hit two more carriers, the *Zuiho* and the *Zuikaku*—Ozawa's flagship. Then, at about 0900, shortly after *Zuiho* was struck by an American torpedo, damaging her rudder, Halsey received another urgent message from Kinkaid: "OUR CVES BEING ATTACKED BY 4 BBS PLUS 8 CRUISERS AND OTHERS STOP REQUEST LEE COVER LEYTE AT TOP SPEED STOP REQUEST FAST CARRIERS MAKE IMMEDIATE STRIKE."

Halsey, preoccupied with the battle against Ozawa, replied to Kinkaid's plea for help with a position report for TF 38 reasoning that Kinkaid, once he knew their location, would know that it was impossible to come to Sprague's aid in time.

Kinkaid replied with a message he didn't even bother to put into code. In plain English, he asked, "WHERE IS LEE? SEND LEE." But Admiral Lee was with Halsey, doing battle with the Japanese Northern Force.

By now Halsey's second wave of American attack aircraft were attacking the carrier *Chiyoda*. It was dispatched later in the day by the guns of closing American ships. The Japanese cruiser *Tama* was also struck and later sank.

About 1000, there was a lull in the one-sided battle and Ozawa decided to move his flag to the *Oyodo*, a light cruiser. He knew that staying with *Zuikaku* was dangerous as well as pointless. His flagship aircraft carrier was already a main target of the persistent 3rd Fleet aircraft. His intuition was correct: Moments after he moved over to the *Oyodo*, two more carriers were sunk—the *Zuiho* and *Zuikaku*.

But the aircraft of the 3rd Fleet couldn't do it all. Some of the remaining Japanese ships were heavily armored, and American bombs seemed to bounce off their decks. Two Japanese battleships—the *Ise* and *Hyuga*—became the targets of the U.S. Navy's big guns.

In the heat of battle, Halsey continued to ignore Kinkaid's requests for help, not viewing it as his responsibility—he'd already advised the 7th Fleet that he was exercising his prerogative of going after the Northern Force.

At 1000 hours, Halsey received a message from Admiral Nimitz in Hawaii, who had been monitoring the two different battles taking place around the Philippine Islands. Anxious to know the answer to Kinkaid's question regarding the whereabouts of Lee's Task Force 34, he sent a dispatch to Halsey: "WHERE IS REPEAT WHERE IS TASK FORCE 34 RR THE WORLD WONDERS."

The message delivered to Halsey contained the usual "nonsense" padding at the front and back of the actual message. These short, frivolous phrases were intended to confuse enemy code specialists. The radio operator aboard the *New Jersey* removed the one at the front of the message, but left in the phrase following the double consonants, which indicated where the padding started. So, the message delivered to Halsey contained the added words of padding: "THE WORLD WONDERS."

Halsey interpreted it as a harsh rebuke—with the "REPEAT" intended for great emphasis and "THE WORLD WONDERS" intended as sarcasm. He was infuriated. To comply with Kinkaid's request for help meant that he'd have to break off his attack on Ozawa and let him get away rather than finishing him off right there.

But Halsey also sensed that Nimitz was alarmed about the fate of Kinkaid's Fleet and was convinced that the 3rd Fleet battleships ought to be in action off Samar with Sprague. So just before 1100, Halsey ordered Admiral Lee's Task Force 34 and Rear Admiral Bogan's carrier group to withdraw from the attack on Ozawa's force and race south to provide support for Sprague.

Four hours into the battle, Halsey's Task Force 38 turned away. The only capital ships Ozawa had left were the six battleships that Halsey wanted to destroy. But now, to the Japanese admiral's surprise, the attackers were turning around and retiring.

Ironically, if the 3rd Fleet had stayed to protect the San Bernardino Strait, Halsey would have had the great battle he'd wished for and Kurita wouldn't have done nearly the damage to Sprague's ships. Or, if he'd have stayed in the area east of Cape Engaño, the Northern Force might well have come farther south and Halsey would have been able to finish off Ozawa's fleet. Either one of the two actions would have been the great victory he sought. He got neither.

✪ HQ PACIFIC FLEET COMMAND
PEARL HARBOR, HAWAII
28 OCTOBER 1944

Despite Halsey's decision to chase the decoy Ozawa had set for him, the four-day Battle of Leyte Gulf was a profound American victory. In the largest naval engagement in history, the Japanese lost almost half their naval forces in the Philippine waters—twenty-eight of sixty-four ships—including four aircraft carriers, three battleships, six heavy cruisers, four light cruisers, and eleven destroyers. More than 10,500 Japanese sailors and airmen were also killed.

The Americans lost just six ships, including two escort aircraft carriers, a heavy cruiser, two destroyers, and a destroyer escort.

When it was all over on 27 October, the Imperial Navy was all but finished. It would never again be able to mount a significant challenge to the U.S. fleet.

✪ HQ 24TH INFANTRY DIVISION
BREAKNECK RIDGE AT ORMOC, LEYTE
PHILIPPINE ISLANDS
26 DECEMBER 1944

The sea battles of Leyte Gulf lasted four days. Taking Leyte, the stepping-stone to the rest of the Philippines, would take four more months. It had begun with a "feasibility raid" against the Philippines by carrier aircraft in September, followed by the decisive sea battles in the surrounding waters. It continued on the ground as foot soldiers pushed across Leyte. In early November, the Japanese were able to get 13,000 reinforcements and hold the American soldiers at bay.

The ten days of brutal combat on Leyte that took place between 7 and 17 November turned out to be some of the bloodiest of the entire war. Soldiers from the 24th Infantry Division had to use rifles, machine guns, hand grenades, satchel charges, and flame-throwers on entrenched enemy emplacements. At a hill dubbed "Breakneck Ridge," the troops of the 24th Infantry Division had to fight for every inch of ground. When the fighting there was over, some 2,000 Japanese soldiers were dead but the Americans had progressed only a mile closer to their objective.

A few weeks later, in desperation, more than 1,000 Japanese troops carried out a banzai charge on three captured American airfields. It was a nightmare of automatic weapons, swords, and grenades. Japanese infiltrators destroyed a dozen American aircraft, burned down buildings, and caused heavy American casualties in a forward hospital. However, by early December nearly all of the enemy soldiers had been killed and the island of Leyte was finally secured by U.S. troops.

The invasion of Leyte cost the Japanese more than 70,000 lives. But more than 15,500 Americans were killed or wounded trying to ensure that General Douglas MacArthur kept his promise to return to the Philippines.

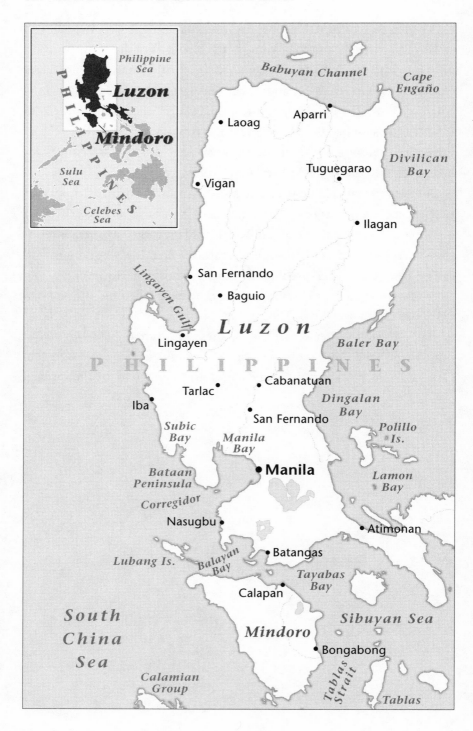

CHAPTER 15

THE DARING RESCUE OF THE GHOSTS OF BATAAN

(JANUARY 1945)

✪ **HQ 6TH ARMY**
TANAUAN, LEYTE
PHILIPPINE ISLANDS
9 JANUARY 1945

MacArthur had landed at Leyte following the great Battle of Leyte Gulf, and it was as if only he had landed: His photograph and "I have returned" was front-page news around the world. Yet lost in the shadow of that headline was the fact that the 6th Army had also landed. General Walter Krueger commanded the 6th Army, tasked with engaging the 250,000 Japanese on the island of Luzon. But first, General Krueger needed a plan to liberate the POW camps on the Bataan Peninsula, where American prisoners—those who had somehow survived the Bataan Death March and the slave labor details—had been kept since 1942.

Krueger had been told about the existence of Camp Cabanatuan as the 6th Army planned their invasion of the Philippines and subsequent push across Luzon toward Manila. He realized that when they marched through the region there was a likelihood that the Japanese would execute the last 500 surviving American POWs.

When Bataan had surrendered in 1942, the Imperial Army took at least 76,000 prisoners. Most of the U.S. and Filipino troops had fought valiantly. Having already suffered defeat by jungle diseases, abandoned by their leaders, and without supplies, rations, ammunition, or fuel, in the end they had no choice but to surrender.

A Japanese execution order was issued in Manila, which caused many of the atrocities suffered by American and Filipino prisoners in the Bataan Death March and their subsequent imprisonment. The execution order read:

Every troop that fought against our Army on Bataan should be wiped out thoroughly, whether he surrendered or not; and any American captive who is unable to continue marching all the way to the concentration camp should be put to death in an area 200 meters off the highway.

One out of every six of those who were part of the Death March died in those first weeks following the surrender, either from sickness or Japanese brutality or a combination of the two. Atrocities took place before and after they arrived at Camp O'Donnell, a processing center where the Japanese decided what to do with their prisoners—whether to keep them there, move them to other POW camps, or ship them out on "hell ships" to Japan, where they would work them as slave laborers until the end of the war.

Initially, more than 54,000 souls started out on the Death March, and the road to their POW internment was littered with American and Filipino corpses—*one dead body every ten to fifteen feet along the way*. The prisoners who survived the sixty-five-mile trek from Mariveles to San Fernando suffered from heat and disease. Many survived only to be tortured and killed at Camp O'Donnell, Camp Cabanatuan, and other prison camps.

At Camp O'Donnell, 54,000 POWs were crammed into an area smaller than one square mile. When Corregidor fell a month after Bataan, Imperial Army general Masaharu Homma had an additional 26,000 POWs to deal with after General Jonathan Wainwright surrendered his troops.

Without medical attention, the POWs were left to fend for themselves or die. The prisoners got no bedding and sanitation was almost nonexistent—a single water spigot served thousands. Medical attention, medicine, and supplies were also lacking. The Japanese usually confiscated whatever supplies were sent through the Red Cross before the packages reached the POWs.

By May 1942, six months after Pearl Harbor, Camp O'Donnell was overwhelmed. On 1 June transfers began from Camp O'Donnell to Cabanatuan, Palawan, or other Japanese POW camps. Camp Palawan was the most notorious place for atrocities. Prisoners there were often beaten unconscious with clubs for trying to steal a tiny amount of rice. Any POWs with compassion who tried to alleviate the pain and suffering of their comrades by bringing them a few morsels of their own meager rations were severely punished, often beaten senseless by the guards.

The prisoners were forced to work in every camp. They were assigned to bury their dead, carry water, collect firewood, and work in the kitchen or on farm detail. The Japanese told them, "No work, no food." If they could move, they worked, usually at burial detail.

This detail was quite toxic and hazardous. The decaying corpses piled up faster than the weakened prisoners could bury them. As a consequence, a number of diseases spread throughout the POW camps. There was another terrible consequence of the backlog of the burial details: The rotting bodies made the camps reek of death twenty-four hours a day, seven days a week. Not even the light evening breezes or a drenching tropical rain could take that smell away.

In June 1942, a POW known simply as "Captain Wilson" somehow finagled a bag of cement from a prison guard and built a cross inside Camp O'Donnell, near the mass graves, to commemorate the heroes on Bataan. The words he etched into the cross were:

In Memory of the American Dead, O'Donnell War Personnel Enclosure 1942 will forever remind everyone of the sacrifice of life the brave Bataan veterans gave for our freedom.

Wilson later died when he was transferred to a prison "hell ship" headed for Japan.

The Americans who survived the Bataan Death March often said that the ones who died along the way were the lucky ones. The "survivors" were already half-dead by the time they arrived at Camp O'Donnell, and hundreds more died in the following weeks. Every one of the men who arrived at O'Donnell had at least one serious health problem, and most had two or three: malaria, malnutrition, dysentery, beriberi, or diphtheria.

Over the next three years, the American POWs suffered and died under the iron fist of the Japanese army. More than 8,000 Americans passed through the barbed-wire gates of Camp Cabanatuan. One-third of them died there, most of beriberi, a terrible and painful thiamine deficiency disease that causes swelling in the arms and legs. The victim eventually drowns in his own pus.

Each day that dawned over the jungles of Bataan was agonizingly similar. The Japanese anthem was played over a loudspeaker and the prisoners were forced to stand at attention and salute their captors. The men struggled to survive on 200 grains of worm-infested rice each day, and to cope with the harsh work details assigned to them. Beatings were random and frequent.

The only thing that kept the POWs alive on the Death March and through the additional horrors was hope. They hoped they wouldn't starve, hoped they wouldn't die of disease, and hoped that they'd have the strength to put one foot in front of the other and live one day after the other.

But three horrific years is a long time to hope. And after three years in a Japanese prison camp, even some of their loved ones back home had lost hope. And now the question was: Could these surviving POWs manage to cling to their hope for a little while longer?

✪ 6TH RANGER BATTALION
U.S. 6TH ARMY FORCE
LINGAYEN GULF, PHILIPPINE ISLANDS
15 JANUARY 1945

Perhaps the American POWs would have had more hope if they had known that the Battle of Leyte Gulf in late October 1944 had demolished the Japanese hopes of ever completely destroying the American fleet. Without aircraft, and with fewer ships, the Japanese had to adopt new tactics to deal with the Americans. The only effective new tactic was the kamikaze attack.

In November, seven suicide attacks struck seven Task Force 38 aircraft carriers, resulting in great damage, along with the killing of 300 Americans and the wounding of hundreds more.

During the same period, the 7th Fleet incurred thirteen kamikaze attacks, damaging all thirteen ships and sinking one of them. However, the American air superiority in aircraft and skilled pilots allowed the U.S. Navy, and Task Force 38 in particular, to keep its planes in the air over Luzon around the clock, attacking Japanese airplanes on the ground and destroying hundreds of bombers and fighter planes.

On 15 December, soldiers from the 6th Army landed on the island of Mindanao, southwest across the gulf from Leyte. They secured dry, flat areas that could be used for airstrips and stiffened their offensive actions against the Japanese with land-based planes to support the coming invasion of Luzon in the north.

Also in December, a massacre happened on the island of Palawan, where American prisoners were burned alive by their Japanese guards. It was reported that POWs had been put into rude shelters. A group of Japanese soldiers entered the compound armed with guns, bayonets, grenades, and dynamite, and then they attacked the prisoners in the shelters. They tossed gasoline onto the American POWs and incinerated them while they were still alive.

Explosions couldn't drown out the screams of dying American POWs. If any escaped the massacre, machine gun fire cut them down. Altogether, 151 prisoners were slaughtered. News of this terrible atrocity reached the 6th Army headquarters and underscored the urgency to rescue the POWs at Cabanatuan.

On 9 January 1945, the American invasion of Luzon was launched. It occurred at Lingayen Gulf, the same spot where the Japanese had invaded exactly three years earlier. Troops from the 6th Army, with support from MacArthur's 7th Fleet, led the assault. There were no Japanese naval forces in the area to challenge the invasion. Most of the enemy soldiers on Luzon had fled inland, to the north, and into the mountains, where they'd make a final stand. The 6th Army invasion force had virtually no opposition.

The only resistance to the American invasion was continuing attacks from kamikaze pilots, which were terribly effective. Suicidal Japanese pilots damaged more than forty U.S. ships, almost half of them seriously, and sank five of them. Nearly 800 Americans were killed in the kamikaze attacks and 1,400 were wounded.

Still, by January 1945, the tides of war in the Pacific were shifting more definitively. The successive recent victories by the Americans and Allied forces had pushed the Japanese back from their forward defensive perimeters, throwing Tokyo into a panic.

In addition to continuing kamikaze attacks, the order to execute all prisoners was emphasized once more to the commanders at the various garrisons. U.S. intelligence uncovered disturbing signs that the various Japanese camp commanders were making arrangements for mass killings of the American prisoners.

At Cabanatuan, the prison population had already been seriously reduced during the past three years. Of the original 9,000 POWs sent there, only 500 or so were still alive. None of the POWs knew that the Americans had already returned to the island to retake it.

The surviving POWs called themselves the "Ghosts of Bataan." They already knew that escape was not an option—simply because there was no place for them to go. If any were lucky enough to get out of the prison camp, they would immediately come into contact with tens of thousands of their unforgiving enemies.

From 1942 to 1944, the war had raged in both the European and Pacific theaters, and there seemed to be some hope among the Americans that an end to the war was on the horizon. But that was still some time away. If it were even possible to rescue the POWs, it would have to be done soon—before the Ghosts of Bataan were dead.

It fell to General Krueger to decide what had to be done. The men had already suffered enough, and he had to do something to prevent a massacre at Cabanatuan. But what? How could anyone take enough soldiers forty miles behind the enemy lines to rescue POWs?

✪ 6TH RANGER BATTALION
VICINITY GUIMBA VILLAGE
LUZON, PHILIPPINE ISLANDS
28 JANUARY 1945

The American command was aware of the "execute the prisoners" order and had graphic evidence of it on Palawan. Like General Krueger, the rest of the military leadership felt that these American POWs had been through enough suffering. There may even have been feelings of guilt and remorse among some of the politicians and war planners in Washington for having abandoned the men three years earlier.

Those in authority decided that they couldn't let anything else happen to them. No more massacres could take place. Yet an unspoken fear troubled the Army planners. They were afraid that when they entered Cabanatuan, the prisoners could be caught in the crossfire of a battle between their liberators and the Japanese.

General Krueger turned to the 6th Army G-2, Colonel Horton Smith, who in turn pulled in a remarkable team drawn from the 6th Ranger Battalion, Filipino guerrillas, the Alamo Scouts, and Army intelligence and combat units. When the front lines of the 6th Army on Luzon were thirty to forty miles from Cabanatuan, Smith and his team quickly planned a mission to free the POWs.

Colonel Smith had organized the Alamo Scouts who worked with the Filipino guerrillas. They were led by Army Major Robert Lapham. Lapham, a survivor of the Bataan Death March himself, had escaped from the Japanese and had become a guerrilla, living and fighting with the Filipinos.

The rescue plan was devised, and the mission fell to a new breed of soldiers to carry it out. They called themselves the Rangers, and a unit of 121 volunteers was picked from the 6th Ranger Battalion. The assault commander was twenty-five-year-old Captain Robert Prince of Seattle. His commander, Lieutenant Colonel Henry Mucci, had personally selected him for the mission.

The Alamo Scouts went on ahead to do recon of the area, and the Rangers were to follow by truck to Guimba by the afternoon of 28 January. There they would rendezvous with the Scouts and guerrillas and get the latest intelligence before moving out across the open grasslands and flat forestland. General Krueger was counting on competent recon and meticulous planning for a mission he prayed would conclude with a swift, well-implemented attack and a safe rescue.

The Rangers represented a new kind of soldiering, created in World War II as an American answer to the British Commandos. The word "ranger" had a certain resonance and sounded like something masculine and American, like the legendary Texas Rangers. But the high command still wasn't quite sure how to use the Rangers, or what their role would be.

National Archives

The men of the 6th Ranger Battalion pulled off the daring rescue of U.S. POWs.

The 6th Ranger Battalion consisted of men who had been part of a pack-mule unit of the "old" army, and apart from their initial invasion action in the Philippines, they'd never fought in any combat situations. This would be their first real combat mission. General Krueger gave the assignment to Mucci, and Mucci told C Company commander Robert Prince to ask for volunteers. The volunteers would leave the next day.

Cabanatuan was a central POW camp. The camp population had dwindled to just a fraction of its original numbers. Only the weakest and sickest had remained behind. If any had any strength at all, they would have been sent off as slave laborers.

But because these POWs were virtually no use to the Japanese as laborers, it became more and more logical that the "execute the prisoners" order would be carried out—sooner rather than later—because now the American 6th Army was breathing down the necks of the Japanese.

✪ 6TH RANGER BATTALION
LUZON, PHILIPPINE ISLANDS
29 JANUARY 1945

There were about 250,000 Japanese soldiers on the island of Luzon, preparing for a final confrontation against the 6th Army. The Japanese still controlled the roads, so they could complete their withdrawal to the north.

The enemy also had large concentrations of troops at Cabanatuan City, a small city four miles from the prison camp. The Filipino guerrillas and American intelligence found out that at least 8,000 Japanese troops were in the immediate vicinity of the POW camp, and perhaps as many as 300 Japanese soldiers were actually staying in barracks inside the prison compound itself.

In the course of planning for the mission, Major Bob Lapham tried to find out everything he could about the American prisoners. His intel confirmed the number of American prisoners still being held in the camp.

Major Lapham also made certain that the Rangers had maps and some aerial photographs. He was greatly disappointed when he was not allowed to join the Rangers for the raid, but his superiors felt that if he were to fall into Japanese hands, the results would be disastrous.

Lt. Colonel Mucci coordinated the two different units commanded by Filipino guerrilla officers Captain Juan Pajota and Captain Eduardo Joson. Both had been fighting the Japanese for years, and now they were offering their help to rescue POWs with the 121 American Rangers.

It was a real-life "Mission Impossible." The Rangers had to slip behind enemy lines, cross at least thirty miles of hostile territory—while surrounded by 8,000 troops of the Imperial Army, who were stationed within four miles of the prison camp—and then get inside, neutralize the 300 soldiers guarding the camp, and, finally, rescue the prisoners. But that was still only half of it. The other half of the mission was to get the prisoners back safely—so they'd have to repeat the entire process in reverse.

The mission began at 0500 on 28 January 1945. Before the Rangers started out, fourteen Alamo Scouts and a band of some 200 Filipino guerrillas—who had been keeping track of enemy positions and troop movements—rendezvoused with the Rangers.

Captain Juan Pajota, the brilliant Filipino resistance leader, knew every square inch of the land and its dangers. Drawing diagrams in the dirt, Captain Bob Prince and Lt. Colonel Mucci rehearsed the plan with their officers and non-coms over and over again. The element of surprise was the key, and it was all set for the night of 29 January.

But last minute intel indicated that the Japanese were going to be on the move: Hundreds of trucks, tanks, armored vehicles, and troops would be right outside the prison camp. The enemy troops were on the retreat, and the Americans feared that before the Japanese left Cabanatuan they would carry out Tokyo's order to kill all the prisoners.

Still, despite their intentions to get to Cabanatuan right away, trying to undertake the raid that night would be a meaningless suicide mission. Mucci took the matter upstairs and was given a twenty-four-hour delay for the Rangers. They would just have to pray that since the Japanese were on the move, they wouldn't take the time or initiative to kill the prisoners before the Rangers got to them. The more likely scenario was that the prison commandant and guards would be assigned that responsibility, and that the Rangers would get to Cabanatuan in time to stop it.

Mucci and the Rangers began their trek to the prison camp with Captain Prince and a handful of Rangers bringing up the rear. They knew it would be an arduous mission. They spent the night at Balincarin, barely avoiding detection by the Japanese. The second night they reached the village of Platero, not far from the prison camp. The last major physical obstacle was the Pampanga River. The Americans held their weapons above their heads and half-waded, half-swam the river, hoping that all 121 of the Rangers would get across safely without being seen.

Now came the tricky part. From the nearby barrio of Platero—where the Rangers were hidden during the day by friendly Filipinos—and for the rest of the way to the prison camp itself, the Rangers had to crawl on their bellies to avoid detection by the Japanese. The land itself was unforgiving during this part of their efforts; the ground was barren and offered practically no cover. So the Rangers crawled, cradling their rifles, measuring their distance in inches, and as they wriggled across through the tall grass, time seemed to stop.

Then the Rangers could see the guard towers of the prison camp, and sometime later they were in sight of the barbed-wire fences. But the gaze of the watchtower guards covered the very area from which the Rangers were approaching the camp.

Lt. Colonel Mucci was hoping that they wouldn't have to wait long for the diversion that he'd ordered, code-named "Black Widow." It happened within a minute or two of the plan—at about 1940 hours.

An American P-61 suddenly appeared in the skies near the prison camp, opposite the side where the Rangers approached. The pilot swooped in at 200 feet above the compound and zoomed past, making a few high loops. Then he cut an engine and restarted it, causing a loud backfire, the actions designed to alert whatever guards hadn't sighted the plane initially. The P-61 made a few more noisy passes in the sky, just out of machine gun range, making certain that the Japanese knew that he was there—and distracting them from the fact that the Rangers were there, too.

The diversion worked perfectly. While everyone looked up at the American P-61, two Rangers ran up, shot and killed the gate guard, blew the lock off the front gate to the prison compound, and then threw open the gates. Simultaneously, C Company Rangers raced down the "main street" of the POW compound. Their weapons blazing, they took out Japanese guards with a merciless barrage of automatic fire. Another unit of the Rangers had surrounded the prison camp to prevent any Japanese inside from escaping or going for help.

The POWs heard the massive amount of gunfire and assumed it was the end. They heard rumors that the Japanese were on the move, and didn't recognize the uniforms of the Rangers, so they feared the worst—that these were enemy troops come to kill them. The prisoners were reluctant to come out of hiding—which probably saved them from getting caught in the crossfire.

The POWs crouched in ditches and under the shacks; they hid wherever they could. They couldn't believe that this was really a prison break—these were actually Americans. They thought it was a trick to lure the prisoners out so they could all be gunned down. It took some persuading on the part of the Rangers to get them to move toward the main gate.

While Krueger and Mucci were considering ideas and options, American soldiers John Cook and Ralph Rodriguez, Jr., Bataan Death March survivors and prisoners in the Cabanatuan POW camp, couldn't believe that this was the hour of their liberation.

▯   ▯   ▯

PRIVATE JOHN COOK, US ARMY
Camp Cabanatuan
Luzon, Philippine Islands
30 January 1945

I was sitting outside and leaned against the side of the mess hall. There were 512 of us in this place.

The Rangers cut the fence beneath the nearby Japanese guardhouse. Lieutenant Richardson fired the first shot, after which all hell broke loose.

The Rangers came up the road into camp from the outside, on the gravel road coming into camp. They had to get past quite a few Japanese there. They also had to deal with the guard tower.

We didn't know what was happening. The first guy that burst into our quarters said, "Let's go. You're free!" I didn't recognize the uniform. He had a funny cap on, and a green uniform. And he kept yelling, "Let's go! Get out the main gate!"

I said, "Who in the hell are you?"

He said, "We're Yanks!"

They wanted to put me on an oxcart, but I said, "Like hell! I walked into that damn place. I'll walk out!"

I ran to the Pampanga River through the rice fields with them and I asked, "How deep is the water? I can't swim." And someone said, "It's waist-deep. Get your butt in here and get across there. Don't you hear the Jap tanks coming?"

From that moment on, I kept walking, all night long. And the next morning we were at the American lines.

◻   ◻   ◻

CORPORAL RALPH RODRIGUEZ, JR., US ARMY
Camp Cabanatuan
Luzon, Philippine Islands
30 January 1945

Every evening, about seven o'clock, I'd type out my diary.

I started typing what I saw to the west of our camp; there were some flares way out there in the distance, and I'd been watching them, typing in the diary about the flares getting closer.

So, this night, I finished the typing the account and something about the new Japanese soldiers coming in and the other ones leaving. That was my last page, and I pulled it out from the typewriter. I had already written a lot but I wouldn't put my name on it. The Japanese warned us that anybody caught with a diary would be shot.

I'd been hiding it for years and couldn't allow it to be found. That's how I had the diary that night we were rescued.

About twenty minutes later, when I'd put my diary away, suddenly, it was the time that somebody had to ring the time. Someone came out and instead of hitting the time bell in pairs (you know, ding-ding, ding-ding), he came in there and he hit it hard, fifteen times, as loud as he could.

Well, for the last hour, there had been Rangers at the end of the building, hiding in a ditch but none of us saw them.

The other Rangers thought that somebody had been discovered. So they started shooting the Japs and I saw two Japs fall off the guardhouse.

And then, at the guardhouse, they dropped three hand grenades inside and that's how it started.

I got shot at there but they hit a pipe, so I turned and kept on going. By this time, I'm the last man, or next to the last man, to leave the camp. And then suddenly I saw a shadow and heard somebody yell, "Any more Americans?" And these guys were big guys. They had cartridge belts draped over their shoulders and one or two handguns. And I don't know what else.

I was afraid to say, "Here I am!" But this guy says, "Well, get out of here!" Then he jerked me up and I stood up, and I walked out. So that's how I got introduced to the liberators.

✪ 6TH RANGER BATTALION
POW CAMP
CABANATUAN, LUZON
30 JANUARY 1945

The whole thing was all over in twenty minutes. There were 225 Japanese dead, while the Rangers suffered just two casualties. They rounded up the American POWs and tried to organize them into a military formation and complete the rescue by getting them back to friendly territory quickly and safely.

Before the Rangers had left on the mission, Captain Juan Pajota had suggested using caribou, ancient beasts of burden in the Philippines, to help move the weakened prisoners. So now, old wooden-wheeled oxcarts were waiting when the Rangers got the prisoners out of the POW camp and across the river.

But 1,000 Japanese soldiers, camped across the Pampanga River and alerted by the noises of battle, were stunned that Americans were attempting a rescue at Cabanatuan. The Japanese officers got their troops into formations and started to go after them.

However, the Filipino guerrillas were waiting for the Japanese at Cabu Bridge on the single road to Cabanatuan. And it was a perfect ambush. Captain Pajota's 200 guerrillas and Captain Joson's eighty men were set up in a

"V" formation across the road and spread out across the area flanking it. The Japanese troops rolled into the ambush and it was a slaughter, despite the guerrillas' nearly four-to-one disadvantage.

Meanwhile, the Rangers and the prisoners were going as fast as the ailing POWs could move or be carried, toward the river. With effort and time, they all made it across safely. Slowly, the dazed former captives emerged from the water and were herded into the waiting caribou carts. Others, who were able to walk, tagged along behind the ancient oxcarts stretching for almost two miles.

Over the next twenty-four hours, the Rangers—with the help of the guerrillas and friendly Filipino villagers—moved their odd-looking caravan back to the safety of the American lines, all the while dodging some 8,000 Imperial Japanese soldiers.

Led by Lt. Colonel Mucci, the first "Ghosts of Bataan" stumbled into American-held territory on the morning of 31 January 1945. It took two and a half hours for the procession of weak, weary, and wounded American POWs to pass. Their next stop would be an Army evacuation hospital, and after they'd recovered from their three-year ordeal, the last stop on this operation would be home to America.

Captain Bob Prince drew great satisfaction from that successful and remarkable raid on the Cabanatuan POW camp.

                  □   □   □

CAPTAIN ROBERT PRINCE, US ARMY
6th Rangers Rescue Raid
Vicinity Camp Cabanatuan
28–31 January 1945

We were on Leyte just a few weeks and then we embarked for Luzon, landing at Lingayen Gulf.

For a few weeks we acted as guard for the 6th Army headquarters. As missions arose we were sent out. At that time we hadn't had much information on other actions that had taken place. We'd heard that a number of POWs had been moved to Japan and Manchuria as slave laborers.

On 28 January through the last day of the raid on 31 January, I was aware that there were many POWs but I had no idea where they were. I knew simply that we were there to rescue prisoners.

We had to study the layout of the prison camp, how we were to approach it, and what we would use for protection on our flanks. We had one guerrilla force that was to be our flank protection and another on the side where we knew there was an active battalion of Japanese soldiers camped.

The makeup of my unit consisted of all of C Company, and one platoon of F Company. Our mission, if we succeeded, would be a great thing because we were going to release our own men and that made it unique from almost any other mission in the war. Usually you were trying to kill the enemy.

Colonel Mucci insisted that there be nothing but volunteers, so I went out in front of my company and said, "I want all the people that want to go on this raid to take one step forward." When I turned around they were in the same formation. Every one of 'em had stepped forward to volunteer.

We marched eight or ten miles inland from Lingayen Gulf on the road to Manila, and then we continued by truck on that road, about forty miles, to near Guimba. At that point the trucks discharged us and we spent the afternoon talking to the two guerrilla captains, Pajota and Joson. Major Lapham and the Alamo Scouts were also there. They'd prove to be instrumental in the success of this mission.

We started off about five in the afternoon. When we got to Rizal Road, the main road that the Japanese were using, we went under a culvert to get across the road past a Japanese tank.

We spent the first night at Balincarin and the second night in Platero, waiting for a concentration of Japanese to move out of the area. On the evening of the raid we waded the Pampanga River and crawled across this field.

Murphy and his F Company platoon were crawling up a dry riverbed, under the cover of the bank, until one of the tower guards spotted 'em and that started the whole thing.

Our men killed the man in the guard tower, opened the gate, and we went through. The second platoon out farther lined up, firing everything they had—BARs, tommy guns, rifles—at anything that moved in there. And in one case they took a bazooka and blew up a truck that some Jap was trying to move out of there.

Anyway, then all the firing stopped and we began moving the POWs out. We went out the same way we went in. We crossed the river and it was a good thing it was so low at that time of year. We had carts waiting, and during the night we picked up a lot more carts, thanks to the Filipino civilians.

There were two main highways that we crossed. We were told to approach them with Filipino guides out ahead of us and we had one place we had to stop while some traffic went by. And then, we'd go across two or three at time and run and hide in the jungle just off the road, so it took a while to get across those roads.

Mucci was at the head of the column and I had the rear—our flanks were covered by the guerrillas and they became a rear guard on our way out.

First Sergeant Anderson said, "I think that we should fire the flare, now that we're through at the prison camp and moving out." So Anderson shot a red flare, which not only alerted our people ahead of us, but signaled the guerrillas on each side of us that we were withdrawing.

And a medic came up and said, "This man's wounded. We need to find Captain Jim Fisher (the medical officer)." And the wounded man on the ground said, "I'm Captain Fisher!"

Captain Fisher was taken to one of the Filipino villages where Dr. Liog, the Filipino doctor, tended to him. Then, one of the POWs, First Lieutenant Merle Musselman from Omaha, Nebraska, who'd spent three years in the prison camp, volunteered to stay and help take care of him. And I think that took a special bit of courage.

A British soldier who was deaf was in the POW camp latrine and couldn't hear the firing, and missed us. He was found by Filipino civilians the next day and repatriated later.

There was enormous jubilation when we got back to American-held territory. MacArthur had been there and greeted the first ones across, and General Krueger had been there, and Lt. Colonel Mucci had already gone back to headquarters. That was the time-lag between the top of the column and the bottom.

✪ ✪ ✪

But there were a lot of POWs who didn't make it. Many would die before they could be rescued; others languished in prison camps like Cabanatuan until the war ended months later. Sergeant Richard Gordon had once been a prisoner at Cabanatuan, and survived the brutality there, but was sent to a slave labor installation in Japan until a month after the war ended.

▯ ▯ ▯

SERGEANT RICHARD GORDON, US ARMY
Japanese POW Camp
Hydroelectric Dam Construction Site
4 September 1945

I was at Cabanatuan from 5 July until late October of '42; most of my time taken up on burial detail because we had so many Americans to bury in that camp. In the first month I was there, something like 500 Americans died and then it escalated, it kept climbing, until it reached over 780 in the month of August.

That situation was unbearable. You'd go out in the morning on a detail to dig one mass grave that took many men. And then in the afternoon you'd come back out and carry these bodies from underneath the hospital out to the cemetery, and throw one body on top of another body. Then a different detail was ordered to cover them up. Many times they were not very well covered up either. And sometimes when it rained in that camp, the water would be discolored from blood mixed with it as it ran along the road.

Once a body rolled over as we carried it and landed on me, and then the skin broke and the gases escaped. The odor was unbelievable.

You couldn't even recognize the corpse that you were burying. They were beyond recognition. You'd see a picture of the man, now an emaciated corpse so thin there was nothing but skin and bones... so it was hard to recognize somebody looking like that. I could've very easily buried friends and never knew it.

But I may not have been around to tell my story if I'd stayed in Cabanatuan. We left there on 31 October 1942, and went to a prison in Manila, the staging area before we went on the ship. I was on the initial work detail of 1,600 Americans to be sent to Japan.

They truly were hell ships. I went on an old ship that the British had sold to the Japanese in 1932 as scrap metal.

They put us aboard the same ship that had come from Japan to the Philippines carrying livestock. So we were sleeping on the filthy straw, with the stench of animals that had been in those holds.

They packed us in so that you had no room to turn around. And then twice a day they'd pass food down—a bucket of rice and what they called *mislau* soup, made out of soybean paste.

We had a submarine attack a couple days out of Manila, and we weren't allowed on deck after that. And when the submarine attack came, they'd given us lifejackets, which God knows would never have kept us afloat—they were that old.

I was on that ship nineteen days and had some pretty bad experiences. We used buckets for latrine purposes but the rolling of the ship upset those buckets, so we lived in a mess that's beyond description. Seven or eight men died on the ship. They were dumped overboard with no ceremonies.

We got to Moji, Japan, on Thanksgiving Day, 1942. And then the Japanese took us off and made us undress and stand on the pier. In

November, Japan is very cold. They brought a number of women with tanks on their back, who sprayed us for body lice. When we left that port area where we landed, we left behind about 150 prisoners who were too sick to go any further. They just left 'em on a pier. From every check that I've made, nobody's ever found those 150 men. They just disappeared.

I stayed in Japan from November of '42 until September, '44.

We were building a hydroelectric dam, the fourth largest in Japan, built mainly with prisoner-of-war labor. The worst part of that place was a very frigid climate—men without proper clothing and proper shoes. We lost a lot of men to pneumonia, real fast.

You were beaten without provocation. When the war ended, the Japanese guards all took off. And we ran the camp ourselves for awhile. About a week after the war ended we learned about the bomb.

On 4 September we all walked to the railroad station, climbed aboard a train, and headed down to Hamamatsu, a seacoast town where the American navy had come ashore to locate and help repatriate prisoners in the area.

Pretty soon I was on a hospital ship, the *Rescue*, sitting out in the bay. They kept us there a couple of weeks, then took us home to America.

✪ ✪ ✪

Sergeant Richard Gordon spent time at U.S. Army hospitals and aboard hospital ships heading back home, finally ending his journey at Madigan General Hospital in Fort Lewis, Washington. Gordon finally boarded a train in Seattle and crossed the country to arrive at Penn Station in New York City. His wife and other relatives were not allowed to see him yet, and Dick recalls a poignant moment when an older woman came up to the railroad car window and peered inside. He describes the moment: "I saw my mother come up and look through the window. . . she had put on weight, and her nose was all smudged from the dirt on the windows. And I saw a kid standing next to her about eighteen years old. It was my kid brother. I didn't recognize him, 'cause I hadn't seen him in some time."

An ambulance took Dick Gordon to Holland General Hospital in Staten Island. There a proper reunion with his family took place. Two weeks after that reunion, Dick's mother died.

Dick Gordon stayed in the hospital another four months before being discharged. Then he reenlisted, received a commission as second lieutenant, and remained on active duty until 1961.

✪ ARMY EVAC HOSPITAL
PHILIPPINE ISLANDS
14 FEBRUARY 1945

By mid-February 1945, six weeks after the successful prison break, the former residents of Camp Cabanatuan had recovered enough in the Army evacuation hospitals to begin the long trip home. They boarded the USS *General Anderson* for the long trip back to the United States. With no escort, the 20,000-ton troop transport ship was virtually defenseless in the Pacific lanes on its way back. Ordinarily, it would've been a major target for Japanese subs and other enemy ships. But there were no Japanese ships and the *Anderson* pulled into San Francisco Bay with her precious cargo intact. The city went wild in celebration and gratitude.

The 121 young American Rangers, the Alamo Scouts, and the Filipino guerrillas who went on the raid to rescue the "Ghosts of Bataan" at Cabanatuan were a remarkable lot—and they were all volunteers. They all made a choice—believing that the value of the lives of their comrades was worth putting their own lives at tremendous risk.

Captain Bob Prince and Lt. Colonel Henry Mucci were awarded the Distinguished Service Cross, the nation's second highest award for valor, and the other officers were awarded the Silver Star. All the other men from the 6th Ranger Battalion were awarded the Bronze Star for their courageous acts during the raid. But the Rangers had chosen to dare the difficult and dangerous not for personal glory, fame, or fortune, but simply because if they didn't do it, who else would?

The American military, war correspondents, and the American public alike celebrated the remarkable achievement. The raid had touched a nerve among Americans who cared about the fate of those long-suffering defenders of Bataan and Corregidor.

To this day, the 6th Rangers' raid on Camp Cabanatuan has remained the largest and most successful rescue mission of its kind ever conducted.

CHAPTER 16

IWO JIMA: THE BLOODIEST BATTLE OF WORLD WAR II

(FEBRUARY–MARCH 1945)

✪ **U.S. JOINT CHIEFS OF STAFF**
WASHINGTON, D.C.
D-DAY MINUS TWENTY
31 JANUARY 1945

After the Battle of Leyte, the Joint Chiefs of Staff in Washington began to plan for the invasion of Iwo Jima. This tiny spit of land, called "sulfur island" in Japanese, was eight square miles of volcanic rock.

The battle for Iwo Jima would turn out to be perhaps the bloodiest combat in American history. Two out of three of the boys (most of them were just seventeen, eighteen, or nineteen) who landed on the island were killed or wounded. Twenty-two thousand Japanese soldiers defended Iwo Jima. Most were older and more experienced than the Americans, but nearly all of them were killed as well.

To put that in perspective, almost 7,000 Americans were killed in action at Iwo Jima. If the battle had lasted nine months, it would have equaled all those killed in ten years of war in Vietnam. Despite its relatively short duration, Iwo Jima would truly be the bloodiest battle in the Pacific.

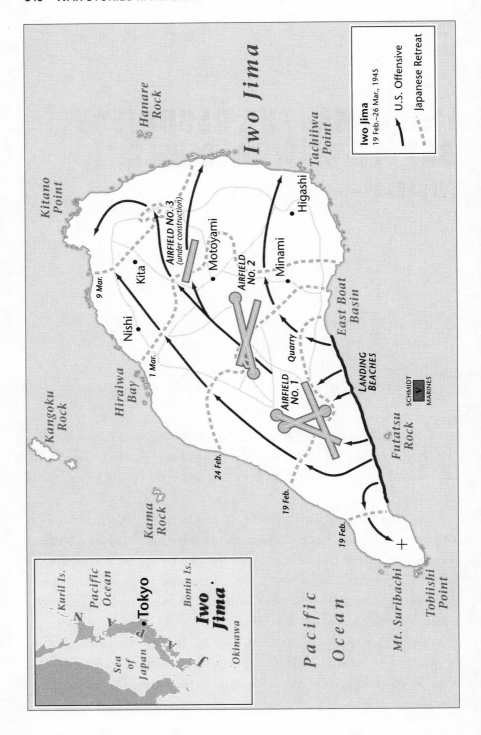

The European front in World War II was governed by a set of traditional rules. The two sides fought intensely but simultaneously observed polite protocols. They took time out for each side to collect their dead and wounded and observed cease-fires for "reasonable" causes. On Christmas, both sides would quit warring and mark the season of "peace and goodwill" with a brief interruption of hostilities. Then, with a sense of heavy-handed irony, they would resume shooting after the short respite.

But there were no rules of warfare in the Pacific. Japanese soldiers had been ingrained in the samurai code, which sent them into "heroic" battle with great ferocity and no fear of death. Throughout the war the Japanese would fight until the last man was dead. They knew that there could be no surrender. A Japanese soldier trying to surrender was likely to be shot by his own officers or fellow soldiers. A soldier who surrendered brought dishonor not just upon himself, but also upon his family, his village, and his emperor. Any soldier who surrendered would have his name taken from the village records, and his family would disown him.

The Japanese had also rejected the Geneva Conventions, which prescribed various "rules of warfare." When the time came to invade the Pacific Islands, both sides understood that it would be a battle of "no holds barred."

The Joint Chiefs of Staff decided to overrule General MacArthur's recommendation to swing south and retake the rest of the Philippines as well as the East Indies. They decided to concentrate on Luzon instead, ratcheting up the pressure on the Japanese mainland with attacks by American bombers, some of which would be based on the recaptured territory of Luzon.

But winter monsoon rains foiled American plans to establish air bases on Leyte, thereby making it impossible for U.S. aircraft to operate from there. The 6th Army made steady progress in clearing the smaller islands with offensive assaults, however.

In June 1944, the Joint Chiefs decided to invade and capture the islands of Iwo Jima and Okinawa, which lie in the northern waters between the Philippines and Japan. The strategic value of these two islands was still in flux. MacArthur would have his hands full trying to retake Luzon. The invasion of 9 January at Lingayen Gulf was only the beginning of the hardscrabble struggle to regain control of Luzon. The battle to overcome the

250,000 troops of the 35th Imperial Army would last until the Japanese surrendered in August 1945.

The 35th Imperial Army, led by General Sosaku Suzuki, put up a skilled resistance to the American invasion of Luzon. It was here that the Japanese war plan had changed. The old plan was to throw everything against the American and Allied troops to keep them from getting ashore. The reason was simple: If the Americans took the small outlying islands, it was an easier step to invade the Japanese Home Islands, as they were able to put more bombers and fighter planes within range of Japan.

However, now it was too late for that. The current Tokyo strategy was to save all war matériel and troop strength for defending the Japanese homeland. Hence, General Suzuki was fighting an ongoing "hide and seek" war with MacArthur and General Walter Krueger, not wanting to engage the Americans and risk any major war resources.

In January 1945, the Americans finally landed on the main Philippine island of Luzon. After a bitter battle, they reached the capital city of Manila on 2 February. Over the next six months, the Japanese would lose 170,000 troops in the Philippines, in contrast to the American losses of 8,000.

Meanwhile, the Joint Chiefs began to consider Iwo Jima more seriously after the Japanese showed lighter resistance to the initial U.S. landings on the Philippine islands. Iwo Jima served as an early warning station for the Japanese; from there they could detect approaching aircraft and radio reports of the incoming bombers to mainland Japan. When the U.S. and Allied bombers arrived over Japanese cities, Japanese air defenses could be ready for them.

Japanese aircraft still based on Iwo Jima also continually harassed the Americans in operations across the northern Pacific. The Joint Chiefs believed that taking Iwo Jima could neutralize those air attacks, make other U.S. operations in the region less risky, and provide another launching site for B-24s and B-25s headed for Tokyo.

The Joint Chiefs had postponed the operations to take Iwo Jima and Okinawa because of the monsoons and the difficulties encountered in taking Leyte and Luzon. Now seemed to be the right time to dust off those plans.

Their decision was made: Iwo Jima would be first and Okinawa next. The islands were to be taken rather than bypassed. Recon planes showed that Mount Suribachi was being dug in, with gun emplacements and pill-boxes both above and below ground. Because so many enemy troops were dug in and couldn't be seen by the recon aircraft, reports grossly underestimated the Japanese troop strength. The naval air bombardment would blast away at the island until D-Day for the Iwo Jima invasion.

✪ HQ 5TH AMPHIBIOUS FORCE
VICINITY IWO JIMA
D-DAY MINUS FOUR
14 FEBRUARY 1945

On 14 February, U.S. ships were on their way to an undisclosed location. The Marines aboard had no idea where the battle would be fought, only that it was a top-secret location known as "Island X."

Vice Admiral Raymond Spruance's 5th Fleet dominated the air and sea around Iwo Jima, softening up the island for the Marine invasion. The U.S. was sending 72,000 Marines of the 3rd, 4th, and 5th Marine Divisions to "Island X"—more troops than were sent to any other Allied island assault. The convoy of 880 American ships—the largest naval armada in history at the time—took forty days to sail from Hawaii to Iwo Jima. Aboard the troop ships, the Marines received communion and prayed during brief services held by the chaplains. Others wrote letters home; some of these letters would contain the last words ever expressed to their loved ones back in America.

D-Day was approaching. This D-Day was not unlike its counterpart in Europe nine months earlier. The invasion of Normandy had been terrible, with appalling costs in dead and wounded troops. But the Normandy assault lasted just twenty-four hours, though to its participants it must have seemed much longer. Yet writer-historian James Bradley said, "Any time a bullet is near your head, that's a bad battle. Normandy was awful, but at the end of twenty-four hours you and your grandmother could have had a tea party on the beach at Normandy. Iwo Jima, a much smaller beach, had a thirty-six-day battle on a four-mile-long island, and it was the most intense battle of World War II."

The defending troops figured out that "Island X" was Iwo Jima even without coded messages and intelligence. They saw Admiral Spruance's ships on the horizon for two and a half months, with troop carriers edging ever closer to the small island.

The average age of a Japanese soldier in World War II was a battle-hardened twenty-four. Most of the Americans were teenagers; many of them at Iwo Jima were seeing combat for the first time. These young Marines had been told by naïve American war planners that the typical Japanese soldier was five feet, three inches tall, wore glasses, and weighed 117 pounds. They were painted as small, inept, and completely unskilled in jungle warfare.

That caricature did not even come close to the reality of the Japanese soldiers. In truth, they were fearless, some of the world's most effective fighting men, defending their emperor and their homeland.

But what did the Japanese know about the Americans, especially the Marines? Their superiors told them fearful myths: that for a young American to become a Marine he had to kill his parents; that Marines ate dead babies. Japanese leaders warned civilians that if the U.S. Marines ever invaded the homeland, the women would be raped and killed and their children slaughtered and eaten.

No doubt these grisly myths had inspired Japanese civilians on Peleliu to throw their children off cliffs and jump to the rocks below. But if these Japanese civilians had seen the Marines weep when they witnessed these terrible acts—including Japanese civilians being machine-gunned when they hesitated or didn't jump—perhaps there might have been a little less horror on Peleliu.

The responsibility for killing the Marines on Iwo Jima was given to General Tadamichi Kuribayashi, a sixth-generation samurai personally selected by Emperor Hirohito. Kuribayashi had been a victorious general in the Japanese campaigns in China and Manchuria, and before the war he had been a Japanese military attaché in the United States. He'd traveled throughout the U.S. and returned to Japan with intelligence about America's industrial and economic might. He wisely told his superiors, "The last country that Japan should ever go to war with is the United States." But the Japanese political and military leaders never really considered his advice.

But now, here he was, about to defend the island of Iwo Jima against that mighty sleeping giant. General Kuribayashi must have known in his heart that his 22,000 men would not be able to prevail against 72,000 Marines. Tokyo knew. It's not known if the general was told that this was a suicide mission, but Kuribayashi wrote to his wife that he did not expect to come home. Kuribayashi ordered his troops that they were to each kill ten Americans before they died.

The general inspired his men with talk of the samurai code, the honor of dying for the emperor, and the terrible dishonor of surrender. He told them that this would be a "heroic" battle for the defense of Japan herself. All they had to do was kill ten Americans before each of them died in battle.

Their cause may have been "heroic" in his eyes, but it was also hopeless. The only thing General Kuribayashi had going was that the Americans had underestimated his troop strength on Iwo Jima, which would turn out to be a significant flaw in their battle plan.

Leading the American troops was another hand-picked general, selected by FDR. He was nicknamed the "Patton of the Pacific"—his Marines had never lost a battle at any place they had stepped ashore. He'd directed assaults on Tarawa, Eniwetok, Tinian, Saipan, and Guam, often leading his troops ashore himself. Now he faced the assaults of Iwo Jima and Okinawa. He was General Holland "Howlin' Mad" Smith, an Alabama lawyer who had received his commission forty years earlier and had even fought in WW I.

This down-to-earth commander of the Pacific Fleet Marine Forces knew more about amphibious assault landings than any other American officer. General Smith knew that he'd have to sacrifice some of his Marines but he also knew the consequences if he didn't. Without the use of Iwo Jima for air bases, it might take many more years to conquer Japan. Formosa and Thailand could be enslaved for decades. General Smith believed that most of Asia was already enslaved and he and his Marines had to do something about it.

✪ 5TH AMPHIBIOUS FORCE, AFLOAT
VICINITY IWO JIMA
D-DAY MINUS THREE
16 FEBRUARY 1945

Iwo Jima was a stinking hulk of volcanic rock located 650 miles south of Tokyo, between four and five miles long and two miles wide. A car traveling at sixty miles per hour could traverse its entire length in five minutes.

Iwo Jima had just a few notable characteristics: Mount Suribachi, a small extinct volcano about as high as the Washington Monument, on the south tip of the island, and two crucial airfields, with another under construction. These airfields were needed as landing fields for U.S. aircraft returning from bombing runs, especially planes damaged from AA gunfire or encounters with Japanese fighters, and planes that were running out of fuel. As it was, too many American pilots were becoming casualties. Having no place between Japan and the American-controlled islands to land safely, a number of them could only ditch. Some were picked up but most simply went to a watery grave.

Key to the invasion were the seventy-two consecutive days of bombing by American B-29 Superfortresses and B-24 Liberators. They dropped more than 5,800 tons of bombs on Iwo Jima in a little more than two months. In fact, Iwo Jima would set the record for the most sustained and heavy bombardment in all of the Pacific war.

At dawn on D-4, the gunnery ships, along with escort carriers commanded by Rear Admiral William Blandy, had already arrived on the scene and began to blast the small island in preparation for the invasion.

✪ HQ 3RD MARINE DIVISION
WEST OF KAMA ROCK, OFF IWO JIMA
D-DAY, 19 FEBRUARY 1945
0820 HOURS LOCAL

Nearly 500 Navy ships laid down more shelling of the island from before dawn until just before 0800. Aircraft from Task Force 58, just off the coast of Iwo Jima, sent in their dive-bombers and fighters to bomb and strafe the small island.

Offshore to the southeast, there was a mix of fresh-faced, newly arrived Marines and battle-hardened Leathernecks who'd already experienced combat on other islands in the Pacific. They were waiting for the word to go in. For the Marine combat veterans, this was their fourth assault in thirteen months, and they were ready to take and hold the beachhead's right flank.

But the Japanese had terraced the beach, and after the Navy guns and bombers had rearranged the coarse, coal-black volcanic sand, it was almost impossible to dig in. When the typical Marine, wearing a seventy-five-pound pack on his back, tried to dig a foxhole for cover it was like digging a hole in a barrel of ball bearings. The best he could hope for was to burrow into the sand like a beetle and hope it was deep enough. As it turned out, the only real practical but grim protection from Japanese bullets was often the lifeless body of a fallen comrade.

The troops from the 3rd, 4th, and 5th Marine Divisions began reaching the Red, Green, Yellow, and Blue beach landing zones. The 4th Division would take the quarry south of Airfield 2. The 5th Marine Division would surround and capture Mount Suribachi. The 3rd Marine Division consisted mostly of reserves, but some scouts and headquarters personnel went ashore.

The first troop-carrying Amtracs rode the low waves onto the black sands of Iwo Jima by 0905 on 19 February 1945. For the next hour or so it was a flawless landing. But then all hell broke loose. Marines from the second waves of Amtracs waded ashore amidst unbelievable chaos. There was broken debris from blasted equipment—landing craft, armored vehicles, and supplies—scattered across the beach and washing up on shore.

Scores of dead Marines were also bobbing in the waves and washing onto the black sands. Body parts were almost as commonplace as the chunks of volcanic rock. The scene was one of absolute pandemonium and mayhem. As one eyewitness Marine said, "I can't describe it to you. All I could think was, this is not the movies."

General Kuribayashi had waited until several waves of Americans were ashore before letting the Marines know that they had company on the island. Then Kuribayashi's guns triangulated on the Marines on the beach, mowing them down like a buzz saw. Rockets, anti-aircraft fire, and anti-tank guns were also trained on the landing beaches. The Japanese opened fire from almost everywhere on the island.

Marines everywhere on the island were pinned down or cut down. Casualties began to mount, and it was an impossible mission for the Marines during those first few hours of combat. In fact, in the first seventy-two hours of combat, there was one Marine casualty every forty-five seconds.

U.S. intelligence had pegged the Japanese troop size on Iwo Jima in late 1944 to be somewhere between 4,000 and 11,000. That's why FDR and the Joint Chiefs were optimistic that the Marines could master the island in short time. No one knew it, but the enemy troop strength was in fact at least twice the highest number given by military intelligence.

General Kuribayashi had constructed his command center with five-feet-thick walls and a ten-feet-thick roof, seventy-five feet underground.

The Americans were not prepared for the horrendous numbers of killed and wounded Marines. Nor had they been prepared for the barbarous ferocity of the Japanese counter-attacks. To General Kuribayashi, this would truly be a "heroic" battle. By that he meant that he expected every one of his soldiers to die, but not before killing 220,000 Marines first—ten for every Japanese soldier, as he had inspired them to do. Kuribayashi would have been even more encouraged if he'd known that the Americans were sending "only" 100,000 Marines ashore—his troops could turn the tide by just killing five Americans apiece.

At the end of the day, the Marines had progressed only a few feet—at a tremendous cost of 10 percent of their forces. Of the first 30,000 men who landed on Iwo Jima that day, 3,000 were already casualties. About 40,000 Marines followed, and were met with the same percentage of casualties. Every one of the nearly 100,000 combatants on Iwo Jima would be caught up in the viciousness of the fighting.

Twenty-four-year-old Marine Captain Fred Haynes was the operations officer for the 28th Marine Regiment as the showdown on Iwo Jima's beaches drew near.

❑   ❑   ❑

CAPTAIN FRED HAYNES, USMC
D-Day, Iwo Jima
19 February 1945
0800 Hours Local

I was the tactical control officer on a patrol craft offshore, and it was my job to see that all of the numbered waves of invasion troops were dispatched properly.

As soon as the numbered waves went, I went in with Colonel Williams and landed in the middle of Green Beach. We had two command groups and set up a command post but we were getting a tremendous amount of fire and the casualties were just incredible.

Nobody really knew that the Japanese were in bunkers below ground. We didn't really wake up to that fact until after we had gone ashore. Our whole regimental staff and their communications people just stood up and went straight across.

It was fairly smooth until the caves on Suribachi opened up. Within about twenty minutes, the Japanese began to pound the beaches with artillery.

When they opened up, we realized we had a problem. We couldn't call for naval gunfire, air support, or artillery, the critical elements of fire support. We were too close to the Japanese, face-to-face with them. The 105 mm artillery gunfire was more than I had ever seen in any Marine operation.

And from Suribachi, they were firing everything they had—artillery, mortars, machine guns—raking the beach. It was the first real battle I had been in. And it quickly taught me that they meant business.

We, the fighting troops, were really not affected by the number of casualties. We were given the orders to take the island, so that's what we had to do. There were huge casualties. This was the bloodiest battle that we fought during the Pacific war.

After four days of battle, the casualties dropped off slowly as we got across the ridgeline. Instead of 100 to 200 a day, which my regiment was having, it dropped off to maybe thirty a day.

At the end of the operation in late March, when we were doing a rout march down to get to the beach, a group of Japanese came out of somewhere, probably 200 of them. They came right down the airfield and caught us totally by surprise. The Army Air Corps pilots were sleeping above ground, unfortunately. About thirty-five pilots were killed in that attack.

Lieutenant Martin and our air battalion, which happened to be back in that area, took the challenge and killed all the Japanese, and that was the end of that.

Pacific intelligence did not realize that we were going to fight the devil on Iwo Jima. But we did, and it was a very, very difficult campaign.

✪ U.S. MARINE ASSAULT FORCE
IWO JIMA
D-DAY PLUS TWO
21 FEBRUARY 1945
1100 HOURS LOCAL

When President Roosevelt saw the casualty figures from Iwo Jima D+2 for the first time, he wept. He found it hard to believe that the Marines had lost so many men in just two days ashore. Over 4,000 Marines were wounded and more than 600 were dead. Another 560 were MIA—in just the first two days of battle.

By now the Marines were coming to grips with a painful reality. The enemy soldiers were not on Iwo Jima—they were in it. General Kuribayashi's island defense plans were ingenious.

He had built sixteen miles of tunnels, some several stories below the ground. These tunnels were wide and tall enough for soldiers carrying rifles to walk or run erect. There were also nearly 1,500 rooms spread throughout the subterranean sprawl, big enough for barracks, ammunition and fuel storage, bunkers and pillboxes, affording plenty of places to hide from American bombs, flame-throwers, naval guns, and other offensive actions. The Japanese had also constructed the tunnels and rooms with electricity, water storage, and even ventilation systems. They were ready to stay put and hold out for many months.

General Kuribayashi also improved on the German D-Day defenses. Instead of trying to blast the invaders while they were still coming ashore, he waited until they were already on the island so as to have more precision in using his guns. He had set up a vast, protected "killing machine." From inside concrete pillboxes situated all across Mount Suribachi, he could unleash every manner of weapon, including spigot mortars that could hurl a 675-pound shell almost a mile. Heavy machine guns set up a crossfire, and other big guns inside bunkers could fire down on the concentrated American forces. Every square foot of the invasion beach had interlocking sectors of fire where machine guns and small arms fire could crisscross.

Night brought a new kind of nightmarish hell. Mount Suribachi resembled a monstrous Christmas tree, with cannon and mortar fire, tracers, and flares exploding all along the rise of the ancient extinct volcano. When the firing stopped, General Kuribayashi sent out terror in the form of his prowling wolves—each warrior intent on killing his quota of ten Marines.

Some of the Japanese soldiers carried hand grenades in addition to their rifles. Others strapped land mines to their chests. After emptying their rifles at the Americans, and trying to kill others with a grenade, bayonet, or sword, they'd run into a foxhole containing several Marines and throw themselves down onto their enemies. The mine exploded and eviscerated everyone within six feet of the blast.

But despite heavy casualties, the Marines held their ground and kept pushing the enemy back, inch by inch. They attacked the Japanese pillboxes with grenades, satchel charges of TNT, and flame-throwers. Many times this just drove the enemy soldiers deeper underground, keeping them alive to fight another day.

One day after the landing, the Marines took the southern end of Iwo Jima around Mount Suribachi and made plans to take the summit. By the end of the day on 20 February, the Marines had secured one-third of the island and Motoyama Airfield No. 1.

Three days after the landing, a teenage Marine from Cleveland assigned to Combat Intelligence made his own landing on Iwo Jima. Private Don Mates experienced combat, death, and the aftermath of the war.

◻ ◻ ◻

PRIVATE DONALD MATES, USMC
Iwo Jima
D-Day Plus Three
22 February 1945

I ended up on Iwo Jima on February 22. It was one of the most scary, hellish places on the earth. It sort of looked like a moonscape, with the burning sulfur and haze that hung over it. And when we got ashore it was just absolute chaos.

There were bodies all over, wounded Marines. There was broken equipment and broken men. They hadn't picked up the bodies yet. So they were in the water, on the beach, they were on the rise going up from the beach. There were parts of men all over.

Wounded men were being evacuated but they were still on the beach. The corpsmen were working feverishly, the doctors were hacking away, and it was just terrible.

The Japanese controlled the high ground on Iwo. They knew where we were going to come in. They had their big guns, mortars, and everything triangulated. They were able to pick us apart and cause tremendous casualties.

Our Marines were working their way up Mount Suribachi. I remember Jim Trimble turning to me and saying, "If we have to go up that hill, Don, we're gonna die."

When we saw that flag go up on 23 February, it was just marvelous, because we knew the hill was secure, and that we wouldn't have to go up there. It was a relief to see that flag go up, even though we knew there was still much more ahead of us.

From 23–27 February, we just did guard duty. On 28 February, G-2 wanted to find out where the huge rockets were coming from. The Japanese were sending up rockets the size of fifty-five-gallon oil drums. They weighed about 168 pounds, and they had a motor that burnt out, causing the rockets to tumble in the air. Wherever it hit it created absolute chaos. They'd send up five or six at a time and just shoot them towards our lines.

So G-2 and General Erskine sent us out on patrol the afternoon of 28 February, to see if we could spot where these tremendous rockets were coming from. We got north of the second airfield and dug in between Hill 362A and 362B on a ridge.

The radio was at the top of the ridge. I was a secondary radioman. Joe McClusky was first radioman and he was in the hole. So he ran a telephone wire down to my hand, and when he yanked that telephone wire, that let me know that he was coming.

He'd take my spot, and I'd go back up and be the radioman for the second shift with Corporal William Reed.

Just before midnight, a flare went off and there they were! We had maneuvered ourselves to be in front of the lines. The Japanese came up out of their holes and came at us hand-to-hand. You couldn't use a rifle from where I was. Thank God we had hand grenades. That's the only thing that stopped them for a while. One Japanese soldier got within two feet of my foxhole while the battle was going on. He was wounded by one of the hand grenades, and he lay there dying.

Fifteen minutes later, Jimmie Trimble was bayoneted, McClusky and Reed were dead, and Nitsell was wounded. Warren Garrett, the old man out of the outfit at twenty-four, was dead.

When Jimmie Trimble got bayoneted he said to me, "Grenades . . ."

He'd heard the clicking of grenades. To ignite a Japanese grenade you have to hit it against something hard. This Japanese soldier hit two of them together and threw them in the hole. I was lying flat when I heard the word "grenades" and Jimmie Trimble was sitting up. He turned and caught the full blast of one of the grenades in the back, and the other one went off between my legs.

I pulled myself out of the hole, and Trimble was still alive. He put his hand out to be helped. At the same time, a Japanese soldier jumped in with a mine strapped to his body, and he wrapped himself around Jimmie. The Japanese soldier just evaporated. If I'd been in the hole I would've been behind the Japanese soldier and I would've gone up with him.

Jimmie didn't catch the full blast of the mine, but it was enough to kill him. Lee Blanchard, a seventeen-year-old private who enlisted when he was sixteen, was much smaller than I was. But he crawled out, put me on his back, and dragged me into his foxhole.

Waiting for me was another guardian angel, Jim White from Michigan. Jim took his bandages and Lee's and wrapped up both my thighs.

That meant they'd used their bandages; if anything happened to either of them they'd be in trouble.

I lay there for about three and a half hours and the Japanese still came at us. Jimmy White got a mortar platoon to move up and fill in the line where we were. And he got a tank to come up, and that's what saved our skins.

There was another man named Brown, who ended up in our foxhole. A machine gun raked the foxhole and killed Brown and hit me a second time.

About nine-thirty that morning, they got a corpsman to come and give me plasma and morphine. About noon, litter-bearers were able to get to me and move me about 150 yards behind the front lines. I lay there for the rest of the day until a litter-bearing Jeep came for wounded Marines.

There were nine of us in line there. One of the fellows had died. I didn't make the first trip, but I made the second trip of four to an aid station.

When I got to the aid station, they gave me whole blood. I lay there all that day and into the next day outside the aid station. They didn't take me down to the beach until 2 March, forty-eight hours later, and gangrene had set in. There were so many wounded men lined up waiting to go aboard hospital ships that they looked like railroad ties. I'd say there were maybe 400 wounded men waiting to go on the hospital ships.

They took me out to the USS *Leedstown*. I lay on the deck for an hour or two, and then they took me down to the galley and put me on a dining room table.

It turned out that because I had gangrene and fractured legs, they had to do a lot of cutting. I was out for three days.

I stayed on that ship until March 11. Then they took me to Army Hospital 127 in Saipan. It wasn't really a hospital, but a series of tents on Guam filled with 21,000 casualties.

After three days on Saipan, I was flown to Iea Heights Hospital in Honolulu. Again, the hospital was just jammed full of wounded Marines. They were all over the place—even in the hallway. Ironically I ended up in a VD ward because that's where the beds were.

From there I went to Oak Knoll Hospital, California, and then to Great Lakes Naval Hospital near Chicago. I spent the next year at the Marine Hospital in Cleveland, Ohio. My getting wounded didn't mean the battle for Iwo Jima was over. There was still a lot of fighting ahead, but D and E Companies, of the 2nd Battalion, 28th Marines, they're the ones that cleaned up that mountain.

In my squad there were ten men, and there were two of us who survived Iwo Jima. Six were killed on Iwo; one died of wounds, and so did another one later. Seventy percent of the casualties of our headquarters company were deaths from our platoon.

✪ U.S. MARINE ASSAULT FORCE
IWO JIMA
D-DAY PLUS FOUR
23 FEBRUARY 1945
0830 HOURS LOCAL

Early in the morning of 23 February, Navy aircraft dropped napalm on Mount Suribachi. Later, the mountain was strangely quiet. At its base, Colonel Chandler Johnson ordered a forty-man combat platoon up the slopes of the extinct volcano. When they landed, the platoon was only 400 yards from Mount Suribachi. It took them four days to cover that scant 400 yards of beachhead.

Led by First Lieutenant Harold Schrier of E Company, 2nd Battalion, the forty Marines of his 3rd Platoon gathered below Mount Suribachi.

Their mission was to take Suribachi from the Japanese, and once that was accomplished, to raise the U.S. flag there on its peak.

Among those forty men of E Company's 3rd Platoon were six Marines and a Navy corpsman that were about to make history, including nineteen-year-old Navy Pharmacist Mate Second Class John "Doc" Bradley, from Appleton, Wisconsin, and USMC photographer Lou Lowery. The men of 3rd Platoon made it to the top at around ten that morning, and by 1020 had fastened a U.S. flag to a long, heavy piece of water pipe they found in the rubble. They raised the Stars and Stripes over that contested Japanese real estate for the first time in history.

Marine photographer Lowery snapped several photos to record the event and headed back down to the combat command area.

"Doc" Bradley was a corpsman assigned to treat wounded Marines in battle. From down below, Colonel Johnson looked up at the flag on Mount Suribachi and felt that it ought to be larger, so it could easily be seen from any part of the island.

Johnson had an American flag from one of the ships that was 96 x 56 inches, and he called over PFC Rene Gagnon. Gagnon had been ordered to go up Mount Suribachi along with four of his buddies to set up a communications post. Joining them were two other Marines and a civilian photographer who had missed the first flag raising.

Gagnon took the flag and the men started up the slippery slopes of the volcanic rock. Joe Rosenthal, the AP civilian photographer, had missed getting the first picture and figured this would be a good opportunity. He was carrying a huge, bulky Speed Graphic camera that used 4 x 5 inch carriers of sheet film. As he was stacking sandbags to secure his camera, the Marines had already gotten to the site and were struggling with the heavy water pipe "flagpole," which weighed at least 150 pounds.

Rosenthal grabbed his camera and instinctively shot a photo. Within seconds, the flag was fluttering in the wind at the peak of Mount Suribachi. He took another photo with the entire group posing and recorded the names of the men who raised the flag.

"Doc" Bradley had stayed after raising the first flag and helped the five Marines hoist the new one. In that famous Pulitzer Prize–winning photograph, the most published picture in history, were Bradley, Sergeant Mike Strank, Corporal Harlon Block, Private First Class Rene Gagnon, Private First Class Ira Hayes and Private First Class Franklin Sousley.

Strank was the "old man" of the platoon—at twenty-four he was a non-com and the senior in the squad. Block was just eighteen years old, a hardscrabble oil worker from Weslaco, Texas, who had joined the Marines a year earlier along with thirteen graduates of his high school football team who all volunteered together. Rene Gagnon, from Manchester, New Hampshire, eighteen years old and far from home, carried a photograph of his girlfriend in the webbing of his helmet liner to give him encouragement. Ira Hayes was a young Pima Native American from River Indian Reservation, Arizona. And Franklin Sousley, a nineteen-year-old, found himself far from the quiet and peaceful hills of Kentucky.

These young men were just emerging from boyhood, and not quite a year earlier, all of them had been part of a huge wave of more than 21,000 who poured into California's Camp Pendleton. "Doc," Mike, Rene, Harlon, Ira, and Franklin became a part of Company E, destined for an appointment at Iwo Jima that would make them all famous.

The man who carried the flag ashore that was raised on Mount Suribachi on 23 February was a young officer from F Company, 2nd Battalion, 28th Marines, 5th Marine Division. Lieutenant G. Greeley Wells came to Iwo Jima with that group of 21,000 replacement troops from Camp Pendleton.

□   □   □

LIEUTENANT G. GREELEY WELLS, USMC
Vicinity Mt. Suribachi, Iwo Jima
D-Day Plus Four
23 February 1945
0800 Hours Local

I hadn't been in combat. I was called before Colonel Chandler Johnson, and he looked me over and said, "I'm going to make you my adjutant and you're going to rue the day. Report on time tomorrow." And that's how I started in the 2nd Battalion, 28th Marines.

I didn't know anything about being an adjutant, so I read the manual, and it said, " . . .the adjutant carries the flag." Someone asked, "Why the flag?"

I said, "I don't know, but I'll have it if you need it." So everybody kidded me about being this flag-carrying adjutant.

Then the training increased, and we got on board a ship to go into combat.

A third of us were paratroopers, a third were combat veterans, and another third were novices. And we had all our orders. We were on an LST and knew we were to land following the 1st Battalion. There were two battalions to take Suribachi.

So we got out into the water, waded, and ran up forward. There were a lot of wounded, and a lot of dead—it was mayhem. The beach was completely covered with Marines, struggling, crawling, trying to go up in the black sand, that slowed everything down. It was difficult. People were in shock. We were told to get off the beach as fast as we could, and then suddenly we were hit with a barrage that knocked everybody down.

There was complete confusion and it took us several hours to get settled. I had my blanket and my ammunition and hand grenades, so we were loaded down, and it was tough.

The Japanese hoped that they could make things so bad that we would withdraw. We landed over 30,000 men and a lot of the supplies that first day, but at a terrible cost.

When I first got out of my LST, with artillery shells and everything going off, I hit the deck. The man next to me was dead. Another guy was wounded; machine gun fire was going, and so we just got up and said, "We've got to keep moving."

I turned and was shot through the arm and across my back. The bullet went through my arm but didn't touch the bone. I felt lucky.

But there was all kinds of gunfire and activity going on all over that island. We had to fire star shells that illuminated and use them all night long, because when we didn't we found some of our men had had their throats cut in the dark.

Our planes were dropping napalm on Mount Suribachi. Suribachi got an awful beating, and our naval vessels were pounding away at the side of it. It took us two and a half days just to get to the base of Suribachi. It was only a short distance, but it was slow going.

Colonel Johnson sent a patrol from F Company to go up and reconnoiter. He didn't say, "When you get to the top, raise the flag." He said, "If you get to the top, raise the flag."

So we got up there, looked around and found a pole, and started to put up the flag, which then was raised.

People on the hundreds of vessels around us, plus the Marines ashore, had heard that we were going to raise the flag that day. And when we did, all the ships' horns and whistles blew. It sounded like Times Square on New Year's Eve. The whole battle suddenly stopped for a moment and you could hear Marines cheering. It really was an amazing scene.

We can never forget the tremendous battle that the Marines fought on Iwo Jima. They went in heroically, without hesitation, at an enemy that they couldn't see, buried below the surface of the island. They were almost impossible to get out, and we spent thirty-six days accomplishing the mission. I think that we can also never forget the flag raising—but as far as the Marine Corps and the people who fought there, we can never permit anything to overshadow their heroic actions.

✪ U.S. MARINE ASSAULT FORCE
IWO JIMA
D-DAY PLUS FIVE
24 FEBRUARY 1945
1330 HOURS LOCAL

Many of the Marines thought that the famous flag raising was a signal that the battle for Iwo Jima was almost over. However, there were still another thirty-two days of brutal combat ahead as the Marines and General Kuribayashi's soldiers slugged away at each other. Sadly, half of the flag-raisers were among the casualties. A week after planting the flag on Mount

Suribachi, Sergeant Mike Strank was killed by friendly fire from an offshore ship. A Japanese shell exploded near PFC Harlon Block just hours later, killing him. His body was misidentified for two years, and it wasn't until after the war that he was finally identified. Four weeks after the flag raising, Franklin Sousley was picked off by a Japanese sniper while waiting to be shipped out for the trip back home.

Private John Cole, barely eighteen, was a Marine whose only previous combat experience was just prior to Iwo Jima, on Guam. It may have helped him survive. He was part of the new group from the States assigned to the 3rd Marines for graves registration detail. He and his buddies recovered bodies of Marines and soldiers killed on Iwo Jima. It was a grisly task.

◻   ◻   ◻

PRIVATE JOHN COLE, USMC
Iwo Jima, D-Day Plus Eighteen
9 March 1945

Most of us had only been in the Marine Corps six or eight months. When I landed it was the sixth day of the battle. The beachhead had been occupied for almost a week. I went back down to the beach, where the first supplies unloaded were ammunition—machine gun ammo, rifle bullets, mortar shells, and shells for the howitzers. Then all kinds of rations.

After a week in shore party, we were sent to various regiments of the 3rd Marine Division. When we did that, we came under mortar fire almost immediately, which was a frightening experience.

Some of us went off with an NCO and we were blowing caves. Our task was to take white phosphorous grenades, throw them into the caves through whatever openings there were, and follow that up with blocks of TNT, which we used to collapse and seal the openings of the caves. And if that didn't kill them, the smoke and the fumes would asphyxiate them. Sealing the caves prevented them from climbing or digging out.

Then a group of us were assigned to work with the graves registration detail. We did not dig graves or put people in graves; we never saw the graves the bodies ended up in. Our task was to carry the dead off the battlefield and get them back to regimental headquarters, where they could be identified, if possible. We checked their dog tags, their last name stenciled on the breast pocket of their uniforms, and sometimes their equipment, packs and so on. Besides that, and by means of their personal effects, identification was generally established.

We had a four-wheel-drive truck with an open bed in the rear. It carried about a dozen stretchers, which were so stained with blood and bodily fluids from the wounded that they were no longer suitable for that purpose. These were given to us to carry out the bodies. So our task was to climb aboard the truck and ride as close to the line as we could get. Then we'd park the truck and get somebody to tell us where the last known men had been killed. We'd take the stretchers and walk until we found them.

As long as there was light, and there were bodies to be found that could be gotten out, we'd go get them. Carrying the bodies down the terrain was difficult. The ground was completely broken by all the shellholes and gouges. The terrain was rugged and rough to begin with so it was a physical burden to carry these guys.

And then we'd roll them or lift them onto a stretcher, typically two men on a stretcher. We'd go back to the truck, load the bodies, maybe eight men, and we'd have to hold and balance the load as the truck bounced along.

Typically the bodies that we picked up had been dead for anywhere from three to six days. It wasn't until that ground was taken and held that anyone could get in and recover the bodies.

Because of that delay, the bodies were bloated and crawling with maggots. The maggots were under the skin and crawling in their eyes, and beyond that, bodily fluids leaked out and skin was separating. Things would swing against you, and you'd get these fluids on your body, on your uniform. And we only got to wash them once in thirty days. So we learned to live in that atmosphere, eat our food, ignoring the flies buzzing off the bodies and onto our food.

But the smell was probably the worst. It's so intense that sometimes you'd literally gag and have dry heaves. You shut down your emotions and your feelings to the extent that you can, because you have a task to do. It is shocking, and at one point or another you say to yourself, "I wonder if they'd send me to the line, it might be better to be dead than to be doing this."

It was mind-boggling to see the destruction. It gives a feeling that life is cheaper than dirt. And since I only dealt with the dead, all I saw was the inevitability of death.

I did that from about 3 March through 27 March, the day I left the island. By the time we came under fire and started to deal with the dead, the idea of war as a romantic adventure was long gone.

If I had been one of the guys who ended up in a line company, I heard that the probability of being wounded or killed was ten times higher.

Yes, the worst is the smell. When I finally left the island, I escaped the smell but not the memory of the smell. I promised myself never to forget that smell, never forget the men, and never let it happen again.

✪ U.S. MARINE ASSAULT FORCE
IWO JIMA
D-DAY PLUS FORTY
31 MARCH 1945
1330 HOURS LOCAL

The total of thirty-six days of fighting on Iwo Jima resulted in 19,000 U.S. troops wounded or MIA and 6,825 killed in action. The Marines had been fighting in combat for four years, but here—in just a month—the U.S. Marines suffered a third of all their casualties of World War II.

"Doc" Bradley, the Navy corpsman, in a letter home to his folks, wrote: "I never realized I could go four days with no food, sleep, or water, but now I know it can be done."

Bradley was the only one of the three surviving flag-raisers on Iwo Jima who resumed a normal life after the war. He summed up his assessment of the battle when he told his nine-year-old son upon his return, "James, I want you to always remember—the heroes of Iwo Jima are the guys who did not come back."

Bradley returned to America to a hero's welcome by President Harry Truman, who sent Bradley and the other two survivors of the Iwo Jima flag raising on a war bond tour of thirty-three cities. Truman gave the men the impossible task of raising $14 billion in war bonds, which represented 25 percent of the national budget. The men accepted the responsibility and raised not $14 billion but $26 billion in two months—amounting to 47 percent of the U.S. budget.

Iwo Jima was one of the bloodiest battles in modern history. More Marines died there than in any other battle in the Pacific in WWII. And more U.S. Marines earned the Medal of Honor on Iwo Jima than in any other battle in U.S. history, while thousands of Marine veterans of that battle were awarded the Purple Heart. Twenty-seven Medals of Honor were awarded to Marines and sailors of Iwo Jima, many of them posthumously. Admiral Nimitz would remark after the battle, "Among the men who fought on Iwo Jima, uncommon valor was a common virtue."

The Navy also lost two of its carriers at Iwo Jima. The famed USS *Saratoga* was hit by a kamikaze aircraft and sank. The escort carrier USS *Bismarck Sea* was likewise sunk. The Navy lost more than 1,000 sailors to the kamikaze attacks.

The Japanese defenders suffered 21,000 casualties, most of whom were killed in action. Surprisingly, in contrast to other island battles, more than 1,000 Japanese soldiers surrendered, despite their strong adherence to the samurai code.

And, as was the case on Tarawa and Peleliu, some Japanese stragglers hid in the caves until well after the war ended. The last two Japanese soldiers on Iwo Jima surrendered four years after the battle.

After the initial assault, the Marines didn't break through the last Japanese lines until 9 March. Iwo Jima wasn't declared secure until 26 March, following a banzai attack near the beaches. The Army's 147th Infantry Regiment relieved the Marines and assumed ground control of the island on 4 April.

After Iwo Jima was declared secure, more than 2,000 B-29 aircraft were able to make emergency landings on the island during later bombing raids of the Japanese mainland. These actions saved as many lives as there were total casualties in the Battle of Iwo Jima.

Chaplain Roland Gittelsohn said it best during the dedication of a battlefield cemetery on Iwo Jima:

Somewhere in this plot of ground, there may lie a man who could have discovered a cure for cancer.

Under one of these Christian crosses, or beneath a Jewish Star of David, there may rest now a man who was destined to be a great prophet. Now they lie here silently in this sacred soil, and we gather to consecrate this earth in their memory.

Here lie officers and men, black and white, rich and poor... here are Protestants, Catholics and Jews. Here no man prefers another because of his faith, or despises him because of his color. Here there are no quotas of how many from each group are admitted or allowed. Theirs is the highest and purest form of democracy.

Unfortunately, at the end of March, although the Marines of the 3rd, 4th, and 5th Marine Divisions had secured Iwo Jima, they had no time to celebrate or even catch their breath.

The next island assault landings—on Okinawa—were just days away.

CHAPTER 17
OKINAWA: THE LAST BATTLE
(APRIL 1945)

⭐ **U.S. MARINE ASSAULT FORCE**
OPERATION ICEBERG
1 APRIL 1945
1030 HOURS LOCAL

The morning of 1 April 1945 was Easter Sunday. It was also April Fools' Day.

Events on the two fronts were irrevocably bringing the world war to an end. In Europe, U.S. troops had encircled remaining German troops in the Ruhr Valley and the Soviet army had surrounded the capital city. In a Berlin bunker, Adolf Hitler and his henchmen were preparing for an ignominious end to their evil campaign for conquest of the West. 1 April was also D-Day for the Allied offensive into northern Italy, as the Axis began to crumble.

But for the more than 200,000 American soldiers, sailors, and Marines heading to Okinawa, it was "L-Day"—Landing Day—for a campaign the war planners called Operation Iceberg. Okinawa is the main island in the Ryukyu Islands group, halfway between Formosa and Kyushu. Tokyo was

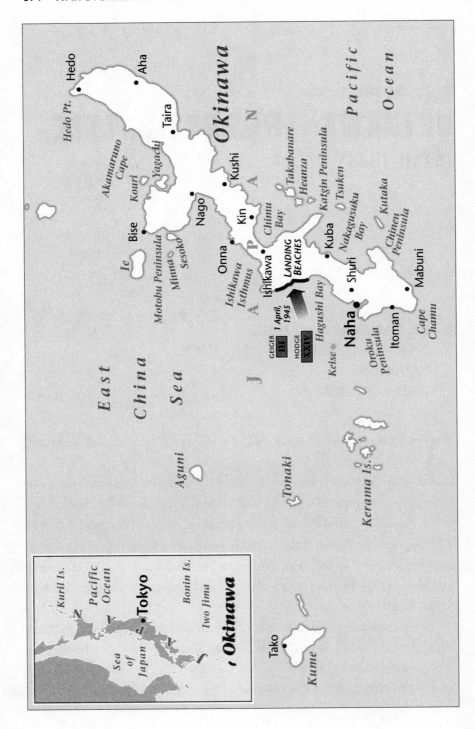

committed to the defense of Okinawa as long as they could. They sealed that determination with plans for maximum use of kamikaze attacks.

As the Allied troops aboard the invasion ships pressed closer to Okinawa, their officers stressed the importance of taking this final island, that it would help end the war. But they were also brutally honest. In light of the casualties inflicted at Iwo Jima, there was no reason to expect anything less at Okinawa. The question plaguing the Americans was how to fight an enemy so dangerous and so desperate that he was willing to kill himself in order to destroy you. The answer seemed obvious: The only option was to fight to the death—just as the enemy planned to do.

On the island of Okinawa, that's exactly what the U.S. soldiers and Marines did, in a gut-wrenching final showdown with the Japanese forces that spring of 1945. This would become Japan's brutal "last stand" against the American forces.

The Americans had fought World War II on two fronts on opposite sides of the globe. Both Germany and Japan had refused to give in, and the casualties of bloody battles in both theaters mounted. The number of American military dead or wounded had risen to more than a million. Yet the American fighting men still pushed on. Because the U.S. Armed Forces were waging a two-front war, they desperately needed matériel and reinforcements in order to keep going.

Yet although things were tough for the Americans, they were worse for the Japanese. The Imperial Army was getting even more desperate than they had been at Iwo Jima. They knew that if they failed to push the Americans back into the sea at Okinawa, the next place they would be fighting them would be on the beaches of Japan.

All across the Pacific, Emperor Hirohito's time was running out. Fighting the Americans and their allies over the past three years had taken a huge toll on the Imperial Army, Navy, and air forces. They were out of nearly everything—fuel, ships, aircraft, munitions—and each day they were running lower and lower on their most essential war component: the Japanese fighting man.

The American public got behind their men in uniform, now numbering sixteen million troops fighting Hitler and Tojo (including a smaller number of noncombatant women in the WACs, WAVEs, and WAFs). The tide of war in Europe had turned in the spring of 1945, when the Allies had Hitler on the defensive, but the war wasn't over in that theater just yet. The Joint Chiefs had planned for an all-out offensive against Nazi aggression to end the war in Europe in weeks rather than months.

If Germany could be forced to surrender, taking Okinawa could force an unconditional surrender from the Japanese as well. Okinawa's proximity to Japan's main islands was strategically critical to the Allied invasion plan, so the Joint Chiefs were willing to risk huge casualties in order to capture it.

A year earlier, the Joint Chiefs had considered Iwo Jima and Okinawa as targets for a final takeover—especially Okinawa. Not just because the tiny island was within striking distance of the Home Islands of Japan by American B-24s and B-25s, but also because of the psychological value of capturing a piece of real estate that for 5,000 years had never known any other ruler but Japan. With the acquisition of these two islands, the military planners in Washington felt they could move the war in the Pacific to a quicker end.

Capturing Okinawa would set the stage for the invasion of Japan. Owning Iwo Jima would help too, but it was more than 750 miles from the Japanese mainland. Okinawa was closer and would give the Americans a decided edge. Control of these islands cut Japan off from her crucial refueling supplies and repair stations and made them available to American ships instead.

America's strategy of "island-hopping" had created stepping-stones for its forces to jump from island to island, each step bringing them closer to Japan. Okinawa was the final hop. At Okinawa, the Marines, Army, Navy, and U.S. Army and Navy air forces all united in a final battle that prepared them for the invasion of mainland Japan.

Americans saw Joe Rosenthal's Pulitzer Prize–winning photograph of the flag raising on Iwo Jima's Mount Suribachi in their newspapers and in movie newsreels. They were cheered by the fact that the Marines had taken Iwo Jima and secured its airfields, giving the United States yet another strategic air base close to the mainland of Japan.

Okinawa was much larger—more than sixty miles long—and hilly, honeycombed with caves, tunnels, and tombs. It was arguably going to be even more costly to take than Iwo Jima.

General Simon Bolivar Buckner Jr., the son of a Confederate general, was selected to lead the invasion. He led the massive 10th Amphibious Force. Admiral Ray Spruance and Vice Admiral Marc Mitscher headed up Task Force 58 and Admiral Kelly Turner led Task Force 51 naval forces. The British Royal Navy's Vice Admiral Sir Bernard Rawlings was assigned to the 5th Fleet and led Task Force 57—a British fleet of four carriers, two battleships, five cruisers, and fifteen destroyers. Marine Major General Roy Geiger would lead the invasion force with three Marine divisions and four Army divisions.

General Buckner's nemesis, Lt. General Mitsuru Ushijima, a senior member of the Imperial Headquarters, led the 32nd Imperial Army—probably one of the most effective combat teams ever assembled, consisting of more than 100,000 troops.

During March 1945, the U.S. Navy began air and sea attacks against Okinawa with such ferocity that the Japanese called it a "typhoon of steel." Six days before the planned invasion, the Navy increased its shelling intensity, pounding the island with more munitions than the 20,000 shells that they'd dumped on Iwo Jima. This time they also pumped tens of thousands of rounds onto the sites where naval recon photos showed evidence of Japanese emplacements. But the weeklong bombardment did little damage to the dug-in Japanese.

Also during March, Rear Admiral Alexander Sharp's fleet of 122 mine patrol craft began minesweeping operations. Continuing night and day until the invasion began, Sharp's operation swept 2,500 square miles of ocean. They found and destroyed six enemy minefields and nearly 200 mines. But Sharp's fleet paid a price for their efforts: His ships and men accounted for 15 percent of all U.S. naval casualties during the Okinawa operation.

Nineteen-year-old Seaman Third Class Larry Delewski joined the Navy to do his part. When he was assigned a stateside, landlocked, noncombatant job, he requested sea duty. His request was granted, and Larry saw perhaps more action than he'd bargained for. He was first aboard the destroyer

USS *Laffey* when it was sent to Normandy for the D-Day invasion of France. The *Laffey* was one of just sixteen (out of 300 destroyers built during the war) to receive a Presidential Unit Citation.

When Delewski's destroyer returned from Europe, it was refitted in the Boston Navy Yard and then given orders to head for the Pacific and Okinawa. The Navy was about to lose more ships and men in Okinawa than it had lost at Pearl Harbor.

□ □ □

SEAMAN THIRD CLASS
LAWRENCE DELEWSKI, USN
Aboard USS *Laffey*
1 April 1945
1115 Hours Local

I'd been trained in the gunnery school and I never got notification that I'd made third class until we were going through the Panama Canal heading to the Pacific.

On the way over, we practiced with the big guns. The gun would fire, then it recoiled fifteen, eighteen inches with hydraulic brakes to stop it. After the gun fired, the hot shell, about thirty inches long, came out. The "hot shell man" wore asbestos gloves up to his shoulders, and it was his job to clear that shell. Once it cleared, he'd trip the ramming shoe down so the gun could be reloaded. And then the "powder man" would load the powder in. This is a five-inch gun, so the powder for the shell itself was like a great big loaf of bread but it weighed over sixty pounds. Then you put the powder and shell in, hit the ramming shoe, and then hit the lever.

The ramming shoe came forward. The bridge closed and you're ready to fire again. Now everything I've just described took place every three seconds, so it took a lot of teamwork.

We had six five-inch guns and twelve 40 mm guns. We also had ten torpedoes and some depth charges. So we were armed and built to protect all those other ships as well.

I always had a globe and I'd hold it up and I'd say, just look—all you see is water. The Pacific Ocean is big. You can go for days and days and not see anything but water.

It was common knowledge that we were moving progressively north toward Okinawa. And sooner or later, we'd go for the Japanese homeland.

Destroyers like the *Laffey* seemed to always be in short supply so we were switched back and forth from fleet to fleet. Sometimes we'd be operating with the 3rd Fleet, other times with the aircraft carriers, and sometimes with the bombardment groups. And another time, we might be with the ships actually taking part in a landing.

This landing was on Easter Sunday, 1 April, and was fairly uneventful. The *Laffey* was landing reinforcements day and night.

We saw the damage that a single kamikaze could do. We saw people who were burned and mutilated.

On 12 April the *Laffey* took a tremendous beating, and there were four other destroyers knocked out the same day. At the worst of it, we had as many as eighty enemy planes on our radar screens at one time.

They started coming in big numbers and we started taking some hits. This plane hit on the blind side and blew me up onto the deck, maybe fifteen, eighteen feet, but I had no broken bones.

Another plane hit just forward of my gun mount. I saw this thing crash and saw the wing as it hit the back of the gun mount, causing a terrible gasoline fire just inside my gun area. Once we got the fire under control, I reported to the bridge that we were ready to resume firing.

I had shrapnel in my back and in the back of my head, with burns on my back. And the fiery explosion burned the hair off the back of my head.

The communications officer, who's standing there, found an unexploded shell. It was fairly common for these suicide planes to just fly over, rigged with shells, and drop them as bombs. And some hit the *Laffey* and went right through the main deck, through the lower deck. The rivets flew and the sheet steel opened up.

And so everything from the engine room aft was flooded because we had holes in the bottom. Later that day, two seagoing tugs came alongside. At that point, we must've had somewhere between eighteen and twenty-four inches of water below decks.

We were taken to a beach area where we dropped anchor, and then the next morning some underwater welders put patches on the outside so we could pump out the inside.

We lost six men out of that gun crew of thirteen that day. One was a young man who went to gunnery school with me in Newport, up by the bridge. They took a direct hit up there and he was killed. There was another gunner, Joe Mealy from Brooklyn, and shrapnel went right through him. He was dead in seconds.

We just knew that sooner or later, people on our ship were going to be lost. There was no escape. That's the thing when you're in the Navy: There's no place to hide.

✪ U.S. MARINE ASSAULT FORCE
OKINAWA
1 APRIL 1945
1915 HOURS LOCAL

By 1 April, more than 1,300 Allied ships had carried hundreds of thousands of men across the Pacific to assemble off Okinawa—more than at Normandy in June 1944.

General Ushijima had spent many months turning Okinawa into a fortress. His troops dug elaborate networks of tunnels that connected to and protected his strategically located artillery. He hoped to delay the Americans' ultimate invasion operation—the assault on the mainland of Japan—for as long as possible.

Ushijima stored enough water, rations, and essential supplies and munitions to last months. His plan was to let the Americans come ashore and then move inland. As at Iwo Jima, the Japanese would not oppose the American landing at first. But once they were far enough inland, he'd have them boxed in with his triangulated artillery and machine guns. Then Ushijima planned to hit them with all the strength of the 32nd Imperial Army in an unparalleled trap.

Still, it was easy at first—the Americans moved quickly into the hills above the beaches. The landing on Okinawa was so different from Iwo Jima that Admiral Turner actually believed that the Japanese had already given up. The Americans secured the beachhead and two airfields by that first morning with minimal casualties.

The Marines had also feigned a landing on Minatoga, completely hood-winking General Ushijima, who mistakenly radioed Imperial Headquarters that his troops had successfully repulsed the Americans, who had "suffered numerous casualties."

But then the U.S. Army's 96th Infantry Division was confronted by soldiers of Ushijima's army—most of them hidden in the hills of the south end of the island. It was the first major combat on Okinawa, with the American soldiers attempting to take the high ground one hill at a time, especially up on Kakazu Ridge. In the first four days, American troops suffered 3,000 casualties. But in the coming days, their casualties would top 3,000 each day.

The American armed forces desperately needed reinforcements, and during 1944 young Americans had lined up at the recruiting stations to serve. One of them was seventeen-year-old Dan Barton, who went to boot camp and was sent directly to the Pacific.

◻ ◻ ◻

PRIVATE FIRST CLASS DAN BARTON, USMC
Vicinity Higashi, Okinawa
1 April 1945
1135 Hours Local

From my personal experience—although Guam was bad enough—compared to Okinawa it was child's play. At the southern end of Okinawa, the Japanese made us pay for every inch of ground we took.

We landed on Okinawa with seven officers and 235 enlisted men. Eighty-one days later, there was one man in that group of 235 that stood muster. All the rest had either been killed or wounded.

Because of the heavy casualties at Peleliu and Iwo, we were expecting heavy casualties in the first waves. But when we walked ashore there was nothing.

Our regimental objective was Yontan Airfield. They gave us three days to take it but by nine-thirty that morning I was standing in the middle of the airfield. Ushijima had decided that instead of trying to meet us at the beach where we had overwhelming firepower, he'd meet us on the southern end of Okinawa, where he had the edge with 110,000 Japanese soldiers dug in. There's an old military axiom: Always take and hold the high ground. Well, Ushijima had done that.

We were under the impression that after we took the northern end we'd be through and could go home. But then when we started south and looked into the eyes of the fellows coming back, we started to understand. They looked like they'd run into a buzz saw.

The Japanese had registered their artillery and machine guns on our positions. So whenever we tried to seal one cave and take another, we usually drew fire from two or three directions. Plus, they had the high ground so we were right out in the open.

We called Okinawa the emperor's doorstep. It was the door to Japan. And they knew that even better than we did. So they were going to make it as difficult as they could.

For us, anything moving at night was enemy. You got into your foxhole; you stayed in it. If you heard something outside of it, you threw a hand grenade. You didn't want to fire a weapon because the muzzle flash gave away your position.

The biggest thing in your mind is, "I cannot let the guy next to me down." Still, you're scared to death. Somehow you manage to do what you have to do.

I got wounded on Horseshoe Hill. Mortar and artillery started coming in. My squad leader and my assistant gunner were hit and killed almost instantly.

I was down on the ground, and before I passed out, the sergeant put a compress on my hip. About that time a shell hit behind us, killing him and wounding me again. I got two pieces of shrapnel through the chest and abdomen. Well, the worst part of that is that we were pinned down and couldn't move. Anybody who stood up was cut down by machine gun fire. So I had to lie there all day and shoot myself with morphine.

The way I felt is that I wasn't going to die for my country, but I wanted to make the other guy die for his. And I kept that idea before me all the time. I said, "Hey, somehow I'm going to come through this." And I did.

The thing I remember most were the heavy casualties. You get the feeling that the law of averages is going to catch up. The other thing you never forget is the stench of fighting on Okinawa, because you're fighting over the same piece of turf day in and day out. You can't evacuate and pick up the dead. And there's a smell that you can't describe but you never get it out of your nostrils. For the rest of your life, you remember it.

✪ 10TH ARMY ASSAULT FORCE
VICINITY ISHIKAWA ISTHMUS, OKINAWA
9 APRIL 1945
1615 HOURS LOCAL

On the first day of the landing, the USS *Indefatigable* was hit by a kamikaze but was saved from serious damage by its armored flight deck. The Japanese launched the first of ten hordes of kamikaze attacks that continued until June. U.S. losses in both men and ships were severe. Between 1,500 and 2,000 kamikaze flights were flown from Kyushu to attack the American ships.

On the sixth day after the landing, the British aircraft carrier HMS *Illustrious* was hit by another kamikaze attack but did not sink. General Ushijima's fleet of kamikaze pilots and planes scored only a few crucial hits, including the U.S. aircraft carriers *Wasp* and *Franklin*. When the *Wasp* was hit, the resulting explosions and fires killed more than a hundred sailors and wounded 269. Nevertheless, within fifteen minutes, the fires aboard the *Wasp* were extinguished and her remaining crew began bringing back their aircraft.

The carrier *Franklin* was hit hard, but the cruiser *Santa Fe* heroically stayed alongside her throughout the afternoon, despite explosions and flames, to rescue those who jumped off the deck to escape from the fiery heat. Damage to the *Franklin*'s flight deck was extensive, but the ship got under way within hours and was able to return home under her own power. Casualties included 724 killed or missing and 265 wounded. Lieutenant (jg) Donald Gary was awarded the Medal of Honor for leading two sailors below the blazing decks in order to wet down a five-inch gun about to explode. He later found 300 men trapped below decks and led them to safety.

On 6 April, the "super battleship" *Yamato*, along with the Japanese cruiser *Yahagi* and eight destroyers, set sail for Okinawa. The *Yamato*, the largest warship ever built, was sent to Okinawa with no protective air cover and only enough fuel for a one-way trip. Their orders were to locate American and Allied ships and destroy them before they were destroyed.

From the very beginning of hostilities around Okinawa, the Japanese were intent on making life miserable for the Allies. In addition to at least 2,000 kamikaze aircraft, the Japanese had also created a fleet of kamikaze ships that included the *Yamato*, the *Yahagi*, and the eight destroyers. But these kamikaze ships were met and overwhelmed by aircraft from the 5th Fleet.

The American submarine USS *Hackleback* tracked the *Yamato* and her escorts and then alerted carrier-based bombers. Vice Admiral Marc Mitscher launched air strikes on the *Yamato*. Aircraft from the USS *San Jacinto* sunk the Japanese destroyer *Hamakaze*, while the light cruiser *Yahagi* was hit and went dead in the water. The small Japanese naval force was under incessant attack. The *Yahagi* was sunk after American carrier-based Hellcats and Avengers made a final attack.

The *Yamato* also finally succumbed to American air power. It took twelve bombs and seven torpedo hits to finally kill her, but she sank in the East China Sea. Three of the Japanese destroyers were also hit and were so badly damaged that they had to be scuttled. Even the four remaining destroyers could not make the return trip to Japan.

Of the *Yamato*'s crew of 2,747, all but 269 men were lost. The *Yahagi* lost about 450; *Asashimo* lost 330; and the seven destroyers suffered casualties of 391. There were few Japanese survivors. Losses to the Americans were ten planes and a dozen men.

This was the last Japanese naval action of World War II.

Giving support to the Okinawa landing was the most costly naval engagement in U.S. history. Thirty-four American ships and landing craft were sunk and almost 400 others were seriously damaged, many beyond salvaging. Worse, nearly 5,000 sailors were killed in action and an equal number were wounded—most of them burned by flaming gasoline that incinerated the skin of their faces, bodies, and limbs.

By 8 April, the American forces on Okinawa were stopped in their tracks by the line of Japanese defenses in concrete reinforced pillboxes with steel doors unaffected by flame-throwers. Casualties on both sides were growing along with civilian deaths. Additional reinforcements were landed on 9 April, and American troops on the island now numbered 160,000.

Attention now focused on taking Shuri Castle, the key Japanese defensive position of resistance. The "castle" was another reinforced concrete fortification located in the southern part of Okinawa on high land between the eastern and western coasts. As usual, General Ushijima had prepared defensive positions with interlocking fields of fire and could direct his men across the island underground without having to encounter American troops.

The interconnected tunnels were almost impossible to get into. However, against these fortifications was the combined firepower of six U.S. Navy battleships, six cruisers, nine destroyers, and some 650 American aircraft—in addition to the 160,000 Marines and soldiers on the ground.

✪ 10TH ARMY ASSAULT FORCE
OKINAWA
21 APRIL 1945
0915 HOURS LOCAL

On 12 April, a major loss had occurred far from the battlefield on Okinawa. Word was communicated from the War Department in Washington that President Franklin Delano Roosevelt was dead of a massive stroke after serving twelve years in office. Many of the young men fighting could remember no other president than FDR. Not many of them knew anything at all about their new commander in chief, Harry S. Truman.

Six days later, war correspondent Ernie Pyle headed to the front lines with GIs from the 77th Division. When Pyle joined the fight in the Pacific in early April, he had sought to become acquainted with the Marines. He wrote that their battles in the Pacific had been so brutal, and the Marines' reputation so fierce, that he was almost afraid of them. But after meeting the Marines in person he wrote that, "they have fears, and qualms and hatred for the war the same as anybody else. They want to go home as badly as any soldier I've ever met."

Pyle tried to understand the minds of the Marines he had chosen to follow. He found them to be young, polite, and compassionate. They bowed to civilians on the roads and did what they could to help them. They were Americans, after all. Pyle finally concluded that, "the Marines do not thirst for battles. I've read and heard enough about them to have no doubts whatever about the things they can do when they have to. They are okay for my money, in battle and out."

Pyle's dedication to getting his story in the heat of battle led him directly into machine gun crossfire on 18 April on the island of Ie Shima. He was with an American officer when a Japanese machine gun opened up on their vehicle. Both men jumped out of the vehicle and headed for a nearby ditch. But Pyle raised his head too soon, and enemy bullets from the machine gun pierced his head just below the brim of his helmet. He was killed instantly, and was later buried on the island.

The inclement weather reduced visibility and cut down on Allied aircraft assaults and recon. But it also helped to keep the kamikaze away. Yet without the recon to improve their handmade maps, the Americans had badly underestimated that only 50,000 to 65,000 Japanese troops were on the island. In truth, there were almost twice that many hiding in the maze of tunnels and caves.

One American general remarked to his superiors, "It's going to be really tough. . . . I see no way to get them out except by blasting them out yard by yard."

Okinawa's torrential rains, mudslides, poisonous snakes, mosquitoes, and disease only added to the hell experienced by the American troops. While on Okinawa, the Marines and soldiers also had to endure the constant stench of rotting human flesh.

Nevertheless, in almost three weeks, on 21 April, the soldiers and Marines had put an end to resistance at the northern end of Okinawa. The Japanese defensive line was finally breached on 28 April. General Buckner's troops attacked the two flanks of the enemy forces and fought ferociously against the Japanese soldiers, whose fortifications were beginning to weaken.

The battle for the rest of the island would continue through the end of June. Before hostilities were over, more than half a million Americans of the 5th Fleet and the 10th Army would be involved.

There would be more casualties right up to the last day of battle on Okinawa. Private First Class Herman "Buff" Buffington, an Army infantryman, had been lucky before shrapnel hit him on that last day.

◻   ◻   ◻

PRIVATE FIRST CLASS
HERMAN "BUFF" BUFFINGTON, US ARMY
Vicinity Machinato, Okinawa
27 May 1945
1330 Hours Local

For the last two weeks, we had briefings that were puzzling to an eighteen-year-old kid. They were asking if we had drawn up our wills.

I had my nineteenth birthday on 7 May when we were right in the middle of this thing. The original first and second scouts had been wounded, so I was our platoon's new first scout. And it got rougher and rougher.

There was a convoy coming up the road with five or six trucks coming back from the lines. After the first one passed, we noticed that they were stacked with dead American soldiers, stacked like wood. That was extremely hard to take. It really hit home as to what we were doing there.

The lieutenant said, "Well, would you like to say a prayer with me?" You never hear this ordinarily. But this was the front lines. Then the lieutenant pulled off his helmet and kneeled down and said the Lord's Prayer.

My buddy pulled a letter out and gave it to the lieutenant and said, "Be sure and get this mailed because I won't live beyond this afternoon."

We encountered a lot of destruction. Bodies would be so thick you'd have to crawl over them sometimes and we couldn't always see the enemy.

While I was up there, someone came up and stood behind me. I knew it was some kind of brass. He kneeled down and asked me, "Soldier, how's it going?" Then he said, "Could I borrow your rifle?"

I said, "Yes, sir, you may." You have to keep in mind that no one wore their rank on them anywhere. But anyway, I didn't recognize him. He was about fifty years old. And he pulled off his binoculars and let me have them. And he says, "I want you to tell me if I'm still a pretty good shot."

It was just like out at the firing range. So that's what I did. And he shot for what seemed to me like ten or fifteen minutes. He was good—a sharp shooter.

As he'd shoot and hit one of the Japanese I'd tell him. He hit quite a few. When he got ready to leave he thanked me and wished me well. I gave him his binoculars back, and he handed me my rifle.

After he left, a few of the guys came up from the squad and one said, "Buff, do you know who that was?" I said, "No, I didn't know him. I assume it's some brass though." They told me that it was General Simon Bolivar Buckner.

Combat here was a lot different than it was in Europe. We crawled most of the time. Sometimes it might take two or three weeks to take one spot. And to take those hills you'd have to have enough people left to hold the hill once you took it. When we took a place and got kicked off, we'd always try to go back. We'd be seesawing back and forth quite often. And in all those times you're getting people killed and wounded. It's just really unbelievable.

When you're taking a hill and there are machine guns and small arms shooting at you, you haven't got much of a chance. You use a sense that's rarely ever used, a sense of survival. After several weeks, you act like there's no tomorrow. There's no tonight. There's not even the afternoon. It's only now. Now is all you think about, and how you're going to survive and help your buddies survive.

That's all you do; you didn't think about home. You didn't think about your girlfriend. You didn't think about anything but "now." And you ask, "Am I going to make it?"

I was hit in the leg with shrapnel and got what they call "the million-dollar wound," meaning I'd be going home. Well, it didn't always happen like that. Guys wounded the night before were up the next morning picking up their packs and weapons.

I was hit in the leg, in a spot where it went right under my knee and went to the bone and stopped there. But the thing that you don't realize is that the hot piece of shrapnel "fries" your flesh just like cooking bacon. You can hear it. And it does hurt. They cut the shrapnel out and in my case they said that they didn't have time to wait for a morphine shot to deaden the pain of that wound.

Finally the Japanese started to collapse. But they would not come through our area. There's a cliff on the southern end of Okinawa, and they were jumping off rather than surrendering.

I couldn't believe the Japanese would ever surrender. You'd think when they did that we went out, threw our hats up, and hollered all over the place. We didn't do it. It was about eleven o'clock in the morning when we found out that they'd all surrendered. Instead of celebrating, we just stretched out on our bunks and stayed there until late that afternoon, even missing our noon chow time.

I remember praying, "God, I might just live yet." And thinking I might even get home.

✪ 10TH ARMY ASSAULT FORCE
VICINITY SHURI CASTLE, OKINAWA
31 MAY 1945
1330 HOURS LOCAL

In Europe, things had happened rapidly. On 28 April, Italian dictator Benito Mussolini was captured and killed, and his body was hung in the street by Italian partisans while the Allies were taking Venice.

Two days later, Adolf Hitler committed suicide in his Berlin bunker while Soviet troops entered the city, and a week later an unconditional surrender of German troops to Allied forces was announced. These events brought about the official end of the war in Europe.

Three days after V-E Day, General Buckner launched an attack against the Japanese Shuri Castle line, bringing about the fiercest fighting yet on Okinawa. General Ushijima asked Tokyo to send more reinforcements and supplies, but he was refused. Tokyo could not spare any more troops, and had already begun to plan how to deploy all remaining soldiers to protect the Home Islands from an American invasion.

On 20 May, the Japanese had begun their withdrawal from China, getting ready for the inevitable invasion of Japan. Ushijima knew now that it was over. After two months of brutal combat, incurring over 50,000 American casualties, the soldiers and Marines of the 10th Army secured the Shuri Castle line.

Japanese Premier Suzuki announced to the people of Japan that the entire nation "will fight to the very end" rather than accept unconditional surrender. But the Japanese people had to be aware of the obvious.

On 11 June, General Buckner sent a message to General Ushijima to surrender. The Japanese leader dismissed it with great disdain—surrender meant endless shame.

Corporal Mel Heckt was at Shuri Castle as part of the 4th Marine Regiment, made up almost entirely of Marine Raiders. He was a squad leader when his replacement company was sent in to help take Shuri Castle and the rest of the Oroku Peninsula. By the time the combat ended, Heckt had been promoted to platoon leader, a job for a sergeant, simply because the Marines' heavy casualties had used up all of the sergeants.

◻ ◻ ◻

CORPORAL MELVIN "MEL" HECKT, USMC
Oroku Peninsula, Okinawa
18 June 1945
0940 Hours Local

We made the landing at night. We got up to the hill and as soon as we got there, I remember mortar fire killed our BAR man. I lost two of my machine gun ammo carriers on the second day. The Japanese artillery was great when we were on top of Sugar Loaf Hill. An artillery shell came over that ridge and killed three of my machine gunners. I'd just left the wounded with a corpsman and was going toward Naha when we came to a bridge. We lost all kinds of men in trying to take that bridge.

One fellow had a leg blown off, and Tex Durasole took out his K-bar knife and cut off the guy's leg in order to extricate him and save his life.

On Oroku Peninsula, one of the worst experiences happened one night on a ridge toward the end of the island. I took the last watch on the gun and about 5 AM I heard a banzai attack. They were coming right at me. My machine gun jammed and then my rifle jammed. Fortunately some A Company guys were standing in a semicircle—like they were at a firing range—and they picked off all these guys.

The next morning, Eddie Dunham from Detroit went up early to drop a satchel charge over the ridge. A bullet hit him right in the head and I helped carry him down. I thought he was alive, but my corpsman said later, "Mel, he was dead. You were feeling your own pulse." And he was such a close friend of mine that I broke down and cried.

One of my machine gunners, Bobby Banker from Racine, Wisconsin, was firing at quite a long distance and doing really well, and he got a bullet right in his neck. We got a corpsman up there and we tried to clamp the artery and stop the bleeding. Finally the doctor came, but he had died.

I lost a heck of a lot of men. Out of my fifty-three-man machine gun platoon, only four didn't get hit or killed. I was one of the four.

✪ 10TH ARMY ASSAULT FORCE
OROKU PENINSULA, OKINAWA
8 JULY 1945
1100 HOURS LOCAL

After a month of bloody and violent combat, American Marines and soldiers finally broke through General Ushijima's defenses and conquered Okinawa by the end of June.

Back in the States, America's new president, Harry Truman, wanted to end World War II quickly, with minimal casualties. After witnessing the quick, unconditional surrender of Germany, Truman hoped that Japan might be convinced to do the same.

Mopping-up operations began on the southern end of Okinawa, and Winston Churchill spoke directly to Americans to tell them just how important the Battle of Okinawa was to the world. He said, "The strength and willpower, devotion and technical resources applied by the United States to this task, joined with the death struggle of the enemy... places this battle among the most intense and famous in military history."

Okinawa was supposed to be the hoped-for turning point that essentially ended the war in the Pacific. But the Imperial Army was unquestionably well fortified and had enough supplies to hold out for many months. The Americans, on the other hand, didn't want to prolong the combat on Okinawa any longer than necessary. Finally, with guts, determination, and commitment, the Americans gave it their all. Both sides sacrificed many lives, but in the end, the Americans finally broke through.

It was said that one Marine division assaulted a hill about a dozen times, taking the hill, losing it, and retaking it again and again in what seemed to be a never-ending cycle. In the process, the division lost twice the number of men in their original troop complement.

Japanese casualties also grew steadily. The Americans slowly pierced the Japanese lines, and they retreated, charging the Americans in a futile suicidal attack. A few actually surrendered. Nevertheless, the Marines and soldiers had to seize the island inch by bloody inch.

Then, by late June, General Ushijima and his officers knew it was utterly hopeless. Still, unconditional surrender seemed out of the question—true to Japanese tradition. Most of the Imperial Army wanted no part of surrender, and they continued to throw themselves into hopeless suicidal charges. Finally, even General Ushijima recognized that by now the battle was over and his cause was lost. Believing that he had embarrassed himself before his emperor, he determined to end his life in an honorable way. So he brought together his officers and said his goodbyes to them. Then he and his chief of staff, General Cho, took part in the traditional ceremonial feast, after which each of them wrote a *haiku* poem. Then the two officers dressed in their white robes and went out to the front of the cave in which Ushijima had his command headquarters. Each of the two officers knelt and disemboweled himself with a sword. A Japanese junior officer then took his own sword and cut off the heads of the two generals.

The American commander, General Simon Bolivar Buckner Jr., was killed by Japanese artillery fire on 18 June. That same day, Marine General Roy Geiger assumed command of the 10th Army on Okinawa, the first time a U.S. Marine would command a field army.

Failure to stop the Americans at Okinawa meant that Japan had to face the unimaginable—an American invasion of the Japanese homeland.

On 21 June, the 10th Army pushed through to take the only part of the island still not in American hands, the southernmost point on Okinawa. Hundreds, if not thousands, of Japanese troops followed the lead of General Ushijima in ritual suicide. On the next day, the American flag flew over Okinawa. The eighty-two-day Okinawa campaign was finally declared officially over on 2 July.

The cost had been horrendous for both sides. American casualties amounted to more than 68,000 sailors, soldiers, and Marines, with some 16,000 killed or missing in action. The Navy lost more men than the Marines did in the Battle of Okinawa, mainly from kamikaze attacks.

The Japanese lost some 131,000 men, with about 108,000 killed in action and another 24,000 sealed in caves or underground fortifications.

Fewer than 11,000 Japanese soldiers, most of them wounded, surrendered or let themselves be captured.

Tragically, some 150,000 Okinawa civilians—about one-third of the population—also lost their lives. And before the battle ended, another third to half of the civilians had been wounded. Many were caught in the cross-fire of combat between the two armies, although the Japanese killed many of the civilians when they tried to surrender to the Americans. Only the Battle of Stalingrad, in the European theater, saw a greater loss of civilian lives.

In the Battle of Okinawa the U.S. fleet lost thirty-four ships and more than 600 were damaged. The U.S. lost almost as many aircraft. However, the Japanese lost nearly 8,000 aircraft and nearly all of its remaining Imperial fleet.

Victory on Okinawa brought no rest for the battle-weary soldiers, sailors, Marines, and Coast Guardsmen. They were told to prepare for the massive invasion of Japan itself. They'd won the battle for Okinawa, but the war itself was definitely not yet over.

From Potsdam, after the surrender of Germany and the Nazi war machine, the Allied leaders warned Japan of the destruction of their homeland when the invasion came. The Japanese still would not bend. Their military leaders would rather die than surrender.

But the casualties of the Battle of Okinawa helped President Truman confirm his decision to use the atomic bomb on Hiroshima and Nagasaki. Truman reckoned that although the new devices would probably kill thousands, using them to force a capitulation by Japan would be the more humane route in the long run.

More people were killed on Okinawa than were later killed at Hiroshima and Nagasaki combined. The Okinawan civilians and Japanese and American dead at Okinawa numbered nearly 300,000.

Those numbers must have seemed horrendous to Truman, yet they would only get worse if the bombings continued over Tokyo, and if the planned invasion went forward. The president had also been told that at least one million American deaths would occur during an invasion of Japan. The Allied leaders projected that another one to two million Japanese lives would be lost in defending against an invasion.

These projections did not even include the 400,000 American and Allied POWs, slave laborers, and civilian detainees held by Japan; most would be executed if an invasion began. Nor would it include the half million to a million Japanese troops virtually stranded on various Pacific islands, who would likely starve if Japanese supply ships did not get through—which was now the case since the Japanese had no ships and the Americans controlled the sea lanes.

The Washington war strategists agreed that they couldn't sacrifice millions of lives, but they weren't sure about the atomic bomb, either. In any event, as the sign on Truman's desk put it, "The buck stops here." The president would make the ultimate decision. And by now, Truman knew that the atomic bomb was only viable alternative.

Japanese-Controlled Areas
Pacific Theater • August 1945

CHAPTER 18
MacARTHUR AND WAR'S END
(JULY–AUGUST 1945)

✪ **OFFICE OF THE U.S. JOINT CHIEFS OF STAFF**
WASHINGTON, D.C.
22 JUNE 1945

Okinawa, the last battle of World War II, yielded horrific losses of life on all sides. President Truman decided that if they were going to press Japan into submission any time within the next ten years, the United States would have to use the atomic bomb.

Truman and the Joint Chiefs wanted the war to end right away. The idea of another decade of the horror was too much to contemplate. They also felt it was imperative to save American lives, but were also concerned about the loss of Japanese lives. That was the main factor in the decision to drop atomic bombs on two Japanese cities, leading finally to Japan's full surrender.

The U.S. soldiers and Marines also wished for an end to the war. The beleaguered American troops who survived Okinawa had never experienced such extreme carnage. Admiral Nimitz had noted, "It was the worst fighting of the Pacific war, its sustained intensity surpassing even the brutal combat of Tarawa, Peleliu, and Iwo Jima."

But since Okinawa was so vital to Tokyo's last stand, the Japanese felt compelled to defend the island to the death. They did so with a desperation equal only to the unrelenting resolve of the Americans, who were even more determined to guarantee a victory of their own.

Toward the end of the bloody fighting on Okinawa, the Joint Chiefs of Staff approved Operation Olympic—the ultimate invasion of Japan. Military planners scheduled it for 1 November 1945. Under the joint command of General MacArthur and Admiral Nimitz, the U.S. forces would launch an assault on Kyushu, the southernmost Japanese Home Island. The Joint Chiefs had approved an invasion force of 650,000 troops, 2,500 ships, and 6,000 planes to attack the southern coast of Kyushu.

The Imperial military intelligence had correctly guessed the sites of American actions before and after Okinawa. They had expected the Americans to land in the Philippines and ordered their troops there to move back into the mountains and jungles. These troops were to hold out in a defensive operation while they prepared the Home Islands for the expected invasion. They were planning to fortify the coastlines and determine strategies for turning back the Americans when they landed on the beaches.

Fox Movietone

President Truman

By August, the Japanese high command planned to station nearly 250,000 troops on Kyushu, where they planned to counter-attack with 6,000 kamikaze aircraft. These suicidal missions would attempt to destroy a quarter of the Allied invasion force before they landed, while American troops were still aboard their amphibious troop carriers.

Meanwhile, American code-breakers, still unknown to the Japanese, were intercepting messages that indicated Russia and Japan were holding secret talks. Russia, although a U.S. ally in the European theater, had signed a neutrality agreement with Japan before the events of Pearl Harbor.

These behind-the-scenes negotiations between the Soviet Union and Japan took place during the first two weeks of June 1945. At Emperor

Hirohito's behest, Japanese diplomat Koki Hirota met with the Russian ambassador to Japan to discuss a possible new relationship between the two countries. Hirota offered to share all of Asia with the Soviet Union, telling the Russian ambassador, "Japan will be able to increase her naval strength in the future. That, together with the Russian army, would make a force unequaled in the world."

The idea of a Russia–Japan alliance complicated the American plans for Operation Olympic. Would an agreement between the two nations mean that Russian troops might come to the aid of the Japanese in the event of an Allied invasion?

✪ U.S. SOUTHWEST PACIFIC COMMAND
MANILA, PHILIPPINE ISLANDS
29 JULY 1945

MacArthur's headquarters announced the end of all Japanese resistance in the Philippines, and the liberation of the Philippines was declared on 5 July. By 10 July preparations for Operation Olympic were under way, and 1,000 bombing raids against Japan were planned. Four days later, they began. The first naval bombardment of the Japanese Home Islands also commenced.

Meanwhile the U.S. was secretly considering the use of an incredible new weapon, capable of destroying an entire city. Destroying a city wasn't a new concept. American B-29s under General Curtis LeMay, who had assumed command of the 20th U.S. Army Air Corps in the Mariana Islands, had leveled cities. After three months of bombing Japanese cities, however, few targets had been destroyed. General LeMay suggested that it would take his air force until October to destroy the fifty most important cities in Japan.

By late July, U.S. bombers had been dropping bombs on Japanese cities for several months, and although 300,000 casualties resulted from these raids, it took many missions and numerous tons of bombs to do it. These bombing raids did nothing to dampen the enthusiasm of the Japanese.

The U.S. now had the means to destroy an entire city with a single device—the atomic bomb—in a single bombing run. Such a weapon would certainly demonstrate to the Japanese warlords that continuing the war was futile. When MacArthur was briefed on the atomic bomb project, he was surprised. It seemed to him to have suddenly appeared as simply another military option, while it had in fact been decades in the making.

While the Manhattan Project is credited for the creation of the first atomic bombs, the concept was at least twenty years old. The first scientific papers were offered following World War I and throughout the 1920s and 1930s. The idea of an atomic bomb came first to Leo Szilard, a native of Budapest who immigrated to Great Britain, in 1933. His idea was patented and the patent was secretly transferred to the British Navy. The secrecy and patents did not put an end to the study and experiments toward nuclear fission. A number of countries took more than a passing interest in the project.

In fact, in October 1940, Imperial Army Commander Sosaku Suzuki had sent Tokyo a report "on the possibility of Japan developing an atomic bomb" based on uranium deposits in its newly acquired Chinese and Burmese territories. And in April 1941, seven months before Pearl Harbor, the Imperial Army had given its approval for the Japanese development of an atomic bomb.

U.S. war leaders were concerned that both the Germans and the Japanese might be working on atomic weapons of their own. Fortunately for the Allies, the Japanese war leaders had taken a more traditional route, focused on building ships and aircraft and using highly trained, thoroughly committed troops. Their scientists had not actively pursued the idea of making atomic bombs.

In the United States, FDR had approved the top-secret plan for exploring nuclear fission as a basis for an atomic bomb, rather than moving forward with a plan for a nuclear energy reactor. The Manhattan Project was years ahead of any other nation's quest for the atomic bomb. American scientists worked around the clock for the duration of the war to build the atomic bomb. They would soon see the culmination of all their efforts.

In April, Truman had informed Russian premier Josef Stalin that America was completing work on an atomic bomb; Stalin's spies in the U.S. had already told him.

On 16 July, near Alamogordo, New Mexico, the first atomic bomb was successfully tested a few seconds before 0530 at the "Trinity" site in the middle of the desert. Code-named "Gadget," the detonation yielded over twenty kilotons of explosive energy. In the process, the steel tower holding the "Gadget" was vaporized.

Word was sent to Truman, who was in conference with Churchill and Stalin at Potsdam to discuss the Allied efforts for ending the war. Truman told the other leaders that the United States now had a way to end the war swiftly, once and for all.

The next day, 17 July, the Allied leaders met once more at Potsdam to consider the possibility that Japan might be open to surrender terms.

Ten days later, Truman issued the Potsdam Declaration. It demanded that Japan unconditionally surrender to the Allies, and without going into any details about the atomic bomb, it warned the Japanese that the alternative to a full surrender was "complete and utter destruction."

Meanwhile, components of "Little Boy"—a working atomic bomb—were carried to Tinian Island in the South Pacific aboard the cruiser USS *Indianapolis*.

A few days after the bomb components had been safely offloaded, a lone Japanese submarine managed to sink the *Indianapolis*, resulting in the loss of nearly 900 sailors. The *Indianapolis* went to the bottom so quickly that a radio distress call wasn't even sent. Survivors were left adrift for two days, resulting in an even greater loss of life.

That week the tragedy of the *Indianapolis* was the dominant story in the headlines, along with Truman's Potsdam Declaration. On 28 July, Tokyo rejected Truman's call for an unconditional surrender.

Nevertheless, General MacArthur was already thinking about the end of the war. Both the Americans and Japanese knew that it was inevitable. The Japanese refused to accept the idea of surrender. In previous wars, the parties had merely declared an armistice. But Truman's mandate to the Japanese called for an unconditional surrender.

Churchill, Stalin, and others had tried to talk Truman out of making Japan submit to an unconditional surrender. The Allies' argument was that the Japanese would likely accept an armistice or conditional surrender, so they could negotiate terms for peace. It was the concept of unconditional surrender that made them choke.

The U.S. State Department and the president had sent MacArthur a list of reforms they wanted to achieve; their consensus was that the only way to achieve these goals was to mandate them through unconditional surrender terms. MacArthur had added his own ideas. While he had his own problems with Truman, this wasn't one of them. He agreed that the reforms had to be made, and without an unconditional surrender, the Japanese could find allies who might help them negotiate their way out of the Americans' terms.

The reforms presented in the Potsdam Declaration dealt primarily with destroying Japanese weapons, giving feudal farmers an opportunity to own land, ending the clan monopolies on industry, giving women equal rights, and replacing the imperial form of government with a democracy. To Truman and MacArthur, these were non-negotiable.

✪ U.S. 20TH ARMY AIR CORPS
TINIAN ISLAND AIR BASE
5 AUGUST 1945

After Tokyo's rejection of the Potsdam Declaration, Truman must have assumed that the Japanese government was in a total state of denial. They apparently believed the war was still winnable.

As Japan seemed prepared to commit national suicide rather than surrender or negotiate seriously with the Americans, Truman decided to follow the only course of action offering him the opportunity to end the war quickly and save the most lives.

Truman consulted with Secretary of War Henry Stimson and the Joint Chiefs' General George Marshall the day before the first atomic bomb fell on Japan. Later that day, General LeMay received the word from Washington confirming the mission for 6 August.

Colonel Paul Tibbets was the pilot for the new B-29 Superfortress that would carry the bomb, which he named "Enola Gay" in honor of his mother. Colonel Tibbets told his B-29 crewmen, "You will be delivering a bomb that can destroy an entire city." He didn't know any more about the inner workings of the device than they did, but told his men simply, "It's something new called 'atomic'."

"Little Boy" was loaded on the Enola Gay that evening. At midnight on 6 August, the crew got its final briefing. The twelve-man flight crew consisted of Colonel Tibbets, commanding officer and pilot; Captain Robert Lewis, copilot; Major Thomas Ferebee, bombardier; Captain Ted Van Kirk, navigator; Lieutenant Jacob Beser, radar countermeasure officer; Navy Captain William "Deke" Parsons, a Manhattan Project scientist; Staff Sergeant Wyatt Duzenbury, flight engineer; Sergeant Robert Shumard, assistant engineer; Sergeant Joe Stiborik, radar operator; Staff Sergeant George Caron, tail gunner; Lieutenant Morris Jeppson, bomb electronics test officer; and Private First Class Richard Nelson, radio operator.

The Enola Gay started its takeoff checklist and took off at precisely 0245 on 6 August. The flying time to mainland Japan would be about six hours. At about two hours from the target site, Captain Parsons supervised the arming of "Little Boy." The Enola Gay, still flying at just over 31,000 feet, approached Hiroshima at about ten minutes before nine. The morning was clear and the skies were empty of enemy fighters or anti-aircraft flak. By now the navigator, engineer, and pilots could see the target, Aioi Bridge. At seventeen seconds past 0915 (0815 Hiroshima time) the bomb was released.

It took exactly forty-five seconds for "Little Boy" to fall six miles to the explosion altitude of 1,850 feet, closer than 650 feet to the landmark bridge. It exploded above the city with an effective yield of fifteen kilotons. In an instant, a brilliant, awful, blinding light filled the cockpit of the Enola Gay. Reflex action caused the crew to turn and look back at the light. But it faded as quickly as it came, and after it an angry, dark, and fiery form roiled across the landscape, rising skyward in a slowly forming mushroom cloud of debris, smoke, and fire that obscured Hiroshima.

For what seemed to be a long while, no one spoke. Then, they all began shouting at once: "Look at that! Look at that! Look at that!" Copilot Lewis said that there was a strange taste in his mouth. "It tastes like lead," he observed.

"It's the taste of atomic fission," Deke Parsons explained.

As the Enola Gay headed back toward Tinian Island, Paul Tibbets wrote a few notes in his logbook. His entry concluded with the words, "My God, what have we done."

✪ U.S. 20TH ARMY AIR CORPS
TINIAN ISLAND AIR BASE
10 AUGUST 1945

There was no official Japanese response following the bombing of Hiroshima. The U.S. had earlier begun printing and dropping millions of leaflets on Japanese cities, warning its citizens of the destruction to follow if their leaders did not surrender unconditionally. The day after the first blast, leaflets warned of more atomic bomb attacks.

The U.S. had originally planned to wait for some time before using another atomic bomb, but a forecast of bad weather pushed up the schedule. The confirmation came to the Tinian air base, where the second atomic bomb—nicknamed "Fat Man"—was kept. The mission would be for 9 August; the target was the Kokura Arsenal.

As the Americans prepared to give "Fat Man" a ride into history, the Japanese and Russians were still frantically negotiating. Until 8 August, the strategy was to somehow convince the Americans to accept negotiated terms rather than an unconditional surrender. That would buy more time for the Russians and Japanese to work things out once the Americans and Japanese stopped the war.

Japanese foreign minister Togo was still hopeful that Ambassador Hirota was making some headway with the Soviets when the Russians abruptly cancelled the talks. The Soviets later informed Tokyo that Russia was declaring war on the Japanese, effective the next day.

Togo and Hirohito were not told the rationale for the Russians' sudden about-face. Perhaps the awesome power and effectiveness of the atomic bomb made Stalin reconsider plans to side with Japan. The equation had suddenly shifted. Even if Japan could rebuild its navy, and even if the USSR could muster an unprecedented army, both parties now had to consider the new tactical advantage of the United States. The Americans had a bomb that made conventional warfare obsolete. It changed everything.

As Russia declared war on Japan, it immediately invaded Manchuria, which by now was just a shell of Japanese military occupation.

Meanwhile, throughout 7 and 8 August, the Americans continued to warn the Japanese of imminent destruction with leaflets and through radio broadcasts from Saipan. A second atomic bomb was coming.

Another aircrew, commanded by Major Charles Sweeney, had the responsibility to ferry "Fat Man" to its intended target over the Kokura Arsenal. This time, the B-29 was named after the man who was originally supposed to fly the plane, Colonel Frederick Bock, who at the last minute didn't make the flight. The crew nicknamed the B-29 "Bock's Car." Sweeney was the commanding officer and pilot for the mission. Others on the flight crew included Captain C. D. Albury, copilot; Second Lieutenant Fred Olivi, third pilot; Navy Commander Fred Ashworth, weapons officer; Master Sergeant John Kuharek, flight engineer; and Sergeant Ray Gallagher, assistant flight engineer.

At 2200 hours on 8 August, "Fat Man" was loaded into Bock's Car for the mission. The last briefing took place just after midnight, and at 0345 on 9 August, the pilots were rolling down the runway to lift off and head for Japan.

Shortly after takeoff, Major Sweeney discovered that the 600-gallon reserve fuel tank switch was not working. After some failed attempts to fix it, they knew that they now had 600 fewer gallons of fuel for the mission. This would seriously limit their range and time over their target. Sweeney even thought that they might have to make an emergency landing at a recently captured Okinawa airfield.

The flight seemed plagued by Murphy's Law. In addition to the malfunctioning reserve fuel tank, their fighter escorts were late at the rendezvous point. The flight engineer also reported a number of shorts in the B-29's electrical system. When the plane approached Kokura and the arsenal that was to be their target, the entire area was obscured by thick clouds

Associated Press

Atomic-bomb cloud.

and smog. The crew was unable to locate the necessary landmarks for targeting.

Sweeney knew that they couldn't wait for the clouds to clear. The navigator and flight engineer did the math: With their remaining fuel minus the 600 gallons in the reserve tank, and the time lost waiting for their escorts and looking for an opening in the clouds, they had fuel and time only for a single run on a secondary target. They picked Nagasaki, knowing that it would be risky for them to change course, find Nagasaki, drop the bomb, and then turn and make it to Okinawa for an emergency landing.

When Bock's Car approached Nagasaki, the crew saw that clouds obscured the city. However, as they approached, a break in the clouds appeared. It was almost eleven o'clock in the morning. The break in the clouds held, and the bomb bay doors were opened and "Fat Man" was dropped over Nagasaki. The Americans made a sixty-degree turn and headed south.

Forty-five seconds after leaving the bomb bay, "Fat Man" exploded 2,000 feet above the city with a force of twenty-one kilotons of energy. The bomb detonated near the outer edge of Nagasaki, taking out the Mitsubishi Steel and Arms Works. At the instant of the explosion, there was a glare brighter than the sun. Seconds later, Bock's Car was shaken with terrible turbulence caused by the intense shock waves of the explosion.

Fire and smoke enveloped the city and over 70,000 people—one-fourth of the population—were killed instantly. An equal number were injured in the blast and thousands of others would suffer radiation sicknesses over the next fifty years. The size and fury of the fiery blast widened out across the city and then began to rise above it. Lieutenant Olivi saw the column of flames and smoke rising and feared that it might envelop the plane, even at 30,000 feet.

The crew managed to escape the mushroom cloud of fury and set a direct course to Okinawa. There they refueled and took off for their home base on Tinian, returning there about three in the afternoon, nearly twelve hours after the mission had begun.

✪ IMPERIAL PALACE
TOKYO, JAPAN
10 AUGUST 1945

On 10 August, the Japanese government and military leaders met again to discuss their strategy and response to the surrender terms. The bylaws of the Japanese cabinet said that they had to have a unanimous decision on such matters, and members were at an impasse, with six favoring surrender, three willing to continue the war, and five neutral votes. Then the word came about the destruction of Nagasaki by another atomic bomb.

The cabinet moved to the Imperial Palace to present the matter to the emperor and seek his counsel. Hirohito listened to all of the arguments and offered his conclusion that the time had come for the Japanese people to "bear the unbearable."

There were peace and war factions within the cabinet. As their country continued to lose battle after battle, leading politicians tried to inspire the people into supporting the country's lost cause and national pride of not being defeated. To even discuss surrender, let alone consider accepting it, was difficult. The "war faction" believed that Japan could still win one final battle to prevent the invasion of their homeland.

These militarists had created their own "super weapon"—not quite an atomic bomb, yet still a powerful weapon: the kamikaze. At first, aircraft were used as manned bombs. Later, various kinds of ships and submarines were sent on suicidal attacks. Next, the leaders tried to convince the Japanese people to consider the kamikaze of last resort—resisting the invasion themselves with spears, rocks, and whatever else they could find to kill Americans. They were told that if they didn't kill an enemy soldier before they were killed, they would die in shame.

The "peace faction" simply reminded the militarists that even if the citizen kamikazes repulsed an invasion, the Americans and Allies would simply launch a second invasion when the kamikazes were all dead, and then they would succeed. Those who sought a peaceful end to the war reminded the others what might happen if the U.S. decided not to invade but instead used more of the terrible bombs. They pointed out to the war faction what a tremendous waste of lives such actions would spawn. They urged their comrades that despite surrender, the country could at last have peace and save countless lives in the process.

Emperor Hirohito and Prime Minister Suzuki were in favor of accepting the terms of the Potsdam Declaration, even though they believed it would be a national humiliation to do so. Yet the idea that the emperor would support the idea of surrender was unimaginable to most of the Japanese military leaders.

The war faction stuck to their position. The three military leaders of the cabinet were adamant. One urged the cabinet to implement the kamikaze plan and commit twenty million Japanese lives in an effort to achieve victory. To offer to sacrifice one-fifth of Japan's population to such a lost cause must have sounded ridiculous and insane.

It was obvious: The time to surrender had now come, even though many in the military still wanted to fight to the end. In a sobering break with Japanese tradition, Hirohito intervened and told the cabinet that he could no longer bear to see his people suffer in war. Following another leaflet bombing of Tokyo with papers outlining surrender terms, Hirohito decided to issue an Imperial Edict accepting the unconditional surrender.

Prime Minister Suzuki quietly warned the emperor that if the militarists thought there was any hesitation or weakness in the Japanese government, he might be assassinated and replaced in a takeover coup.

As the Japanese leaders debated, Emperor Hirohito secretly recorded a radio broadcast accepting the terms of the surrender and announcing it to the Japanese people. When one of the opposition generals got word of the secret recording (to be broadcast on 14 August), he attempted a coup. His men assassinated the commander of the palace guards, put Emperor Hirohito under virtual house arrest, and sent troops to search all of the palace and government offices for the recording. The guards turned over nearly every room and office in the palace and government office building but couldn't find the recording.

The attempted coup unraveled by morning, however, and the general who started the coup shot himself and the Japanese war minister committed ritual suicide. The cabinet then voted unanimously to accept the terms of the surrender.

The recording of the emperor's address to the Japanese people was broadcast at noon, announcing acceptance of the unconditional surrender and the end of the war. This was followed by a news release from a Japanese news agency confirming that the unconditional surrender had been accepted.

That message was released at mid-afternoon Tokyo time, but it was just 0149 in Washington when American leaders were awakened to receive the news that Japan had accepted the terms and provisions of the Potsdam Declaration.

The American government responded with a release announcing V-J Day and that General Douglas MacArthur had been appointed by President Truman and the Joint Chiefs to be the supreme commander for the Allied powers for the occupation of Japan. This was followed by exuberant celebrations across the world, with automobile horns, church bells, factory whistles, and every other kind of noisemaking marking the occasion in every American and Allied city.

On 16 August, Lt. General Jonathan Wainwright, who had been taken prisoner at the surrender of Corregidor and held in Manchuria as a POW for the duration of the war, was released. Two weeks later, the British returned to occupy Hong Kong, and American troops aboard Navy ships were anchored in Tokyo Bay to begin the occupation of Japan.

✪ ABOARD USS MISSOURI
TOKYO BAY, JAPAN
2 SEPTEMBER 1945

On the morning of 2 September 1945, Japan formally surrendered. The thirty-minute ceremony took place on board the battleship USS *Missouri*, at the time the flagship of Admiral Halsey. The *Missouri* was anchored with other U.S. and Allied ships in Tokyo Bay, and over a thousand carrier-based

American planes flew overhead. The Stars and Stripes fluttering on the *Missouri* was the same flag that had flown over the U.S. Capitol on the day Pearl Harbor was attacked.

The deck was crowded with dignitaries, sailors, officers, and correspondents from around the world. Japanese foreign minister Mamoru Shigemitsu, accompanied by General Yoshijiro Umezu, represented the Japanese. They had been chosen by the Japanese Supreme War Council and Emperor Hirohito to sign the documents on behalf of the nation. With great flourish and dignity, Shigemitsu and Umezu each signed the surrender documents—one set in Japanese and another in English. Then General Wainwright signed the documents along with Lt. General Sir Arthur Percival. Also signing were Admiral Nimitz and other Allied forces delegates.

The far-reaching surrender document was clear and to the point:

We, acting by command of and in behalf of the Emperor of Japan, the Japanese Government and the Japanese Imperial General Headquarters, hereby accept the provisions set forth in the Declaration issued by the heads of the Governments of the United States, China, and Great Britain on 26 July 1945 at Potsdam, and subsequently adhered to by the Union of Soviet Socialist Republics, which four powers are hereafter referred to as the Allied Powers.

We hereby proclaim the unconditional surrender to the Allied Powers of the Japanese Imperial General Headquarters and of all Japanese armed forces and all armed forces under the Japanese control wherever situated.

We hereby command all Japanese forces wherever situated and the Japanese people to cease hostilities forthwith, to preserve and save from damage all ships, aircraft, and military and civil property and to comply with all requirements which may be imposed by the Supreme Commander for the Allied Powers or by agencies of the Japanese Government at his direction.

We hereby command the Japanese Imperial Headquarters to issue at once orders to the Commanders of all Japanese forces and all forces under

Japanese control wherever situated to surrender unconditionally them-selves and all forces under their control.

We hereby command all civil, military and naval officials to obey and enforce all proclamations, and orders and directives deemed by the Supreme Commander for the Allied Powers to be proper to effectuate this surrender and issued by him or under his authority and we direct all such officials to remain at their posts and to continue to perform their noncom-batant duties unless specifically relieved by him or under his authority.

We hereby undertake for the Emperor, the Japanese Government and their successors to carry out the provisions of the Potsdam Declaration in good faith, and to issue whatever orders and take whatever actions may be required by the Supreme Commander for the Allied Powers or by any other designated representative of the Allied Powers for the purpose of giving effect to that Declaration.

We hereby command the Japanese Imperial Government and the Japanese Imperial General Headquarters at once to liberate all Allied pris-oners of war and civilian internees now under Japanese control and to provide for their protection, care, maintenance and immediate trans-portation to places as directed.

The authority of the Emperor and the Japanese Government to rule the state shall be subject to the Supreme Commander for the Allied Pow-ers who will take such steps as he deems proper to effectuate these terms of surrender.

Signed at TOKYO BAY, JAPAN at 0904 I on the SECOND day of SEPTEMBER, 1945:

MAMORU SHIGEMITSU   YOSHIJIRO UMEZU

By Command and in behalf of the Emperor

By Command and in behalf of the Nation of Japan and the Japanese Gov-ernment and the Japanese Imperial General Headquarters

Colonel Frank Sackton was in the 33rd Infantry Division, part of the army accepting the surrender of the Japanese troops on Luzon. He expected to be transferred back to the States following many long months of combat. Instead, he was told to report to Tokyo along with his commanding officer. The two of them would be on the staff of General Douglas MacArthur.

◻ ◻ ◻

COLONEL FRANK SACKTON, US ARMY
Office of the Supreme Commander
of the Allied Powers
Tokyo, Japan
22 September 1945

We were going to Japan, not to attack it but to occupy it. I got in there in early September 1945. The first occupation duty was disarming the troops. But they were following the emperor's direction pretty carefully, laying down their arms so there was no hostility.

I was transferred to Tokyo because my division commander had become chief of staff to General MacArthur and he took me with him. That turned out to be a good career move for me, because I became a staff secretary to General MacArthur, a key spot in the occupation.

The Allies established MacArthur's authority as being absolute—as sort of a dictator. The Joint Chiefs sent a short message to General MacArthur saying, "Your authority is absolute, so do not entertain any questions about the scope of your authority." Still, he preferred working through the Japanese bureaucracy, although there was never any doubt about his authority.

There was an international tribunal in Washington that gave broad guidance to the general. It favored the democratization of Japan and bringing it into the fold of the Western nations as a friendly country. In Japan, there was the Allied Council, an international group that advised the general. The general never paid any attention to the Allied Council. On that body was a lieutenant general of the Soviet Union who was always against everything. As a matter of fact he even tried to introduce Communism to the country. So things were left pretty much up to the general, and he operated without their guidance, developing his own program.

For example, the question came up about reparations. The Soviet Union said, "We defeated this country, now they must give us reparations." But the Joint Chiefs dealing with the Allied Council said, "No, we're not going to do that." So even with this amalgamation of the international commands, General MacArthur's authority was supreme.

And by and large, when I look at the thing from a global point of view, the whole thing ran extremely well. The people were happy, the bureaucracy was happy, and the emperor was happy. That became the "bottom line" for the occupation.

When the war was over, the Allies developed a list of criminals, people to be tried in a court tribunal in Tokyo. At the top of the list was the emperor, considered responsible for what Japan did or failed to do during the war.

MacArthur thought about it. He had no problem with the generals and admirals on the list. But he did have a problem with the emperor being on it, because he understood the Japanese customs and mores. The emperor was the spiritual leader of the people, and MacArthur was sensitive to that.

The staff told MacArthur that the problem of the emperor for the occupation was a question in the minds of the Japanese people: Who is the authority here? They told MacArthur, "You should abolish the office of emperor and make it clear to the people that you're in charge."

Well, the general demurred and said, "Leave it alone for a while."

The general was right. In late September, MacArthur indicated that he wanted a visit with the emperor to take place in his home. And the general said, "Have the emperor select an interpreter, and he'll be the only one present besides me."

The general's staff researched all about the emperor, his likes and his dislikes. We found that he was a marine biologist and had written things about sea life. We got his published articles and translated them for the general. He wanted to know all about this person before he met him. When we found that the emperor liked cigarettes, the general said, "Get me a cigarette case with some cigarettes." Now, the general didn't smoke but he wanted to accommodate the emperor.

When the emperor came in, things were a little stiff. (General MacArthur later told us what had occurred.) After the cordial hellos, General MacArthur offered the emperor a cigarette, and he took it. The general lit a cigarette for the emperor and one for himself. After that, the emperor spoke first. He said, "General, I want you to know, that I, as emperor, am responsible for everything that occurred in the war. And you must do what you feel you must do."

This impressed General MacArthur, because surely the emperor knew that he was on the war criminal list, and maybe the general expected a plea for mercy. But the emperor accepted complete responsibility.

General MacArthur was so impressed with his attitude that later he grappled with the problem of what to do with the emperor. The American, British, Soviet, and Australian press all assumed that the emperor would be tried as a war criminal. But MacArthur reasoned that the emperor could be very helpful in the reconstruction of Japan. So he announced to the Joint Chiefs of Staff that the emperor's name should come off the criminal list.

This created a furor among the Allies. Oddly enough, Winston Churchill was one who said, "The general should make the decision, and not the press or the attitudes of the people." The emperor's name was taken off the list.

Now, the general had also made a decision on the model to be used in the occupation. He considered two models. One resembled the model used when the Allies took over Germany. But General MacArthur didn't like that model. He said, "Military people are not governors, mayors, police chiefs, or judges in a court of law. We'll only use the military government teams to ensure that our orders are carried out in the field. But we will operate through the existing mechanism of government. We'll purge the bureaucrats, and get people in there that we can train and trust, and work through them." That second model, of a civilian government, was the one we used in Japan. In that model, the emperor proved very helpful.

The people of Japan were pleased about the way the general had handled his visit with Hirohito. He'd shown kindness and courtesy and did not insult the emperor. He allowed him to save face. The general established a relationship between himself and the emperor. They'd meet every six months and he would ask for and get advice from the emperor. And on one occasion, it really paid off.

During the development of a new constitution, the general couldn't get anywhere with the Japanese cabinet. He was blocked by a committee of scholars and government people, who were supposed to work out a constitution. They didn't come up with anything acceptable.

The general staff consensus was that the Japanese were dragging their feet. They simply didn't want to change their way of life, which the constitution change would do. I said, "I don't think it's that. I think the Japanese just don't understand a constitution based on the principles of democracy. Maybe we'll have to impose a constitution on them."

The general accepted that and said, "Okay, let's write a constitution based on the principles of the American Constitution." And that's what he did. He had some sharp lawyers to help him and they developed a constitution that General MacArthur liked. He tooled it personally for a week or so. Then he gave it to the Japanese cabinet and said, "I would like your concurrence with this. But if you don't concur, I'll probably do it anyway."

They knew that he had the authority to do it. He wanted not to simply impose it on them—he wanted them to bring it to the people in a referendum. He wanted the people to vote on it. Well, the cabinet didn't know what to do. So they sent it to the emperor.

In a few days the emperor came back and said, "I like it. This is the way Japan should go." With that, the cabinet then put it before the people in a referendum, and it was overwhelmingly approved. General MacArthur had written it, but it turned out to be the Japanese people's constitution because they and their emperor had approved it. There was a shift of power, very clearly, from the emperor to MacArthur.

I think that MacArthur had a sense that this was his show. But he had never done anything like this before. He had been a great military hero. And now he was thrown into this job. He built it from the ground up. And he had a sense that it was going to work. And he did make it work.

✪ ✪ ✪

Following the Pacific war, despite thousands of documented atrocities, only twenty-eight Japanese war criminals stood trial, compared to six times as many German war criminals. And to the surprise of Allies and others in the American chain of command, MacArthur had taken Emperor Hirohito's name off that list. Geoffey Perret, author of *Old Soldiers Never Die: The Life of Douglas MacArthur*, explained part of the difference. "You cannot run a prison without the cooperation of the prisoners. You cannot run an occupied country without the participation of the people who live there. MacArthur did not go after and seek prosecution of more Japanese war criminals, because he did not believe it was possible to provide anything resembling a truly fair trial for Japanese war criminals."

Perret said that MacArthur was critical of the Nuremberg trials. "I think it's important to remember this whole business of trying people for war crimes is absolutely new in international law. There wasn't much in a way of precedent. And the concept of these crimes against humanity is open to interpretation.

"The prosecution of war crimes in both the Far East and in Europe was to some degree simply punitive or exemplary justice where people are being punished as much to set an example as for anything else. Well, if you're going to use people as examples in that way, how many do we have to execute?"

Perret believes that this is why MacArthur went after just a few of the full possible list of people who could be charged with war crimes. "These were people he really wanted to see executed," he says. "Beyond that, he didn't see much point to it. He did not see this as really a service to history."

EPILOGUE

The soldiers, sailors, airmen, Marines, and Guardsmen who fought during the Pacific campaign were tested in many ways—and persevered. They were a part of a "generation" who set an amazing example for others to follow. Here is what happened to the brave defenders after the war.

FIREMAN FIRST CLASS KEN SWEDBERG, whose ship the USS *Ward* fired the first shots of World War II against a midget Japanese submarine, came home to Minnesota with a sense of genuine humility and patriotism. When asked, as a Pearl Harbor survivor, how he wanted to be remembered, he said, "I guess I would like to be remembered as somebody who volunteered for my country."

LIEUTENANT STEPHEN WEINER captured the first Japanese prisoner of World War II at Pearl Harbor, before Kazuo Sakamaki could release the torpedoes from his midget submarine on 7 December 1941. Following the war, Weiner was promoted to captain and stationed at Redding Air Base, where he met his wife. After that, he became successful with the first Kaiser-Fraser automobile franchise in Pennsylvania. He later went into banking. Today, he's an active consultant for the First Republic Bank of Los Angeles.

LIEUTENANT KAZUO SAKAMAKI, the first Japanese POW of World War II, spent the war in an American POW camp. Sakamaki wrote a book about his experiences in 1949. He joined the Toyota Motor Company in the late 1940s and was sent to South America, and later worked for Toyota in Texas.

SERGEANT RICHARD GORDON, a survivor of the Bataan Death March and a slave laborer in Manchuria, was liberated at the war's end. He spent months recuperating aboard various hospital ships. After he recovered, he reenlisted, received a commission to second lieutenant, and went back on active duty. He remained in uniform until 1961.

CORPORAL RALPH RODRIGUEZ, JR. received a business degree after the war and went to work as a lumber company supervisor. Five years later, he was managing the company. In 1946, he attended the first meeting of Bataan Veterans, a group of survivors of the Bataan Death March. He also served as national commander of the American Ex-Prisoners of War in 1964. He never missed a national convention in twenty-five years.

PRIVATE ANDREW MILLER was promoted after his release from POW camp and was discharged in July 1946. Back home, he entered the University of Nebraska, earned a mechanical engineering degree, and was hired by the GE Corporation. In 1951, he left GE, moved to New Mexico, and took a civil service position with the U.S. Air Force (4925th Test Group–Atomic), where he worked for twenty-six years. Miller remains active in the American Defenders of Bataan and Corregidor, and serves today as its national commander and national historian.

PRIVATE JOHN COOK lobbied for a memorial plaque to be placed in the Ranger Hall of Fame after his rescue in January 1945 from Camp Cabanatuan. It was finally unveiled on 11 August 2000, more than fifty-five years after that daring rescue. Since the dedication of the memorial plaque, Cook appeared on several national television programs supporting the Alamo Scouts and Rangers. He died in May 2003.

GENERAL JIMMY DOOLITTLE was picked up by friendly Chinese, who helped him return to the U.S. weeks after bailing out over China when his B-25 ran out of fuel. He was expecting to be court-martialed for a mission that he felt was a failure. Instead, he was honored by FDR, promoted to general, and went on a war bond tour. After the war, he held a number of "Raider Reunions." Jimmy Doolittle died on 27 September 1993, fifty-one years following his audacious bombing raid over Tokyo.

SERGEANT JACOB DESHAZER was one of the Doolittle Raiders held as a POW. He was captured following the Tokyo Raid that inspired Americans and terrorized Japan. DeShazer experienced a dramatic conversion to Christianity following his reading of the Bible while imprisoned. After the war, he came home to become a missionary, then returned to convince the Japanese people to follow Jesus Christ. Amazingly, one of his converts was the famous Japanese fighter pilot Mitsuo Fuchida, who had led the attack on Pearl Harbor. DeShazer spent over thirty years as a missionary to the Japanese people and retired to Oregon.

LIEUTENANT ROBERT HITE dropped to just eighty pounds during his forty-month stay in a Japanese prison. He endured captivity, torture, and starvation before his release on 20 August 1945, nearly a week after the war ended. Hite went on to serve in Korea and Morocco. In civilian life, he had a career managing hotels in Arkansas, Oklahoma, and Texas. He and his wife, Dorothea, live in Camden, Arkansas.

LIEUTENANT RICHARD COLE served out his time until the end of World War II as an Army Air Corps pilot. Dick flew transports over "the hump"—the menacing Himalayan mountain range—until June 1943. Then he came home, reenlisted, and stayed in the service for twenty-six years, after which he retired to his home in Dayton, Ohio.

LIEUTENANT HENRY POTTER came back home with the four other crew members from the lead aircraft of Doolittle's Task Force 16, and shortly afterwards was reassigned to his old unit and a B-26 bomber. This time he headed for North Africa until the end of World War II. Potter stayed in the Army for thirty years, reaching the rank of colonel, then retired to his home in South Dakota.

FIRST LIEUTENANT JOHN ALISON made the first night kills in the CBI theater, for which he was awarded the Distinguished Service Cross and the Silver Star. Ending his tour as commander of the 75th Fighter Squadron, Alison left as an ace with seven confirmed "kills" and a number of "probables." After the war, Alison served as an assistant secretary of commerce, president of the Air Force Association, and a major general in the U.S. Air Force Reserves. He recently retired as vice president of the Northrop Corporation.

LIEUTENANT CHARLES TURNER was discharged in July 1945 and returned to the States, where he accepted a sales position with a Chevrolet dealership. He later accepted a position with a new company and stayed with them for eighteen years. In 1968, Turner formed his own company and sold it in 1976. He remained active on its board and has served as chairman since 2000. He and his wife, Dorothy, have two daughters, five grandchildren, and four great-grandchildren. Turner and his wife live on a ranch outside Waco, Texas, where he has been ranching since 1971.

STAFF SERGEANT RAYMOND "STUB" BLUTHARDT returned from the war to join his wife's parents in operating a Phillips 66 filling station and garage. He later took a civil service position at nearby Ft. Riley, where he stayed for twenty-five years. Bluthardt served as a committee chairman with the Boy Scouts and was the fire chief for the local volunteer fire department. He married his sweetheart, Geraldine, and they had a daughter and a son, four grandchildren, and four great-grandchildren. Ray Bluthardt passed away on 28 March 2004.

PRIVATE FIRST CLASS KYLE THOMPSON returned to the U.S. and wrote a book about his experiences, *A Thousand Cups of Rice*, the story about the "lost battalion" and their survival as slave laborers for the Japanese. After the war he became a journalist, serving as Austin bureau chief for United Press International and as an editorial writer for the *Fort Worth Star-Telegram*. Kyle Thompson passed away 5 March 2004.

CAPTAIN JOSEPH ROCHEFORT was the code-breaker whose expertise made the difference at the Battle of Midway, but he never received recognition by Washington. After the war, he settled in Manhattan Beach, California. He remained in the Navy and was called to duty for the Korean War and later for the Vietnam War. He finally retired from the military at age forty-nine and returned to his home in California, where he died in 1976. In 1985, Admiral Mac Showers took it upon himself to "right a big wrong" and recommended the World War II code-breaker for a medal. President Ronald Reagan awarded the Distinguished Service Medal, the nation's highest civilian honor, to Rochefort posthumously.

ENSIGN LEWIS HOPKINS received the Navy Cross and was promoted following his exploits at Midway, Guadalcanal, and other South Pacific battles. After World War II, Hopkins reenlisted in the Navy, achieving the rank of admiral. He retired in 1974.

PETTY OFFICER WILLIAM SURGI, JR. taught aviation for the Navy in Jacksonville, Florida, in 1945. Some time later he was given the responsibility of training Argentine pilots. In 1981, he was part of Operation Unitas and was sent to Chile. After forty-three years in the Navy, he retired in 1984 on his sixtieth birthday.

SEAMAN SECOND CLASS FRANK HOLMGREN was discharged 7 December 1945—exactly four years to the day after Pearl Harbor was bombed. He was assigned to duty at the U.S. Navy's Earle Ammunition Depot in Colts Neck, New Jersey, to finish out his tour, and took a civilian position at EAD after the war for a thirty-five-year career there.

CAPTAIN JOHN SWEENEY returned to Ohio following World War II but would never forget his experiences on Edson's Ridge, or Bloody Ridge, as it was later called. For his actions on Guadalcanal, Sweeney was awarded the Navy Cross.

PLATOON SERGEANT MITCH PAIGE received a battlefield commission following his heroism at Guadalcanal and made the Marine Corps his career. He has spent more than two decades working to expose frauds who claim to have been awarded the Congressional Medal of Honor but who were never cited for the award. He has exposed a large number of frauds, including one highly publicized on *60 Minutes*.

CAPTAIN JOE FOSS, a highly decorated Marine fighter pilot, moved up the ranks to general. He held the records as the top World War II ace, with twenty-six confirmed enemy kills. Foss stayed in the Marine Corps until his retirement and then began several other productive careers: president of the National Rifle Association, Major League Baseball commissioner, and governor of South Dakota. He died in January 2003.

MAJOR GREGORY "PAPPY" BOYINGTON was awarded the Congressional Medal of Honor for his exploits in the South Pacific. After the war, he penned his autobiography, *Baa Baa Black Sheep*, and in 1976, Hollywood producer Steven J. Cannell launched a dramatic television series loosely based on Boyington's book and the exploits of the Black Sheep Squadron in the South Pacific. "Pappy" was hired as a technical consultant for the show. He died of cancer in January 1988, at the age of seventy-five, in Fresno, California.

LIEUTENANT HENRY "HANK" MCCARTNEY stayed in the Marine Corps for twenty-six years and retired to Florida to begin another entirely new career. Hank founded a citrus company, managed it for a number of years, and recently sold it.

LIEUTENANT HENRY "BOO" BOURGEOIS was an ace in many of the South Pacific battles and was another career Marine, spending twenty-one years in the Corps. He left when his eyes were no longer what they'd been when he was a twenty-two-year-old pilot in the Solomon Islands. He then took a sales engineering position with a division of the Singer Company and moved up the corporate ladder until he recently retired.

FIRST LIEUTENANT JOHN F. (JACK) BOLT was promoted to captain and returned to the U.S. in 1944, right after his first tour of duty, to marry his high school sweetheart. Then he returned to combat. After World War II he stayed in the Marines and served in the Korean War, where he became an ace all over again—shooting down six MIGs piloted by Russian aces. He retired from the Corps as a lieutenant colonel after twenty years and went back to school, studying law and earning his degree from the University of Florida.

LIEUTENANT W. THOMAS (TOM) EMRICH finished his stint in the South Pacific and returned to the United States. He stayed in the Marines until he was offered the opportunity to become an airline pilot with TWA. That began a wonderful, although less exciting, career in aviation.

LIEUTENANT ED HARPER was wounded and shot down during his stint with the Black Sheep Squadron but returned to duty. He remained in the Marines and served in both Korea and Vietnam. When he retired from the Corps, he went to work for McDonnell Douglas in California, where he worked on the Marine Harrier aircraft. He retired after eighteen years there.

LIEUTENANT DEAN LADD recovered from wounds received at Tarawa and returned to duty with the Marine Corps. He achieved the rank of lieutenant colonel before he retired. Thirty-nine years after being wounded at Tarawa, Ladd returned to that tiny atoll, ferried to the remote site in a landing craft very similar to the LCR that had carried him away. Following that visit in 1982, Ladd helped convince the Marine Corps to put a memorial on the atoll honoring the young men killed in the three-day battle there.

MAJOR MIKE RYAN was nominated by his regimental commander, General David M. Shoup, to receive the Navy Cross, the nation's second highest award, for his heroism in the Battle of Tarawa. Ryan finished out the war and then served in the Korean War. He spent time at the USMC headquarters, completing an illustrious career as a Marine Corps major general.

SERGEANT NORMAN HATCH stayed in the Marine Corps, was promoted to warrant officer, and went to Japan as part of the occupying American force after the war. He later joined the Bell & Howell Corporation, handling government projects, and still later returned to Washington, D.C., where he freelanced as a photographer. From 1956 to 1979 he became the first civilian to head the Public Affairs Department at the Pentagon.

LIEUTENANT DON LILLIBRIDGE returned to the States after the war and went on to graduate school at the University of Wisconsin in Madison, where he earned a Ph.D. He became a professor of history at California State University at Chico and taught until his retirement in 1981. He is also the author of six books, many articles, and a published war memoir.

CORPORAL HARRY NIEHOFF was awarded five battle stars, two Purple Hearts, one Silver Star Medal, and one Bronze Star Medal for his heroism and exploits at the Battle of Tarawa. When discharged, he went home to Portland, Oregon, and enrolled in the Chouinard Art School in California. Niehoff pursued the home furnishing business, working with design, manufacturing, and sales until he retired in 1998. He often goes to public schools to tell students about his firsthand experiences in World War II.

PRIVATE FIRST CLASS RICK SPOONER stayed in the Marines and retired in 1972 as a major. After retirement, Spooner decided to go into the restaurant business. He now owns and operates the Globe & Laurel Restaurant, just outside the gates of Quantico.

LIEUTENANT ALEX VRACIU put in twenty years with the Navy, retiring in 1963. After that, he started another successful career with the Wells Fargo banking firm.

SERGEANT CYRIL "OBIE" O'BRIEN left the Marines after the war but stayed in the Marine Reserves, putting in a total of twelve years of service and rising from sergeant to captain. He continued his work as a reporter, helping Americans understand everything from the politics of Washington to applied physics research at Johns Hopkins.

DON SWINDLE left the Marines at the end of World War II. He returned to his home in Indiana and went back to work with General Motors until he retired in 1980. After a few restless years, he went to work for Ace Hardware for another six years. He works today as a security guard, more than sixty years after the battles he fought in the South Pacific.

MAJOR GORDON GAYLE rose through the ranks of the Marine Corps and was promoted to the rank of brigadier general. He retired from the Corps in 1968. He then went to work with the Georgetown Center for Strategic Studies, where he worked on a study of the U.S. involvement in Vietnam. He later wrote a book about his Pacific war experiences, *Bloody Beaches: The Marines at Peleliu.*

PRIVATE FIRST CLASS FRED FOX went to college on the GI Bill and was given a disability pension because of the wounds he received in the Battle of Peleliu. He returned to Peleliu in 1964, twenty years after he fought there, and exorcised his demons of combat. He also went back for the fiftieth anniversary of the Battle of Peleliu in 1994.

PHARMACIST MATE THIRD CLASS JOHN J. HAYES was awarded the Purple Heart and the Bronze Star for his actions at Peleliu. After recovering from his shrapnel wounds, he served again in the invasion of Okinawa, where he was also decorated. After the war, he was discharged from the Navy and joined the Coast Guard. Thanks to the GI Bill, he got a degree from the University of Missouri and his master's in hospital administration from Washington University in St. Louis. He served in hospital administration for the next thirty-eight years.

CAPTAIN EVERETT POPE met President Harry Truman when he presented him with the Congressional Medal of Honor in June 1945, even as plans were being made to end the war by the first tactical use of atomic bombs. Pope left the Marine Corps after the war and became the youngest bank president in Massachusetts. He says he had to retire in 1980 because he was about to become the oldest.

FIRST LIEUTENANT PAUL AUSTIN returned to Ft. Worth, Texas, after the war and spent thirty-one years in a career with the telecommunications business.

 **LIEUTENANT (JG) JAMES (JIM) HALLOWAY** remained in the Navy and eventually achieved the rank of admiral, followed by service on the Joint Chiefs of Staff as chief of naval operations.

 **LIEUTENANT RICHARD (DICK) ROBY** spent five years in active duty service and another five years in the organized Reserves. He moved to Texas, where he worked thirty-two years in the insurance and investment business while also being active as a rancher on a 1,000-acre ranch outside of Austin. He retired in 1982. He and his wife, Mary Evelyn, who died in 1998, raised three children and have five grandchildren and five great-grandchildren.

 **LIEUTENANT THOMAS (TOM) STEVENSON** survived the shark-infested waters of the Pacific Ocean after his ship USS *Samuel B. Roberts* was sunk by the Japanese. After the war ended he returned to his family's shipping business in Long Island, New York.

CAPTAIN ROBERT PRINCE saw virtually no combat prior to helping to lead the Rangers' rescue raid of POWs at Cabanatuan, but he returned to the U.S. a hero. He and the other officers who took part in the raid were debriefed at the Pentagon and then honored by President Roosevelt. Prince is still shy about being in a spotlight that he neither seeks nor believes he deserves. But he says, "A new generation is learning about the sacrifices that were made. I'm glad to see that happening."

PHARMACIST MATE SECOND CLASS JOHN "DOC" BRADLEY was awarded the Navy Cross and will always be remembered as one of the six men who raised the U.S. flag on Mount Suribachi. After the war a movie was made about his life, and he was often invited to dedicate a war memorial or lead a parade honoring America's heroes. He downplayed his actions in World War II until his death in 1995.

LIEUTENANT GEORGE GREELEY WELLS returned to his home in Green Village, New Jersey, after the war. For his heroic service on Iwo Jima in 1945, where he was wounded in action, Wells was awarded the Purple Heart.

PRIVATE JOHN COLE, after serving two and a half years in the Marines, returned home after the war to fight another battle—finding a job. He and many other nineteen-year-old veterans hadn't been trained in anything but combat, and it took some time to find other work. In 2000, Cole returned to Iwo Jima, where he visited the graves that he and others from Graves Registration had filled. He grieved that there was no one to mourn the brave men who had died and now rested on this lonely and scarred island.

PRIVATE DONALD MATES was hospitalized until 1946, recovering from wounds he received on Iwo Jima, where he was awarded the Purple Heart. He returned to the U.S., went to Arizona State, graduated in 1951, and went into business. Mates is retired and lives in Palm Beach, Florida. On the fifty-fifth anniversary of the Battle of Iwo Jima, he returned to the island with other Iwo Jima survivors and hardly recognized the land, now lush and green with sixty years of new vegetation.

PRIVATE FIRST CLASS DAN BARTON recovered from his wounds and went home after the war. He worked in oil exploration in Kuwait, the Khyber Pass, Pakistan, and then in Venezuela and the Oronoco and Amazon jungles. Barton later worked for the TRW Corporation, an aerospace company in Redondo Beach, California, for twenty-five years.

SEAMAN THIRD CLASS LAWRENCE DELEWSKI recovered from the explosion on the USS *Laffey* but his nerves would never be the same. He suffered from what came to be called "post-traumatic stress syndrome" after the Vietnam War. Back home, Larry became a teacher and coach and taught special-ed kids for twenty-five years.

PRIVATE FIRST CLASS HERMAN "BUFF" BUFFINGTON went back to finish high school and took advantage of the GI Bill to go to college. He married his wife, Helen, in 1949, and the couple had two sons. Buffington and his wife worked for the *Summerville* (Georgia) *News*, where they learned the newspaper business. They purchased a newspaper in Jefferson, Georgia, and now own four weekly newspapers and a commercial printing operation. Buffington is still involved in the business but has been semi-retired since 1978; his sons now run the business.

CORPORAL MEL HECKT landed in San Francisco on 3 August 1945, completing exactly twenty months of continuous combat in the Pacific. After a few days of celebration, he headed for his hometown in Iowa, getting there in time to celebrate V-J Day and the end of World War II.

COLONEL FRANK SACKTON, after helping MacArthur with the occupation, returned to Washington after the war, serving as deputy director for national security affairs for the Secretary of Defense, then as deputy director of planning for the Joint Chiefs of Staff, and deputy chief for military operations, U.S. Army. After an illustrious military career, he turned to higher education. Today he is Professor Emeritus at Arizona State University and said, "I'd like to be remembered as a man who remained in the workforce until I was ninety." Still active at ASU, Sackton turned ninety-two this year.

ENSIGN DONALD ("MAC") SHOWERS decided that after World War II he would make a career in the U.S. Navy. He retired as a rear admiral and in 2002 returned to Midway atoll to commemorate the sixtieth anniversary of that pivotal battle.

ENSIGN WILLIAM (BILL) TANNER was reassigned to the European theater after he took part in the hunt for midget subs at Pearl Harbor. On 1 August 1943 his plane was attacked by a group of eight German Luftwaffe in air combat and Tanner was shot down with two of his crew. All survived.

TIMELINE OF WORLD WAR II
IN THE PACIFIC

1937

28 July
Japan Invades Chinese Capital
Chinese and Japanese troops skirmish in Peking (Beijing). Japan bombs three Chinese cities and "terror bombs" Shanghai in August.

12 December
The Sinking of the USS *Panay*
A U.S. gunboat and three other ships evacuating Chinese citizens of Nanking are attacked by Japanese planes. A U.S. sailor on the *Panay*, Charles Ensminger, becomes the first American to die in the Pacific War.

13 December
Nanking, China, Captured by the Japanese
Over the next six weeks 300,000 civilians are brutally killed, mostly elderly, women, and children. The event is captured on newsreels and is dubbed "the rape of Nanking."

1938

4 February
Japan Continues Its War with China
The Japanese subdue the eastern third of the nation.

20 February
Roosevelt Revises the Pacific War Plan
The U.S. War Plan (Plan Orange) transfers part of the American fleet to the Pacific, and uses the 1933 "Trading with the Enemy Act" to develop a plan to freeze Japanese assets in the event of war.

20 February
Hitler Supports Japan in Its Plans for Asian Conquest
Nazi leader Adolf Hitler proclaims his unilateral support for Japan in its war for Asia.

March–June
Japanese Launch Total War in Asia
They claim their military aggression is to "free Asia from colonial rule and communism." Public opinion in the U.S. opposes Japanese aggression and is determined not to permit the kind of appeasement that America had condoned in its dealings with Germany. The U.S. indicates that its citizens will not permit Japan's war efforts to continue unchecked.

17 May
The Vinson-Trammel Naval Expansion Act
This bill is passed, authorizing $1 billion for building a "two ocean" U.S. Navy of sixty-nine new ships and 3,000 airplanes.

August
U.S. Fortifies Its Pacific Possessions
The U.S. takes steps to protect its possessions in the Pacific (Midway, Wake, and Guam Islands) by constructing strong defenses. Earlier, U.S. politician William Borak decried the expense of such efforts as "decoration of a useless sand dune."

16 August
Birth of the Atomic Era
Enrico Fermi receives the 1938 Nobel Prize in physics for identifying new elements and discovering nuclear reactions by his method of nuclear irradiation and bombardment. It is one of the precursors to creating the atom bomb.

23 August
Flying Tigers Created
U.S. retired Army Air Corps general Claire Lee Chennault begins a "secret" air war in China using funds covertly approved by President Roosevelt. He recruits and organizes volunteer pilots, calling his air force the "Flying Tigers." He uses American P-40 fighters, which perform better in dogfights with the Japanese Zero.

1939

7–15 April
Congress Cuts Off Trade with Japan
The U.S. Congress introduces a resolution to cut off trade with Japan.

1940

9 April
Nazis Occupy Denmark, Invade Norway
Continuing their run across northern Europe, the Germans storm into Denmark and Norway. They will also take Belgium and Holland, and march into Paris in May.

May
U.S. Pacific Fleet Ordered to Pearl Harbor
The Pacific Fleet makes Hawaii its base instead of San Diego, California.

3 June
Dunkirk
British and other Allied troops send thousands of ships to evacuate the retreating army at Dunkirk, and 350,000 are rescued from the Nazis, although the next day 40,000 are captured by the Germans.

30 June
British Appeasement for Asia
Great Britain continues its policy of Japanese appeasement and Churchill agrees to a Japanese demand to close the Burma Road, a key China army supply route. Churchill acquiesces in order to avoid war with Japan.

5 July
Nazi U-Boats Extend Their Range
German submarines extend their range ever closer to the United States and Canada in their attempt to blockade British shipping.

10 July
Battle of Britain Begins
Winston Churchill becomes the new prime minister after Chamberlain resigned on 10 May. Germans attack British shipping and their *Luftwaffe* begins bombing raids that will later come to be called the "Blitz" by Britons.

17 July
Japanese Troops Occupy Hong Kong
Part of the Hong Kong territory is seized by the Japanese and they blockade the British colony. The governor general of Hong Kong issues an evacuation order for women and children to be moved to the Philippines.

3–7 September
Hitler Plans to Invade Britain
The Nazis are committed to invading Great Britain and extinguishing the opposition to German conquest. The plan, Operation Sea Lion, is unveiled on the third, and the "Blitz" begins on the seventh. In October Hitler decides to postpone Operation Sea Lion until spring 1941.

16 September
America Introduces the Draft
Military conscription starts in the U.S.

22 September
Japanese Troops Invade Indochina
French Indochina (present-day Vietnam) is taken by Japanese troops crossing the border. The Axis-controlled French Vichy government accedes to their action.

25 September
Japanese Secrets Stolen
The Japanese seek a way to improve the security of their signals. Their solution to the security problem is radical: They decide to abandon using codebooks and began instead to encrypt their most confidential and secret messages on a machine. Ironically, this decision eventually enables the U.S. to read Japanese diplomatic messages with great ease once the Americans break their new code.

27 September
Axis Powers Formed
Japan, Germany, and Italy announce the Tripartite Pact and become known as the Axis Powers.

30 November
Flying Tigers Group Gets Funding Help
China's leader, Chiang Kai-shek, gets a $100 million loan from President Roosevelt to purchase fifty more war planes for Claire Chennault's Flying Tigers.

1941

January
British Victories in the Mediterranean
British and Australian troops capture Bardia, take 48,000 German prisoners, then take Tobruk and another 25,000 Germans.

7 January
Yamamoto Plans Pearl Harbor Attack
Admiral Isoroku Yamamoto outlines his war plans, and suggests that an air attack of Pearl Harbor and other American bases, along with raids against British colonies and bases in the Pacific, will convince the Americans and British to abandon their interests in the Pacific and concentrate on the war in Europe.

27 January
U.S. Ambassador Warns of Attack
Ambassador Joseph Grew warns his government that the Japanese intend to attack Pearl Harbor, but U.S. naval intelligence believe that the threat is not credible.

2 February
The "Desert Fox" Prowls
General Erwin Rommel, Hitler's brilliant tactician for desert warfare, arrives in North Africa to oppose the British and Australians.

14 February
Ultimatum to Japan
Eugene Dooman delivers FDR's ultimatum to Foreign Minister Ohashi in Tokyo that if Japan attacks Singapore, it would mean war with the United States.

15 February
Discovering "Magic"
"Magic" (the nickname for American code-breakers' ability to read Japanese signals communications) intercepts a "shopping list" for spies in Hawaii, but Pearl Harbor is not informed.

3 April
Ships for the Atlantic
Admiral Harold Stark, chief of naval operations, orders three battleships, one carrier (*Yorktown*), and four cruisers transferred from the Pacific to the Atlantic due to emerging "Europe-first" strategy and the need to send war matériel to Britain as part of the Lend-Lease convoys.

10 April
Start of the Air War
Admiral Yamamoto creates the Japanese First Air Fleet, with four aircraft carriers and 200 carrier-based aircraft. Starting with Pearl Harbor, carrier-based aircraft will play an increasing role and ultimately end traditional ship-to-ship warfare.

13 April
Japan and Russia Sign Neutrality Pact
The USSR and Japan sign a five-year neutrality pact, allowing the Soviet Union to concentrate on imminent war with the Nazis.

22 June
Hitler's Armies Invade Russia
Hitler breaks his neutrality pact with the Soviets and declares war. Nazis invade Russia and destroy Stalin's air force.

11 July
Coming of the Spooks
William Donovan is named as the "coordinator of information" for President Roosevelt. This service is the forerunner of the OSS (Office of Strategic Services), a U.S. government agency, which in World War II eventually evolves into the CIA.

26 July
FDR Names Pacific Commander
President Roosevelt appoints General MacArthur as commander of the Philippine Islands; he officially commits Claire Chennault's Flying Tigers as the "Chinese Air Force" using 100 pilots of the American Volunteer Group; he freezes Japanese assets in the U.S.; and he offers Japan a proposal for a neutral Indochina.

31 July
Hitler Gives "Final Solution" Order
Hitler issues an order for a "final solution" to deal with "Jews, gypsies, communists, and homosexuals" but which is primarily aimed at eliminating the Jewish race. A little more than a month later, the gas chambers at Auschwitz are used for the first time.

4 September
FDR Closes Panama Canal to Japan
President Roosevelt closes the Panama Canal to all Japanese shipping.

11 September
Hitler's U-Boats Test U.S. Neutrality
The U.S. Navy is given orders to "shoot on sight" any U-Boats close to U.S. coasts or ships.

24 September
"Magic" Intercepts Attack Plan
Picked up this day, but not translated until 9 October, the message reveals ship berths, location of torpedo nets, and the harbor layout for an air attack on Pearl Harbor—but the warning is ignored by Washington.

16 October
Tojo Takes Over Japanese Government
Extremist Japanese army commander Hideki Tojo takes over as prime minister when former prime minister Fumimaro Konoye is dumped. Described as a dictator, Tojo becomes principal director of Japanese war operations.

3 November
Yamamoto's Attack Plan Approved
The Japanese government approves Admiral Yamamoto's War Plan, and decides to implement the plan by December. Yamamoto's primary strategy lists the priorities of attacks: the First Air Fleet is to attack Pearl Harbor; the Second Air Fleet is to attack the Philippines, Malaya, and the East Indies; the Fourth Air Fleet is to attack the island of Guam. The Northern Force is to stay behind in Japanese waters to guard their national interests, along with the Main Force. U.S. Ambassador Joseph Grew says that war between the U.S. and Japan is not only likely but imminent.

10 November
Churchill Warns Japan
In a tone that departs from the usual British diplomacy of appeasement, Churchill warns Japan that a war with the United States will also mean war with Great Britain.

20 November
Final Plans for Pearl Harbor Attack
Japan's impending attack of Pearl Harbor is made official and attack orders are issued, but military commanders are told to wait until diplomatic negotiations are completed before these orders are carried out.

26 November
Japanese Carrier Force "On the Move"
The Japanese First Air Fleet sets sail from the north coast of Japan with an armada of six aircraft carriers carrying 423 aircraft, twenty-eight submarines (including six SPS "midget" subs), eleven destroyers, two battleships, and two cruisers. The fleet is ordered to maintain strict radio silence. The next day, Secretary of War Henry Stimson sends a "hostile action possible" warning to U.S. Pacific bases. Pearl Harbor issues only sabotage alert; no anti-torpedo nets, ammo for AA guns, etc. It seems no one is seriously concerned about what the Japanese might do.

1 December
Heading for War
The Japanese set 7 December as the date to attack Pearl Harbor. Their diplomats are told not to end negotiations so the Americans won't get suspicious.

7 December
The "Day of Infamy"
Pearl Harbor is attacked by two waves of Japanese dive-bombers and torpedo bombers led by Mitsuo Fuchida. The air attack on Pearl Harbor devastated the American fleet and killed 2,388, and 1,200 were wounded. Of the ninety-six ships in the harbor, eighteen are sunk, including the *Arizona* and *Oklahoma*,

or suffer serious damage. Of 394 aircraft at Hickam, Wheeler, and Bellows airfields, the air attack destroys 188 and damages 159.

7 December
More Japanese Attacks
The Japanese Combined Fleet Order No. 1 also includes the invasion of Malaya. This invasion began twenty-five minutes before the first wave hit Pearl Harbor. An attack on Hong Kong begins six hours after Pearl Harbor. Another air attack, on the Philippine Islands, six hours after Pearl Harbor, destroys all the P-40s at Clark Field and pits 108 Japanese bombers and 84 Zeros against 107 P-40s and 35 B-17s, but most U.S. planes were caught on the ground and destroyed.

8 December
America At War
The U.S. and Allies (except Soviets) declare war on Japan. Japan promptly declares war on the U.S. and Britain; a Japanese air attack hits Wake Island. On tiny Wake Island, a small U.S. Marine detachment commanded by Major James Devereaux heroically fends off the aggressors and gives the only real opposition that the Japanese run into during their substantial attacks.

10 December
Japanese Troops Invade Philippines
General Masaharu Homma lands Japanese troops on Luzon and quickly moves south to Manila. Guam surrenders. On 22 December Homma will bring in another 43,000 troops, landing at Lingayen Bay.

11 December
Hitler Declares War on America
Nazi Germany declares war on U.S. The U.S. declares war against Germany and Italy.

23 December
Manila Evacuated
U.S. troops evacuate Manila and then fall back to Bataan. Japanese troops also take the American possession of Wake Island, which then surrenders.

24 December
MacArthur Forced to Flee to Corregidor
General MacArthur moves his headquarters to Corregidor, leaving General Jonathan Wainwright to defend Bataan.

1942

9 January
Manila Captured by Japanese
Enemy troops enter Manila, while nearly 80,000 U.S. and Filipino troops try to defend Luzon despite critical food and supply shortages and crippling diseases.

26 January
Japanese Troops Take Solomons
After a month-long swing through the South Pacific, the Japanese invade the Solomon Islands, after having captured the Dutch East Indies and Rabaul in New Britain. They also cause the American and Filipino armies to retreat into the Bataan Peninsula on Luzon, and capture the Manila naval base.

15 February
Singapore Falls Into Japanese Hands
The British possession is lost, due in part to improper dispersion of forces by the British army.

19 February
U.S. Internment Camps Begin
Executive Order 9066 signed by FDR orders internment of all Japanese-Americans. U.S. locks up 110,000 Japanese-Americans, mostly in California.

22 February
MacArthur Flees the Philippines
President Roosevelt orders General MacArthur to leave the Philippines and set up his command headquarters in Australia.

23 February
America Under Fire
A Japanese submarine shells Ellwood Beach, twelve miles west of Santa Barbara. The sixteen shells fired by the sub cause no injuries and only $500 damage along Goleta Beach, yet the appearance of the enemy so near creates fear.

25 February
U.S. Navy Raid on Rabaul
The USS *Lexington* tries to raid the Japanese supply port of Rabaul, but is driven off. Admiral Halsey and USS *Enterprise* raid Wake and Marcus Islands with only minimal success.

27 February
Battle of Java Sea
Results in the loss of USS *Houston* and HMS *Perth*.

10 March
Fall of Rangoon
The British close the Burma Road, giving way to the fear that invading Japanese troops may result in the Brits "losing India."

2 April
Surrender of Bataan and Philippines
Japan begins final bombardment of Bataan. A Japanese offensive breaks through U.S. and Filipino lines on 9 April. General Ernest King surrenders Bataan against MacArthur's orders. Two thousand escape in small boats, and 78,000 (66,000 Filipinos and 12,000 U.S.) troops surrender. It is the largest contingent of U.S. Army troops ever to surrender in history.

April–May
Bataan Death March
This horrible ordeal of atrocities is kept secret until 28 January 1944. Of the 80,000 Filipino and U.S. troops, along with 26,000 civilians who had surrendered, there are thousands who die during the Death March, and then 5,000 more Americans die in POW camps. Japan is not a signatory of 1929 Geneva agreement on treatment of POWs.

5 April
Indian Ocean Raid
Admiral Chiuchi Nagumo's First Air Fleet attacks twenty-nine British warships, sinking seven, including two cruisers. Japanese plane losses are high. British are able to keep Japanese navy out of the Indian Ocean.

18 April
The Doolittle Raid
Eighty American fliers in sixteen B-25 two-engine bombers from USS *Hornet*, led by Colonel Jimmy Doolittle, fly over 700 miles to Tokyo in a daring bombing raid designed to create fear in the Japanese. The B-25s take off from a 470-foot carrier deck, drop their bombs in broad daylight, then escape to the coast of China. The mission's success lifts Americans' spirits when most war news is bad.

29 April
Station Hypo Breaks Japanese Codes
Lt. Commander Joseph Rochefort puts together "Station Hypo" code-breaking operation to break Japanese codes before the war. Rochefort and colleague Commander Edwin Layton work night and day on the codes, and in particular on a code called "JN-25." The men ingeniously find a way to test their results in breaking the code and successfully learn intelligence about the Battle of Midway in time to give Americans an edge going in.

5 May

Luring the Americans Into a Trap

Imperial Japanese General HQ Order No. 18 expands their defensive perimeter to Midway and Samoa, forcing a decisive battle with the U.S. fleet. Japan is overconfident as they've had no losses of any of their eleven battleships, ten carriers, eighteen heavy cruisers, and twenty light cruisers. Their plan is to entice the U.S. fleet to areas near Midway where the ships and carriers can be picked off.

6 May

Wainwright Surrenders Corregidor

General Jonathan Wainwright and 15,000 troops have no choice but surrender after heavy Japanese bombardment and invasion that overwhelms the garrison on Corregidor.

7–8 May

Battle of the Coral Sea

This is the first naval battle fought without either party seeing the other. The enemy was beyond gun and torpedo range—but not beyond aircraft range. Admiral Nimitz sends the carriers *Lexington* and *Yorktown* under Admiral Jack Fletcher for the first naval action fought entirely with aircraft. U.S. loses thirty-three planes but shoots down forty-three Japanese planes. The *Lexington* sinks 8 May when an overheated motor ignites gasoline.

15 May

Women in the Military

President Roosevelt signs a bill creating WACs. The bill, opposed by the military, leads to WAVEs, WASPs, SPARs, and Women Marines. Some 300,000 women will eventually serve in the military during World War II.

23 May

Costs of A-Bomb Research Soar

On 6 December 1941 the government approved $2 billion for the Manhattan Project to build a secret bomb. J. Robert Oppenheimer's physicists and scientists have spent much of this fund by this date.

1 June

Germans Work to Test "Flying Bomb"

At a site in Peenemünde, the Nazis are working to test their V-2 rocket to be used as a "flying bomb" by giving it a payload of explosives. The first fire test on 13 June fails, but the Germans will perfect the rockets to be used to rain terror bombs over London.

3–4 June

Battle of Midway

This is a turning point of the Pacific war. Before Midway, Japan's legendary First Air Fleet was considered the strongest air unit in the world. After Midway the core carriers of the First Air Fleet are sunk and Japan's offensive capabilities are severely weakened. Many American planes miss their targets completely, but enough are successful that in less than five minutes they sink three Japanese carriers (*Akagi*, *Kaga*, *Soryu*). U.S. bombers also sink a fourth carrier, *Hiryu*. However, Japanese planes sink the *Yorktown* in a counterstrike. U.S. loses 147 planes and 307 men while Japan loses 322 planes and 3,500 men—many are their best pilots. Japan failed to entice the U.S. Navy to engage them. The U.S. didn't take the bait, and Japan never recovers from loss of its carriers and pilots at Midway.

7–9 August

Invasion of Guadalcanal

The 1st Marine Division and Allied units go ashore from eighty ships and are mainly unopposed on the beaches, but the U.S. Navy ships providing cover are routed by the Imperial Navy. Fierce fighting will be a sign of the overall Battle of Guadalcanal. Americans killed number 1,600 while 25,000 Japanese lose their lives. The Japanese also lose two dozen ships and 600 aircraft. The Japanese defeat at Guadalcanal marks the end of their efforts to take New Guinea.

11 October
Battle of Cape Esperance (Part of the Battle of Guadalcanal)
The U.S., unable to stop the Tokyo Express—troop transports making nightly trips through "the slot" between the islands—prompts Americans to attack and destroy two Japanese ships. U.S. loses two of its own ships by friendly fire. It was a victory for the Americans, but a bittersweet win. FDR is determined to hold Guadalcanal—the first "toehold in the South Pacific."

24–25 October
Battle of Bloody Ridge (Part of the Battle of Guadalcanal)
Americans use new weapons—the flame-thrower and Garand M1 rifle—for the first time at Guadalcanal. Outgunned and outnumbered, the Americans hold their own in a Japanese suicide charge, where the enemy loses a fifth of their troops against Marines at the line protecting Henderson Field.

25–27 October
Battle of Santa Cruz Island
The two great naval forces meet near the 165° latitude near Santa Cruz Island and engage each other in another sea battle. It was fought south of the New Hebrides, 1,000 miles from Guadalcanal. U.S. carriers *Hornet* and *Enterprise*, along with their escort ships, take on the Japanese. The battle ends in a draw, but the Americans damage two Japanese carriers, two battleships, and three cruisers. They also shoot down a hundred enemy aircraft.

November
Naval Battle of Guadalcanal
This is actually a series of five naval battles in which the U.S. loses nine ships, but prevents Japanese reinforcements from getting through, guaranteeing America's eventual triumph in the battle for the island. New radar warns Americans of enemy approach fifteen minutes before they arrive, proving the worth of radar.

2 December
Manhattan Project
Enrico Fermi's lab in Chicago makes an important stride in an effort to produce an A-bomb. Elements go "critical" for four-plus minutes, and produce neutrons.

1943

14 January
Casablanca Conference
The ten-day Allied conference regarding World War II in both theaters changes the allocation of resources for the Pacific from 15 percent to 30 percent.

February–December
Plan 9 Glider Operation
General Hap Arnold picks two brilliant young aviators, Phil Cochran and John Alison, to head a new risky operation called "Plan 9." That proposal calls for using American-built CG-4A Waco gliders to ferry men, mules, supplies, and matériel behind enemy lines in Burma to attack Japanese and build jungle airstrips.

1–17 February
Japanese Evacuate Guadalcanal Troops
In between naval and air skirmishes with the Americans, Japanese commanders evacuate troops from Guadalcanal—a lost cause for them.

28 February
Nazi A-Bomb Research Setback
German scientists thought to be working on a nuclear bomb receive a major setback when commandos destroy their "heavy water" facility.

March
Japanese Occupation of Alaska Islands
Japan invades and occupies Attu and Kiska, the two westernmost islands of the Aleutian Islands, as the northern anchor of their "ribbon defense."

2–4 March
Battle of Bismarck Sea
U.S. bombers destroy eight Japanese transport ships and four destroyer escorts while evading Zeros. It is a major defeat for Japan and ends the "Tokyo Express" means of bringing in supplies. Now they have to be brought in by subs.

12 March
South Pacific Strategy
The conference in Washington offers a plan called "Operation Cartwheel" to continue a dual advance against the Japanese in the Solomons and New Guinea.

18 April
Yamamoto Killed
American intelligence learns of a secret flight that includes Admiral Yamamoto. A squadron of P-38s shoots Yamamoto down, ending his illustrious military career.

8 May
Joint Strategic Plan
An Allied meeting in Cairo approves a plan putting MacArthur in charge of an area from the South Pacific to the Philippines; Chiang Kai-shek is named top military leader from China to Hong Kong (including the B-29 air bases in his area); Nimitz is to oversee the central Pacific area to Formosa (and the B-29 bases there). The goal is to retake Luzon, strategically located near China, Formosa, and Japan.

11–29 May
Recovery of Attu Island
Landings by the 7th Infantry Division are successful. Japanese troops fight desperately, and on 29 May, launch a futile 1,000-man suicide charge.

30 May
The New Fast Carriers Arrive
The USS *Essex*, the first of twenty-four "fast carriers," arrives in the central Pacific. These new ships will have a huge impact on the war.

30 June
"Operation Cartwheel" Begins
American troops land at Rendova Island; the 43rd Division engages the enemy but Munda on New Georgia is not taken until August.

22 July
Black Sheep Squadron Formed
A U.S. Marine fighter pilot is chosen to head a new squadron to provide air protection for Admiral Halsey's task force. Major Gregory Boyington is the new leader. He is nicknamed "Pappy" by his squadron because at age thirty-one he's the oldest man in the unit. The Black Sheep Squadron has many pilots who become "aces" in shooting down Japanese bombers and fighter planes.

6–7 August
"Island-Hopping" Begins
Halsey skips Kolombangara for Vella Lavella en route to Bougainville. "Island-Hopping" strategy takes advantage of Pacific geography and lets American troops bypass the strongest Japanese garrisons, sealing them off by air and sea from getting supplies and reinforcements, while U.S. troops take more strategic islands.

15–16 August
U.S. Retakes Kiska Island
American soldiers land at Kiska Island in the Aleutian chain and discover that the Japanese have evacuated their 5,000-man garrison.

3 September
Italy Surrenders
After Fascist leader Mussolini is ousted and a new Italian government is formed, Italy surrenders to the Allies. A month later, Italy will declare war on Germany as the Allies occupy most of the country, except for Rome, which the Nazis still hold.

1–2 November
Invasion of Bougainville
One "hop" in the "Island-Hopping" toward Rabaul lands U.S. troops on Bougainville.

5 November
U.S. Navy Hits Four Enemy Ships
Task Force 38 air strikes against four Japanese heavy cruisers, with ninety-seven carrier aircraft in attack; the U.S. loses only eight. All four Japanese cruisers are heavily damaged. It will mark the last time heavy Japanese warships come to Rabaul.

11 November
Battle at Truk
The Japanese fleet is crippled at this battle in the Pacific. The Japanese lose all their cruisers and half their fighter planes. It will require at least six months for Japan to train fresh pilots.

20–24 November
Battle of Tarawa
Landings for this battle start with fighting that becomes so intense that the four-day battle is called "Bloody Tarawa." U.S. Marine total casualties are 3,301, including more than 1,000 who are killed. In contrast, nearly 5,000 Japanese are killed; only thirteen surrender.

1944

29 January–23 February
U.S. Attacks Marshall Islands
Landings are made on Majuro Island, which is captured by U.S. Marines—the first Japanese territory to be taken by the United States. Kwajalein and Eniwetok islands are also taken. The invasion task force includes 297 ships with 84,000 troops. U.S. Navy ships and planes shoot down some 200 enemy aircraft and sink 15 enemy ships.

17 February
U.S. Task Force Attacks Truk
American navy destroys 250 Japanese planes and sinks fifteen warships in a battle to isolate the Japanese supply port at Truk Island, dubbed "the Gibraltar of the East" because of its impregnability. But the U.S. raids leave the Japanese base vulnerable, isolated, and increasingly impotent as a source of supplies.

6 June
Allied Invasion of Europe
After months of secret, intensive planning, the U.S. and its Allies launch a "D-Day" invasion of Normandy with thousands of naval ships and even more conscripted vessels to ferry the troops and matériel. There are terrific losses, yet it marks the turning point in the European theater.

19–21 June
Battle of the Philippine Sea
This three-day battle, nicknamed the "Great Marianas Turkey Shoot," is one of the biggest battles of World War II. This "greatest carrier battle of the war" costs the U.S. only thirty planes. But Japan loses a total of 346 planes *plus two carriers*. Japanese naval air forces can never again engage the U.S. in the Pacific on "any terms other than suicidal."

15 June–9 July
Battle of Saipan
Saipan is "taken at a high price," and as many as 3,000 Americans are killed. Lt. General Saito commits suicide after convincing his army and civilians (men, women, and children could push the total to as many as 22,000) to make one last suicidal charge at advancing Americans. Enemy troops and civilians jump off cliffs when American lines do not break. Nimitz sees the carnage, including thousands of civilian suicides, and believes that similar problems will face the U.S. if it invades Japan.

18 July
Japanese Retreat from Northeast India
After heavy losses in the China-Burma-India theater, Japanese troops withdraw from the northeast India cities of Imphal and Kohima, and a month later all Japanese resistance is ended.

21 July–8 August
Battle of Guam
Guam, largest of the three Mariana Islands, is liberated by U.S. Marines after nearly three years of Japanese occupation. Guam becomes Nimitz's headquarters for the central Pacific offensive. More than 18,500 enemy soldiers are killed or captured. The Marines' casualties are in the 1,000 range but only about 200 are killed.

24 July–1 August
Battle of Tinian
The majority of 13,000 Japanese troops on the island are killed in the battle to take Tinian. Saipan is the staging area for taking the nearby island with its prized airfields. These airfields put our B-29s within striking range of the Japanese Home Islands. With a range of 1,500 miles they are a genuine threat. They could fly from Saipan to Tokyo and back in about 1,300 miles, and the Japanese know and fear this.

26 July
FDR Meets with MacArthur and Nimitz
President Roosevelt schedules a meeting in Hawaii with Admiral Nimitz and General MacArthur to finalize objectives for taking the war to the main islands of Japan. It is at this meeting that the U.S. decides to retake the Philippine Islands rather than isolating them and going to islands closer to Japan, such as Formosa.

11–16 September
Quebec Conference
FDR and Churchill meet to discuss war strategy. Miscalculations render many plans a waste of time and they delay a number of postwar strategies, including the plan to invade and occupy Iwo Jima and Okinawa, primarily to provide air bases and staging areas for the bombings and invasion of Japan. Churchill insists that the Royal Navy be "in at the death" of Japan, alongside the U.S. Navy.

15–21 September
Operation Stalemate
The invasion of Peleliu Island is part of a larger exercise dubbed Operation Stalemate as a component of an overall plan to take all of the Palau Islands. On 10–11 September the U.S. 3rd Fleet attacks the Palaus prior to the invasion. Marines suffer 6,500 casualties and the Army loses another 3,000. But for the Japanese it is even more terrible. Of the 10,000 troops of the original garrison, fewer than a hundred are alive at the end. Nearly 600 men of the 1st Marine Division and 81st Army Division receive awards for their heroism.

15 September
U.S. Invasion of Leyte Set
The Joint Chiefs of Staff approve MacArthur's plan for landings at Leyte on 20 October using the 7th Fleet and Admiral Halsey's Navy Task Force 38. As a prelude to the invasion, Marine Rangers are to invade nearby islands. Japan is wary about the U.S. efforts to retake part of the Philippines. Weakened by the loss of most of their warships and two-thirds of their tankers, they fear a U.S. invasion. Japan starts to maintain a "Home Fleet" with nine battleships and five carriers to patrol Japanese waters.

10 October
"Beginning of the End" for Japan
As air raids by planes from 3rd Fleet carriers start on Formosa, Okinawa, and Luzon, Americans destroy at least 500 Japanese aircraft in a week. Despite heavy losses, the Japanese government reports instead that they sank fifteen American ships. Imperial General Headquarters, which invents the myth, actually believes its own propaganda.

15–27 October
Battle of Leyte Gulf
U.S. Marine Rangers invade Suluan and Dinagat Islands near Leyte in preparation for the Leyte invasion. Three Japanese naval forces try to oppose the landings and engage the U.S. fleets. When it ends on 27 October, the Japanese naval forces are repulsed and the U.S. Navy is undisputed victor. No longer will the Imperial Navy be able to make any significant challenge against the U.S. fleet.

25 October
Kamikaze Attacks Begin
The first "organized" kamikaze attack on U.S. escort carriers *Santee* and *Swanee* occurs during a battle off Samar. These frantic suicidal missions accelerate, as the Japanese grow more and more desperate.

14 December
Palawan Massacre
On the island of Palawan, American POWs are burned alive by their Japanese guards. Japanese soldiers armed with guns, bayonets, grenades, and dynamite attack the POWs. They toss gasoline onto the American POWs and incinerate them while they are still alive. Altogether 151 prisoners are slaughtered.

16–25 December
Battle of the Bulge
The U.S. and Germany go toe to toe in combat in the Ardennes in the Battle of the Bulge. On 17 December the Nazi SS massacres U.S. prisoners of war in Malmédy. On 26 December General George Patton and the U.S. 3rd Army come to the rescue of beleaguered troops in Bastogne. Germans finally withdraw in January.

1945

2–7 January
"Burma Road" Reopened
Chinese forces join to reopen the Burma Road, now renamed "Stilwell Road."

9 January
Americans Return to Luzon
General Walter Krueger's 6th Army begins landings on Luzon at the same location that Japanese forces had landed in December 1941. The only resistance to the American invasion is continuing attacks from kamikaze pilots. They are also effective. Suicidal Japanese pilots damage more than forty U.S. ships, almost half of them seriously, and they sink five U.S. ships. Nearly 800 Americans are killed in kamikaze attacks, and 1,400 are wounded.

13 January
MacArthur Returns
General MacArthur wades ashore on Leyte beachhead to fulfill his promise to the Filipino people, "I shall return."

29–31 January
Rescue of Bataan POWs
In a daring raid behind enemy lines, Colonel Horton Smith, Lt. Colonel Henry Mucci, Major Robert Lapham (a Bataan Death March survivor), Captain Robert Prince, and 121 volunteers execute a risky plan—the greatest prison escape ever attempted—rescuing 500 American POWs from a Japanese prison camp on Luzon.

19 February–26 March
Battle of Iwo Jima
The battle for Iwo Jima is one of the most terrible of the Pacific war. It costs the Marines casualties of nearly 7,000 killed in action and 21,000 wounded. Japanese dead total 20,000 and only 1,000 survive to surrender or be captured.

10 March
Tokyo Firebombed
In the start of "1,000 bombing runs" on Tokyo, some 334 American B-29s drop 2,000 tons of incendiary bombs, resulting in 100,000 deaths and a million homeless.

26 March–2 July
Battle of Okinawa
Okinawa, an island that has been in Japanese control for 5,000 years, is invaded when 458 American ships land almost 200,000 U.S. troops. American casualties total 68,000, including 16,000 soldiers, sailors, and Marines killed or missing in action and nearly 50,000 wounded. More than 131,000 Japanese troops die, along with some 150,000 Okinawan civilians. The battle is called "an awful warning" of what it will take to invade Japan's homeland. Many push to drop the A-bomb.

11 April
Allies Liberate German Concentration Camps
American forces liberate two of the most notorious German concentration camps of World War II—Belsen and Buchenwald. On 29 April they also liberate Dachau, another infamous prison camp.

13 April
FDR Dies of a Stroke
Franklin D. Roosevelt dies during his fourth term as president. Some call it "Black Friday." The new president, Harry Truman, keeps pushing FDR's policies and war efforts.

18 April
Correspondent Ernie Pyle Killed in Action
Veteran war correspondent Ernie Pyle heads to the Pacific theater after the war in Europe ends. He steps ashore on a small island just west of Okinawa. Traveling with a group of infantrymen, Pyle is killed by a sniper's bullet. Saddened, the soldiers pay tribute to their fallen friend with a simple plaque reading: "At this spot, the 77th Infantry Division lost a buddy, Ernie Pyle, 18 April 1945."

28 April
Mussolini Killed
Italy's deposed fascist dictator, who was originally freed from an Allied prison by Germans, is captured by Italian partisans and killed. His body is hung upside down in a city square.

2–4 May
German Armies Surrender
As the infamous Third Reich begins to crumble, German forces begin to see the futility of trying to stop the inevitable. In Italy, German armies surrender to the Allied forces, and two days later all German troops in Holland, Denmark, and northwest Germany also surrender. On 7 May the German High Command signs an unconditional surrender and the next day is proclaimed "V-E Day," for Victory in Europe.

15 June
American Bombers Destroy Japanese Cities
American B-29s begin destruction of sixty mid-sized cities in Japan. These attacks kill at least 250,000, more than will be killed at Hiroshima and Nagasaki combined. Japanese militarists are not persuaded to surrender.

18 June
Truman Plans to Use A-Bomb
President Truman approves "Operation Downfall," the code name for dropping the atomic bomb. No one knows exactly what will happen, although the Joint Chiefs predict some 200,000 casualties.

16 July
First Successful A-Bomb Test

American scientists working at the "Trinity" site near Alamogordo, New Mexico, conduct a successful test of a twenty-kiloton atomic bomb. Word is sent to Truman, who is on his way to attend the Potsdam Conference the next day.

6 August
First Fiery Destruction from A-Bomb

Over the city of Hiroshima in Japan, the B-29 named Enola Gay drops the first atomic bomb to be used in war. "Little Boy" explodes with the destructive energy of fifteen kilotons and kills 140,000 and injures another 70,000.

9 August
A-Bomb Explodes at Nagasaki

A twenty-two-kiloton "Fat Man" atomic bomb falls on Nagasaki after its B-29 crew is prevented from striking the primary target at another Japanese city. This blast kills 70,000 and leaves hundreds of thousands homeless. Russia, which had been discussing the possibility of joining Japan in the war, instead declares war on Japan.

15 August
War's Over!

Emperor Hirohito surrenders on a radio broadcast. The message is recorded the day before for broadcast the next day. During the night a military plot to unseat the emperor and seize the surrender recording is narrowly averted. A Japanese general, determined to defend his homeland to the last man, still has at least 5,000 kamikaze planes and men to fly them. They have more than a million men under arms throughout the island but the general suggests calling on twenty million Japanese to become kamikazes to kill American invaders with sticks, stones, spears, and pitchforks.

2 September
Japan Formally Surrenders

Surrender documents are signed on the deck of the U.S. battleship *Missouri* anchored in the Pacific just outside Tokyo, as over a thousand carrier-based American planes fly overhead. The Stars and Stripes that fly that day on the mast of the *Missouri* is the same flag that had flown over the U.S. Capitol on the day that Pearl Harbor was attacked.

GLOSSARY

Amtrac: Amphibious tractor, used to ferry troops in assault landings ashore

AP: Troopship (non-landing)

AVG: American Volunteer Group (the "Flying Tigers" unit in China)

AVT: Aircraft Carrier (Training)

BOGEY: Unidentified (possibly enemy) aircraft

CA: Heavy (armored) Cruiser

CBI: China-Burma-India; an operational area for Allied Forces in WW II

***Chutai*:** Japanese word for "squadron"

CL: Light Cruiser

D-DAY: Day on which an operation is to commence and/or on which troops will depart (Day of Departure). *See also* H-Hour

ECM: Electric Coding Machine
A top-secret device for encrypting messages

ETA: Estimated time of arrival

GQ: General Quarters (battle stations)

H-HOUR: Time at which an operation is to commence. *See also* D-Day

HMS: His Majesty's Ship (designation with ship's name)

HMAS: His Majesty's Australian Ship (designation with ship's name)

HIGGINS BOAT: An amphibious landing craft. *See also* Amtrac

HIKO: Japanese word for "air" that was generally used in describing something else, such as *chutai hiko* (air squadron)

KIA: Killed in action

LCC: Landing craft command ship

LCI: Landing Craft Infantry
Capable of carrying up to 200 infantrymen at 216 feet long

LCM: Landing Craft Mechanized
For carrying mechanized equipment

LCT: Landing Craft Tank(s). *See also* LST

LCVP: Landing craft carrying vehicle(s) and personnel

LCVR: Landing craft carrying vehicle(s), ramped

LHA: Amphibious Assault ship

LST: Landing Ship Tank
At 316 feet long, capable of carrying tanks, troops, and supplies onto a beach in an amphibious assault

MIA: Missing in Action

MOTHER SHIPS: Ordinary ships, usually submarines, that carried so-called "midget" submarines (*see* SPS) to sites close to their attack objective

OSS: Office of Strategic Services
World War II intelligence agency, forerunner of CIA

PBY: Patrol Bomber aircraft
The "Y" in the designation signifies the manufacturer, Consolidated Aircraft Corp

POW: Prisoner of War

RAF: Royal Air Force (Great Britain)

RENTAI: Japanese word for "regiment"

RISKOSENTAI: Japanese word for Imperial Navy marines

SAR: Search and Rescue

SEABEES: Nickname for CBs (Construction Battalion personnel)

SENTAI: Japanese word for "wing," as in *Sentai Hiko*

SORTIE: A single mission flown by a single military aircraft

SPS: Special Purpose Submarine(s)
The "midget" submarines—seventy-eight feet long and six feet high—that were developed by the Japanese for special missions in World War II

SS: Submarine

TBS: Talk Between Ships
Radio used on amphibious assaults

VMF: Designation for USMC Fighter Squadron

USAAC: United States Army Air Corps
World War II predecessor to U.S. Air Force

USS: United States Ship
Abbreviated designation used with ship's name to identify country of origin

ZERO (AKA ZEKE): Nickname given by American pilots for the Japanese Mitsubishi A6M *Reisan* (pronounced ray-san) that ruled the skies over the Pacific. A later model of the Zero was nicknamed Zeke.

ZERO WARD: Where wounded, sick, and dying patients were sent when nothing could be done to save them

ACKNOWLEDGMENTS

P resident Franklin D. Roosevelt, in one of his fireside chats to the American people in February 1942, said, "Never before have we had so little time to do so much."

That's the way I've felt during this past year and a half after agreeing to do a series of books based on my FOX News Channel, *War Stories* television documentaries. The initial book was based on eyewitness accounts and reports filed while I was embedded with U.S. military units for FOX News from the middle of February through April 2003. Thanks to my producers in New York, my Iraq combat cameraman Griff Jenkins, and my friend Joe Musser, that initial work, *War Stories: Operation Iraqi Freedom*, stands as a first draft of history for a war that is still being fought.

For this second book in our series, my publisher asked me to focus on the Pacific theater during World War II. Since none of us involved wanted this to be just another historical review of major battles or key events, we agreed that it must offer the kind of in-depth, first-person observations by participants for which *War Stories* has been acclaimed.

That proved to be no mean task. It required reviewing hundreds of interviews, thousands of pages of transcripts, and miles of videotape in order to accurately capture the heroic experiences and subsequent reflections of those who fought these terrible battles. It was likewise important that the final product provide a context for their compelling eyewitness observations.

Accomplishing all that in the time available was a goal that could only be achieved with the assistance of those whose help I acknowledge here. It is their commitment and hard work that makes these war stories so compelling—and inspiring.

Foremost among those who made this book possible are the remarkable veterans who agreed to recount their experiences in the Pacific theater. All of us involved in this project have been enriched by their intensely personal recollections. We have all been moved by the way so many of them endured terrible privation, loneliness, fear, and savagery—and yet describe it all simply as "a job that had to be done."

The participants explain their victories, so critical to the outcome of the war, in a selfless, matter-of-fact way, with modesty and grace. Many told me things that they had never shared before—not even with their wives or children. I am grateful to them for that and grateful for their valor, dedication, and service to our country. These brave Americans are featured in every chapter, and recognized in the epilogue. You will find their names listed there.

My admiration and gratitude also go to my wife and best friend, Betsy, and to our children and their spouses: daughters Sarah and her husband Martin; Tait and her husband Tom; and Dornin; and our son, Stuart and his wife, Ellen. There were all too many times when husband/dad was absent because of an always-impossible schedule, but they continue to show consummate understanding, devotion, and forgiveness.

This book would not have happened but for the team at FOX News led by Roger Ailes. He had the vision to make *War Stories* a reality and a great success. Kevin Magee, Bill Shine, and John Moody have made it possible for me to hang around with heroes—past and present—so that I can document what they do and have done. Jack Abernethy pays the bills and in between hurricanes, Dianne Brandi tries to keep me out of trouble.

Our *War Stories* Unit, headed by senior producer Pamela Browne, ensures that every televised documentary is flawless. Pamela personally made certain that the DVDs included in this book illuminate the eyewitness accounts of our participants. Producers Martin Hinton, Greg Johnson, Steve Tierney, Cyd Upson, and Ayse Weiting have all spent countless hours with each of the individuals we interviewed for this work, and in many cases built deeply personal relationships with these heroes and their families. My assistant producers were likewise essential to the success of this work. Kelly Guernica, Jason Kopp, and Bevin Mahoney devoted themselves to finding unique material for each of these heroic stories that otherwise might never have been recorded for posterity, while Michael Weiss mined hundreds of public and private sources for the historical photographs that appear in this book. My appreciation also goes to Peter Bregman for his help on the photo archives at Fox Movietone News, and to Don Brown for his contributions to the timeline.

Joe Musser, my friend, collaborator, and research partner of many years, pored over hours and reams of *War Stories* tapes, transcripts, maps, and interviews and did months of research in order to pare down mountains of excellent possibilities to a workable outline. Joe also found in David Deis a cartographer of great talent, who rendered the superb maps for each chapter to help readers comprehend the events more easily.

I'm more than grateful for the extraordinary assistance and forbearance of Marji Ross and her team at Regnery Publishing. Editor Miriam Moore and art director Amanda Larsen encouraged me with their patience and faith that this book really could get finished. Their associate, Paula Decker, ably assisted in that effort.

This book, a collaboration between FOX News Channel and Regnery Publishing, could never have come about but for the work of Williams & Connelly, where Bob Barnett and Kathleen Ryan dotted all the "i"s and crossed every "t" in all the requisite documents.

All who have worked on this project are indebted to the authors, historians, museum directors, and curators who have participated in our Pacific campaign *War Stories* documentaries. Helen McDonald, at the National

Museum of the Pacific War in Fredericksburg, Texas, deserves more than thanks for all she has done to support this work. We have also been aided in this effort by the wisdom and experience of:

- Colonel Joe Alexander, author of *Utmost Savagery: The Three Days at Tarawa*
- James Bradley, author of *Flags of Our Fathers*
- Burl Burlingame, author of *Advance Force Pearl Harbor*
- Robert Cressman and Mark Horan, authors of *A Glorious Page in Our History*
- Benis Frank, Marine historian and author of several books on Okinawa
- Richard Frank, historian and author of *Guadalcanal: The Definitive Account of a Landmark Battle*
- Carroll Glines, author of *Attack on Yamamoto* and *Jimmy Doolittle: Daredevil Aviator and Scientist*
- Donald Goldstein, author of *At Dawn We Slept*
- Jack Green, curator and historian for the Naval Historical Center
- Eric Hammel, author of *Bloody Tarawa*
- Bradley Hartsell, military researcher
- E. B. Potter, editor of *Sea Power*
- Colonel John Ripley, director, U.S. Marine Corps History and Museums Division
- Hampton Sides, author of *Ghost Soldiers*
- R. D. Van Wagner, author of *Any Time, Any Place, Anywhere*
- John Wiltshire, director, Hawaii Undersea Research Lab

In order to even attempt such a project as this book without the help of all these people would have been foolhardy on my part, and I bow to these dedicated experts and friends who have made such worthy contributions to this work.

Semper Fidelis,
Oliver L. North

INDEX

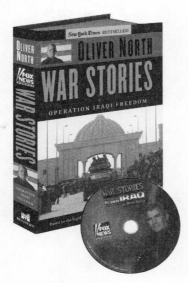